Simon Gray

PLAYS FIVE

Simon Gray was born in 1936. He began his writing career with *Colmain* (1963), the first of five novels, all published by Faber. He was the author of many plays for TV and radio, also films, including the 1987 adaptation of J. L .Carr's *A Month in the Country*, and TV films including *Running Late*, *After Pilkington* (winner of the Prix Italia) and the Emmy Award-winning *Unnatural Pursuits*. He wrote more than thirty stage plays, among them *Butley* and *Otherwise Engaged* (which both received *Evening Standard* Awards for Best Play), *Close of Play*, *The Rear Column*, *Quartermaine's Terms*, *The Common Pursuit*, *Hidden Laughter*, *The Late Middle Classes* (winner of the Barclay's Best Play Award), *Japes*, *The Old Masters* (his ninth play to be directed by Harold Pinter) and *Little Nell*, which premiered at the Theatre Royal Bath in 2007, directed by Peter Hall. *Little Nell* was first broadcast on BBC Radio 4 in 2006, and *Missing Dates* in 2008. In 1991 he was made BAFTA Writer of the Year. His acclaimed works of non-fiction are *An Unnatural Pursuit*, *How's That for Telling 'Em, Fat Lady?*, *Fat Chance*, *Enter a Fox*, *The Smoking Diaries*, *The Year of the Jouncer*, *The Last Cigarette* and *Coda*. With Hugh Whitemore he adapted his *Smoking Diaries* for the stage: *The Last Cigarette* was directed by Richard Eyre in 2009. Simon Gray was appointed CBE in the 2005 New Year's Honours for his services to Drama and Literature. He died in August 2008.

For more information please visit
www.simongray.org.uk

*also by Simon Gray*

*collected editions*
PLAYS ONE
(*Butley, Wise Child, Dutch Uncle, Spoiled,*
*The Caramel Crisis, Sleeping Dog*)

PLAYS TWO
(*Otherwise Engaged, Dog Days, Molly, Pig in a Poke, Man in a Sidecar,*
*Plaintiffs and Defendants, Two Sundays, Simply Disconnected*)

PLAYS THREE
(*Quartermaine's Terms, The Rear Column, Close of Play,*
*Stage Struck, Tartuffe, A Month in the Country, The Idiot*)

PLAYS FOUR
(*Hidden Laughter, The Common Pursuit, The Holy Terror,*
*They Never Slept, After Pilkington, Old Flames*)

*stage plays*
MELON, MICHAEL, SEPARATELY AND TOGETHER, JAPES TOO, THE PIG TRADE,
HULLABALOO, THE LAST CIGARETTE (with Hugh Whitemore)

*television plays*
DEATH OF A TEDDY BEAR, THE PRINCESS, A WAY WITH THE LADIES,
SPOILED, THE DIRT ON LUCY LANE, THE STYLE OF THE COUNTESS

*radio plays*
THE HOLY TERROR, THE RECTOR'S DAUGHTER, WITH A NOD AND A BOW,
SUFFER THE LITTLE CHILDREN, LITTLE NELL, MISSING DATES

*television films*
THE REAR COLUMN, QUARTERMAINE'S TERMS, THE COMMON PURSUIT,
RUNNING LATE, FEMME FATALE, UNNATURAL PURSUITS

*non-fiction*
THE EARLY DIARIES
(*An Unnatural Pursuit, How's That for Telling 'Em, Fat Lady?*)
FAT CHANCE, ENTER A FOX, THE SMOKING DIARIES,
THE YEAR OF THE JOUNCER, THE LAST CIGARETTE, CODA

*fiction*
SIMPLE PEOPLE, COLMAIN, A COMEBACK FOR STARK,
LITTLE PORTIA, BREAKING HEARTS

*films*
BUTLEY, A MONTH IN THE COUNTRY

*audio books*
THE SMOKING DIARIES, THE YEAR OF THE JOUNCER,
THE LAST CIGARETTE, CODA

# SIMON GRAY

# Plays Five

*Cell Mates*
*Life Support*
*Just the Three of Us*
*Japes*
*Little Nell*
*The Old Masters*
*The Late Middle Classes*

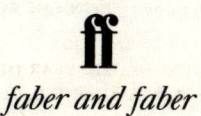

*faber and faber*

This collection first published in 2010
by Faber and Faber Limited
74–77 Great Russell Street, London WC1B 3DA

Typeset by Country Setting, Kingsdown, Kent CT14 8ES
Printed in England by CPI Bookmarque, Croydon, Surrey

All rights reserved

*Cell Mates* first published by Faber and Faber Ltd, 1995

*Life Support* first published by Faber and Faber Ltd, 1997

*Just the Three of Us* first published by Nick Hern Books Ltd, 1999

*Japes* first published by Nick Hern Books Ltd, 2000

*Little Nell* first published by Faber and Faber Ltd, 2006

*The Old Masters*, in an earlier vesrion as *The Pig Trade*,
included in *Four Plays*, published by Faber and Faber Ltd, 2002,
and in the present version first published by Faber and Faber Ltd, 2004

*The Late Middle Classes* first published by Nick Hern Books Ltd, 1999,
and included in *Key Plays*, published by Faber and Faber Ltd, 2002

The right of Simon Gray to be identified as author of this
collection and the works in it has been asserted in accordance
with Section 77 of the Copyright, Designs and Patents Act 1988

*Cell Mates* © Simon Gray, 1995
*Life Support* © Simon Gray, 1997
*Just the Three of Us* © Simon Gray, 1999
*Japes* © Simon Gray, 2000
*Little Nell* © Simon Gray, 2006
*The Old Masters* © Simon Gray, 2004
*The Late Middle Classes* © Simon Gray, 1999

*This book is sold subject to the condition that it shall not, by way
of trade or otherwise, be lent, resold, hired out or otherwise circulated
without the publisher's prior consent in any form of binding or cover
other than that in which it is published and without a similar condition
including this condition being imposed on the subsequent purchaser*

A CIP record for this book is available from the British Library

978–0–571–25490–3

2 4 6 8 10 9 7 5 3 1

# Contents

Cell Mates, 1

Life Support, 85

Just the Three of Us, 139

Japes, 213

Little Nell, 317

The Old Masters, 401

The Late Middle Classes, 479

All rights whatsoever in the plays are strictly reserved and application for performances etc., other than the amateur rights as stated below, should be made in writing, before rehearsals begin, to Judy Daish Associates Ltd, 2 St Charles Place, London W10 6EG. No performance may be given without a licence being first obtained.

For *Japes* and *The Late Middle Classes*, applications for performance by amateurs in English throughout the world (except in the United States of America and Canada) must be made in advance, before rehearsals begin, to Nick Hern Books Ltd, The Glasshouse, 49a Goldhawk Road, London W12 8QP (e-mail: info@nickhernbooks.demon.co.uk).

All other applications for performance by amateurs should be addressed to Judy Daish Associates Ltd, address as above.

# CELL MATES

**Cell Mates** was first presented at the Yvonne Arnaud Theatre, Guildford, on 17 January 1995 and transferred to the Albery Theatre, London, on 16 February 1995. The cast, in order of appearance, was as follows:

**Sean Bourke** Rik Mayall
**George Blake** Stephen Fry
**Philip / Viktor** Paul Mooney
**Miranda / Zinaida** Carole Nimmons
**Sparrow / Stan** Sam Dastor

*Directed by* Simon Gray
*Lighting Designer* Mick Hughes
*Set Designer* Eileen Diss

# Characters

Sean Bourke
George Blake
Philip
Miranda
Sparrow
Zinaida
Stan
Viktor

# Act One

## SCENE ONE

*Bourke's office in Wormwood Scrubs. There are boxes of magazines on the floor. Bourke has his feet on the table, looking through a pile of typescripts. He has a pot of tea beside him, a mug in his hand. He picks out one typescript, begins to read.*

**Bourke** (*aloud*)
'Oh, spare a thought ye people there
For all of us who dwell in here.
Sinners all, we must endure
Until again our souls are pure.

And then the gates will open wide
And out we'll go from dark inside . . .'

*Blake enters, unseen by Bourke. Stands watching him.*

'To dash about the valleys green
And by our loved ones brightly seen
As we clasp them to our pounding hearts
Our wives and children, those better parts
Whom we left in shame, our heads held low,
But now return to, though the healing's slow.

And listen judges, juries all –'

*Bourke breaks off with a laugh, drops typescript back on table.*

And listen judges, juries all –
Listen when my heart does call!
Oh pray don't sentence me to poems so bad
That listening at them makes me –

*He is suddenly aware of Blake.*

**Blake** Glad? Mad?

**Bourke** No, sad, I think it was going to be. It was written by a young house-burglar. Doing five years for greivous bodily harm. If I publish it he'll be able to show it to his wife and two daughters – it'll give him and them a lot of pleasure and pride, more than anything else he's done in his life, almost. That's what's sad.

**Blake** So you'll publish it?

**Bourke** I'm the editor of the Wormwood Scrubs magazine, sir! The world expects the highest literary standards from me – I can't let my personal feelings get in the way of true judgement, can I?

**Blake** In other words, you're going to publish it.

**Bourke** He's six foot three, he has a violent temper, he believes on the basis of this that he has a great, great talent – would you care to deliver the rejection slip yourself, sir?

**Blake** No. But then I wouldn't be fool enough to reject it, my standards not being as high as yours.

**Bourke** Then I compromise! I publish it as long as he changes the title.

**Blake** Which is?

**Bourke** (*picks up typescript*) 'All is Not Lost if All is Forgiven'.

**Blake** And what would you change it to?

**Bourke** (*thinks*) What about 'An Unpublishable Poem by Steve Lewis'.

**Blake** I think that tells the whole story.

**Bourke** Good. Because that's what we care about — telling the whole story.

**Blake** These are the rejects, are they?

**Bourke** They are indeed, sir.

**Blake** Ah, well, in that case . . .

**Bourke** It's a pleasure to meet you at last, Mr Blake. You're something of a celebrity in this institution, I expect you realise. To my knowledge almost every fellow convict thinks you're a national disgrace.

**Blake** Thank you, Mr Bourke. Becoming a national disgrace is the reward of a lifetime's endeavour. I've earned every one of my forty years.

**Bourke** (*laughs*) I think you know what I meant, that your *sentence* – is – a national disgrace. A disgrace to this nation, anyway. It's not my nation, thank God – but to what do I owe the – the privilege?

**Blake** I asked my custodian if I could pop in for a moment. To pick up a copy of the last issue. He's having a cup of coffee with a colleague. If he wants me he'll blow on his whistle. I wanted to pick up a copy of the last issue.

**Bourke** You don't want to read it. But why not consider writing for it? Autobiographical piece. Telling your side of the story. Then I might enjoy reading it myself.

**Blake** Thank you, but you'd be disappointed. I write badly. Very stilted. Over-guarded, probably. A habit acquired in my profession.

**Bourke** Then tell me about the Turk.

**Blake** Oh, the Turk! There's nothing much to tell there.

**Bourke** It's made you a legend.

**Blake** A legend *and* a celebrity. With thirty-three years to go. If I keep up this level of achievement –

**Bourke** You could end up editing the in-house magazine. Your own teapot. A table to put your feet on. Peace and quiet. A room with a view, But what happened with the Turk, Mr Blake? Is it true you disarmed him, threw him over your shoulder, pinned him to the wall while you talked to him in Turkish –

**Blake** Only the last bit's true. He ran amok in the canteen – he had a sudden fit, you see, at the thought that he'd never see his family again, never see Turkey again. So while he was shouting and baying and swearing and threatening and waving his knife I tried to explain to him in his own language that if he calmed down and gave me the knife, all was not lost, all might be forgiven. Anyway, that he'd have a decent chance of getting home eventually.

**Bourke** So he gave you the knife – and went quietly over to the guards.

**Blake** Who'd maintained a respectful distance between themselves and his knife. He bowed in submission –

**Bourke** – whereupon they probably kicked and beat and throttled the – bejesus out of him.

**Blake** I expect so. But that he'll survive.

**Bourke** I've seen you walking with the other two – Dick and Nigel – the other prisoners of conscience, as you're called. Also a national disgrace – thrown in jail for marching against the bomb! And Nigel married, with children – (*Suddenly realising.*) Sorry. I was forgetting. You're married yourself, aren't you? And with children.

**Blake** (*briskly*) I've told my wife to get a divorce as soon as possible. Anyway, I won't be walking with them much longer, he's out in a few months, Nigel. Home to his wife, Annie. And so's Dick too. I don't mean that Dick's off home to Nigel's wife Annie.

**Bourke** It's a lovely thought, though – and you can just see her, their Annie, without ever having seen her – the type – so English –

**Blake** – the two short-term prisoners of conscience sharing –

**Bourke** – and her fitting them both in in the middle of the bed, Nigel on one shoulder, Dick on the other – then off on their marches, their picnics. God, I love the middle-class English.

**Blake** Careful. I was almost one myself, remember. (*Laughs again.*)

**Bourke** Makes a change to have someone to enjoy a harmless joke with.

**Blake** And it is harmless! Nobody could have more respect –

**Bourke** – for Annie –

**Blake** – and her jailbird lovers. Perhaps when you're out you'll join them. But will she wait for me?

**Bourke** You know, the odd thing is, Mr Blake, I've been expecting this kind of conversation with you. Imagining it, even.

**Blake** Yes, that is an odd thing. Because so have I, Mr Bourke.

**Bourke** You know, I've seen you often in the cafeteria, in the courtyard –

**Blake** I've seen you seeing me. But it's been difficult to make the approach. A matter of – of – (*then with surprise*) shyness, perhaps.

*They laugh again. There is a pause.*

**Bourke** Will you have a cup of tea?

**Blake** I'd love one but I don't think I'll be allowed the time. Tell me, Mr Bourke, when *do* you get out?

**Bourke** Not soon enough. A year or so.

**Blake** That means I have a friend for a year or so. So I hope.

**Bourke** You have a friend for at least a year. Count on it.

**Blake** And Nigel's wife aside, what will you do when you're out and about again?

**Bourke** Try my hand at writing. I'm already trying my hand but – (*Shakes his head.*) The atmosphere here isn't conducive. So the first thing I'll do is get myself home. Back to Dublin, and among my own people again. And who knows – perhaps being there'll help me to become a fine and successful author, the genuine article. So there I'll be, strutting along the streets of Dublin – laughing, joking, singing songs in the pub – a famous book or two behind me – another one in my head – (*Laughs.*)

**Blake** Well, why not? It could happen. If you make it happen.

**Bourke** Yes, well – it's a hope I have to cling to. I've wasted too many years of myself. On what? Being a petty criminal. What's worse, a failed petty criminal. Well, there's going to be no more of that, because I'll tell you something, Mr Blake, whatever my record shows, I'm a man of intelligence. Resources and intelligence. Believe me.

**Blake** I do. I know it. From what I've heard about you. From what I've heard from you.

**Bourke** Thank you. (*Little pause.*) Well, as for you, Mr Blake – I know what you want, of course.

**Blake** Yes.

**Bourke** Any idea how to get it? I mean, what about your, um, foreign friends?

**Blake** Oh, the Russians, you mean? What can they do? Fly down in a helicopter, pluck me up and away to my freedom? Well, they haven't done it so far, have they? And I don't think I can wait around for them too much longer. (*Little pause.*) It did cross my mind that someone with outside contacts might find me some sort of – of professional group –

**Bourke** A gang you're after, are you? How much could you pay them?

**Blake** I could raise a little – not much. There's my family to provide for – the mortgage, children's education –

**Bourke** So you're looking for a gang to spring you, with almost no money to pay them.

**Blake** Yes, it does seem preposterous, doesn't it, when you put it like that. They don't exist –

**Bourke** Oh yes they do. And you wouldn't have to pay them – the government would pay them for you. In return for information received. The Home Office would know about your plans before you did. Then you'd be off to a maximum security prison where you'd never get a chance at a human conversation again. Not once in the rest of your thirty-five years.

**Blake** I see. Thank you. Thank you for telling me.

**Bourke** What you need is a single fella. One who knows the insides here, and a bit about the workings of the outsides, too.

**Blake** I see. But – well, how do I find this fella? This single fella.

**Bourke** I don't know, Mr Blake. He'd have to be a fella you could trust. But I tell you what – I'll keep an eye – my mind and my memory and my eye – open.

**Blake** That's very good of you, Mr Bourke. Thank you. My name's George, by the way. *George* Blake.

*He holds out his hand.*

**Bourke** And mine's Sean. Sean Bourke. Sean Alphonsus Bourke.

*Taking hand. A whistle sounds.*

**Blake** Ah, I'm being summoned. I'll be seeing you, Sean.

**Bourke** You will, George. You'll be seeing me.

**Blake** Thank you.

*Blake exits.*

**Bourke** Well, why not, Sean? Why not?

*Lights.*


## SCENE TWO

*Winter 1966. About eight in the evening. Bedsitter in London: a bed, a kitchenette, door to bathroom off.*
  *Blake is sitting in his underwear, slumped. Clothes are scattered around him. Other clothes neatly piled beside him. The television is on. From television, ballroom dancing, music. Commentator's voice.*

**Commentator** And this is Linda and Sidney from Luton, third in last year's finals. And now Frederick and Alison from Purley – this is the first time they've competed.

Frederick's a schoolteacher and Alison is a social worker. Ah, and here's Herbert with his new partner Daphne from Sidcup. Daphne has taken over from Marguerite, who has given birth to twins since last year's competition – but doesn't she look cool? Not a sign of nerves – ah, and now Harold and Lynette, in some ways the most remarkable couple on the floor –

*Blake gets up, totters to set, turns it off. Commentator's voice fades down.*

Lynette is a deft mover – (*Voice becomes almost inaudible, vanishes.*)

**Blake** (*stands unsteadily, staring at television*) What, deaf mute? Lynette is a deaf mute? That can't be right. It must be my head, Sean. (*Looks around, sees room is empty.*) I must be hearing things – (*Begins to make his way back to chair.*) Sean, Sean, where are you?

*Bourke enters.*

Where have you been, where have you been, Sean? Why did you leave me?

**Bourke** George, George, I've been stashing the car. I told you I was going to. Don't you remember? I've put it in Harvist Road, looks like all the others in the street, it could be there for years and –

**Blake** What? What are you talking about, Sean?

**Bourke** The car, George. It's in Harvist Road, George –

**Blake** Why was that on television?

**Bourke** Television? There's been something about you on television?

**Blake** No, no, not me, the music. And the grinning faces in chiffon. And a voice like treacle telling us about a deaf mute. In a ballroom competition. That sort of thing.

**Bourke** You've gone feverish. I was afraid you would. Come on, George, let's get you to bed.

**Blake** No, no, Sean – (*Pushing Bourke away.*) Something I haven't finished. Something I have to do. (*Stares around agitatedly, then looks down at himself.*) Oh yes. Get dressed. I've got to get myself out of uniform – into decent clothes. Street clothes. Where are my decent street clothes? I need them.

**Bourke** They're here, George, on the bed. (*Picks up pile of neatly folded clothes.*) So let's get to it, eh? (*Picks up trousers.*) Lift your leg – and the other one – that's a good fit now, that's a good fit, George, considering they're from off the peg and guesswork. Arm now, sleeve a bit short – and the other one – (*Buttoning up shirt.*) Well, the collar's all right, a little snug – (*Stands back, surveying him.*) What's it like, too snug, George?

**Blake** Yes, snug. Nice and snug. Thank you, Sean. Togging me up –

**Bourke** Time to tog you up inside. Here. Wrap yourself around this.

*He opens bottle, hands it to Blake.*

**Blake** Do you think I should?

**Bourke** Not if you don't want to.

**Blake** I don't know what I want, Sean. There's something – something I always want. But I don't think it's this. (*Lifts bottle to lips, takes a swig.*)

**Bourke** No, no, steady, George –

*He snatches bottle back from Blake.*

A few sips, a few careful sips –

**Blake** Mmm?

*He stands swaying, lurches sideways suddenly.*

**Bourke** Oh, Jesus! Oh, *Jesus!*

*Catches Blake. There is a ring on the doorbell.*

Oh, Jesus! That's not the signal! Three short and one long is –

*Another ring.*

(*Dragging Blake towards lavatory door.*) Come on. Let's get you to the toilet.

**Blake** (*stumbling eagerly towards it*) Oh, the toilet! Yes. Yes, please – that's what I need.

*There are three short rings. One long.*

**Bourke** Ah, that's it! Thank God. Don't worry, it's only Nigel and Annie – or Dick –

*Puts Blake into a chair, hurries to door, opens it.*

**Blake** Who is it? Who is it?

**Bourke** Actually, it's Philip!

**Blake** (*in feeble alarm*) Philip? Who's Philip?

**Philip** Gosh, sorry, Nigel told me the signal but I forgot –

**Bourke** I wasn't expecting you just yet.

**Philip** I know, but I couldn't resist. So, there you are, Mr Blake . . . Mr George Blake himself. What a great moment for true British justice . . . Miranda's not here yet, then?

**Bourke** Miranda's just your wife, Philip.

**Blake** Miranda – Miranda – who's Miranda? Sean – Sean, I thought nobody knew where we were except Nigel and Annie. And Dick.

**Bourke** Philip's a great friend of Nigel's and Annie's and Dick's too. In fact, he gave some money to the cause.

**Blake** The cause, what cause?

**Bourke** You, George – the cause of you. I needed financial support, you see. While I was on the job. Food and accommodation. And for renting the car. Philip was very generous.

**Philip** Well, I gave what I could. Nothing on the scale of Nigel and Annie. Or Dick even. (*To Bourke.*) She'll be here in a minute, I'm sure.

**Blake** Who?

**Philip** Well, Miranda.

**Blake** Miranda? Who's Miranda?

**Bourke** She's the wife, George, that's all.

**Blake** The wife, *the* wife, whose wife? This can't be real, can't be, must be my head –

**Bourke** Rest your head, George, don't upset yourself, no need, it's all under control –

**Blake** Whose wife? (*Almost screaming.*) Whose wife?

**Bourke** His.

**Philip** Well, actually she's not my wife, Sean, didn't you realise that? But she would be if she wanted to get married. She's taking her time, you see. Finding out. She's very independent. Quite right too. Actually, to tell you the truth, we're going through a bit of a bad patch at the moment.

**Bourke** Oh no, Philip, not again.

**Philip** Anyway, please don't be put off by her manner. Obviously you're a rather awkward proposition for her, professionally, she has to protect her interests –

**Blake** (*gapes at Bourke*) What professionally? What?

**Bourke** (*evasively*) She's a lovely girl, George. With a good heart.

*He gives Philip a warning look, which Philip doesn't notice.*

**Blake** Good heart? Good heart?

**Philip** She's not doing it just for me, you know. She's doing it for you too. She feels as strongly about you morally as I do. Though we can't go all the way with you, ideologically speaking, we both respect – no, speaking for myself, more than respect, I admire the courage with which you've acted on your principles. As you believed, so did you live. And so shall I write to that effect.

**Blake** Write, write, you'll write –

**Philip** Yes, I'm a journalist.

**Blake** (*in a moan*) A journalist. Yes, please. And a camera, could we have some cameras here too? I could get back into my prison garb –

**Bourke** George!

**Blake** – and pose with the police before they take me back to jail.

**Bourke** Philip's not that sort of journalist, George. Will you trust me, trust me, will you –

**Philip** I write on matters of conscience. Strictly matters of conscience.

**Bourke** Conscience. There. You see.

**Philip** That's how I met Nigel and Annie. And old Dick too. Covering all the CND rallies – the marches,

Aldermaston for the *New Statesman* – so I wasn't sent to jail. Like Nigel and Dick. Shameful. Shameful. Sent to jail for their beliefs. Just like you. I often wish I had been – (*Laughs.*) Well, just for the eighteen months. So I could have met people like you.

**Bourke** There aren't any people like George, Philip.

**Blake** No, I'm very special. I wasn't doing eighteen months. I was doing forty years. And probably will again. Sean! Sean!

*He clutches Bourke's arm.*

I'm sorry, Sean. Just testing. For reality.

**Bourke** I'm real enough for our purposes, George. You're safe. And you'll be sound. I promise it.

**Blake** Thank you, Sean. But there's a question hanging about somewhere in my head. About – about – the girl with a good heart, is that it?

**Bourke** George, you'll oblige me by sitting down. And stop fretting, eh?

*There is a pause.*

**Philip** (*to Bourke*) Am I allowed to know how you did it?

**Blake** Don't tell him, Sean! You mustn't.

**Bourke** It's no secret, George. It'll be public knowledge tomorrow. If it isn't already. The how of it.

**Blake** Yes, yes, the how of it, but not the who of it – you mustn't tell him who.

**Bourke** George, George, he knows the who. He's looking at the who and asking about the how.

**Blake** But he's not to tell anybody who –

**Bourke** He knows that, George.

**Blake** Does he? Do you? Do you know that?

**Philip** Yes, of course I know it. I mean – I mean, well I'm not actually mad. (*Laughs slightly.*) If they find out it's Sean, they'll find out about Nigel and Annie and Dick and Miranda and me. And we'll go to jail.

**Bourke** There. That's settled then. Eh, George?

**Blake** The wife, the wife – what was it he said about the wife?

**Bourke** That they're going through a bad patch, George, and they're not actually married. Now, Philip, you wanted to know how we did it. Just as I planned. George sawed through some bars, I threw my rope ladder over the wall. George climbed up it. George fell down the other side. That bit I didn't plan. His missing his footing.

**Blake** He tried to catch me. Went through his arms.

**Bourke** Broke the fall though, George.

**Blake** Yes. Broke the fall, Sean. Thank you.

**Philip** And then you just got into the car? And drove here?

**Bourke** That's it. That's the whole story, Philip.

**Philip** But that's – that's – (*Laughing.*) It's like something out of a – a comic book!

**Bourke** Comic book!

**Philip** Sawing through bars, a rope ladder –

**Bourke** (*suddenly angry*) A comic book! That's what you think, is it?

**Philip** Well, so simple –

**Bourke** Here. Here, you listen to this! Listen to this!

*Bourke goes to table, picks up tape recorder, winds it back, presses 'Play' button.*

**Bourke** (*voice on tape recorder*) Traffic lights to take notice of. The real bugger is at Halcyon Road where they take two minutes to change from red to green and about twenty seconds to change back to red – you could be stuck for six to eight minutes –

*Bourke turns off recorder, stares at Philip, points to piles of tapes.*

Look at them, hours and hours of them, me walking around the Scrubs, driving around the Scrubs, detailing all the details, until I knew exactly when, exactly where, to the minute – one chance, I had one chance for George. It took work, work, work to work it out. The precise minute. What does it matter that it was with a hacksaw, a rope ladder, a hired car if it was the only way? It was the precise minute that mattered. Comic book – comic book – you get that in your comic books, do you? Eh, Philip?

**Blake** See this man here? He's a genius. Don't you understand that? Sean Bourke. Sean Alphonsus Bourke. Sheer genius. And a great gentleman. Do you understand? Or don't you? Eh? (*Aggressively, if faintly.*)

**Philip** Yes, look – I'm terribly sorry – the last thing I meant – I can't tell you how much I admire you. Both of you.

**Blake** There's only one of you at last, Sean, thank God. So my head's clearing at last. (*Looks at Philip.*) Who did you say you are? There's almost none of *you* that I can see. Oh, that's it! I've got it now, his wife, his Miranda, she's against me professionally, isn't that what he said, Sean? What does that mean?

**Philip** Only that seeing you professionally puts her in a dodgy –

*Doorbell rings once.*

That's probably her.

**Bourke** It's not the signal.

**Philip** I can't – can't remember whether I remembered to pass it on – the signal –

**Bourke** Oh God, Philip!

*Doorbell rings again.*

Well, answer the door. If it's not her, send them away.

**Philip** (*goes apprehensively to the door*) I'm not good – not very good – at lying, I'm afraid. (*Goes to door, hesitates.*) I'll – I'll –

**Blake** Not very good at lying? Who are these people? What's going on? Sean!

**Bourke** (*goes to stand in front of Blake.*) Sit down, George. Not another word from you. Not a word. (*To Philip.*) You – open the door . . . open the door.

**Philip** (*opens the door*) Oh, Miranda, love, thank God!

*Miranda enters, carrying a black bag.*

**Bourke** George – Miranda's a doctor, George.

**Blake** What? A doctor! But I told you – no doctors. No doctors. I told you –

**Bourke** I know, George. But a head injury's a head injury – I couldn't take the risk.

**Blake** She's the risk you shouldn't have taken.

**Miranda** Look, do you want to see me or don't you?

**Bourke** (*coaxingly*) Miranda – Miranda, love –

**Miranda** Dr Joseph, if you please. (*To Bourke and Blake.*) And I've never seen you two before in my life.

**Bourke** Dr Joseph, right, Miranda, but whatever he says, he needs you to look at him – he fell off the wall of the Scrubs –

**Miranda** That's already more than I need to know about the cause of his injury. Now, do I examine you, or don't I?

**Bourke** George! You'll do it for me.

**Blake** As you're here – and been put to such trouble – I would be greatly obliged, (*smiles charmingly*) Dr Joseph.

**Miranda** You've drunk alcohol from the smell of your breath. Bloody stupid.

*Examining Blake's forehead.*

Nasty but superficial. Should heal quickly.

*Checks Blake's eyes and reflexes.*

You're probably in shock and have got mild concussion. (*To Bourke.*) But he's right, a head injury's a head injury. You should go to a hospital for an X-ray.

**Bourke** But Miranda, he can't possibly go to a hospital.

**Philip** No, of course he can't, Miranda, love.

**Miranda** I've given my professional opinion. Whether it's taken is not my responsibility. Then I suppose I'll have to give you a shot of penicillin. (*Takes syringe out of bag.*)

**Blake** What? I hate needles. They – they –

**Bourke** You've got to have it, George.

*He begins to roll up Blake's sleeve.*

**Miranda** No, I need a buttock.

**Bourke** Come on, George.

**Blake** (*trying to push Philip away*) I can do it – I can do it – (*Tries futilely to undo his belt.*)

**Bourke** No, you can't, George. Leave it to me.

*Philip supports Blake. Bourke undoes Blake's trousers, pulls down his underpants, bends him over.*

Go on now, George – a bit lower – bend over.

*Blake is bent over, held by Philip and Bourke, buttocks exposed.*

**Miranda** (*jabs syringe*) There. (*As she packs up.*) I've one last thing to say. What this man needs above all is sleep. Plenty of it. If he gets it, he shouldn't require further medical treatment. Which he won't be getting from me, anyway. Please remember I've never seen any of you before. And I shan't be seeing any of you again –

**Philip** You've been absolutely wonderful, love.

**Miranda** (*to Philip*) And that includes you.

**Philip** What? Oh, Miranda, love – (*Takes her arm.*) You can't mean it!

**Miranda** (*snatching her arm away*) Oh, yes, I mean it. How could you, how could you let me? Did you give a single thought to my future?

**Philip** But Miranda love – Dr Joseph – I didn't make you come. It was your choice, your own personal choice.

**Miranda** You told me where he was and how he was. You told me he needed help. So you knew I wouldn't have any choice – none at all.

**Philip** But we agreed we'd always tell each other everything. And we're always saying people can't go through life not knowing things deliberately. The truth is the truth, facts are facts. It's no good being angry at all the injustices in our society, including him – (*pointing to Blake*) if it's just a matter of principle, but when it comes to the actual living and breathing victim – George Blake himself – the George Blake who needs something practical done for him – not just slogans and high-minded debates – but there, *that* George Blake –

**Miranda** Why do you keep on saying his name? Are you trying to ruin my life, is that what this is about? Because you resent my independence, my having a career – so you'd rather see me struck off and go to jail –

**Bourke** Miranda, darling, we'll never mention your name. Even if we're caught, we'll never mention it, will we, George?

**Philip** You see? You're just overwrought, love. So why don't you go back to the flat, have a cup of tea and an aspirin and lie down – and when I get back, we'll talk the whole thing through.

**Miranda** When you get back to the flat, you'll find all your things outside the door. You're moving out, Philip.

**Philip** Oh, no, I'm not! No, I'm not! For one thing, it's my flat, I own the lease.

**Miranda** I'll buy it from you. Don't worry, I'll give you a fair price.

**Philip** There isn't a fair price. I'll never get another flat like 21E Phildeep Gardens for that money – not with a patio and access to the gardens. If you really want us to separate, you're the one who'll have to move out. Back to Mummy and Daddy – the Brigadier and his lady wife and their three dogs and bring back hanging and keep out the blacks and as for that swine, George Blake, let him . . . let him . . .

**Miranda** (*to Blake and Bourke*) I suppose I should be grateful to you. It's because of you I've found out what kind of man he really is.

*She makes to open the door, as doorbell rings.*

**Bourke** No, don't open it!

*Miranda has already opened the door.*

**Sparrow** (*entering, to Philip*) Sorry to call at this late hour, but better than a dawn raid, eh? Sparrow and Week. Property Management Agents. I'm the Sparrow.

*During this Bourke has bent over Blake, not yet taken in by Sparrow.*

**Philip** It's not us. Nothing to do with us. Him you want, I expect. (*Gestures towards Bourke.*) Well, darling, we'd better be going or we'll be late. The theatre . . .

**Miranda** (*pushing past Sparrow*) Yes. *Much Ado.* Zeffirelli's. At the Old Vic.

**Sparrow** Well, do enjoy it.

**Miranda** Thank you.

**Sparrow** (*looks at clipboard in his hand*) Well, the him I want is O'Brien, Mr O'Brien?

*He looks towards Bourke, who turns.*

**Bourke** (*assuming a much stronger Irish accent*) Evening, sir. How can I help you, sir?

**Sparrow** I'm here on behalf of the landlord. Need to look around, make sure everything's roughly as it ought to be.

**Bourke** I hope you don't mind being quick about it, sir. My brother here (*stepping aside*) was told down at the hospital he needed a good, long lay-down.

**Sparrow** Oh, I see.

**Bourke** But you should see t'other fellows, as they say, eh, Seamus?

**Sparrow** Oh. It was a fight then, was it?

**Bourke** Well, he's a peace-loving man, sir, is Seamus, it takes a lot to set him blazin', but down the pub this noon a couple of ill-advised boyos took it on themselves to say somethin' inflamin' 'bout te motter-country, sir, and that did it, d'int it, Seamus?

**Blake** Yes.

**Bourke** Take it from me, sir, they'll be careful what t'ey say about Motter Ireland in future, when t'ey can speak again, t'at is.

**Sparrow** (*laughs nervously*) Um – well, excuse me – there's a question I have to ask. On behalf of my landlords. Um – is he actually living here by any chance, Mr Seamus – Mr O'Brien. O'Brien?

**Bourke** Oh yes, we're just a couple of Paddys living here, aren't we, Seamus? Just a couple of Paddys.

**Blake** Yes. (*Pause.*) Begorrah.

**Sparrow** Be – sorry, Mr O'Brien?

**Bourke** Begorrah. Yes, begorrah, is what he said. He's having a bit of trouble connecting thoughts to words. His head –

## CELL MATES

**Sparrow** And – is he here – on a permanent basis? Sorry, so sorry to pry like this but the landlords specifically insist that this is a one-person occupancy. The rent is agreed on that basis.

**Bourke** (*suddenly uncertain*) Well now, well now, sir, we're not sure of Seamus's plans since the incident at noon, are we, Seamus?

**Blake** Back to ta Emril Isle. Bloddy English. See.

**Sparrow** Mmm?

**Bourke** The Emerald Isle, t'at's Ireland, sir. Going back as soon as he can – because of te – te bloddy English, sir. Pardon me, sir, but in view of what's happened you'll understand –

**Sparrow** Yes, yes of course. And – and on behalf of my fellow countrymen, I'd like to apologise – and if by any chance he's still here when I come around next month, just, well – (*Winks.*) Make a point of being out, eh?

**Blake** Tanks.

**Sparrow** Now I'll get on with it – let you get to bed. (*Glances rapidly round room, checking off on clipboard.*) Bed, cupboard, chest of drawers, mirror, light bulb in place, bookcase, table, lamps, television set – functioning, I'm sure. (*Turns it on.*)

**Voice on TV** . . . two hours ago of the spy, who was jailed for a record forty years. This is the most recent photograph that has been issued. The public are asked to report any sighting to their . . . local police station, or contact Whitehall 1212 . . .

**Bourke** Tat's moine that is! Paid for out of my own money.

**Sparrow** Oh, yes, you're right, quite right – it's not on the list. Oh, I'm so sorry. So sorry.

**Bourke** Are you?

**Sparrow** Yes, yes, very sorry indeed – well now, that's everything, thank you very much, goodnight, Mr O'Brien, Mr O'Brien.

*He hurries to door, exits.*
  *Bourke and Blake stand staring after him, then turn to each other. Bourke lets out a howl of laughter. Blake yelps with feeble laughter.*

**Bourke** Begorrah, begorrah. Oh George, I never in my life heard an Irishman say 'begorrah'!

**Blake** But I'm not Irish, Sean. Half Egyptian, half Dutch. So naturally I say 'begorrah'.

**Bourke** And Emerald Isle – Emerald Isle – (*Laughs again.*)

**Blake** (*also laughing*) No, don't, Sean, please – please – my head!

**Bourke** Yes, the time's come for you to get what the good Dr Joseph ordered.

*He leads Blake towards the bed.*

A long rest. Sleep – she's right. That's what you need. And a lot of it.

*Beginning to undress Blake.*

**Blake** But we've only just put them on.

**Bourke** (*continuing to undress Blake*) But now the company's gone. So we can take them off, George.

**Blake** I may need – need to go to the lavatory, Sean. My bowels, you see –

**Bourke** That's all right, George. Call out when you want to go – I can help you to it.

**Blake** All evening I've needed – and now when I can – I can't.

**Bourke** But when you can I'm here. So don't worry about it, George. We're going to be living together closer than – closer than a husband and wife almost, almost, I mean less privacy than in the Scrubs even, so embarrassment doesn't come into it –

**Blake** The Scrubs! Wormwood Scrubs! I've finally left it, then, have I, Sean, thanks to you?

**Bourke** You have, George. And for ever. I'll see to it. Now you lie down –

*He gets Blake between the sheets.*

And close your eyes – close your eyes now. Try some of this – (*Begins to hum 'Danny Boy'.*) Always works with the English – the nice ones – Nigel and Annie and Dick and Philip – and even Miranda – I've seen their eyes fill with tears, even hers, so relax, George, relax – (*Hums more 'Danny Boy', croons it.*) There you go, George. You're off, aren't you, eh?

*Blake murmurs from bed. Bourke goes on crooning 'Danny Boy'. Bourke gets up from beside Blake, wanders around room, humming. Sees tape recorder on table. Glances towards Blake in bed, then seizes tape recorder, presses 'Play' button.*

**Bourke** (*voice on recorder*) – so allow as much as ten minutes at Halcyon Road lights to be certain – that you're not going to hit any major problems.

*Bourke presses 'Stop' button, winds back, presses 'Record' button.*

**Bourke** (*into recorder*) 'The Springing of George Blake. Chapter One. A Genius and a Gentleman.' That's what he called me. Well, I don't know about the gentleman – I hope I'm always a gentleman – of a sort – even as a thief. But a genius. Sheer genius, didn't he say? Begorrah! (*Laughs.*) But what matters is this. I've got George his freedom. And this. I've got myself a story to tell at last. A story to tell and a story to sell. They'll love me for it in Dublin – there I'll be . . .

**Blake** (*rears up in bed*) Sean, Sean –

**Bourke** (*turning off recorder*) What is it, George? You want the toilet? (*Going to bed.*)

**Blake** Promise me something.

**Bourke** (*sitting on bed's edge*) Anything, George. You know that.

**Blake** Get me to safety, Sean. Complete safety, please.

**Bourke** I've already arranged that. As soon as the time's right, I'm taking you home. To Dublin.

**Blake** No, no. *My* home. Get me to my home.

**Bourke** But – where is your home, George?

**Blake** Moscow. Moscow, please, Sean. (*There is a pause.*) Sean – you promised me anything.

**Bourke** But I don't know how to do it, George. I've got a plan worked out to get us to Dublin.

**Blake** What is it? What is your plan?

**Bourke** Well, you'll be under the kiddies' bunk in Nigel's and Annie's Dormobile, with Dick going along as extra camouflage, a little group of tourists, see, George, and I'll go separately, so there's no connection between us. Then we join up in Dublin –

**Blake** Moscow. Join up in Moscow. You and I.

**Bourke** But you can't keep yourself squeezed under a little bunk all across Europe to Moscow –

**Blake** Yes, I can. I can if I have to. Then you join me separately. Just as you said.

**Bourke** George, I've told you. I'm going to Dublin. I need to be there. Need to!

**Blake** Yes, yes, yes, you go home to Dublin – but come to me in Moscow first, Sean. For a short visit. A holiday. A week or two.

**Bourke** Oh, George, look at you, you should be lying down, you're trembling and shaking –

**Blake** You promised me anything! I want to go to Moscow. I want you to come separately, just as you said. Be with me a week. The thought of that, that'll help me survive under the bunk. Having you to look forward to, that's all I ask. Sean – my Sean.

**Bourke** All right, George. If that's what you want. I'll get you to Moscow. And come for a week myself. Just for a week I'll come. All right?

*There are three short rings, one long one, on the bell. Bourke looks towards door.*

**Blake** (*screams out*) I'm falling, I'm falling!

*He grabs at Bourke.*

**Bourke** (*holds him*) I've caught you, this time I've caught you, George!

**Blake** Gone, gone, gone, gone –

**Bourke** Hush now, George, hush, it's the signal, it's only Nigel and Annie, and Dick too probably, come to see you safe and sound! Let go of me, George, let go of me.

*As again three short, one long ring on the bell. Lights.*

## SCENE THREE

*Three weeks later. Moscow. Lunchtime. Dining room of Blake's flat. Table, chairs. Hatch to kitchen, off.*

*Stage left, Blake's room. Desk on which stands a typewriter, a pile of typescripts, and a very large and sturdy recording machine of the period.*

*Stage right, another room, similar layout to Blake's, a pile of typescripts on desk.*

*Blake is in his room, roaming about as he talks into the recording machine.*

**Blake** (*his speech is slightly stilted*) And so at the age of seventeen, on the run from the Nazis because of my work in the Dutch underground, I managed to escape to England. Although I was born and bred in Holland, my father, being Egyptian, was entitled to British citizenship. As indeed was I. I therefore had no trouble in joining the British navy and was selected to be a member of the submarine service. (*He looks at his watch, sighs.*) Unfortunately, I soon discovered that the sensation of being under water filled me with the utmost terror. I applied, instead, for a post in the Foreign Office, and was immediately accepted. After the war I was sent to Korea. I will give an account of my experiences there in a separate chapter. But ideologically the most significant event of my life was when, back in London again, I was transferred to Intelligence and then to the Russian desk. I was put on a special course at Cambridge University – where all the top British traitors have always been educated (*stifles a slight laugh*) to study the Russian language, Russian culture, and the philosophical principles that lie behind the Soviet Revolution. One of my teachers was Tom Wingard, a senior civil servant. It was he who introduced me to the works of Karl Marx.

'Know Thine Enemy', his series of lectures was called. (*Looks at his watch again.*) An exceptionally objective, fair-minded man, he succeeded, without of course intending to, in converting me completely to Marxism. English teaching at its very best.

*Zinaida enters carrying medals.*

(*In Russian.*) Come in. News of Comrade Robert at last?

**Zinaida** (*in Russian*) Comrade Robert? No. Nothing.

**Blake** (*in Russian*) You've done a wonderful job, thank you, Zinaida.

*Zinaida pulls him up to put the medals on.*

(*In Russian.*) Not now, Zinaida. For the next official dinner.

**Zinaida** (*in Russian*) I want to see what they look like. (*She pins them on.*) There, now you are wearing what you have won.

**Blake** Yes. They positively glow with indecency and vulgarity. Best of all, they clink when I walk. *Spasiba*, Zinaida.

**Zinaida** *Zanyeshna.*

*Zinaida goes into kitchen.*

**Blake** Ah, yes, Tom Wingard. The memory of him brings me to the main point of this section of my book. That for those of us who worked steadily for the Communist cause, the Hitler–Stalin pact, the show trials, the summary executions, the internment, exiling or wholesale massacre of millions were indeed – (*pauses to find word*) sensitive issues. The struggle to reconcile our personal sense of what is just and right with our acknowledgement that there is a greater good at stake –

a country of the future – is a painful one. But in the end that ideal, the country of the future, must prevail. The aphorism 'You can't make an omelette without breaking eggs' is often quoted. To which the frequent reply is: 'But supposing I don't want an omelette?' To this I can only say –

*Viktor, carrying Bourke's suitcase, enters the dining room. He is followed by Bourke, who is followed by Stan, carrying Bourke's overnight bag.*

**Bourke** Well, where is he, then? Where is George?

**Stan** He is probably in his study. Working.

**Viktor** Let us put your bags in your bedroom.

**Stan** And then we will find him.

*Blake, medal still dangling half-attached, hurries into dining room, followed by Zinaida.*

**Blake** At last! Robert!

**Bourke** Who?

**Blake** Well, here you are then.

*Blake goes to Bourke, embraces him. Bourke responds.*

**Bourke** Yes, here I am, George!

**Blake** Ah, Robert.

**Bourke** Robert, that's twice in two sentences you've called me Robert, George, don't you remember me? It's only been three weeks since you saw me.

**Blake** Robert's your – your *nom de guerre* while you're here – *nom de plume* as well, come to think of it. Don't worry – I'll explain it all to you when you've had a chance to settle. You'll be amused –

*He throws anxious glances towards Stan and Viktor, who smile, nod.*

I promise you.

**Bourke** What are those then, George?

**Blake** Oh, just – just a couple of gongs. Given for services rendered. Order of Red Banner. Order of Lenin. And this is Zinaida! My housekeeper. A jolly good one too. (*To Zinaida, in Russian.*) This is our guest, Comrade Robert.

**Zinaida** (*in Russian*) Comrade Robert. (*Nods.*)

**Bourke** (*attempting what he thinks is Russian greeting*) Comrobert. (*Then realising.*) Oh, Robert! Comrade Robert – that's me.

**Blake** Yes, you – (*In Russian.*) Can we have a bottle of champagne please, Zinaida?

**Zinaida** Of course.

*There is an awkward pause.*

**Bourke** And of course you know Stan and – and – (*Gesturing from Stan to Viktor.*)

**Stan** Oh yes. George knows us very well. We have become his great – great –

**Viktor** Chumps is the word. George's great chumps.

**Stan** No, no, chaps. We are great chaps.

**Blake** (*slightly obsequious*) No, Stan – I think the word you're both looking for is chums. We're great chums, the three of us. The four of us, I hope, Robert.

**Viktor** What then is a chump?

**Stan** I believe I know. A chump is a person who does something he knows is foolish. A mistake. (*Looks from Blake to Bourke.*)

**Blake** Yes, yes, an excellent definition, wouldn't you say, Robert?

**Bourke** (*watching closely but with an attempt at casualness*) That's right. 'Oh, what a chump!' we say. 'What a chump you've made of yourself.'

**Blake** Yes. 'What a chump you've –' But why are we all so formal? Let's sit down, um, chaps – (*laughs nervously*) like chums. Zinaida's gone to get us some refreshment, Stan, Viktor, Robert – champagne, you'll be glad to hear there's a plentiful supply of it, thanks to our excellent hosts – (*Almost bows to Stan and Viktor.*) And spirits too, mainly vodka, of course – but champagne's my favourite tipple –

*Zinaida enters with tray, on it a bottle of champagne and glasses. She puts it on the table.*

Russian, of course, but I've come almost to prefer it to the French, which I haven't drunk since my days in the British Consul in West Berlin and so can scarcely remember, but the Russian variety is fruity, earthy, it has a – a ripe peasanty fruitiness and pleasantness – (*opening bottle and pouring*) that I've come to – to prefer. (*Small, awkward pause.*) And as I say, there's lots of it – Oh, Robert, Robert! Robert!

**Bourke** (*gives a start, realising*) Oh sorry, yes, that's me, isn't it? (*Little pause.*) Yes, George?

**Blake** What was your journey like? I was getting quite anxious – wasn't I, Stan?

**Stan** Yes. He was afraid you had changed your mind about coming.

**Viktor** We would not have liked that, Robert.

**Blake** So what was it like, your trip to Moscow?

**Bourke** (*assumes a tone of jolliness, glancing nervously from face to face as he speaks*) Well, George, as it turned out, it was the loveliest trip of my life – 'Have you anything to declare?' asks the man at Victoria Station. 'Only a pint of scotch,' says I, 'and that's inside me' –

*Laughs. Blake, Stan and Viktor laugh.*

– and stamp they go, on my false passport. I got one in the name of Kennedy, George K. Kennedy – I mean, what's the point of spending five years in the Scrubs if you don't know how to get a false passport in the name of George K. Kennedy to take you to where you don't want to go?

*He laughs. Stan and Viktor look at Bourke blankly.*

**Stan** Where you don't want to go?

**Blake** There, that's what I was telling you about, the Irish sense of humour, they love anarchic jokes, jokes that *seem* hostile –

**Bourke** Oh Jesus, yes, chaps – (*Laughs again.*) That's the joke I always made to myself every time I approached a new frontier, out of terror, you see. But I needn't have worried, because stamp they go in Calais, and stamp they go in Berlin – stamp, stamp, stamp, stamping me and old George K. right through Checkpoint Charlie –

**Stan** Stamp?

**Viktor** You put it on an envelope? Or walk heavily, stamp, stamp –

**Blake** No. On your passport. (*Makes passport-stamping motion with his fist.*)

**Stan** (*in Russian*) You have his passport?

**Viktor** (*in Russian*) I forgot to take it.

**Bourke** What? A problem –?

**Blake** Viktor was just saying to Stan that he forgot to take your passport.

**Viktor** Yes. My mistake. Can I have it, please?

**Bourke** My passport?

**Stan** We have another one for you.

**Viktor** And it is not forged.

**Bourke** Oh. Well, in that case –

*Takes passport out of his pocket. Viktor takes it, hands him new passport. Bourke studies it.*

But it's – what is it? I can't make it out.

**Stan** It's Ukrainian.

**Viktor** With your name on it. Robert Adamovich Garvin.

**Bourke** Robert Adamovich –

**Viktor** Garvin.

**Blake** Which is why I've been calling you Robert, you see, Robert.

**Bourke** Robert Adamovich Garvin, eh? (*Makes to put passport into his pocket.*)

**Viktor** Please permit me, Robert.

*Takes passport from him, puts both of Bourke's passports into his pocket.*

**Bourke** But – but I don't get to keep it, then? Not either of them?

**Viktor** It remains in possession of the Department.

**Bourke** But when I go home. I mean, how do I –?

**Stan** It is returned to you.

**Bourke** Oh. Well, I suppose that's – that'll do. As long as I can get it when I need it. But it's a little strange, George. For me, I mean. Here I am, one minute Sean Bourke, with a false passport of my own, and the next I've got a genuine passport in somebody else's name – Robert Adamovich something – and the next I haven't got any passport at all. (*Laughs anxiously.*) If you see. A little strange, eh? (*Little pause.*) George?

**Blake** Yes. Yes, I know. But – well, they want to keep your identity concealed, Robert. There are spies all over Moscow. British, American, West German. They're bound to discover I'm here. Any day now. Isn't that right?

**Stan** It is inevitable. A certainty.

**Blake** (*referring to Stan and Viktor*) And then if they discover I'm being visited by an Irishman called Sean Bourke, late of the Wormwood Scrubs – well, that will lead them to Nigel and Dick, also late of the Wormwood Scrubs. And then to Annie. And Philip. And Miranda – Dr Joseph – they'll all go to jail. We don't want that. Do we?

**Bourke** No. No, of course not.

**Stan** We are very grateful to you and your friends for all that you have done for us. You have brought George Blake here. To us.

**Viktor** You must not be punished because of it.

**Bourke** No. Thank you. You're right –

**Blake** The George that's here – this George – (*passing the glasses on tray*) wants to propose a toast.

*Holds up glass. Others follow suit.*

To Robert Adamovich Garvin! Without whom this George – the George that's here – wouldn't be here!

**Viktor** *and* **Stan** Robert Adamovich Garvin!

*They drain off their glasses.*

**Bourke** Thank you, thank you.

**Stan** Now (*rising*) I have to go home. To arrange for my wife's aunt's husband's funeral.

**Blake** Oh, I'm sorry, Stan. Very, very sorry. My condolences to – to your wife. To . . . Katerina.

**Stan** Oh, she is happy. He was not a nice – chap – you see. In fact, he was a complete chump. Shouting, swearing, drunk, violent. Often I wanted to –

*Points finger at Bourke, makes soft shooting noise.*

**Viktor** (*who has also risen*) I must go home too. My daughter is taking part in her school's display of gymnastics. She is gifted but dumpling. I tell her, 'Starve, my child, starve and become famous and rich.' But like most childs –

**Stan** Children.

**Viktor** Yes, of course, yes, children – like most children she likes to lie on the cushions listening to pop, and who can blame her? I tell you who. Her mother. Also me. (*Laughs.*) So –

**Stan** So. So welcome to Russia, Robert.

*Shakes Bourke's hand.*

**Viktor** Yes, welcome to Moscow. I hope you will be at home with us.

*Shakes Bourke's hand.*

**Bourke** Thank you, I am, I feel I am. Thank you.

**Blake** Goodnight, comrades. See you soon. And thank you for all – all you've done for us.

**Bourke** Yes, thank you.

**Stan** (*in Russian, to Blake*) How is the book coming on?

**Blake** (*in Russian*) Oh, I keep working on it.

*Stan nods.*

**Viktor** (*in Russian*) If you need any help –?

**Blake** (*in Russian*) Perhaps when I get to the end –

*Stan and Viktor go out, calling 'goodnights' to Zinaida, who returns them.*

**Bourke** What was that? The Russian bit at the end?

**Blake** They were asking about my book.

**Bourke** Your book?

**Blake** Yes. They want me to write my autobiography. They think it'll be a great propaganda coup.

*There is a pause.*

**Bourke** So, they're your publishers too, are they? As well as being whatever it is they are.

**Blake** No, they're not my publishers. What they are is officers of the KGB. Rather high-ranking ones. At least, they outrank me.

**Bourke** KGB?

**Blake** Yes, KGB.

**Bourke** I see. (*After a pause, makes an effort.*) But what about your own trip, George? How was that?

**Blake** (*absently*) The worst thing was my bladder. Nigel and Annie – no, it was Dick – only gave me the one bottle. I filled it before we got to Calais, so from then on – well, there were times when I thought of giving myself up, just so I could have a pee. I shouldn't have asked you to come. (*Little pause.*) I shouldn't have been so – so – damned selfish. (*Little pause.*) I shouldn't have persuaded you to come.

**Bourke** (*little laugh*) Well, can you explain further?

**Blake** They don't trust you. Stan and Viktor. And the committee of the KGB.

**Bourke** Committee? What committee?

**Blake** Their job is to analyse your every move, every word. Every aspect of your behaviour. As observed and reported by Stan and Viktor.

**Bourke** Like a parole board, you mean?

**Blake** Oh, they're far more powerful than a parole board. Parole boards can only keep you where you don't want to be. But Stan, Viktor, the committee, they can –

**Bourke** (*after a little pause*) What, George?

*Blake points finger at Bourke. Makes soft shooting noise.*

That's twice in no time I've been shot with a finger and a hiss.

**Blake** Yes. But they don't always use fingers for shooting. And never when they mean it. They use bullets in the back of the neck. If ever a chap owed a chap an apology –

**Bourke** In this case it's a matter of a chap and a chump. I knew it was the wrong thing to do. Knew it in my blood and bones!

**Blake** I didn't. Not for a second. If I had, I wouldn't –

**Bourke** I know, George. Is there anything stronger – ? (*Indicating champagne.*) You mentioned vodka, wasn't it?

*Blake goes to hatch, raps on it. Zinaida raises hatch.*

**Blake** (*in Russian*) A bottle of vodka, please, Zinaida.

*Zinaida passes out vodka, vodka glass.*

Thank you.

*Zinaida closes hatch. Blake opens bottle, pours vodka into glass, hands it to Bourke, puts bottle beside him. Bourke downs vodka, pours more, downs that.*

**Bourke** What do they suspect me of? Why don't they trust me, George? After what I've done for them?

**Blake** Well, to understand it, you have to look at it from their point of view. Supposing they had a top Western agent in one of their high security prisons. And somebody comes along – a Ukrainian – a single Ukrainian fella called Robert Adamovich Garvin, let's say – and the top Western agent saws through a few bars, the single Ukrainian fella, Robert, throws a rope ladder over the wall, drives him around the corner to a flat in Moscow, and then hides him in the bunk of a Dormobile and gets him driven to London. To them the idea is preposterous. Because they can't begin to understand what it means to have incompetent liberal Englishmen for your masters, half-witted and uneducated Englishmen for your jailers, and above all a single Irish fella for your friend –

**Bourke** But why? Why do they think the single Irish fella would do it?

**Blake** One possible explanation – you're a British agent. Planted in Wormwood Scrubs to make friends with me, get me out. With the concealed connivance of the British government. Then you follow me to Moscow. Pick up names. See how the KGB really works – then off to Ireland, and in due course back to London for a debriefing. Unfortunately they have a very high regard for British Intelligence.

**Bourke** But you told them – Stan and Viktor and this KGB committee – you told them it was your idea I come here for this – this holiday?

**Blake** Of course.

**Bourke** They don't believe you?

**Blake** They believe I think that's what's happened. They also believe it's possible you manipulated me into thinking that's what happened. That's their world, you see, Robert. That's how they're paid to think. It's how they earn their pensions.

**Bourke** And what is it I have to do, George? What exactly do I have to do, to survive?

**Blake** The most important thing is – to be natural. Then it's mainly a question of don'ts. Don't ask questions. Don't snoop – not that you would. But don't *look* as if you're snooping. Avoid picking up any Russian. You'll start using it. Then they'll suspect you're already fluent in it. Keep yourself innocently occupied.

**Bourke** What, sightseeing, holidaying, being a tourist? I can do that all right, I'm looking forward to it.

**Blake** You won't be allowed out much, I'm afraid. When you are, you'll be accompanied by Stan or Viktor or both. No – the solution is work.

**Bourke** Work! What sort of work?

**Blake** Editorial work.

**Bourke** Editorial work! (*Laughs, in spite of himself.*)

**Blake** (*also laughs slightly*) It was my idea. I pointed out that you edited the Wormwood Scrubs in-house magazine, so why didn't you help turn some of their translations of political tracts into grammatical and idiomatic English? Stuff with titles like *Tractors, Wheat and Bread: A History of the Economic Revolution in the Ukraine and Belorussia* – stuff like that, making it readable. You can do that, Robert. Easy-peasy.

**Bourke** I can make it grammatical and idiomatic. I doubt I can make it readable. (*Laughs.*) It's the vodka.

**Blake** What?

**Bourke** My thinking it'll be all right. I'll get out of this and through to Dublin.

**Blake** Of course you will, Sean – no, Robert – no, Sean, damn it! Tonight, at least, you're Sean. And look, Sean, we've already got out of a worse pickle than this one! So to us, Sean! To Sean and George! (*Raising glass.*)

**Bourke** (*also raising glass*) To George and Sean! And anyway, what's all the fuss? My being a good boy – see nothing, hear nothing, say nothing – for a week, that's all it amounts to.

**Blake** Six months, Sean.

*Bourke stares at him.*

They want you to stay for six months.

**Bourke** Oh, Jesus.

**Blake** To give themselves time to watch you. Listen to you. Satisfy themselves that you are who and what you claim to be. And actually are. As I know. A single Irish fella –

**Bourke** Six months! Six months of – of acting natural? Every minute of the day? Here? In Moscow?

**Blake** Yes. That's the – the sentence, so to speak, Sean. You'll do it standing on your head. I know you will.

**Bourke** George – George – I believe I've got to lie down for a while. I've gone a bit dizzy –

**Blake** (*getting up*) Here. Let's get you to your room. (*Picks up Bourke's bags.*) You rest until dinner. Zinaida's a terrific cook – her chicken casserole is scrumptious.

**Bourke** Good, George, good. I'll – I'll look forward to that then. Her chicken casserole.

*Blake leads Bourke into Bourke's room, puts down bags, turns suddenly, and emotionally.*

**Blake** It's going to be all right. I'll look after you. What you've been to me, I'll be to you. We're in this together. As always. Trust me. Please, Robert.

*Holds out his hand, takes Bourke's.*

**Bourke** (*taking Blake's hand*) Of course I trust you. It's Sean, though. Sean for tonight, George. Isn't it?

**Blake** Yes. Sean, Robert.

**Bourke** Oh Jesus, oh Jesus, oh Jesus!

*Looks at bag, fumbles to the bottom, pulls out tape recorder, presses 'Rewind' button, stops, presses 'Play' button.*

**Bourke** (*voice on recorder*) I really believe this to be true – that nobody in the whole bloody world could have done what I've done! I, Sean Bourke –

## CELL MATES

*Bourke presses 'Stop' button, presses 'Record' button.*

**Bourke** (*into machine*) This is probably madness, absolute madness.

*He stuffs recorder back into bag, crouches furtively over concealed machine.*

Just the sort of thing George's warned me against – see no, hear no, speak no – And I wasn't going to anyway, not during the little week I was here, this was just going to be an exotic aside in my story, visiting George all safe and sound in Moscow, the two of us in our pomp – but I've already said this, before I left I said it, that first evening out of the Scrubs I said it, I knew in my blood and my bones it was a mistake. I had the chance, all I had to say before he ran out of the flat and down to Nigel's and Annie's Dormobile was, 'Sorry, George, I've changed my mind, I won't be coming to Moscow, home to Dublin for me – and see you – see you some time –'

*Lights dim slightly as he goes on speaking, inaudibly. Blake, meanwhile, has gone back to the dining room, picked up the champagne bottle and glass, gone on into his study. Pours himself a glass of champagne, takes a sip, presses 'Rewind' button, then 'Play' – it is inaudible to audience – rewinds. Presses 'Record'. As Bourke becomes inaudible:*

**Blake** (*into recorder*) No, it's not a question of whether you want an omelette. The egg always gets eaten in some form or other. Or it rots and is thrown away. The thing is to make sure that as many who live, are allowed to live, have an egg, cooked in some fashion, to eat. Sacrifices *are* inevitable for the greater good. Otherwise there's no point to my having done what I've done. That doesn't mean, it does not mean, that there is pleasure to be found in doing what has to be done to those for whom no eggs are available, no eggs allowable, or what is done, indeed, to the egg itself – it is a hateful business, a dreadful habit but I – I insist that I – and others like me – who saw the light, had no choice, no choice but to follow our –

*Lights dim slightly on him as he speaks inaudibly and intensely towards machine.*

*During this Zinaida comes out. Begins to lay table for dinner. Lights fade slowly on Bourke crouched over machine in his bag; Blake roaming around room as he speaks into his machine; Zinaida laying table.*

*Curtain.*

# Act Two

### SCENE ONE

*Six months later. After dinner. Bourke and Blake are sitting slightly away from each other. There is an atmosphere of tension. Bourke has vodka in front of him. Zinaida is finishing the clearing up.*

**Bourke** (*clears his throat, looks at Blake's chest*) I see it's a night for the medals, George.

**Blake** Yes, I promised Zinaida this morning.

*Zinaida, catching her name, glances towards him. Blake smiles vaguely towards her.*

As it gives her so much pleasure and costs me so little effort – (*Gestures coldly.*)

**Bourke** I've never worked out why they mean so much to her. As if she'd won them herself.

**Blake** Because she's very proprietorial, Robert. Like most Russian servants. A legacy from the serf-owning days. The serfs owned the masters as completely as the masters owned the serfs.

*Zinaida looks from Bourke to Blake anxiously, goes to kitchen.*

The same was true of the slaves in the southern states of America, from all historical reports.

*There is a tense and ghastly pause, during which Zinaida looks through hatch, draws it softly down.*

**Bourke** (*in a sudden panic*) Excuse me, George, excuse me – (*Getting up.*) Won't be a minute –

*Hurries to his room.*

*Blake watches his exit coldly. Bourke pulls out bag from under bed, bends over, speaks into tape recorder.*

What's going on, that's what I want to know. Something's going on, as sure as hell's hell. It's never been like this before, he's never been like this before – Look, look, here's something I'm going to say that could be the death of me, but that's what I'm talking about, fretting about, isn't it? The death of me – because that's what it's like, like waiting for my own death – so if anything happens to me before Tuesday, or on Tuesday itself come to that – if any accident befalls me, so to speak – Oh, shut up, Robert – Sean – Sean, nothing's going to happen, boyo, nothing's going to 'befall' – and if it does there's nothing you can say now will help you then, so calm down, calm down – go back and do what you've done this last six months, go back and act natural and don't say another word, don't think another thought about Tuesday. Tuesday's Tuesday and will turn up in due course. Preferably on Tuesday, eh? So keep away from mentioning Tuesday as if your life depended on it.

*Laughs, puts machine away, makes to go to door, stops, goes off. Sound of lavatory flushing. Bourke comes straight out into dining room.*

Sorry about that, George, being taken short like that. A touch of trouble with the old stomach.

**Blake** Would you mind shutting the door properly, Robert? Your door.

**Bourke** Oh, right. Sorry, George.

*Closes door, goes back to chair, sits. Picks up glass, drains contents. Pours himself more. Blake watches him.*

**Blake** (*as Bourke raises glass to his lips*) That can't be doing it any good. Your old stomach. You're making it older by the glassful, Robert.

**Bourke** You're right, George. Dead right.

*Puts glass down, undrunk. Blake raises his glass of champagne, sips from it.*

Look, George, what is it? Is it what I said about Tuesday? Going home on Tuesday. If I did, it was accidental, George, and not meant to be detrimental. Not to you, of all people. Did I say anything accidentally detrimental to you, George? If so, I apologise.

**Blake** What you said was that I'm lacking in normal, human feelings.

**Bourke** I couldn't have said that, George! I couldn't have!

**Blake** Not in those actual words, of course. You didn't actually say, 'George, you're lacking in normal, human feelings.' But it was the implication of what you did say.

**Bourke** Which was what? What did I say?

*Blake takes a sip of champagne, is silent.*

Oh, come on, George – (*Cajolingly.*) What did I say, tell me what I said and I'll apologise for the implications. How's that for a deal, George?

**Blake** (*gets up, goes to his study door*) I must get back to my work. (*Stops.*) What you said actually, Robert. What you actually said. After you'd congratulated yourself on your good fortune in escaping from my adopted country, my flat and my company on this coming Tuesday – what you actually and actually said was: 'It's a good thing for you, George, that you never suffer from homesickness. That you can brush your past aside without another thought.' That's verbatim, Robert.

**Bourke** (*after a miserable pause*) I don't believe I said 'brush', George. I believe I said 'push'. And I didn't mean, the last thing I meant –

**Blake** (*coming back*) What you meant, Robert, was what I've already stated you implied. That I'm some sort of emotionless – (*gestures*) freak. But hasn't it occurred to you, Robert, hasn't it ever occurred to you that the reason I'm not homesick is because I'm finally at home? Morally and spiritually at home. Which is the only kind of home worth having. For me. (*Little pause.*) My past was always in the future. The country of the future. This is where my feelings have always been. Does that mean I have no feelings, Robert? Does it? But of course you've never understood –

**Bourke** Oh Jesus, George, I understand – I understand better than any man alive that you're as human as they come. I mean we've been close, as close as two men could be. I'll never forget you in your concussion back there in London, so helpless, dependent, vulnerable you were, George, but the one thing you fixed on – the only thing you fixed on was getting yourself here.

**Blake** With your help, of course.

**Bourke** However. You'd have done it however, George. With me or without.

**Blake** No, I wouldn't have, Robert. Helpless, dependent, vulnerable. I needed you as a man needs his wife. Didn't I?

**Bourke** (*shocked*) What, George?

**Blake** Well, isn't that what you said at the time? Mumbled it into the fog and headache of my concussion –

that you were looking after me as if you were my wife. Or as if I were your wife. Which way around was it, Robert, come to think of it?

**Bourke** I don't remember, George.

**Blake** Don't remember whether you're my husband or my wife? (*Little pause.*) Oh come, Robert, it's usually quite easy to distinguish between the one and the other – especially in a shortish marriage like ours, eh?

**Bourke** Whatever I said was just a way of speaking about our friendship, George. However I behaved, it was as your friend. (*Little pause.*) What's the matter with you, what's the matter? I've never seen you like this before!

**Blake** I loved my wife. I still do.

**Bourke** Oh, I see, I see. Yes – well, you know, you don't talk about her, so people forget, I forget –

**Blake** Silence on certain personal matters doesn't necessarily come from a lack, Robert. Of normal human feelings. My Madeleine still is, and ever will be, my Madeleine. If she'd had her way she would have stood by me for the whole of my sentence. For every one of my forty years. Or at least as many as she would have survived. Her health is so delicate – she's always afflicted with some sort of rash, on one part of her body or another – and the heroic manner in which she endured her almost constant conjunctivitis. It was I, Robert, I who insisted on releasing her from her vows. For her sake. For the sake of our three children. About whom, you may have noticed, I also do not speak.

**Bourke** That's why I forget you had them – have them.

**Blake** The knowledge that my Madeleine has embarked on a second, equally successful, marriage gives me joy. Not pain. She deserves to live under another name, legally acquired. With a man who isn't, and is unlikely ever to become, a jailbird. (*Pours himself champagne, raises his glass.*) Madeleine, dear wife of my heart and my loins. Mother of my beloved children, I salute and honour you – the ladylike embodiment of all the womanly virtues, including the finest virtue – domestic loyalty.

*Bourke, hurriedly and amply filling his glass with vodka, raises it.*

**Bourke** To Madeleine. The perfect embodiment.

*They clink glasses. Blake begins to shake, then lets out a howl of laughter. Bourke stares at him in bewilderment, then, realising, also lets out a howl of laughter. They rock and shake with laughter.*

Oh, Jesus – Oh, Jesus, George –

**Blake** Oh God, oh dear God –!

**Bourke** I thought you'd gone mad on me, George. Around the bend, I thought you'd gone, and out of sight.

**Blake** Although of course the fact that I don't think about them doesn't mean I wouldn't love them if I did think about them.

**Bourke** But there's no point if you can help it. She's gone. And they're gone. The kiddies.

**Blake** Kiddies. They're not kiddies, Robert. They're children. My *children*. Please.

**Bourke** Sorry, George. Children.

**Blake** And one day I might even see them again. Who knows? And I wonder what I'll make – or they'll make – and on Tuesday, Robert. It's been quite hard for me. To think of you – your heart and mind intent on Tuesday.

As if you're being released from prison at last. The prison of me. You've put in your six months. And so now –

**Bourke** Oh, George! That's not it!

**Blake** You had the same spring in your step, the same roll to your gait, the same *joie de vivre*, humming, singing, almost prancing and dancing, when you were doing your last few days in Wormwood Scrubs. And of course trying not to let me see it – out of delicacy for my feelings. A delicate chap, is our Robert. (*Nods at him.*) When it comes to feelings.

**Bourke** Not delicate enough, it seems. It's not you I'm wanting away from, George. Ever. It's just the need – the need to be home again. You know that. Like some animal, wounded animal –

**Blake** Yes. Some wounded animal. Lolling about in the pubs of Dublin.

*Bourke laughs, slightly shamefaced.*

Lionised you'll be, won't you? That's the only animal part of your future, Robert. (*Smiles at him.*)

**Bourke** I'll stay on a little longer, if you want. A few days. A week even.

**Blake** Oh dear God, this is awful! Awful! (*Paces about in agitation.*) Help me, Robert! Help me!

**Bourke** How, George? How can I? Even if I stay on a bit, our time is up.

*Sound of door opening. Stan's and Viktor's voices in the hall, greeting Zinaida in Russian.*

**Blake** (*under his breath*) Oh, damn! Damn, damn!

*Bourke looks at him, confused. Stan and Viktor enter.*

*There is a tense pause. Stan and Viktor look enquiringly at Blake.*

(*In English.*) Stan. Viktor. Good evening.

**Stan** George. Robert.

**Viktor** Good evening, Robert, good evening.

**Stan** Good evening.

**Bourke** Haven't seen you two for a while. How's everything on the Western front? (*Laughs awkwardly.*) Home front, I meant to say.

**Stan** (*attempting easiness – badly*) Oh, my wife's recently widowed aunt has moved in with us. I begin to understand now why her late husband drank and beat her. She is a terrible nuisance. (*Laughs, shakes his head.*)

**Bourke** Who was it said, 'Nobody ever left me anything but relatives to look after'? Dickens, wasn't it?

**Stan** Dickens?

**Bourke** Charles Dickens. Wasn't it, George?

**Stan** Oh, Charles Dickens! Yes. A great writer. Much worshipped. Here. In Russia.

**Bourke** Yes, I've seen his books when you've taken me out to the shops. Well, I think they must be his, because there's his photograph on the back. (*Laughs.*)

**Viktor** Still making no progress with our language then, Robert?

**Bourke** No, my eyes go funny when I see the letters, and my hearing goes off when I listen to the sounds. Not a word, not a word – but Ludmilla, how's her sprained ankle, Viktor?

**Viktor** Completely cured. So she's probably thinking how to sprain the other one. She's too fat now to be anything but a thrower of the discus.

**Stan** Discus thrower.

**Viktor** Yes. Of course. Discus thrower. So perhaps I'll put her on steroids. For the next Olympics, eh?

*There is laughter. Then another tense pause.*

Well, George? What's the situation?

**Blake** What will you have?

*Raps on the hatch.*

Tea, coffee, a glass of champagne?

**Stan** Nothing, thank you. We're here for a minute only. To see how everything is.

**Blake** Are you sure?

**Stan** Yes.

*Zinaida enters. She looks to Stan and Viktor. Both shake their heads, grimly. Zinaida makes to go out.*

**Blake** Ah! – but there's one thing. Zinaida – just a minute! (*Turns to Bourke. In English.*) Robert, give them a performance, Stan and Viktor! Robert may not have learnt any Russian but – go on, Robert.

**Bourke** Oh now, George, I don't think Stan and Viktor –

**Stan** Oh, no. Please. (*Gestures politely.*)

**Viktor** Yes. Please. Whatever it is.

*Bourke hesitates, then begins to croon 'Danny Boy' at Zinaida. Zinaida, anxious and embarrassed, looks from Stan, to Viktor, to Blake.*

**Blake** (*in Russian*) Please, Zinaida. The comrades want to hear you.

*Stan and Viktor nod unenthusiastic encouragement. Bourke starts 'Danny Boy' again. Zinaida joins in. Bourke drops out, leaving Zinaida to sing through, charmingly, words incomprehensible to her, to the end. Stiff laughter and applause from Bourke, Stan, Viktor, Blake.*

**Stan** (*in Russian, to Zinaida*) Thank you, Zinaida. Now please leave us.

*Zinaida runs off to the kitchen, giggling with pleasure and embarrassment. There is a pause.*

(*In Russian, to Blake*) Well, it's obvious that you haven't told him.

**Blake** (*in Russian*) I was just about to. When you turned up. (*In English.*) It was going to be my next sentence, Robert. Or next but one. If Stan and Viktor hadn't appeared. You see.

**Bourke** What?

**Blake** Stan and Viktor. And their committee. Don't want you to go back to Ireland on Tuesday. Nor – nor – in fact, nor in the immediate future, Robert.

**Bourke** (*after a pause*) But we had an agreement. Six months was the agreement. And they're up. My six months is up.

**Blake** Things have changed, Robert.

**Bourke** Changed? Changed how? Why?

**Stan** They found the car you left in – in – (*Looks at Viktor.*)

**Viktor** Harvist Road.

**Stan** Yes. And they've traced it to you. They have your name. Photographs. Your prison record. They know everything about you.

**Viktor** Except where you are.

**Bourke** But – what does it matter if they know who I am, or where I am, as long as I'm in Dublin?

**Stan** You'd almost certainly be extradited to Britain. To stand trial.

**Viktor** The committee has taken expert legal advice –

**Bourke** I don't believe it, Viktor. I know my own people. They'd never give me up. Not to the old John Bull. They wouldn't.

**Blake** They would in the current political climate, Robert. You wouldn't be a political refugee, you see. Just a criminal. On the run. I do know about these things. My years in the Consulate – you'd be extradited.

**Bourke** Well – well, that's my risk. I'm ready to take it.

**Stan** But you wouldn't just be taking it for yourself, Robert.

**Viktor** You'd be taking it for all those people who helped you in London.

**Blake** Nigel and Annie. Dick. The doctor –

**Bourke** But even if I'm extradited – which I don't accept – I don't accept – you're not thinking I'd give their names to the English police? I'd die before I betrayed Annie and Nigel. And – and the rest of them. You know that, George!

**Stan** We *all* know that, Robert. But you wouldn't only be having deals with the English police. Not once they know you've been to Moscow. Met Viktor and me.

Stayed with George. No, you would be having deals with very different sorts of people. Believe me, Robert. One of our agents in London – not even an important one – when they'd finished with him – (*Gestures to Viktor.*)

**Viktor** I visit him every month. One of my duties of compassion. He is in a clinic. He will be in the clinic for the rest of his life. His nervous system is so 'no hope' that he is almost a complete – what word? (*Says Russian word for 'imbecile'.*)

**Stan** Fool. Idiot. Silly person.

**Blake** Imbecile.

**Viktor** Yes. Thank you, imbecile.

**Blake** Not at all, Viktor.

**Viktor** Sorry? Yes? What – ah – (*Confused.*) Yes, Teodor. Poor Teodor. He can no longer arrange the chess pieces on the board. He was our champion, Robert. Chess champion of the KGB. The imbecile. (*Shakes his head sadly.*)

**Stan** We do not want this to happen to you, Robert.

**Viktor** You are too precious to us.

*There is a pause.*

**Bourke** Well, well – I was just saying to George. I can stay on a few more days. A week. A few more weeks. (*Pause.*) Well then – well then – how much longer? I could do another month. Time for the dust to settle. (*Looks at their faces.*) Two even. (*With an effort.*) Three?

**Blake** It will have to be years, Robert.

**Bourke** Years, years, how many years? How many?

**Blake** Five, Robert.

**Bourke** (*in a whisper*) Five years! (*Staring around at their faces.*) But what do I do here – what do I do – for another five years? Eh, George? (*Little pause, then supplicatingly.*) George?

**Stan** We will assist you to pursue a career in publishing. For which you have great gifts, Robert.

**Viktor** Yes, who is this droll chap from the Ukraine, our Moscow publishers ask. Who is this Robert Adamovich Garvin, who makes such excellent and witty corrections to our old-fashioned English translations.

**Blake** Well, there you are, Robert. Witty and excellent. Words that equally applied to your editorship of the Wormwood Scrubs house magazine. I doubt that they'll ever be applied to my own literary effort. I sound like a pompous liar. In every sentence I – (*Shakes his head.*)

**Bourke** (*interrupting*) It's not the – the notion that I might do a book of my own, is it? These extra five years?

*There is a pause. Blake, Stan, Viktor look at each other, as if puzzled.*

**Stan** What do you mean, Robert? Haven't we explained?

**Viktor** We're thinking of you. And your friends.

**Bourke** Still, I want you to know – and your committee to know – that not a word of my part in George's escape will come out when I get home. As far as I'm concerned all the glory can belong to the KGB. All right? And here's my hand on it.

*He holds his hand out to Viktor, who shakes it. Then to Stan, who shakes it. Then to Blake – then withdraws it.*

No, I don't have to do this with you, do I, George? It would be an insult to the two of us.

**Blake** Yes, it would. Though yours is a hand I always like to shake, Robert. In almost any circumstances.

*Holds his hand out to Bourke. Bourke takes Blake's hand. They shake, solemnly.*

**Bourke** Thank you, George. Well, there we are then. That's settled then. All understood and cleared up. Your real worry you don't have to worry about.

**Stan** (*beaming*) I shall pass your undertaking straight on to the committee. You will publish nothing about George's escape.

**Bourke** That's it.

**Viktor** And you agree to remain with us for another five years.

**Bourke** No. No.

**Blake** It's all settled then, Robert.

**Bourke** No.

**Blake** All settled, Robert.

**Stan** Our thanks, Robert. On behalf of the KGB.

**Viktor** Speaking in person, Robert, I'm glad you agree to stay with us. I would be sorry to lose you. You bring us much funniness.

**Stan** (*to Blake*) Fun is the word, yes?

**Blake** Yes. No. Well, he brings us both.

**Bourke** Fun and funniness I bring you, do I? For the next five years. Thank you. (*Laughs dully.*)

**Stan** You have made a wise choice.

*Embraces Bourke.*

**Viktor**  Yes. Very wise.

*Embraces Bourke.*

**Stan**  (*in Russian*) We will talk about your book, George. Very soon.

**Viktor**  (*in Russian*) If I can give help –

**Blake**  (*in Russian*) Thank you. Goodnight.

**Stan** *and* **Viktor**  (*in Russian*) Goodnight.

*Go out, calling 'goodnights' to Zinaida in Russian en route. She answers them. There is a pause.*

**Bourke**  So you knew all the time. And you couldn't tell me.

**Blake**  I can't tell you how badly, how badly I feel –

**Bourke**  You feel. *You* feel. But I'm the one who's doing the facing here, the facing of five years, so let's talk for once about my feelings here, George. About them. Let's talk about *them*!

**Blake**  Yes. (*Little pause.*) Well – let's talk about them. Your feelings.

**Bourke**  I haven't got anything to say. You know my feelings.

**Blake**  Yes. One thing, though. Why I so much wanted you not to want to go so much – was that you wouldn't mind so much being obliged to stay. You see.

**Bourke**  (*laughs*) Very daintily put, George. Very daintily put.

**Blake**  What I mean is – what I mean is! That I didn't want you to go for my sake. As I've already made clear. But by God, by God, Robert, I did want you to go for your sake. I wanted *that* far more. Far more than what I wanted for myself. Do you think I don't know I owe you that? Do you think I don't know you deserve it! All I've ever wanted since you got me out of Wormwood Scrubs is to pay you back. And all I've succeeded in doing is to trap you in a plight that gets worse. And worse.

**Bourke** Oh well, what the hell. (*Laughs.*)

**Blake** (*looks at him, astonished.*) What?

**Bourke** You've got your bad feelings, I've got my five years, but when you come to look at it, George, the last six months – we've had good times, a lot of laughs.

**Blake** Yes. We have.

**Bourke** And there may be something in this publishing career Stan and Viktor are urging me into. I'll learn everything there is to know about the business. When I get back to Dublin, five years from now, I'll set up on my own. Control the Russian market. That's how I've got to look at it. I'm going to spend the next five years teaching myself a good business. Making a future for myself. I choose – yes, that's it – I *choose* to spend my next five years here. And as I'll be spending them with you, George –

**Blake** They'll pass in a flash. I'll see to it.

**Bourke** We'll have more good times, George. (*Raises his glass.*)

**Blake** To more good times! To all the more good times!

*Blake hesitates, then comes into Bourke's open arms.*

**Bourke** Goodnight, George. Till tomorrow. Until tomorrow. The start of a new day. (*Picks up the vodka bottle.*) By way of a new dawn.

**Blake** A new dawn. And a new day.

*They separate, go to their rooms. Pause at their doors. Turn. Look at each other, make to speak, nod and smile at each other. Blake sits down at his desk, very still. Thinking. Bourke goes straight to the tape recorder, presses 'Record' button, makes to speak straight into it, microphone in one hand, vodka bottle in the other, turns machine off, sits, in distress, thinking. Blake leans forward, stabs 'Record' button, speaks.*

Every time I hear the words 'treacherous' and 'deceitful' applied to me I find myself reflecting on those groups of men who in their day were similarly described and with whom I have much, I believe, in common. Those Roman Catholic priests, say, who during the Reformation were not thought to be just wicked or evil, but were – like me – thought to be agents of the Devil himself. Like me, they were forced to go about their life's tasks in secret. Like me, their purity of intention was only preserved through many forms of duplicity. A sacred duplicity of the heart and of the soul in the name of their God, as they like me, and I like them, sought to bring about a Kingdom of Heaven on earth. (*Little pause, as he loses control of the line of thought.*) Let me proceed with this thought. But do I have to proceed with this thought? What is it about, this thought? It's about justifying the betrayal of the man who brought me out of captivity, back into life and freedom. The only man who could have done it. The single. Yes, the single Irish fella did it. Did do it. (*Little pause.*) How ridiculous. Ridiculous that I should –

*He turns off the machine, sits, thinking.*
　*Makes to start machine again. Stops himself.*
　*Bourke simultaneously makes to start machine, stops himself. Raises vodka bottle to his lips. Notes that it's almost empty.*

**Bourke** Hah! That's it, that's it, of course that's it!

*Goes out, strides to hatch, bangs on it.*

Zinaida, Zinaida! Zin, Zin!

*Zinaida opens hatch, sees Bourke, grins.*

**Zinaida** (*in Russian*) Another vodka?

**Bourke** (*in English*) Another wodka. Yes. Another wodka. Please, Zin.

*Zinaida vanishes then re-enters and plonks a bottle of vodka in front of Bourke, who grabs it.*

That's my lovely Zin. Here's what we're going to work on. Starting tomorrow, my Zin, Zin of my heart. My darling. Here's one to drive any sane man to his doom.

*Begins to croon 'When Irish Eyes are Smiling'. Zinaida stares at him, transfixed. Blake makes to speak into machine, stops, stares towards dining room, as Bourke's voice rises to higher and higher notes on 'When Irish Eyes are Smiling'.*
*Lights.*

### SCENE TWO

*Blake enters, in overcoat and hat. Blake looks at Bourke, the table, in disgust.*

**Bourke** Morning, George. (*Pouring himself a vodka.*)

**Blake** Actually, it's the afternoon. Still at your breakfast, I see.

**Bourke** Only just begun it.

**Blake** (*indicating typescripts*) What's all this doing in here?

**Bourke** Oh, it's become such a muddle in there (*nodding to his room*) I've decided to spill over. I hope you don't mind.

**Blake** Actually I do.

**Bourke** (*catarrh*) Sorry, George.

**Blake** I do wish you'd confine yourself to your own sty. I'll have Zinaida clear up – Stan and Viktor will be here for lunch shortly.

**Bourke** And where have you been, George?

**Blake** Out. For a walk.

**Bourke** Cold, eh? From the look of you.

**Blake** Very. But it helped me to think. About you. About what's happening to you.

**Bourke** What's happening to me, Georgie?

**Blake** Sorry? What did you call me?

**Bourke** Georgie.

**Blake** I'd rather you didn't.

**Bourke** Why not?

**Blake** For one thing it's not my name.

**Bourke** Well, it's a hell of a lot closer to your name than Robert is to mine. But I'll tell you what – if you let me call you Georgie, you can call me Bobbie. (*Chuckles.*)

**Blake** Do you know what you're beginning to remind me of? One of those lifers in Wormwood Scrubs. The ones who'd given up all hope.

**Bourke** God, I love the ways you say 'Wormwood Scrubs' in, Georgie, always the whole name. ''Member that summer, '58, '59, Bobbie, delightful old place, what was it, Shrubs something Shrubs, no, no, Scrubs, that was it, wasn't it, Bobbie, Wormwood Scrubs, delightful accommodation – if a touch cramped – splendid grounds, a mite inaccessible and the staff, Bobbie, in their splendid uniforms –' (*Laughs.*)

**Blake** (*watches him*) I came back with a resolution, Robert. A resolution that I'd help you. As a matter of urgency, actually. The greatest urgency. I was going to try to talk to you as we used to talk – remind you of the publishing opportunities you were so eager to pursue, the need to keep at these properly – (*indicating typescripts*) to put on your best front with Stan and Viktor so they'd start reporting back favourably to the committee –

**Bourke** Oh, bugger Stan and Viktor. Bugger their committee too. If I can't live where I want, I'll live how I want. And how I want is like this. See.

**Blake** Nevertheless I shouldn't – if I were you – let Stan and Viktor see you like this. Not today. Especially not today. I'd go in and spruce up and sober up. If I were you.

**Bourke** Well, you're not, are you, Georgie! You're not me! And that's the whole difference between us!

**Blake** And it's one I'm devoutly grateful for . . . Listen, Robert . . . Is that one of my cigars?

**Bourke** Yes, it is. Thank you, Georgie.

**Blake** Have you been in my study?

**Bourke** I just popped in to see how things were.

*Blake goes into his study. Picks up books from the floor, puts them on bookcase. Rewinds tape recorder and plays it.*

**Blake** (*voice on recorder*) . . . the most sophisticated eavesdropping devices then in existence. Which of course brings me to the Berlin tunnel. The Berlin tunnel was – was – oh, this is unendurable. I can't go on with this –

**Bourke** (*voice on recorder*) Don't worry, George, I'll do it for you. I've heard it from you so often, I know it by heart. Here we go, George. (*Imitating Blake's voice through this.*) The Berlin tunnel, my tunnel as I call it because of the significant part I played in its establishment as a nerve centre for treachery, was undoubtedly the greatest achievement of the propaganda war, providing information from the Germans to the Russians, who gave it back to the Americans, who passed it on to the Turks, who handed it to the Chinese who gave it back to me. And of course the true triumph of it all was that everything that passed from country to country was a pack of lies that concluded with forty thousand top spies in the pay of their Western masters being lined up against the walls of their respective cities and being mowed down. Apart from one or two who were tossed alive into their department furnaces, and roasted before the terrified gaze of their colleagues. *Pour encourager les autres*, so to say. (*Imitates Blake's laugh.*) I spurned such glory as came my way–

> *Bourke pours himself another drink, looks at it, puts his glass on the table without drinking, in a gesture of disgust.*
> *Zinaida has come back into dining room to clear up. Bourke, glancing with apprehensive triumph towards Blake's room, puts his arm around Zinaida's waist.*

**Bourke** Come on then, Zin, Zin, Zin, come on, my old darling, let's have it.

*Begins to croon 'When Irish Eyes are Smiling'. Zinaida struggles, alarmed, looking towards Blake's room.*

You sing, my girl! (*With ferocity. Croons again.*)

*Zinaida, fearfully, starts singing along with Bourke. Blake looks towards their voices, makes as if to go to door, checks himself, goes back and, with an air of determination, rewinds tape recorder. As he does so, he opens bottle of champagne, pours himself a glass, takes a sip as he presses 'Play'. Listens to Bourke's parody. He stands for a moment, thinking, then begins to laugh, turns off machine. Goes into dining room, carrying glass of champagne. He smiles at Bourke and Zinaida.*
   *Zinaida falters.*

**Blake** (*encouragingly*) No, finish, finish please.

*Zinaida and Bourke sing to the end. Blake toasts Zinaida. Then, in Russian:*

Thank you, Zinaida. Now if you'd go to the kitchen –

*Zinaida goes into kitchen.*

Well, it did occur to me. But I couldn't quite believe it. Now it all makes sense.

**Bourke** Really? What makes sense, George?

**Blake** Your deterioration. It's deliberate. An act.

**Bourke** No, it's not an act.

**Blake** But it's deliberate.

**Bourke** I hope so. (*Puts his hand to his head.*) And I hate every minute of it. But you had to see what I could do. When I put my mind to it.

**Blake** But I already know what you can do, Robert. Who better?

**Bourke** Yes. But you had to experience the living with it, didn't you? I mean, there was no point my saying I'm going to fill every corner of your life with my disgustingness – I had to fill it. And today, George, I've really begun – I'll go on and on and on – every day for the next four years, nine months – and I'll get worse. Believe me, George. I'll get so much worse that I won't even have to try. It'll be first nature.

**Blake** Unless?

**Bourke** You know what unless.

**Blake** You really think Viktor, Stan, the committee – they'll put up with it?

**Bourke** What difference does it make to them? They don't have to live with me.

**Blake** So you think I can just go to them and say, 'For God's sake, send him back to Ireland. I can't tolerate another minute of him in my flat. My life.'

**Bourke** That's my belief. It has to be. Otherwise I'm without hope. A lifer –

**Blake** You – without hope! I've seen you do five years in Wormwood Scrubs – (*Nods ironically.*) The Scrubs.

**Bourke** That was then. I'm older now. George – believe me. Please. I've got to go home.

**Blake** You might. Even now. If you bring all your resilience, your determination –

**Bourke** I'll put them to just one end, George. Making your life insufferable.

**Blake** God! It's not a question of my getting them to send you home, it's never been that, it's a question – I told you, I told you right from the start, it's been a question of – of saving your life, Robert. I was hoping I wouldn't have to tell you this. That's what I was doing this morning. I wasn't out for a walk, I was begging Stan and Viktor to beg the committee to let you live.

**Bourke** What?

**Blake** In the name of God, Robert, go and make yourself presentable. Please.

**Bourke** (*shakily*) This is serious, then?

**Blake** It couldn't be more serious. When I left it seemed on a knife-edge. They're not letting me have any part in the decision. Come on, hurry. Hurry!

*They go into Bourke's room.*

**Bourke** But why, why, why now, after they've got me here?

**Blake** They still don't trust you. And then from what they've seen of you recently, and from Zinaida's reports of your drinking –

**Bourke** Zinaida!

**Blake** Of course. Surely you realised that! She goes into the department once every two days –

**Bourke** Oh Jesus, not Zinaida.

**Blake** It's not her fault. She's employed by them. She gives an exact tally of how many bottles you've drunk, describes the state of your room, your behaviour – and of course I couldn't argue with any of it, could I – not when they've seen for themselves? They think you're, well, even if you're not a double agent, they do believe that you've become unstable. And are therefore a security risk.

**Bourke** And so they're going to kill me. Kill me.

**Blake** I don't know, I don't know what they'll decide – it's the picnic factor, you see.

**Bourke** Picnic factor?

**Blake** They may just be coming around to inspect you. (*Inspects him.*) And at least you're not in your underwear and that dressing gown this time – and we can keep it up from there, can't we? I mean, from dressed to respectable, hard-working –

**Bourke** Oh Jesus, George, yes, yes. Yes. But this picnic factor –?

**Blake** If they say, let's not be dull and have lunch here, let's go to one of the KGB's dachas and have a picnic, I'm to say – I've been ordered to say – that I would rather stay here, at home, and work on my book.

**Bourke** And – and I go on the picnic. (*Raises his finger, points it, makes shooting noise.*) Is that what you mean, George?

**Blake** I don't know, I don't know. Perhaps they won't know themselves until they've got you in the dacha and observed you on your own without me to – to protect you.

**Bourke** And if I refuse to go?

**Blake** Refuse to go on a picnic? With the KGB? (*Suddenly remembering.*) Oh, God –

**Bourke** What, what!

**Blake** The tapes! Your voice. If they hear your voice on the tape.

**Bourke** Wipe it, George, please wipe it . . . Please! Please!

**Blake** All right.

*Blake goes out to his room, winds tape back, etc.*

**Bourke** Thank you, George . . . Jesus! I've got to get out of here. Now.

*Pulls on overcoat, crams vodka bottle in pocket, seizes bag with tape recorder, hurries out. As he does so, sound of front door opening. Stan's and Viktor's voices greeting Zinaida. Zinaida returning greeting. Bourke stands frozen. Stan and Viktor enter.*

**Stan** Oh hello, Robert. All ready then?

**Viktor** Well muffled up, that's good. Though the dacha is quite warm –

**Stan** We're lucky to have got it for the afternoon. One of our best.

**Viktor** We're going on a picnic. Didn't George tell you? If we could get a dacha – pity he won't come too. All work, no play, makes boy a dull John.

**Stan** No, no – makes John a dull boy, isn't it, Robert?

**Bourke** Jack, Jack, a dull Jack – (*Moving towards door.*) Makes Jack a dull boy – I'm not going on any picnic. I'm not going on any bloody picnic with the KGB.

*Bourke bursts past Stan, opens the door, hurls himself outside, slamming door.*
*Curtain.*

## SCENE THREE

*Six weeks later.*

**Blake** (*sitting at desk*) . . . but I used to be good at waiting. I mean . . . all those years of waiting to be caught and tried for my crimes, so-called – sometimes it was as if my crimes were merely what I did while I was waiting to be caught and tried for them. And I waited with complete serenity through my trial and sentencing. And patiently in jail until you came to get me out – but the truth is, I never knew what waiting was, Robert, until this last six weeks. It's a very painful thing to have to do – real waiting. And in a few minutes, just a few minutes . . . now in fact.

*Bourke enters main room from front door. Dishevelled and clutching his bag, he bangs on the hatch.*

**Bourke** Zin – Zin!

*Zinaida enters, upstage left, stares out at Bourke. Blake looks towards dining room, stands up.*

A bottle please, Zin – wodka, wodka.

**Zinaida** (*in Russian*) Oh, you poor man, you poor man – look at you!

**Bourke** (*urgently*) Wodka please, Zin.

*Zinaida hands Bourke a bottle of vodka, staring at him, shaking her head anxiously and pityingly. Bourke opens bottle.*

Thanks, Zin, my old darling. Thank you.

*He takes a long swig. Blake comes out of his room. Zinaida closes hatch.*

**Blake** So here you are then.

**Bourke** Been expecting me, have you?

**Blake** Every day for the last six weeks. But with confidence this evening. A traffic policeman spotted you going into a barber's shop.

**Bourke** Yes. That was the last of my roubles. But I couldn't stand all that growth. I've been clean-shaven all my life. I've been short-haired all my life. And I figured that if I was coming back to it at least I'd come back to it looking as I usually do. My face, anyway. (*Little pause.*) So they know, do they, Stan and Viktor? Know I'm back?

**Blake** Oh, yes. They've been called out of some big function. That's how important you are, Robert. You're a much wanted man, you see.

**Bourke** And they're on their way over, are they?

**Blake** They are. As always when they're least wanted, eh? And where have you been, these last six weeks?

**Bourke** Out. And about.

**Blake** Out and about where, exactly?

**Bourke** In the woods, mostly.

**Blake** In this weather! But where did you sleep –?

**Bourke** Under newspapers. Nothing else I could do. No passport. Almost no money – started turning into a tramp. By tomorrow I'd have been a beggar as well. But hard to be a beggar if you don't know the basic words, like 'money', 'food', 'help'. (*Laughs.*) Have to stand there, on street corners, silent, with my hand out. And your boys would have seen me, in the end. So – so why wait, why wait, George? (*Looks at Blake.*) In that condition, why wait?

**Blake** (*after a little pause*) I see you clung on to your – (*Nods to bag.*)

**Bourke** My what?

**Blake** Your machine.

*Bourke takes out recorder, tapes. Pushes them at Blake. Blake hesitates.*

May I? (*Winds back, presses 'Play'.*)

**Bourke** (*voice on recorder*) . . . truth of it is, I need to hear a voice – a voice in my own language – no, the truth of it is I need to hear *his* voice. I've heard it every day for years now, it's become a part of me, a part of my life. God, how I miss him, God, how I miss it, God how I miss him. Even though it's because of him that I've come to this. I dream – almost every night I dream of them there. George and Zin, my darling Zin. And even Stan and Viktor, and in my dreams it's like – like my family – Zin! Wodka, wodka, another bottle, please. (*Laughs.*) Another bottle, please. George, my friend, help me, help me!

*Blake turns off machine, puts it and tapes into Bourke's bag.*

**Bourke** (*in person*) How long have you known?

**Blake** Well, when I saw you talking into it in London. The first day – the day you got me out.

**Bourke** And that's when you planned to get me to Moscow. And to keep me here. Or did you already have it in mind when we were in the Scrubs – and we were discussing how I could help you escape? Did you, George?

**Blake** I can't remember, Robert. But I might have. Even in the Scrubs I was an officer of the KGB. A prisoner of war, so to speak. So I had to consider all the possibilities.

**Bourke** Like the possibility of betraying me.

**Blake** Spies betray people, Robert. That's what we do. It becomes a – a habit. Difficult to break – even when it's not – not strictly necessary.

**Bourke** (*nods to bag*) So it's always been the book that you've been afraid of?

**Blake** Well, it does make us seem absurdly incompetent – that the KGB couldn't do what you did. A single Irish fella. With his rope ladder and the Dormobile.

**Bourke** But they didn't even try, did they, George? That must be a galling thought, eh?

**Blake** It has been now and then. Yes.

**Bourke** And what's the authorised version going to be?

**Blake** We don't know. We can't work it out. I can't, anyway. Every time I try to write it up I get – (*shrugs*) stuck.

**Bourke** Well, now I'm going to be out of the way, you'll unstick yourself, probably.

**Blake** Yes, well this brings me to the – the little matter I should have started with. You see, what happened that morning, six weeks ago – what happened –

*Sound of door opening. Stan and Viktor enter, greet Zinaida.*

(*To himself.*) Oh, damn! Damn, damn!

*Bourke sinks to his knees, lowers his head.*

**Stan** What is this – Robert, what are you doing?

**Bourke** I want my picnic here. Now. In front of him.

**Stan** (*in Russian*) So you haven't told him? (*In English*) On your feet please, Robert. On your feet.

**Bourke** So this is what you wear for an execution.

**Viktor** Robert. This is for the dinner.

**Stan** The reunion dinner. The KGB reunion dinner. Full uniform always.

**Stan** Why didn't you tell him?

**Blake** It must have been – shame, I think.

*There is a pause.*

**Stan** Well, tell him now. Listen to him, Robert. You will hear the truth. I guarantee it.

**Blake** What I was about to tell you, Robert, was that there was never any question of killing you. I – I made all that up. I knew Stan and Viktor were going to invite you on a picnic. In a dacha. And I – used it.

**Bourke** (*after a pause*) Why?

**Blake** To – well, I suppose, to teach you a lesson. A – a small counter-ploy. Your ploy was to turn yourself into something unspeakably less than yourself. So my counter was –

**Bourke** To be yourself.

**Blake** As I said – it's a hard habit to break. I never expected you to run off like that. I thought you'd spend a few terrified hours in the dacha and then come back relieved to be alive, and then you'd, well, knuckle down. I should have known better, shouldn't I?

**Stan** Go on, please, George.

**Blake** As for the KGB committee – Stan and Viktor – they never had the slightest intention of forcing you to stay. Not for five years. Not even for the six months.

**Stan** We hoped you'd stay. We wanted you to stay. We argued – that's all – argued with you to stay. But force – against your will? Never.

**Viktor** Also we liked your company. You are very Russian. To us, Robert, you are the cat's knees.

**Stan** Bee's whiskers. Finish now please, George.

**Blake** I am instructed by my superiors to offer on behalf of the KGB profound apologies for my behaviour.

**Stan** Now everything is understood at last. Yes, Robert?

**Bourke** What is understood – what I understand – what I think I understand is that I'm free to go.

**Stan** Exactly. A free man. You always have been.

**Viktor** But we would like you to stay. Would prefer it.

**Bourke** Now. I want to go now, please.

**Stan** Very well. It will take a few days to arrange your travel.

**Bourke** But go from here now. This place.

**Stan** I understand. We will find you a hotel – (*Looks at Viktor.*)

**Viktor** The Union Hotel. The Department has a suite there. For important guests.

**Stan** The Union Hotel. (*Nods.*)

**Bourke** I need to be away – need to. This very minute.

**Stan** Then this very minute we go.

**Blake** (*in Russian*) You realise he'll publish his book.

**Stan** In English, please, George.

**Blake** You realise, he'll publish his book.

**Stan** Then he publishes his book. (*To Bourke.*) We don't want you to. But we can't stop you. And won't try.

**Viktor** Though you did make a promise –

**Stan** In the wrong circumstances. He thought he had no choice. Robert knows our wishes. He will decide for himself.

**Blake** (*in Russian*) But – but you can't – (*Catches Stan's look. In English.*) Do you really want to go to the Union Hotel? Looking as you do. And, well, smelling as you do.

**Stan** (*to Bourke*) The Union Hotel will be honoured to have you.

**Viktor** Yes, I'll make sure of that.

**Blake** Please – stay, Robert. Just for a few days. So we can – can talk – one last time at least, please, Robert.

**Bourke** The name is Sean. Sean Bourke. Sean Alphonsus Bourke.

**Blake** (*picks up Bourke's bag*) Don't forget this, Sean.

*Hands it to Bourke. Bourke goes out, followed by Stan and Viktor. Blake stands as, from the hall comes:*

**Bourke** Oh, Zin – I must say goodbye to my darling Zin.

**Stan** (*in Russian*) The comrade is leaving.

**Viktor** (*in Russian*) He wants to say goodbye.

*Zinaida makes gasping, wailing noise.*

**Bourke** Now don't take on, my Zin, don't take on – just one more time – for old times' sake.

*Bourke croons 'Danny Boy'. Zinaida joins in. Bourke laughs.*

And a last cuddle. There. Don't take on so. Think of me from time to time, eh . . . Goodbye, George.

*Sound of steps, front door closing. Blake stands for a moment. Goes to hatch, knocks on it. Zinaida opens hatch. She is dabbing at her eyes with apron.*

**Blake** (*in Russian*) Zinaida, a bottle of champagne, please.

*He walks to his room. Sits down at desk. Zinaida appears, carrying bottle of champagne and a glass on tray. Enters. Puts down fresh bottle and glass, picks up empty bottle and other glass.*

(*In Russian.*) Thank you, Zinaida. Oh – (*making an effort at contact*) my medals. (*Picks them up.*) Would you like to give them a polish?

*Zinaida brightens slightly. Breathes on medals, rubs them on her apron, looks at them, shakes her head, puts them on tray, goes out. Blake opens bottle, pours himself a glass. Takes a sip. Looks at tape recorder, rewinds, presses 'Record'.*

(*To machine.*) To the question, in other words, of whether I have in my conscience – in my heart – any remorse, any regrets, I give this answer: how can I have remorse or regrets when I have devoted my life's work to mankind? And thus have the privilege, indeed the honour of being where I am now. Here. Here in this country of the future.

*Presses 'Stop', stares ahead. Picks up champagne glass, holds it out in toast.*

To the country of the future!

*Raises glass to lips. Blackout.*

*Curtain.*

# LIFE SUPPORT

For Nigel

**Life Support** was first performed at the Yvonne Arnaud Theatre, Guildford, on 10 June 1997, presented by Duncan Weldon. The cast was as follows:

**JG** Alan Bates
**Gwen** Georgina Hale
**Pat** Frank McCusker
**Jack** Nickolas Grace
**Julia** Carole Nimmons

*Director* Harold Pinter
*Set Designer* Eileen Diss
*Lighting Designer* Mick Hughes

# Characters

**JG**
**Gwen**
**Pat**
**Jack**
**Julia**

## SCENE ONE

*Lights down.*

**JG** (*over*) If everything had worked out all right, I would have been describing a scene something like this. There I am, sitting in the armchair, checking through the contents of my knapsack, my plane tickets, my passport, my vaccination certificate – and suddenly she comes into the room. From the kitchen, of course. 'OK,' she says. 'OK,' says the little woman, elsewhere also referred to as 'wifey'. 'I'm coming with you this time.' 'Why?' I wonder with my usual air of dependence and devotion. 'Why on earth would you want to waste your time coming with me, sweetling mine?' 'To find out what you get up to when you're on your own, hubby mio.' 'But dearest, dearest heart, you won't find out what I get up to on my own if you come with me.' 'In that case, I'll at least stop you from getting up to whatever you get up to while I'm not there with you. By being there. Won't I?' That's how I might have described it if everything had worked out all right.

*Lights up.*
*A private room in a hospital. Set in darkness, apart from Gwen in bed, on life support.*
*JG, in his early fifties, is walking up and down in front of the set, distraught.*
*Pat appears.*

**Pat** Mr Golding. I'm Dr O'Brien. Pat O'Brien. (*Holding out his hand.*) I'm sure Mr Rolls has told you all there is to know about your wife's condition.

**JG** (*shaking Pat's hand*) Well, there doesn't seem very much to know, according to Mr Rolls. Even where she is, so to speak, in her – her consciousness. Even whether she's there or – or not.

**Pat** But he did explain that she was alive?

**JG** Yes, but that's about as far as he would go. And he used this phrase 'vegetative state' – I couldn't make out whether that was a diagnosis or –

**Pat** No, no, I think it's merely the usual description for people in your wife's sort of condition. It really means that nobody, not even Mr Rolls, knows what sort of condition that sort of condition is. At least at this stage. I'd like to say how sorry I am, how terribly sorry I am, for you. And your wife. But you know, in a sense she was lucky – lucky, I mean, in that sometimes death in these cases is virtually instantaneous. It happened to a friend of mine in a field outside Guildford. His wife drove him to the hospital, fifteen minutes away at the most. He was dead before they got there. But you, with just your bicycles in Guadeloupe, managed to keep her alive! And back here. To Mr Rolls. He's worked a couple of miracles, has our Mr Rolls.

**JG** (*eagerly*) Yes, he said something about miracles – two miracles I think he said there'd been in the last few years. Do you know anything about them?

**Pat** Yes I do. One of them was three years ago, when I'd just started, chap called Humphrey, I can't remember whether that was his first or last name – Humphrey something, something Humphrey. Very tall. White-haired. He cycled over a cliff in Cornwall. Not on purpose, I don't mean. He was caught in a fog. Trying to get out of it. Head down over the handlebars, legs pumping, vision impaired. So over he went, pedalling. On to the rocks below. Whole body smashed, including his head. He lay here – this very room, actually – for four or five months. I used to think it very sad that nobody but me ever visited him – except for his landlady, his landlady came once but only to try to get her rent. He seems to have been rather unpopular, at least according to her. He was a psychiatric nurse. Still is, I suppose. (*Stops.*)

**JG** Well, what happened?

**Pat** Sorry. Well, one day I popped my head around the door and saw that he was scowling. That was the first sign. Then he began to clench and unclench and clench his fists. Like a boxer. Guttural sounds from his throat. Barks, really. And then he was on his way. Extraordinary progress. Complete recovery. Apart from the occasional memory loss. That was Humphrey. The Humphrey miracle.

**JG** I see. And the other one? The other miracle?

**Pat** Sandy. A bonnie lass of nineteen. Went scuba diving. Got into a terrible tangle in a fishing net. Was assumed drowned when she was hauled out. Mr Rolls said that her brain was deprived of oxygen to the point where she should have been – no, he can't have said 'should', can he? – but normally she would have been past the point of no return. But her parents, her boyfriend, her friends, refused to give up on her. They kept at her and at her – they were Scots, so they did all kinds of Scottish things, reels and Highland flings, bagpipes, sang 'Auld Lang Syne', Hogmanay, the lot. Pitiful, I thought it was, pitiful. Until one day, at teatime, they were sitting around her eating freshly baked scones, laughing and joking as if they were picnicking somewhere in the heather, her eyes fluttered. She made a little cawing sound. She smiled. She was on her way back. Well, most of the way back. A good part of the way back.

**JG** Then Mr Rolls didn't really have anything to do with it? With either of them.

**Pat** Well, they were under his care. But I'm sure he wasn't claiming them as his miracles. Mr Rolls would be the first to attribute them to God. Or – or to a fluke. After all, that's the nature of miracles, isn't it? There's nothing to explain how they come about. Though that doesn't mean there isn't an explanation somewhere or other. Like the first car I had, an old Citroën – sometimes it would just stop itself for no reason any garage could discover. They'd change the battery, clean the plugs, fiddle with wires – and me, I'd kick at it, swear at it, beg it on my hands and knees – nothing. And then suddenly it would start up just like that, as if it felt in the mood again, almost. I used to think it was a miracle at the time – at least I always said 'thank God' – but it could have been a fluke. On the other hand there was probably a mechanical explanation, who knows? As Mr Rolls says.

**JG** Well – well, let's suppose there's an explanation for the two miracles you and Mr Rolls – What can I do? Tell me what to do.

**Pat** Well, what people usually do – and what might have done the trick for Sandy – is family. Family and friends.

**JG** Family and friends, yes. But – but the trouble is we haven't really got any. I mean – I mean, we've got friends of course, but they're lunch friends, dinner friends, that sort of friend. And there's Julia, my agent –

**Pat** Agent?

**JG** Yes, literary agent. She negotiates my contracts, that sort of thing. But she and Gwen weren't really particularly close. But the point is, there isn't really anyone –

**Pat** And no family?

**JG** No, none. Well, there's my brother Jack. But he's – he's – well, we only see him occasionally. When he's in trouble. He's an actor, you see – and – and – the point is we're very private, Gwen and I. We cherish our privacy, you see.

**Pat** So it's just you then, is that what you're saying, Mr Golding?

**JG** Yes, that is what I'm saying. Just me when it comes down to it.

**Pat** Well, at least she's nicely settled down. And in a room all to herself.

**JG** Yes, but I don't think she can appreciate – I mean, she won't have noticed, will she? (*With sudden hope.*) Or will she?

**Pat** Well, as Mr Rolls always says – who can say? But at least you'll have your privacy together, won't you? That's the good thing.

**JG** Yes, yes, our privacy. But to do what? What do we do? What do *I* do, I mean?

**Pat** Well, I suppose you should do all the things you always do in your privacy. And hope that one day soon she'll come back from wherever she is all on her own to join in with you.

**JG** Yes, yes, right. (*Pause.*) I'll bring her back. I swear to God I'll bring her back!

**Pat** That's the spirit, Mr Golding. Because whether there are miracles or not, we still need faith.

**JG** I've got faith, I've got faith. (*Little pause.*) May I ask – what is your function? Your specific function?

**Pat** Oh, just to keep an eye on you is what it comes to.

**JG** On me?

**Pat** Yes. On your case.

**JG** On my wife's case, don't you mean?

**Pat** Of course on your wife's case. I'm really here to be around for when I'm needed.

**JG** Oh, I see. Well, thank you, thank you very much.

*There is a pause. Pat, smiling pleasantly, JG wondering what to say.*

**Pat** Well, if there's nothing else I'd better be off to the Wisdens. A lovely couple. Well, I don't know about him of course, but from what she tells me, the way she dotes on him – even in his absence – he must have been quite a man.

**JG** Must have been? You mean – you mean –

**Pat** You're quite right, Mr Golding. Must *be*, must *be* – keep everything in the present tense here, eh? (*Exits.*)

*Lights.*

### SCENE TWO

*Lights down.*

**JG** (*over*) It was hot, very hot. We'd been cycling for hours, and there we were on a country lane off the main road. She had to stop for a widdle. There was a buzzing. I was vaguely aware of the buzzing. It contributed to all the drowsiness, the heat, the peacefulness. But it must have alighted on her neck because suddenly there was no buzzing. She was about to get up when – 'Ow,' she said. 'Ow!' And clapped her hand to her neck.

*Lights up on Gwen, now seen properly. Six weeks later.*
*A small window, stage left, with a sofa under it.*
*A bed upstage, with a chair on either side of it. Also a bedside table, with books, magazines on it. Downstage, a larger table with a couple of chairs. On this table sits a chessboard, more books, magazines, a compact disctape-recorder-radio. Stage right, a sink, a mirror, a razor, shaving foam, etc. In the corner of the room, on a shelf on the wall, a television set.*
*It is about ten in the morning. Spring day.*
*The television set is on, giving a summary of the news. The sound is low.*
*JG enters. He is wearing casual clothes, under a raincoat. He is carrying a bunch of white carnations, a newspaper. There is also a book in his pocket. He takes off raincoat, extracts book, puts it on the table, looks at the television set in disgust.*

**JG** Oh, for Christ's sake – we would agree that you're not the liveliest company at the moment, but surely they can roll you about your bed, change your sheets, mop you up, unplug and replug your tubes, change your drip, drip, drip without needing to keep one eye on the television –

*Goes across to turn it off. His attention is caught by something on the screen. Picks up manual control, raises volume. He is still holding carnations, by the way.*

**TV** – the number of dead has now risen to a hundred and twenty thousand. In Calcutta alone a quarter of a million people are thought to be infected. The British Government has closed the airports to all Far Eastern flights, both inward and outward bound. (*Little pause.*) At home, a London newsagent, Mr Lionel Patel, and his seventeen-year-old son, Sam, were shot dead by two men in balaclavas inside their shop in Shepherd's Bush. The victim's wife, Mrs Violet Patel, says –

**JG** (*turns off television*) See what we're missing, Gwen? Real life. And real death. How pleasant to be cocooned here, in complete safety.

*As he speaks, he puts the fresh carnations on the table, throws the old carnations in the vase into a wastepaper basket, fills the vase with water from the sink, puts the fresh carnations in the vase, stands looking at them uncertainly.*

I'm losing my nerve. About these, I mean. I know there's something floral you particularly loathe because of that time Uncle Percy got you alone in the garden when you were thirteen – so the smell always gives you the willies. (*Sniffs.*) Is it these? What are they, anyway? You know I can't tell one flower from another, except buttercups – I must remember to ask one of the nurses, the tall one with legs, probably – Lydia, I think it is, isn't it? She looks as if she knows about flowers. And lots of other things too, I expect. Actually, she's very nice, isn't she? You like her, don't you? Caring – wouldn't that be our word for Lydia? Yours, anyway. Mine would be attractive, yours would be caring. Caring young Lydia. Pat was telling me the other day – oh, of course, you were here, weren't you? – that they have a very short shelf life in this ward. The nurses, I mean. Because of the strain of seeing – (*Stops.*) And the more caring and attractive they are . . . Some of the others, though – Rosie, for instance – look as if they could tough it out for decades. Already have toughed it out for decades, in Rosie's case. We don't fancy decades more of Rosie – (*Stops, takes book out of his pocket, puts it on the bed.*) There! The new paperback edition at last. Arrived this morning, *Bananas in Borneo*. If you glance at the back,

## LIFE SUPPORT

you'll find some relishable puffs, 'Jeff Golding's witty and vivid travel . . . highly enjoyable . . . more delightful for being offered . . .' That's the *Financial Times*. And here's the *Guardian*. 'The intrepid JG has pulled off another of his small miracles. His eyes and ears ever on the alert, his style effortlessly deadpan, he carries us through the comedies and horrors of an alien land.'

*During this, he goes to sink, begins to shave.*

'But then JG –' notice that, darling, not Jeff Golding, or Mr Golding, or mere Golding, but JG institutionalised by initials, that's what I'm turning into, a national institution – anyway, a kind of pet. What do you say to that? Comment, please. (*Glances towards bed.*) Comment, darling. Please. (*Goes back to shaving.*)

**JG** (*in Gwen's voice*) Fraud! Fraud! You're a fraud, Jeff!

**JG** (*shaves away*) Bit cryptic, that. Can you explain?

**JG** (*as Gwen*) You could write the same book out of going up to Muswell Hill to do the Saturday shopping, you can't tie your shoelaces without making a panto out of it, so when you're finished congratulating yourself on becoming an institutional buffoon, perhaps you'll come over here and give your non-suffering wife a little attention. I've had to get through another night without you. And without a drink. Which is worse.

**JG** You've been without a drink for over three years.

**JG** (*as Gwen*) That's what you think.

**JG** I don't want to know. There's no point in knowing.

**JG** (*as Gwen*) And now it's too late to find out. (*Laughs.*)

**JG** No, it isn't! It is not, Gwen. That I don't want to know doesn't mean it's too late to find out.

**JG** (*as Gwen*) Well, I've been without you for – for how long has it been, Jeff? That I've been without you for?

**JG** You've never been without me. Not for a minute. It's you that's been absent. These last six weeks. For the last six weeks I've been here. But you've been away. (*Pause.*) I believe – I'm determined to believe that it's been three years since you last drank. That afternoon at Simon's. That was the last time – and what a last time that was, eh? For both of us. For Simon too, come to that. Not that he noticed, I expect, he never notices, but still he did come down to see you – I mean, weren't you amazed? I was. Coming through the door, smiling vaguely, but actually getting your name right most of the time – not that he used it often as he scarcely spoke, but he looked benevolent, quite loving. And at least not at all embarrassed like the rest of them – Davina and Roger and Liza trying to avert their eyes from both of us, not knowing what to say to either of us. I hope I made it clear that there's no point, absolutely no point, in their coming back. Though Simon would be all right. I mean, after a time we'd scarcely know he was here, would we, and he was the only one who didn't ask – typical of him, I suppose – about what happened, so I didn't have to go through the bee saga all over again – (*Stops.*)

*Pat enters, unnoticed by JG, who continues.*

**JG** (*as Gwen, voice shaking*) Your fault! All your fault!

**JG** (*finishes drying face, stares into mirror*) Yes. My fault. Yours too. *Our* fault. The way it should be between husband and wife. In sickness and in health. Sharing the fault.

*Turning round towards Gwen, he sees Pat.*

**Pat** (*cheerfully*) Morning, JG.

**JG** (*startled*) Oh – morning, Pat.

**Pat** I didn't know you were in yet.

**JG** I popped into your office but you weren't there.

**Pat** Really? Oh yes, it must have been during the little burst of excitement. Mr Wisden – his wife claimed she heard him singing the chorus from the *Messiah*. He used to do it whenever he felt particularly chipper. Which was most of the time. She couldn't bear it, she told me, his voice baying out Hallelujahs all over the house. Now, of course, she'd give anything to hear them again. His Hallelujahs.

**JG** Well, and she has, you say.

**Pat** No, no, I'm afraid it was her own Hallelujahs she heard. I didn't know you shaved here.

**JG** I've just been trying it. These last few days. I thought it might – well, touch something. We did it every morning, you see. She would stay in bed while I shaved. We'd keep the door open and talk of – of this and that. Her day, my day. Monologues from one side or the other. Complaints. Jokes, quite often. Sometimes rows. So – so –

*Pat, going over to Gwen, stares down thoughtfully.*

**Pat** Oh, did I tell you – I'm having a great time with *A Chump in China*. Sometimes I laugh out loud. And what did Mr Rolls say today?

**JG** Nothing much. No change, anyway. Though he thought he noticed a smile. He was quite interested in that. Not excited. But quite interested.

**Pat** A smile. (*Looking more closely at Gwen.*) A smile. It looks more like a – (*thinks*) a smirk to me.

**JG** Yes, to me too. Odd, she never smirked in life. I mean, in ordinary life. But whether it's a smile or a smirk, perhaps it means she dreams. But Mr Rolls's view is that it's probably merely a slight muscular change, a nerve twitching. But I'm not so sure, I've caught one or two expressions – strange expressions. It's true I don't recognise them – well, anyway . . .

**Pat** You're doing a marvellous job, JG. Nobody could do more, give more –

*There is a knock on the door.*

**JG** What? I thought we'd done them all. Come in!

*Jack enters. He is holding a bouquet of flowers. He is dapperly dressed.*

Oh, it's you. Of course. (*To Pat.*) This is my brother, Jack. (*To Jack.*) This is Pat. Dr O'Brien.

*Jack and Pat nod to each other.*

**Jack** I'm sorry I haven't looked in before but I – well, I wasn't sure – wasn't quite sure what the form is in – in these –

*He gestures towards Gwen, without looking at her.*

**Pat** The form?

**Jack** Yes. (*To JG.*) I've been waiting for a – well, to hear from you. An invitation. Or something.

**JG** Invitation! 'Dear Jack, I'd like to invite you to a party to celebrate our return from Guadeloupe. Six p.m. Drinks and canapés. Dress informal. RSVP Intensive Care Unit, St Michael's Hospital, Paddington.'

**Pat** (*laughs*) Well, I'd better be on my way, I've got to look in on Martin's parents. The little boy in the car crash. They usually want to talk about insurance. But then everyone has their own way of dealing – I'll look in later on, for the usual. If you're up to it.

**JG** Yes, yes, of course. Looking forward to it.

*Pat goes out. There is a pause.*

Well, now you're here, do come and say hello. You haven't seen each other since – since . . . Gwen darling, here's Jack come to see you at last – my brother – remember him?

*Jack holds out flowers to JG.*

For me?

**Jack** Well, for – for – (*Nods towards bed.*)

**JG** Then give them to her. (*Gestures to bed.*)

*Jack hesitates, goes to Gwen's bed, looks down. Is clearly upset. Turns away. Puts flowers on the table.*

**Jack** What's the prognosis?

**JG** Well, Jack, being a vegetable is a grey area. One day, who knows when, she may judder upwards into animal life. Alternatively, she might sink downwards into death. Or she might remain where she is now, for years. That's the prognosis.

**Jack** And all because of a wasp. A bloody wasp.

**JG** It was a bee, actually. And now that we've covered our side of things, you can tell me why you've really come at last.

**Jack** What do you mean?

**JG** Here – let's sit down properly.

*Goes over to chair on one side of the bed, gestures to the chair opposite.*

We don't want Gwen to be left out.

*Jack comes hesitantly over, sits down.*

Off you go then.

*Jack says nothing, his eyes fixed over Gwen.*

The sound of your voice, you see. It might stir something. Are you resting?

**Jack** What?

**JG** I meant professionally. Are you resting again?

**Jack** Oh. Well, I suppose – I was in something at the Kennel. That pub theatre in Islington.

**JG** What was it about?

**Jack** An Aids play. It's become a genre, you know. But quite sharp and touching, I thought. So did most of the reviewers. I had a nice little part. Well, more than little. I survived into a bit of the second act. Two good speeches. (*Stops, unable to continue.*)

**JG** Pity we didn't get to see it, eh, darling?

**Jack** Oh, you wouldn't have enjoyed it much. Nor would Gwen. Neither of you like the plays I very occasionally get offered. Though I was quite good in it. Even if I did over-rehearse myself. As is my tendency, you once told me.

**JG** Actually, that wasn't me. That was Gwen. Wasn't it, darling? She always said that you acted as if you were directing yourself, so you should direct really talented actors who would listen to you but still be their spontaneous selves. Does that put it accurately, darling? (*To Gwen.*) That he can't really act himself because he overreacts to his direction of himself. The actor in him is awed by the director in him and –

**Jack** You're repeating yourself.

**JG** No, no, I'm repeating Gwen. But what we want to know is what happened to the Aids play, don't we, darling? It just closed, did it? No future?

**Jack** Oh, it's got a future all right. A West End management has taken it up. There'll be a short break and then it moves in.

**JG** But that's splendid, splendid. Did you hear that, darling? Jack's bound for the West End again. At last. It's been – what? – ten years since you graced the boards, in the revival of that musical. Cockney Sparrow you were, weren't you? And now here you are, back again, dying of Aids and in the West End –

**Jack** I'm not going to grace the boards, dying of Aids in the West End. They've taken the short break to recast a few of the parts, mine among them.

**JG** (*looks for support to Gwen*) Oh. Oh, dear. What a – a pity.

**Jack** Gwen's quite right. I'm a rotten actor.

**JG** Anything in the offing?

**Jack** I've got an audition this afternoon.

**JG** What for?

**Jack** Cockney Sparrow's father. They're doing a revival. A touring revival. They hope to end up in London. But if they do, I won't be with them. They'll recast me. That's for sure.

**JG** Don't be sure, Jack. Nothing's for sure. That's what we've found out, haven't we, darling? Oh, and how's Esmond? You're still together? In your Hackney bedsitter?

**Jack** Yes.

**JG** Gwen thinks you're one of the cosiest couples she's ever heard of, eh, darling, from the way you describe yourselves. Sometimes we're actually quite jealous, aren't we? Oh, do tell us again about the way you met. You never know, it might, it might – (*Nodding towards Gwen.*)

*Jack says nothing, then:*

**Jack** Oh, for God's sake, Jeffie!

**JG** Well, I'll tell it. You met when he tried to mug you. There he was, Esmond, a black tearaway from Notting Hill Gate, no future, no family, running with the pack, streaming along the pavements, snatching handbags from old ladies, mugging, drugging – You saved him from a life of crime, an early death – and think, it all began then, when he held a knife to your stomach. It takes most couples years to get to that point. But you saw something in each other's eyes – isn't that the way you tell it, doesn't he, darling? The sinner saw the saint, the saint saw a – what did you see, Jack? In Esmond's eyes, as he stood there in the darkness, your back to the wall, his knife to your stomach? More than the possibility of your death in the form of a beautiful young black –

**Jack** I saw a frightened boy.

**JG** So you took his knife away, and ushered him into your heart. And then back to your little flat in Hackney. Where you became the cosiest couple you've ever heard of, darling, from the way he tells it, eh, darling?

**Jack** Jeffie, what are you doing?

**JG** Counting your blessings. Which is one more than we have, isn't it, darling? But we aim to get ours back. Don't we, darling?

**Jack** (*after a pause*) It may interest you to know that my own blessing is currently in jail.

**JG** But you just said you were together.

**Jack** Of course we're together. In the sense that matters. He didn't *choose* jail instead of me.

**JG** What did he do?

**Jack** He went to the job centre, as he does every morning. On his way home. He was stopped by a couple of policemen. They started to manhandle him, incited him to violence, that's what it really was – an incitement to violence – and for once he lost control. I'd told him, told him and told him, to be passive, polite, deferential, just for a few disgusting minutes, and he'd managed it time and again but – I suppose he was depressed, no job on offer, no prospect of a job – and then being mauled and abused for absolutely no reason, apart from being black and young and jobless. They handcuffed him and took him to the station. And of course they found a knife on him, all kinds of dope, which of course wasn't his.

**JG** He'd stolen it?

**Jack** No, they planted it on him. And the knife.

**JG** You can be sure of that?

**Jack** I watched him dress before he left. (*Little pause.*) As a matter of fact I dressed him. One of our little rituals. So I know what he had in his pockets.

**JG** But he might have stopped off somewhere on the way to the job centre. Or on the way back. You can't even be positive he went to the job centre – sorry, darling, but it's got to be said. Whatever you think about men in uniforms. Women too – some of them are honest. Mean well. They do – try to do the decent thing, darling.

As you know. From your own experience. (*As if jogging Gwen's memory.*) With your drunk-driving charge? How long's he going to be in jail?

**Jack** I don't know.

**JG** Well, what's his sentence?

**Jack** He hasn't gone to trial yet. He's been remanded in custody. He could be in for a year before he even comes before a court. Innocent until proved guilty. So he'll rot innocently away in the filthiest conditions, on remand, being punished as if guilty even if he's found not guilty. And there's nothing I can do. Unless I can find him a solicitor. A paid one. Legal Aid's no good – they try their best, but they've seen it all too often – and if you can't offer bail because there isn't the money –

**JG** Ah.

*Looks at Gwen, nods slightly. After a pause.*

How much?

**Jack** (*shrugs*) Two or three thousand.

*Looks away from JG towards Gwen without intending to. Looks away from her.*

**JG** That's quite a lot.

**Jack** I certainly haven't got it.

**JG** I have. Haven't I? I wonder how much, though. Gwen knows all about that side of things. Why don't – why don't you ask her? If she agrees, I'll write you a cheque for three thousand. On the spot.

**Jack** Ask Gwen?

**JG** That's it. Her decision. Not mine. Put it to her, why don't you? See what you can sort out between the two of you. I won't interfere in any way.

*Gets up, goes over to other table, sits down, picks up magazine, opens it.*

*Jack stares towards him, in disbelief.*
  *There is a pause.*
  *Jack looks at Gwen, makes to speak again, then looks towards JG.*

**Jack** But if she can't speak –?

**JG** Oh, you'll hear something. I'm sure you will. If you get her to listen. And then listen hard yourself.

**Jack** But how will you know?

**JG** Well, I'll listen hard too. And if I don't hear her, I'll hear from you what she's said. Won't I?

*He goes on reading magazine.*
  *Jack, after a pause, leans over and forces himself to whisper to Gwen, awkward and embarrassed.*

**Jack** Gwen, Gwen, if you can hear me –

**JG** Don't be afraid of playing – or even preying – on her emotions. She's always a soft touch. Especially where you're concerned.

*Jack hesitates. Tries again. Begins to gesture.*
  *JG watches him surreptitiously, over the top of the magazine.*
  *Jack becomes increasingly eloquent, gesticulatory, then stops, stares down at Gwen, smiles gratefully, bends over her.*

**Jack** Bless you, Gwen. Bless you.

*Gets up, goes over to JG.*

Well, that's all settled then.

**JG** The whole whack? The full three thousand?

**Jack** Yes. Well, actually, she wants it to be three and a half thousand. So there's a little in hand after I get Esmond out.

**JG** Well! Well, well, well!

**Jack** (*boldly*) Isn't that right, Gwen? Three and a half thousand?

*JG goes over to Gwen's bed, bends over it.*

**JG** Is it right, darling? Three and a half? (*Little pause.*) What? Oh, I see. I'll clarify that then. (*Comes back to Jack.*) A little misunderstanding. She meant half the three thousand, not three and a half thousand. We're sorry. Oh, but look, you don't think you overdid it? The presentation, I mean. The actor/director taking over – rather than Jack just being Jack. Have another go, why don't you?

*Jack makes as if to refuse.*

Think of Esmond rotting away.

**Jack** (*goes back, sits down on the bed*) Gwen, I haven't got anything to say, really. I've said it all. I can't bear life without him. That's what it comes to. And I'm so frightened for him in there. I'm desperate, Gwen. That's all it is. Will you help me? Please. Help us.

*Waits, then comes back to JG.*

**JG** And?

**Jack** Why don't you ask her? To avoid any further misunderstanding.

**JG** (*goes to the bed*) He *is* my brother, darling. And though we don't – of course we don't – believe a word he says, and never have, about why he needs it, we are in the habit of letting him have it. You always say it's worth it, just to find out what story he'll come up with next. And Esmond in jail is quite a good one. Far better than his last – the need for an immediate operation on his vocal cords that he couldn't get on the National Health. So – so – (*as if listening*) oh, darling! What a sister-in-law I've acquired for my brother.

*Kisses her, strokes her head.*

Oh, I'm sure he will.

*Comes back to Jack, who has sat down. He sits down too, takes out a chequebook, writes a cheque.*

What *do* you want it for?

**Jack** I told you – (*Stops.*) I need it to pay off my overdraft. To pay my back rent. And to pay the landlord for the damage that little shit and his friends did to my flat when he left. Graffiti on the walls, smashed furniture, urine and crap on the carpet – there. Satisfied?

**JG** Yes, I am. I find that a much more moving story.

*He hands him the cheque. Jack takes it, puts it in his pocket.*

**Jack** Thank you.

*JG nods towards Gwen.*
*Jack nods thanks towards Gwen.*

(*To JG.*) I never thought you believed my stories, only that you pretended to accept them to save me – save me – Well, I didn't tell you the truth this time either. The fact of the matter is I want the money for a two-man show Esmond and I are going to put on at the Edinburgh Festival. That's the fact of the matter, Jeffie. But as it is, I'll take my chances as Cockney Sparrow's father. (*Taking cheque out of his pocket, tearing it up.*) I don't want anything from you again. (*Carries the bits of cheque over to bed.*) Either of you. (*Realises.*) What am I doing?

> *Goes to door, turns as if to say something, goes out.*
> *JG sits down at table. Hums, taps his foot, Picks up magazine.*

**JG** (*after a little pause*) Did you say something, darling? (*After another pause.*) Mmm? (*After another pause.*) Anyway, you don't have to. I know what you're thinking. That I shouldn't have forced you to take the decisions. That's it, isn't it, darling?

**JG** (*as Gwen*) It was disgusting. Quite disgusting.

**JG** Yes, but he can't help it. Couldn't help it. Perhaps he can from now on.

**JG** (*as Gwen*) No, you were disgusting. You used me.

**JG** No. He tried to take advantage of you. And you let him.

**JG** (*as Gwen*) You let him. I'd never have done that to him. You enjoyed yourself.

**JG** Perhaps. But at least he tore up the cheque for once. For once he did the manly thing –

**JG** (*as Gwen*) Manly!

**JG** Grown-up then, that's how you'd put it. Grown-up! Hah!

**Gwen** (*as herself*) I'll speak for myself, if you don't mind.

> *JG suppresses a grin of pleasure and triumph, seeming still to concentrate on his magazine.*

**JG** Then go on, darling. (*Yawns slightly.*)

**Gwen** I hate it when you're unkind. You're not unkind. It's not in your nature to be unkind.

**JG** Oh, I think it must be. Between us we're bringing it out. Besides, if you didn't like it, you should have stopped me, shouldn't you? Just one word would have done the trick.

**Gwen** And what word would that have been?

**JG** How can I say? It would have been *your* word. You ask me to let you speak for yourself, and then you ask me to put words in your mouth.

**Gwen** No. You choose to put them there, as you're doing now. There are no words in my mouth, no hearing in my ears, no thoughts in my head, no impulses in my heart.

**JG** Then how come you're speaking to me? And how can you speak to me if you can't hear what I'm saying, can't think about what I've said, can't feel some impulses in your heart?

*There is a silence.*
   *JG goes over, kisses Gwen on the forehead, takes her hand, sits down beside her, stares at her, kisses her again. Picks up newspaper.*

Ah. A seventeen-year-old's been picked for Sussex.

**JG** (*as Gwen*) Oh, please not the sports pages.

*He tosses newspaper aside.*

**JG** OK, not the sports pages. So where does that leave us? (*Goes to tape machine, picks up tape.*) Shall we do household noises again? If they weren't familiar to you when you were at home, they've certainly become familiar while you've been away. At least to me. (*Laughing.*) Oh, I know – we haven't had this for a bit. Not exactly seasonal but it always brings back memories. At least to me.

*Puts on 'Silent Night'. Picks up book, looks at quotes on back as lights go down.*

## SCENE THREE

*Lights down.*

**JG** (*over*) I passed out. When I came to, they'd gone. Just me and the guards. The odd thing was I still had my passport and wallet. I was sure I'd been defiled in some way. While I was unconscious. But when the British Consul saw me in one of the prison offices and I told him that I'd been raped, he said that it was extremely unlikely, 'extremely unlikely', as the four other men in the cell were members of Amnesty, there on a conference, who'd asked if they could spend a night in prison to experience conditions for themselves.

*Lights up.*
  *Three weeks later.*
  *JG is sitting at table, looking at newspaper. A chessboard is set up nearby, in the middle of a game.*

**JG** Hey – here he is again, that boy! He got six wickets against Hampshire. Six for thirty-one. All the guile of an old master – deceptive, looping flight, the ball cutting back, turning away, fresh-faced, grinning, cocky – well, they've got to be cocky, haven't they, that's the real deception – What?

**JG** (*speaking as Gwen, from the bed*) This isn't fair, you're just taking advantage. You know how I hate sports. Especially competitive sports.

**JG** Yes, yes, yes, I do know. (*Still reading.*) And I'm sick to death of hearing you say it. You don't mind being competitive when it comes to attracting attention to yourself, though, do you? Your behaviour at parties, for instance, in the days when you were an alcoholic.

**JG** (*as Gwen*) I'm still an alcoholic, don't forget. I'll always be an alcoholic. And so will you.

**JG** All right then, in the days when you were an alcohol-drinking alcoholic. You competed with every other woman in the room. Usually successfully. I mean, you were always the first to fall into one of my friends' arms or onto their laps.

**Gwen** (*as herself*) What about you? Working yourself into drunken rages, throwing your drink over girls' blouses so you could rip them off –

**JG** I did not rip them off. They took them off.

**Gwen** They wouldn't have if you hadn't soaked them.

**JG** For God's sake, it only happened once and it was decades ago! Why do you keep going back to it?

**Gwen** Because I only found out about it a few years ago.

**JG** Ah yes. And of course that's an incident you'd be wiser not to mention. That ghastly afternoon when you shamed me – and yourself – in front of Simon.

**Gwen** You were drunk too. Completely drunk when you came to get me at the police station.

**JG** I drank from despair. You drove me to it. And I wasn't the one charged with 'driving under the influence'. You were bloody lucky not to go to jail.

**Gwen** Oh, Jeff, Jeffie, why are you dragging us through all that again? It was just a lapse. You said so yourself afterwards. We'd stopped drinking for years before then and we didn't drink again after then.

**JG** Didn't we? How do I know whether you drank or not? You say yourself that there's no way for me to know. And as I always let you look after the money... Perhaps that's why you wanted to, eh? So I couldn't check on your booze bill.

**Gwen** You let me look after the money because it was the only thing I was good at. The only way I could – I could share – (*Voice trembling.*) And we came through – oh, my darling, we've come through. Look at me, Jeff, look at me. We're talking about us and your eyes are fixed on the newspaper.

**JG** (*after a pause, not looking up*) He also got twenty-three not out. So an all-rounder in the making. An England prospect. Though born in Jamaica. What we'll end up with is two West Indian sides, one based in the West Indies, one based in England, playing each other, while some honky from Yorkshire or Middlesex brings on the drinks –

**Gwen** Why won't you look at me?

**JG** You know perfectly well why.

**Gwen** No, no, I don't. Why, why, why?

**JG** Because you'll stop talking. You won't be there again. (*Looks at her.*) See, Gwen. You've gone. When I don't see you I can make you up. Or you make yourself up. But when I attend on you – *attend* –

*Turns back to paper. There is a pause.*

**Gwen** You can't imagine me.

**JG** That's right.

**Gwen** Does that mean you're in danger of forgetting me?

**JG** (*still reading*) No. That you're in danger of my forgetting you.

**Gwen** What would become of us then?

**JG** I could lead a life.

**Gwen** You haven't got a life to lead. Not without me.

**JG** Don't be too sure, darling. Oh, did I tell you, Julia's coming round today at three – four – sometime today, I think it's today. She's got contracts and – well, you know Julia, always on the ball – (*Glances quickly at Gwen, then back at newspaper.*) Here's the contrary story. Finglebury, forty-three-years-old Middlesex opening bat, scored his second century in three innings –

*There is a long pause. JG stares desperately down at the newspaper.*

Well, darling? Forty-three, his second century – (*Another long pause.*) Well, Gwen? Two centuries, three innings, forty-three years old.

*Another long pause.*

**Gwen** Sorry, JG. Can't think of anything to say. (*Little pause.*) Silly boy. Soppy darling.

**JG** We should have had children. Proper children. Just one would have done. As long as it'd been a sensible one. Even a foolish one would have been better than none.

**Gwen** I suppose you blame me for that.

**JG** No, I don't. I blame both of us. Or neither of us. Couldn't be helped.

**Gwen** According to you, nothing can be helped. Ever.

**JG** Nobody can work out the consequences of sex. Or the lack of consequences. It's entirely random, how the sperm, the eggs sort themselves out – sometimes long-ago genes revive themselves in a fraction of a second, sometimes nothing at all revives itself – (*little pause*) in a fraction of a second.

**Gwen** Try looking at me. Hold me. Hold me in your eyes.

**JG** Your eyes are closed. Your mouth is sealed. You're nowhere, Gwen.

*There is a knock on the door.*
  *JG looks at his watch, surprised. There is another knock.*
  *He goes over to the door, opens it.*

You're early, aren't you? Or are you late?

**Julia** (*enters, carrying a briefcase*) No, I'm exactly on time. Aren't I?

**JG** Yes, yes, I expect you are, you always are. Hours tend to get a bit muddled up in here. Sometimes it seems like the same hour, the same long hour.

**Julia** How are you?

*JG shrugs.*

No change then?

**JG** One lives in hope.

**Julia** (*awkwardly*) I've brought some contracts. (*Begins to open briefcase.*)

**JG** They're not why I asked you here.

**Julia** I know. But they've still got to be signed. There's the American mini-series and – and . . . Do you really want to go through with this?

**JG** What have I got to lose?

**Julia** Well, perhaps – perhaps your marriage.

**JG** If there's still a marriage to lose I'm a lucky man, aren't I?

**Julia** Have you tried this with anyone else?

**JG** Who else is there to try it with – apart from Jack? I had a serious go with him without his knowing it, which means he was true to form, but nothing much came of it. Except that he missed out on a couple of thousand. I expect he'll be back for it. Well – (*Looks at her.*) Would you do the honours, please?

*Julia stares at him uncertainly.*

(*Encouragingly.*) Your move.

**Julia** (*after a pause*) Sorry, I can't. I feel sort of awkward. It seems – seems kind of indecent, really.

**JG** Oh God, I wish you wouldn't say 'sort of' and 'kind of'.

**Julia** Sorry.

**JG** No, I'm sorry. (*Looks at Julia.*) Please.

**Julia** Gwen, Jeff and I are lovers.

**JG** Look, I know it's difficult but I scarcely heard that myself.

**Julia** (*after a pause, loudly*) Gwen, Jeff and I are lovers.

**JG** (*loudly*) Have you got that, Gwen? Julia and I are lovers.

**Julia** Please forgive me, Gwen. I've always wanted you to know. Felt so guilty. Haven't we, darling?

**JG** Yes. Well, I have, anyway. Since – since the bee – I can't bear to think about it. It seems so treacherous now. So squalid and – and –

**Julia** Well, I hope it was never actually squalid. (*Little laugh of anger.*) And as for treacherous, I did everything I could to keep it between ourselves.

**JG** Yes, we really did our best to make it into a hole-and-corner affair.

**Julia** (*to Gwen*) I always knew that you were the one that came first.

**JG** That's true, darling. She meant nothing to me, darling, nothing at all. It was just when we were going through one of our rough patches, so of course I looked for something on the . . . And it seemed practical because she was my agent and a sort of friend. Sort of, kind of – (*To Julia.*) this isn't quite panning out as I – planned.

**Julia** Well, you may not be telling Gwen anything but you're telling me a great deal. When we were in Tonga, for instance –

**JG** (*to Gwen*) We were only in Tonga the once, darling, I promise. I mean abroad together once. The rest of the time it was after-lunch stuff in London, when we'd finished discussing contracts and deals –

**Julia** I used to cancel meetings – important meetings – so that you could have your 'after-lunch stuff'. I mean, for Christ's sake, if we're going to confess to our affair, let's try and give it some – some dignity, or what's the point of the confession?

**JG** You're absolutely right. I apologise, darling. It did have a little dignity in as much as we were in love. For a time. Sexually and – We had fun together, didn't we?

**Julia** Well, I hope so. At least I tried to give you fun.

**JG** Well, I hope you got some fun too. At least your usual ten per cent.

*Julia makes as if to slap JG, suddenly realises. He studies Gwen's face.*

Nothing. Nothing, nothing, nothing. (*To Gwen.*) Don't you mind that I was unfaithful? Don't you – (*To Julia.*) Let's have another go. (*Thinks.*) Oh, yes, I've got something. You know, all the time I was away in all the places neither of you came to, I'd occasionally have a fantasy. An erotic fantasy. That while I was cavorting through Canada, meandering through Madeira, a clown in Columbia, a sot in the Sudan, all on my ownsome, making a mint for you – (*to Gwen*) and ten per cent for you – (*to Julia*) the two of you were lolling in each other's arms, whooping in girlish laughter, playing with each other sexually, having rows in order to have reconciliations, loving and loving and loving –

*He looks at Julia encouragingly.*

**Julia** (*to Gwen*) Yes – yes, I imagined telling you about him – about what we were up to. It would always be an Italian restaurant. And you'd throw a glass a wine into my face, heave your spaghetti into my lap – and after I'd mopped myself up in the Ladies, we'd settle down, yes, settle down, to enjoy our lunch. That's the truth of it. I wanted to be your lover, not his. I wanted you in my arms, not him, and – and . . . I can't, I can't go on with this. I have a life, I have a past too. I'm not going to have them falsified like this – emptied like this – even for – even for – (*Turns away from bed, crying slightly.*)

**JG** You know how much it meant to me at the time. How much it still means to me.

*Goes over to Julia, wipes her tears away.*

Oh, my darling, my poor darling, my poor darling Gwen!

**Julia** (*laughs*) I hope you heard that, Gwen – oh, I do hope you heard that. Because that really was the whole story. Is the whole story. (*There is a pause.*) Oh, the contracts.

*Opens her briefcase, takes out contracts.*

**JG** How's Maxi?

**Julia** He's dead.

**JG** Really? Oh, dear. How?

**Julia** He strolled under a bus.

**JG** Strolled? Strolled under it?

**Julia** Yes. It looked quite deliberate. But he'd been rather depressed. Fatalistic.

**JG** But do dogs commit suicide?

**Julia** Oh, yes. More often than you'd think. But it's not surprising – their best friend is man, don't forget. That's why they have an inner life. Maxi was introspective, gloomy by nature. Ate badly. Slept badly. Low self-esteem.

**JG** On the other hand, he may just have been jay-walking. Are you going to get another one? Dog?

**Julia** I'm keeping an eye open for a bitch. A good-natured, life-loving, dependent and dependable bitch. Whose best friend is woman.

*They laugh intimately, then both look guiltily towards Gwen.*
*Julia hands JG contracts. JG takes them, then hands them back.*

**JG** To hell with them. To hell with all contracts.

*Julia nods, puts the contracts back into her briefcase, and goes out.*

*JG sits at main table, picks up magazine, glances at cover.*

Ah, the television guide. In other words, our weekly guide to murder, pillage, rape. What a foul world. (*Gets up, goes towards window, looks out.*) So that was Julia and I, as we were then and are now. Then what might we have been, you and I, if Julia and I – but what does it matter as you're not here to be anything. Even as you were. And I – and I – what a foul world. (*Stares out of window.*) There she is, going down the steps, back to the office, I suppose, her briefcase full of unsigned contracts. I should have signed them, it would've only taken a minute – and life goes on, doesn't it – and she does try to earn her ten per – Oh, there's Lydia! Caring and attractive. Well, let's face it at last, old cheese, not just attractive but sexy. Throbbingly sexy. And those legs! Sometimes I don't know where to look when she's changing you, in case you're looking at me looking at her legs. I can't say she seems particularly sexy at the moment. Not even caring. No, careworn is what she looks. Poor Lydia, poor, poor girl, day in, day out, death after death, that boy gone –

*Gwen lets out a long sigh.*

I wish you wouldn't do that. You used to do it at night, when you slept like a normal human being. Now it's a provocation.

*Gwen lets out a rasp. JG turns away from window.*

And you used to do that as well. I'd put my hand on your side, you'd let out a rasp of pleasure, of security and – I remember, through the fog of sleep, your hand – open your eyes, damn you. You have no right, no right –

*He goes over to tape machine, puts on 'Silent Night', begins to hum with it, then, as Gwen, hums 'Silent Night'.*
*During this, Pat enters, stands, watching.*

*JG, as Gwen, continues to sing 'Silent Night'. The effect is desperate and grotesque. JG stops, suddenly aware of Pat.*
*There is a pause.*

Just like your Mrs Wisden. Except Gwen's voice was rather lovely. At least it never bayed.

**Pat** May I?

*Going to sofa, sits down, begins to roll a joint.*

**JG** It was her favourite carol. She used to sing it every Christmas. It was a tradition. She at the piano, I listening to her. And I keep remembering that Christmas –

*Pat is vaguely studying the chessboard during this.*

– seven – eight years ago? Before I went to Tonga. For my first book. She looked so beloved, eyes wicked, her head back, not having to watch her fingers – oh, the sight of her. And yet I – it's the Hardy poem, isn't it, do you know Hardy?

**Pat** Yes, yes – 'Kiss me, kiss me, Hardy' –

**JG** The poet. The poet. 'Everything glowed with a gleam; Yet we were looking away!' And that's it. I was looking away. Looking at her in joy, but within myself, looking away, looking forward to all the funny things I'd make sure happened to me as I trekked through Tonga. I even had the title before I went to bed, *By Tube to Tonga*, 'Silent Night' still in my ears –

**Pat** *By Tube to Tonga*. (*Laughs, moves a chess piece.*)

**JG** – and then checking my knapsack, my plane tickets, my passport, my vaccination certificate, then – then to bed, where she lay reading, eyes half closed, waiting, and still I could hear it, will never not hear her voice – even while I was looking away – just like Mrs Wisden – I wouldn't look away again. Not if she let me see her at the piano one more time. How long has he been gone now? (*Goes over to chessboard.*)

**Pat** Mmm?

**JG** Mr Wisden. When was it he died finally?

**Pat** Three weeks, isn't it? Two, anyway.

**JG** (*sitting down at chessboard*) So she's, um, liberated at last, is she?

**Pat** N-no. Not really. Keeps coming back as if he's still alive. Completely baffled when she realises. Spent all those months, you see, willing him, willing him, and now there's nothing left to will. But she still goes on willing. Like a muscle, you see. Keeps flexing itself.

**JG** (*moving a chess piece*) Sometimes I think you only come in here so you can dope yourself safely.

**Pat** That's only partly true. I also come in for this – (*Moving a chess piece.*)

**JG** One of the nurses noticed the smell the other day.

**Pat** The tall, leggy one, very pretty. (*Nods.*) Very pretty. Linda.

**JG** Lydia. She smelt it and I could tell she knew what it was.

**Pat** Yes, I know. She reported you to me. I said that you were probably trying to reach Gwen through a favourite memory. I explained that people of your generation started the whole fashion. That's right, isn't it – you all did it, didn't you?

**JG** Just now and then, eh – (*Checks himself.*) We were a very old-fashioned couple. Stuck strictly to booze and tobacco. Until we gave them up.

**Pat** A dish, isn't she? Those legs –

**JG** I wouldn't know, I haven't noticed.

**Pat** Haven't noticed! Haven't noticed her legs! Her –!

*JG looks away, looks back at Pat, laughs. Pat laughs.*

**JG** You respond to it very quickly, don't you?

**Pat** (*looks at his joint, inhales*) Yes, something in my chemistry, I suppose. The downside is that it wears off very quickly too.

**JG** So what are you going to say to Mrs Wisden?

**Pat** Nothing any more. I've sent her on to Mr Rolls, to explain the facts – well, the fact. That her husband is dead. So it's his can of worms.

**JG** And how's he going to calm her down? Tell her that because she's missed out on one of his miracles, it doesn't mean that there isn't another one around the corner? A really big one. A resurrection! There isn't the bedside any more but there's always the graveside. Try baying out a few Hallelujahs there.

**Pat** (*studying chessboard*) Hallelujah. That's right. Keep the faith.

**JG** (*intensely, as if to himself*) Is there ever a time when one can say enough? Enough. I've had enough.

**Pat** Mmm? (*Moves a chess piece.*) Check. No, mate, isn't it? Yes, it's mate. Hallelujah and amen.

*Lights.*

## SCENE FOUR

*Lights down.*

**JG** (*over*) 'Quiete ya – silencio.' Then I was being dragged up the steps of some institution and hustled down a corridor, tossed into an anteroom, and left there with a couple of guards. I assumed – what was I to assume? – that I was going to be executed. I was crying, I think, yes, I'm afraid I was crying. And then he came in. The doctor. He was angry. I've never seen anyone so angry. He stood in front of me and another guard opened a door and some little man came in, unshaven, fat, cheerfully malignant he looked, and I thought – I thought – is this my executioner? But he was the interpreter, actually.

*Lights up.*
  *Jack is sitting beside Gwen, holding her hand to his forehead.*
  *Pat is lying on sofa, apparently asleep.*
  *JG enters, unshaven, carrying a carrier bag.*

**Jack** I came to ask – to ask for – for your forgiveness. And Gwen's. I'm so ashamed, so ashamed. Ashamed at having failed you as a brother. A proper brother. I've been trying to imagine what it's like for you – well, of course I saw for myself. Crazed. Crazed with despair, that's what you've been, haven't you? (*Pause.*) Look, Jeffie, I'm going to talk. Brother to brother. About you. What's happening to you. What's going to become of you? I'm going to say what I've got to say whether you want me to or not. You can't go on in here, Jeffie, you can't. Look, I know how much you loved – love Gwen, and how much she loved – loves you. But she would have hated the thought of you in here every day. She would have wanted you to get on with your life. To get back to your work. Think of Daddy. How much he loved Mummy. When she was dying – all those months of ugly dying – and she was conscious for most of them, she could speak, could reach out for his hand – she insisted he got on with his life. She insisted on it. Into classes every day, marking papers every evening after he came back from the hospital. When the school offered him compassionate leave he refused to take it. She wouldn't let him. If we hadn't heard him sobbing at night, we wouldn't have known how deeply he felt – and then immediately after the funeral, back to the classroom. Getting on with his life saved his life. He told us so. And that's what Gwen would want for you. I mean, you're not blaming yourself, surely?

*JG, during this, has sat down and is writing a cheque.*

It was an accident. A one-in-a-million accident! You're not God, Jeffie, you can't – can't rule bees and know where they're going to visit and who they're going to sting and why they choose one person as opposed to another –

**JG** Over-rehearsed. Over-rehearsed, as usual.

*Hands Jack cheque. Jack takes cheque, looks at it.*

**Jack** I – I –

**JG** She was widdling into the dust. By the side of the road. The bee alighted on her neck. She clapped her hand to her neck. 'Ow,' she said, 'Ow!' Bzzzzzz –! (*Slap.*) Ow! Bzzzzz –! (*Slap.*) Ow! Bzzzzz –! (*Slap.*) Ow! (*Begins to shake.*)

**Pat** (*to Jack*) I'll see to your brother. He'll be all right. I'll see to him.

*Jack hesitates, pockets the cheque, leaves.*

*Pat begins to roll a joint.*

*JG winds down. Still trembling, he sees bottle in his hand, pours it down the sink, goes to chair, sits, huddled.*

**JG** Sorry. Just my way of baying at the graveside.

**Pat** What? Oh, Mrs Wisden you mean. No, no, she's not at his graveside. Not at the moment anyway. She's in Majorca. I had a postcard from her this morning. Doing a lot of swimming, she says.

**JG** She was widdling into the dust. The bee alighted on her neck. She clapped her hand on her neck. 'Ow,' she said. 'Ow!' (*Pause.*) Over-rehearsed. A liar. Still, the truth will out, eh? (*Looks at Pat.*) It wasn't an accident, Pat.

**Pat** (*after a pause*) Ah. Is this a confession, then? Is that what I'm about to hear?

**JG** It was unbearably hot. We stopped at a café to have a lemonade, and instead of lemonade I ordered beer – the first time we'd drunk alcohol – well, together – for years. As far as I know. It went straight to our heads, as always, so – so there we were, the two of us, and the beer warm and flat, flies everywhere – on our eyelids, our nostrils and there were some military types shouting and laughing – and when it came simmering up, why didn't I go and demand cold beer, and I said, what's the use, they won't have any, and she said, and I said, and so it went, until I don't know, we were snarling, snarling, on our feet snarling, and they'd gone silent, watching us. And suddenly one of them, the one with a scar, got up, pushed me out of the way, and told Gwen to shut up, stand still, '*Quiete, silencio,*' that sort of thing, and she went at him, demented, and he took out his gun, and pointed it straight into her face – 'Ow!' she said. 'Ow!'

And fell. And he – he unzipped his flies and stood over her, his cock in his hand, grinning down at her, grinning with the strain of trying to pee over her face – I grabbed a jug and smashed it over his head and – and – do you understand?

*Pat, who has surreptitiously lit another joint during this, nods seemingly dopily.*

**Pat** Yes, yes. Drew his gun to keep her still. Tried to urinate over her to neutralise the poison. And you buggered him up.

**JG** If it hadn't been for me, he might have saved her.

**Pat** But then how were you to know? Most people don't. Though everybody should. (*Nods to himself.*) Should. First-aid handbook stuff.

**JG** But don't you see the joke? The joke of it? Endearing old JG at it again. Heroically and comically preventing his wife's life from being saved. It's like one of the things I make up in my hotel rooms. Because that's how I really do it. I don't go out and about on bicycles looking for trouble, getting involved in scrapes and misunderstandings, getting myself lost – I hate trouble of any kind, I always have. Except the trouble I make up in my hotel rooms. I just sit there, in an armchair if I'm inside, or in a deckchair on the terrace, speaking into my tape recorder, making up trouble. So she's quite right to call me a fraud. That's what she calls me, you know – sometimes as a term of endearment, her 'little fraud', sometimes – sometimes to wound me. So when she insisted on coming with me for once, it just seemed like vindictiveness. Typical, I thought. So I responded vindictively. For the first time I really did do all the things I'd only pretended I'd done. I hated every minute of it – and so did she – cycling in the heat, actually getting lost, rows in the bank over the rate of exchange – but even so I would have made it all a good read. Highly entertaining. Even the bit about my wife being stung – she'd have been my partner in buffoonery. That would have been my revenge. And she'd have laughed, I know she would. So it would have been a nice revenge, the two of us laughing at ourselves. Back home. (*Pause.*) My last words to her were full of poison.

**Pat** But that doesn't matter. You love each other. That's what matters.

**JG** We don't love each other enough to love her back to life. So what is the good, what is the good of our love if it's got poison in it and no antidote?

**Pat** Well, that's it really, isn't it? That's the whole issue, the fundamental question itself. I mean, look at you, JG, going on and on, on and on creating, recreating her out of the void in this room, the void on the bed, the void in yourself – and all the time you're asking the fundamental question: why do we have to love if love is the cause of our greatest suffering? Without love there'd be no grief, no guilt, and above all, no hope. That would be the best of it – no hope. Then you'd be free, wouldn't you? Free to move on. Goodbye Gwen, hello Lydia.

**JG** (*stares at him in momentary disbelief*) Goodbye Gwen, hello Lydia!

**Pat** Well, it's goodbye Lydia too, as a matter of fact. She asked to be transferred to another ward. Much better hours too. So I might make a move soon. Been on my mind. Though I've heard she's tangled up with some married bloke.

**JG** Tell me – is this what you do with the others? What you did with Mrs Wisden and the parents of that boy? Sit smoking a joint, rambling on about the hopelessness of their love, planning your – your sex life? Do you play chess with them too? Is that really all you have to offer any of us?

**Pat** Well, yes, JG, that's what I have to offer. Though you're the only one I play chess with. I used to play Scrabble with the Norris twins – well, they were triplets actually, but the third one was in bed – and Beggar My Neighbour with –

**JG** And that's the point of you, is it, the whole point of you? That's what you're employed to do?

**Pat** Oh, no, JG. The point of me is you. You're the point of me. You see?

**JG** No, I don't see.

**Pat** I'm doing research on people in your sort of condition. How you all cope and fail to cope. Well, we might learn from it. The more data we get the more likelihood there is that we'll eventually be able to help people in your sort of condition.

**JG** And are you going to get a book out of it?

**Pat** I've published a few articles and one day, who knows, as Mr Rolls says. But don't worry, I shan't be using any names – just case numbers or alphabetically – Case One or Two, Case A, Case B –

**JG** Are you saying – are you saying that you've kept her alive just so that you could study me in my – in my –

**Pat** Oh, no, JG. No, no. It's Mr Rolls that's keeping her alive. Or allowing her to continue. That's his work. Mine is to observe the consequences.

**JG** Observe, observe – how can you observe anything in your sort of condition?

**Pat** Well, that might be true. It's sometimes a strain, you know. It's more than I can bear sometimes. I need to relax myself.

*He sucks on his joint. JG stares at him, goes over, snatches joint from Pat's fingers, sniffs it, then inhales.*

**JG** This isn't – what is it?

**Pat** It's very bad for my throat is what it is. Dry it makes it. Dry, raw and thirsty.

**JG** It wasn't yourself you were trying to relax, it was me. Is that it?

**Pat** I was trying to be – family, you see. So that you had someone to relax with. It's not just for my career, JG, it's for you too.

**JG** Family. My family's there. On the bed.

**Pat** Now is the time you can say enough. You've had enough.

**JG** Yes, I've had enough. Enough of you. So go, please. Please go.

*Pat gets up, goes to door, turns.*

**Pat** Look, you're not serving a custodial sentence. You're free at least to give yourself a break. Take a holiday.

**JG** But if I did and she did one or the other, I wouldn't be there to be with her, would I? But you would. And I wouldn't like that.

*He turns, begins to put away chess set.*
 *Pat goes out.*
 *JG puts away a few more pieces, then suddenly goes over to Gwen, kneels beside her, presses her hand to his forehead.*

Oh, Gwen, my darling Gwen, please – please –!

*He gets up in desolation, goes back to chess set, puts a few more pieces away.*
 *Gwen sings 'Silent Night, Holy Night'.*
 *JG makes as if to turn towards her, remembers, forces himself to stand, not looking at her, as Gwen continues to sing.*
 *On this, lights fade down.*


## SCENE FIVE

*Lights down.*

**JG** (*over*) 'Our little country can't afford to keep your vegetable.' He spat it out, full of anger and – and contempt, and there was the meaning coming at me, almost idly, from the interpreter. And they went to the door, the doctor and his interpreter, then stopped suddenly. He spoke again, his eyes fixed on me. Not angry eyes, now, but insinuating – a – a tempter's eyes.

*Lights up on JG speaking into a tape recorder. On the table, a typescript, exercise book, pen, a bottle of whisky. He is holding a glass from which he is sipping as he speaks.*
 *The door is open. Pat is at the door, watching and listening. JG, who has his back to Pat, is not aware of him.*

(*Into tape recorder.*) 'He says that probably in your country there are all kinds of laws that complicate situations,' the interpreter interpreted. 'If you wish – he can offer you the advantages of a primitive society.' Very offhand, the interpreter was, but there was the other pair of eyes, the doctor's eyes. 'If you go now,' the interpreter interpreted, 'he will finish it for you.' Not a cruel man, the doctor, even when offering a cruel choice. I wonder if he knew it was cruel, how I'd go back to it – time and again. That decisive offer that I decisively –

*Becomes suddenly aware of Pat, turns off tape recorder. There is a pause.*

How long have you been there?

**Pat** I don't know. I was listening so I didn't mark the time. Am I allowed to come in?

**JG** You seem to be already in.

**Pat** Then may I sit down?

**JG** (*hesitates, then gestures towards sofa*) But no herbal cigarettes.

**Pat** Oh. Pity. I discovered I'd become quite addicted.

**JG** (*raising his glass to his lips in acknowledgement*) Well then, I suppose you'd better have one.

**Pat** Thank you. (*Rolls a cigarette.*) Though it isn't actually a herbal. It's the real thing.

**JG** And how's everyone else since we last spoke?

**Pat** Some have come, some have gone. So it's as usual.

**JG** And Mrs – Mrs –?

**Pat** Wisden. She stayed on in Majorca. Something's happened but I don't know what it is. Her last postcard was evasive – excited but evasive. A waiter, do you think?

**JG** And Lydia?

**Pat** Not much fun. No sex. By inclination she's a patient, not a girlfriend. Falls in love with people in your sort of condition.

**JG** Really? Lucky I didn't know, I suppose. So what do you do when you're together?

**Pat** She sits in fairly expensive restaurants grieving by proxy. I nod away uselessly.

**JG** And the married man?

**Pat** Not married, widowed. Got two grown-up children. Rethinking his whole life in Bermuda.

**JG** So you have a widow in Majorca and a widower in Bermuda and – what are you doing here?

**Pat** Rolls sent me.

**JG** But he looked in this morning. He didn't say anything in particular.

**Pat** No, there was nothing in particular to say. That's the point.

**JG** Wants to pull the plug, does he?

*Pat nods.*

And you?

**Pat** He's the miracle worker and he's lost faith. He's not a cruel man either, even though he's offering you a cruel choice too. Take it, JG.

**JG** I'm used to it here. I'm getting on with my life and staying in touch with my past. What more could a man want?

**Pat** The past is memories. Let them live in you. And not as a lump on the bed. You don't have to hang around here for your grief, it'll come at you when it will – in Majorca, Bermuda, wherever you are. Anyway, where and when you least want it. That's the thing about grief, it –

**JG** What do you say to a game?

**Pat** (*after a little pause*) Well, it seems I've got nothing better to do.

*They move to the table, JG taking the bottle of whisky and glass with him, Pat sucking on his joint. JG puts a cassette into the tape recorder.*

*They begin to set up the chess pieces. Pat picks up a black and a white piece, puts them behind his back, then holds them out in his fists. JG points to one of the fists.*

*Curtain.*

# JUST THE THREE OF US

For Ian Hamilton

**Just the Three of Us** was first presented by the Peter Hall Company at the Theatre Royal, Windsor, on 7 October 1997, and subsequently at Brighton, Guildford, Nottingham, Wolverhampton, Swansea and Newcastle. The cast was as follows:

**Enid** Prunella Scales
**Ronnie** Dinsdale Landen
**Terri** Carli Norris

*Director* Peter Hall
*Designer* Ti Green
*Sound Designer* Matt McKenzie
*Lighting Designer* Ben Ormerod

# Characters

**Enid**
**Ronnie**
**Terri**

# Act One

## SCENE ONE

*Late evening.*
 *A cottage studio, with an open-plan kitchen and bathroom off. A bed on stage, a table, two chairs, one armchair, French windows opening on to balcony. Shelves crammed with books (Dickens, Tolstoy, etc.), a cassette player and various tapes and compact discs of classical music.*
 *Hanging from the ceiling, stretching down from the highest point in a corner, is a considerable length of chain which goes through a pulley and vanishes as if leading up to the roof. The chain is not particularly noticeable. The door of the studio is open.*
 *There is a bottle of scotch on the table. Also a bottle of dandelion wine.*
 *Enid is standing at the French windows. She has a glass of scotch in her hand.*
 *Ronnie is walking up and down studio, agitatedly, puffing at his pipe, glass of wine in his hand.*

**Enid** (*coming in*) Now, what were you saying, Ronnie? Oh, yes, something about your church roof, I expect, whenever I can't remember what you've been talking about it's always the church roof, people being rained on during your sermons, plaster falling into their hair – is that it?

**Ronnie** No, my dear, I wasn't talking about the church roof. I was asking you if you're sure her name is Toni Gray, it seems to me it hasn't been Toni Gray until now.

**Enid** Nonsense, Ronnie, she's always been Toni Gray, of

course she has. (*Takes a long drink.*) For as long as I've known her.

**Ronnie** But, my dear, you've never even met her. You've only talked to her once. On the telephone.

**Enid** But I know her. Through and through. Indeed I do.

**Ronnie** Well, be that as it may, I still don't think she's Toni Gray. Nearly but not quite. She's got a chap's name, yes, beginning with a 'T', yes – and a colour – yes, a colour – The note! Did you remember to put out the note?

**Enid** Note? What note?

**Ronnie** The note telling her to come down here and not to the Big House.

**Enid** Yes, yes, of course I did, I must have done, I remember quite distinctly making a note to myself to put a note on – on the front – You're flustering me with all these questions, Ronnie, why are you flustering me? Why do we have to talk about it? I don't want to think about it even. It'll happen as it happens, when it happens, whatever arrangements I've made or forgotten to make, and that's all we need to know. (*Makes to pour herself another large drink.*)

**Ronnie** My dear! (*Checks himself.*) Um, would you like a glass of dandelion, Mrs Price's dandelion instead – (*Picking up bottle.*)

**Enid** Oh, don't be ridiculous, Ronnie! (*Pouring whisky.*)

**Ronnie** But – but do you really think that that's wise?

**Enid** Of course it's not wise. Wise doesn't come into it.

**Ronnie** But if you're going to do this, if you're really going to do this, my dear, you're going to need a clear head.

**Enid** No, I don't. I don't. A clear heart, a clear will, that's all I need.

**Ronnie** Very well, my dear.

*Watches Enid taking another gulp of whisky, then looks at his watch.*

She'll be here any minute, I'd better get going. I'll look in – I'll look in in an hour or so. As – as planned. All right, my dear, and – and good luck or – or –

**Enid** Yes, yes, in an hour. No, earlier. Half an hour! Come in *half* an hour!

**Ronnie** Half an hour. Right, my dear. (*Moving to door.*)

**Enid** No, no, don't go at all. Stay here, Ronnie, I may need you.

**Ronnie** My dear, we agreed that this bit has to be entirely private. I can't possibly watch, I mean, I'm a vicar, after all –

**Enid** Well then, well then – don't watch, go in there! (*Indicating door.*)

**Ronnie** What – in the lavatory! Hide in the lavatory! Really, Enid! No, no, I can't – I can't.

**Enid** Ronnie, if you want me to go through with this –

**Ronnie** My dear, I don't want you to go through with anything you don't want to go through with. That's been my position. Right from the very start.

**Enid** Well then, if Fred wants me to go through with it –

**Ronnie** Fred's position would probably be exactly the same as my position – that is, if he had any idea of what it is you're thinking of going through with. But as he doesn't, he can't be blamed for not having the position he would have if – if – he knew, um –

**Enid** So you're blaming *me*, is that it? Blaming me, on top of everything else. Hah!

**Ronnie** No, no, of course I'm not, Enid my dear, we're not talking about blame, blame doesn't come into it –

**Enid** 'Oh, Enid, Enid, I'm sinking into the marsh,' he said. 'Going straight down the tubes, into the marsh. Save me, Enid, my dearest and last hope, as always.' And he was crying when he said that, Ronnie, yes, I could see tears trembling down his cheeks. And you, Ronnie, you went down on your knees in that way you always do when you're shocked and moved – 'Oh, save him, save him yet again, Enid, I beg you. Only you can do it!' Isn't that true, Ronnie? Isn't that what you said, and what he said?

**Ronnie** Well – not quite as I remember it, my dear. Certainly not in those words anyway. 'Down the tubes' possibly, because that's his usual phrase when he has a crisis – and perhaps something about a marsh, yes, I remember being struck by the marsh, not having heard it before, but as for tears and crying – no, no, I think he was his quiet matter-of-fact self, and as for me, I may have gone down on my knees but that was merely to add a little weight, there was no question of begging for him, not at all – and besides, we weren't talking about what you're thinking of doing now, we would never have dreamt of asking you to do this, good heavens, I mean a criminal act! No, no, this has nothing to do with what we were talking about, we were talking about, well, the hope that you'd return to your trusty typewriter and give Fred a new Lady –

*Enid lets out a scream, puts her hands to her ears.*

**Ronnie** Sorry, my dear, sorry. I didn't mean to mention – I was just trying to explain – that there's no connection, really, between the one thing and the other.

**Enid** There is a connection, indeed there is! If I'm going to be deprived of my calm, my happiness, my health itself, then Fred's going to be deprived of something too, that's only fair! And that's all I ask, tit for tat, his tit for my tat. (*Lets out a yap of laughter.*) And if you're going to deny me, Ronnie, then we can just go back to where we were. Me, to my peace and good health, and he to his – his tit, as he goes down the tubes into his marsh, yes, I'll really not begrudge it to him, not at all, so you phone him, Ronnie, go and phone him –

**Ronnie** My dear, my dear, please – if all this is simply about my going into the lavatory, why then – why then, of course I'll go into it.

**Enid** Thank you, Ronnie. (*Calmly, then emotionally.*) You're a dear, dear man, Ronnie, I don't know what we'd do without you.

**Ronnie** Thank you, my dear. I don't have to tell you how much, how very much you and Fred –

*Sound of car approaching.*

Oh, there she is! But that's – that's Fred's car!

**Enid** Fred! What do you mean! He hasn't come too!

**Ronnie** No, no, my dear, what are we thinking of, it can't be him – impossible. Well, I'd better – (*Hurrying towards lavatory.*) I just hope she doesn't want to use it – (*Goes into lavatory.*)

**Enid** (*tries to take up a dignified position, stumbles slightly*) Oh – oh, dear.

*As sound of car door slamming, footsteps on gravel, Enid rushes to sink, splashes water onto her face, then unable to help herself, runs to bottle, turns away from door and gulps down scotch, as:*

*Terri enters, briskly. She is in her mid-twenties, carrying handbag-briefcase. Sees Enid with her back to her.*

**Terri** Mrs Parkhurst?

**Enid** (*puts glass down, turns*) Yes, can I help you? Oh, you're my husband's PG, aren't you?

**Terri** Well, his PA. Personal Assistant.

**Enid** Oh, of course. PA. Not PG, PG used to be a paying guest, and we don't have those any more, do we? But the name's Gray, isn't it? Toni Gray. Ms Toni Gray, as we have to say these days.

**Terri** Green actually, Mrs Parkhurst. Terri Green.

**Enid** Ms Green, I'm so sorry. And Terri, you say. Well, we knew it was a 'T' and a colour, didn't we – (*As if to Ronnie.*) Anyway, you saw my note, that's the main thing.

**Terri** Note? What note?

**Enid** Didn't I put a note on the door of the house – the Big House – saying that I'd be down here in the studio and not up there in the Big House. I'm sure I put it up because I made a note –

**Terri** Well, I didn't see any note – I didn't stop at the house, you see, because when we talked on the telephone you told me to go past it, around the bend to your studio. Actually, you said that I couldn't miss it because if I did I'd be over the cliffs onto the rocks and I'd be dead.

**Enid** Oh, we wouldn't want that, would we, you down there, dead on the rocks.

*They laugh together.*

**Terri** But what a lovely place.

**Enid** It was the bottom part of an old lighthouse, you know, I come down at all hours of the day and night, when I want to get away from the Big House and mull things over, mull them over all by myself, it's my mulling place. Mulling place. Do you have one of those?

**Terri** No – no. I wish I did.

**Enid** What a nice answer. And I'm sure you will. Yes, I'm sure you will. (*Smiles at Terri.*) Well, anyway, here you are, safe and sound, for this – this surprise business. This birthday surprise. For my husband. He's looking forward to it enormously. No, no, what am I saying, how can he be looking forward to it if I'm going to surprise him with it? Where is he at the moment, by the way, my husband?

**Terri** He's – he's in Frankfurt.

**Enid** Oh yes, Frankfurt. Of course he is. Why?

**Terri** Well, he's gone to the book fair.

**Enid** Is that it? – Yes, I find it so difficult to follow his comings and goings at the moment. Sometimes he seems to be all over the place all at once. But why are we standing? Let's sit, shall we – and what about a drink? (*Pouring herself one.*) There's this or (*Seeing wine.*) Ronnie's daffodil – (*Shudders.*)

**Terri** Oh, no, I'd better not, thank you. Driving, you see.

**Enid** Oh yes, of course you are, we heard the car, didn't we? (*As if to Ronnie.*) I mean I did, I heard the car. Did it take ages?

**Terri** An hour and a half about. To hit the middle of Dover.

**Enid** An hour and a half! To hit the middle – *hit* the middle of poor old Dover! You must have driven like a demon, my dear. What sort of car is it?

**Terri** A Porsche.

**Enid** A Porsche. I don't know about cars but it rings a bell. A Porsche – is it blue and very expensive, like Fred's?

**Terri** Well, it is his, actually.

**Enid** Oh, I see, you've got my husband's car then, have you?

**Terri** Well, it's the company car, actually. So we're allowed to use it when – Mr Parkhurst's away.

**Enid** Well, I never let him use it down here, except at weekends when he usually comes down, not his company car nor any other kind of car. Absolutely forbidden. We're bicycling folk down here, go everywhere by bicycle. Or on foot. Except when we take the train. To go to London – and such places. And how do you get around normally, my dear, when you haven't got my husband's company car? What methods do you use?

**Terri** Well, I live out in Harlow so I've been taking the train to Victoria and then the tube to Sloane Square and then a bus to World's End. And there I am. Apart from a bit of a walk. But there may be simpler – methods, I've only just moved there.

**Enid** What, my dear?

**Terri** I've only just moved there. Harlow.

**Enid** Harlow? Moved to Harlow? Why would you do that, my dear?

**Terri** Well, I don't know, really, come to think of it. It must be the nomad in me, or something – but just when I'm really settling down somewhere and making a proper little home for myself, then I'm up and off to somewhere else starting all over again – I mean apart from Harlow now, I've lived in Willesden, Neasden, Ruislip, Finchley –

**Enid** Hamburg, did you say?

**Terri** Hamburg? Oh, Freddie – your husband, I mean. No, Frankfurt. For the book fair.

**Enid** And he doesn't take you with him? To such a seedy, sad and lonely place, Frankfurt? Doesn't he need you there?

**Terri** No, no, he needs to have me in the office. Especially when he's away.

**Enid** Needs to have you in the office especially when he's away. Must be difficult for him. (*Lets out a hysterical yap.*)

**Terri** Pardon?

**Enid** What, my dear?

**Terri** I thought you said something.

**Enid** Oh, no. It was a yap. I do that sometimes, yap. What do you make of the moustache?

**Terri** The moustache?

**Enid** Yes, the moustache. His. Fred's. His moustache. What do you make of it?

**Terri** Um, well – I – I haven't really thought about it. (*Laughs.*) But it's very – very – well, it seems to suit him.

**Enid** Suit him, yes, yes, that's the secret of it, isn't it, that it just belongs there. Well, it could hardly belong anywhere else, could it, being a moustache. (*Laughs*.) He grew a beard once, you know, black and ginger, thick, black and ginger stubble is what it was really, made him look like something out of *Macbeth*, especially when he was drunk. Oh, how you must adore working for him, Fred, and his moustache. Tell me, what are your precise duties, my dear, as his personal – or are they all merely personal, too personal to talk about? (*Laughs*.)

**Terri** No, no, not at all. Well, I do some editorial things as well, quite a few recently, I mean recently he's asked me to look at manuscripts – oh, not the highbrow ones – the philosophy, the religions and the – the – (*Gestures*.) I'm useless for those, don't understand a word of them – but the romantic fiction. What Freddie – (*Checks herself*.) Mr Parkhurst calls the bread and butter *and* the jam.

**Enid** Oh! bread, butter, jam. Yes. That's what romance is to Fred, bless him, butter, jam, that's all it is, is that what it's to you too, jam, butter, bread?

**Terri** Well, well, I absolutely love reading it myself. I mean – I mean I'm a sort of addict. The perfect reader, Mr Parkhurst says. If someone like me likes it, it'll make a million. I remember the first I ever read, it was when I'd just started working, it was by Lizzie Heartbourne, one of her Lady Goforths –

*Enid lets out a scream, puts her hands over her ears.*

**Terri** Mrs Parkhurst?

**Enid** (*checks herself, laughs*) Oh, I'm sorry, my dear, it was just that I knew you were going to say that somehow, I just knew it.

**Terri** Yes, well, she's so famous and brilliant, isn't she, I've read everything she's ever written, some of them again and again – *Love is a Dragon, Oh, Heart, Oh,*

*Heart, Oh Hunting Heart* – and her Lady Caroline Goforth series – *Go Forth with Courage, Go Forth with Hope, Go Forth with Honour* – I wish she'd write another one soon, I miss her. So does Mr Parkhurst. He says we – well, his company, what it desperately needs right now is a new Goforth from Lizzie Heartbourne so he can stop worrying about not being able to pay for all his really important books. So you love her too, do you then, Lizzie Heartbourne?

**Enid** Oh well, she may have a talent for telling stories, I suppose, but they're still tosh. Soppy tosh, that's what they are, soppy, soppy, tosh, tosh. (*Viciously.*) I'm so glad she's stopped. A drunken mess of a woman, Heartbourne, revolting. But then look at me! Enid Parkhurst. Also revolting. Quite revolting. But then we're all revolting, aren't we, my dear?

**Terri** (*after an embarrassed pause*) Well, as for the party, the surprise party for – your husband – I've made out a sort of provisional guest list. (*Hands list to Enid.*) And of course we have to discuss the – um – the venue.

**Enid** (*takes list, stares at it, unfocused*) The what?

**Terri** Well, where you want to have it.

**Enid** Have what? (*Studying list.*)

**Terri** Your surprise party. For your husband's birthday, I mean.

**Enid** What's this, I can't make it out, all these names –

**Terri** Well, they're everyone from the office and the agents, and some of the sales people – along with all Freddie's – Mr Parkhurst's writers.

**Enid** But *she's* here, Lizzie Heartbourne! (*Glaring at Terri.*) I've just told you how much I hate her and despise her – (*Strikes name off list.*) We want real people, real friends. The people Fred grew up with, the people who love him. Like me. Like me. His Enid. I'll be there, you know.

**Terri** Well, of course you will. But – (*Awkwardly.*) I don't know any of the people from Freddie's private life. You see.

**Enid** Nor do I. Not any more. (*Begins to cry.*)

*There is a pause.*

**Terri** (*desperately*) Perhaps the best thing would be for me to go away and leave you to – to think about it and – and I'll give you a ring before – um – your husband comes back from Ham— Frankfurt, so you can think about his past –

**Enid** I don't want to think – I don't want to think about Fred's past. That's the last thing I want to think about. His past. Thinking about his presence is bad enough. Present, I mean. What? What do I mean? He's not present – his absence I must mean. Yes. I – I – (*Stops, stares helplessly at Terri.*) My dear?

**Terri** (*gets up*) Well – it's been very nice to meet you, I'll be in touch before – before – he comes back. (*Goes to door.*)

**Enid** Yes, yes, go away, goodbye – oh, no, no, one thing I need you to help me with – come back – come back just – just for a second, it'll only take a second –

*Terri comes back.*

**Enid** Stand there. (*Rocking slightly on her feet.*) Now – here, let me take this –

*Takes handbag from Terri, puts it down. Terri stands, concealing impatience.*

## JUST THE THREE OF US

Now, it's this, you see – (*Lurching around her, picks up chain.*) This. You – you – how does it go, Ronnie? Oh yes, you put it around your waist – your tummy – will you do that for me – really, only a second –

*Ronnie opens bathroom door slightly, peers out, unseen by Terri, as Terri puts chain around her waist.*

Yes – a little tighter, I think, eh, Ronnie? Ah, that's it, perfect. Now, you see –

*Takes padlock out of her pocket, hands it to Terri.*

If you just put this through this – and this –

*Terri clicks padlock around her waist, stands there, patient but bewildered.*

(*Steps away, claps her hands.*) Done it, done it! Didn't think I could do it, did you, my dear? But there, look at her! Just look at her! I've got her!

*Ronnie closes the door quietly.*
*Enid sits down, stares gloatingly at Terri. Terri stares back, bewildered. She attempts a little laugh.*

**Terri** Well, um –

**Enid** How does it feel? I mean, what are you feeling?

**Terri** Well, I'm not feeling anything really except – um – that I really have to go. (*Pause.*) You did say it would only take a second.

**Enid** And it did, didn't it? It did only take a second.

**Terri** Well, perhaps you could spare another second to – (*Gestures to padlock.*)

**Enid** Yes, well, before we get around to all that – would you just walk to the door for me, would you do that, my dear?

*Terri, after a slight hesitation, walks to the door, is stopped by the chain.*

**Enid** Can you reach the handle?

*Terri reaches for the handle, fails.*

**Terri** No, I can't. Mrs Park—

**Enid** You haven't seen my view, please go and see my view. (*Indicating balcony.*)

*Terri crosses the room to the balcony, is stopped before rails, by chain.*

**Enid** See. Perfectly safe. I mean, even if the whole thing came crashing down you'd just hang there until we pulled you up. That's the worst that could happen. Now tell me what you see.

**Terri** Well, there's the sea and – er, and the rocks below and – and some gulls and – and the sea. (*Makes to come in.*)

**Enid** No boats then? Usually there's a boat.

**Terri** Yes, well, there is one. On the horizon.

**Enid** What sort of boat? (*Claps her hands.*) A schooner! Is it a schooner?

**Terri** No, it's small and black, looks more like an oil thing. Well now – (*Makes to come in again.*)

**Enid** And the gulls, you know, you could watch them for ever, you'll find. So there you are, you see, you can't get out that way – (*pointing to door*) or fall out that way – (*pointing to balcony*) and there's the kitchen, you know all about that just by looking at it, and the fridge is bulging with all kinds of – everything – of course you may be a dieting person, I haven't thought about diet but you can probably make a diet by simply not eating a lot of what's in there – and – and there's the – the – (*pointing to the door*) oh, of course he's still in there – constipation, you see, poor dear, but, but really it's yours, it belongs to you, look, I've raised the door slightly for you so the chain can go under, you can be absolutely private, so important to feel absolutely private when he's not in there – that's it, then, I think I've covered everything, haven't I? – unless you can think of something, but we'll find out as we go along if I've forgotten – oh, clothes – you'll be worrying about those, but of course I haven't been able to do anything yet, for one thing I didn't know your size and what sort of things you like, what colours – but once we've had a good think I'll pop up to Marks and Spencer, we've got a very good one in Dover, I get most of mine from there – (*Pours herself an enormous scotch.*)

*Terri stares at her in disbelief.*

This is my last, you know. I promised Ronnie. (*Goes to balcony, throws bottle over. As she does so.*) So goodbye, old friend.

*There is a long, long pause. Then sound of bottle smashing below.*

Hello, new friend.

*Raises her glass to Terri, takes a vast gulp.*

**Terri** Mrs Parkhurst –

**Enid** Enid – (*Groping.*) Toni dear. Enid. Toni and Enid. (*Gesturing between the two of them.*)

**Terri** It's Terri. Terri. Terri Green. Would you mind undoing the padlock, please? I really do have to be going.

**Enid** Come and sit down and we'll talk, shall we?

**Terri** (*after a little pause*) Well, if you – if you just undo the padlock first.

*Enid shakes her head.*

Enid, if I may say, I think perhaps you've had slightly too much to drink.

**Enid** No, no – not slightly. A lot too much. Far too much. But no more. (*Goes to basket, takes out another half-bottle.*) This *is* the last. I promise *you*, just as I promised Ronnie.

**Terri** Look, why don't you give me the key and I'll undo it.

**Enid** No, no, I can't do that, can't.

**Terri** Yes, you can. Give it to me. Please.

**Enid** Don't you understand, it's all arranged – the kitchen and the bathroom – and – this is your home now. Here.

**Terri** The key, please. I don't – I really don't want to make you give it to me.

**Enid** You can never do that. Out of the question.

**Terri** If you don't let me have it, I'll take it from you. By force if I have to. (*Goes towards Enid.*) I mean it, Mrs Parkhurst, honestly I do. (*Grabs Enid.*) Now give it to me!

**Enid** Oh dear, I've been dreading this. I do so hate violence, you know. And your face, it really is very frightening, my dear, all bunched up like a – like a – cabbage, but I can't give you the key, I truly can't.

**Terri** Yes, you can! (*Shakes her slightly.*) So give it to me!

**Enid** I haven't got it, I haven't got it – oh, please don't –

*As Terri continues to shake her.*

I haven't got it, it doesn't matter what you do, I can't give it to you.

**Terri** (*relinquishes Enid*) What do you mean?

**Enid** What I mean, my dear, is that you can search me, shake me, turn me upside down, do whatever you like, but you still won't get the key.

**Terri** Well, where is it then?

**Enid** At home. Up at the Big House. In a safe place, don't worry.

**Terri** Well, go and get it then. Go on.

**Enid** I can go all right – out of that door, yes. But I may choose not to come back, mayn't I? For days and days. Not come back for ever if I choose. And then what would you do?

**Terri** Somebody will come looking for me, they're bound to – Freddie will come. He knows where I am. I told him. All about the party and everything.

*Enid laughs, waves her hand dismissively.*

He does know. I did tell him. And lots of other people. I told lots of other people. Everyone in the office. They'll all come looking for me.

**Enid** (*takes a glug of whisky*) Well, we'll see. But our own view is – this is our view – that you're too nice and honest a person to go blabbing out confidences about something as precious and secret as Fred's surprise, isn't it, Ronnie?

**Terri** But when he comes back from Hamburg –

Frankfurt! Frankfurt! – and I'm not in the office – and anyway he'll be phoning all the time while he's away and if I'm not there answering the phone and people say they don't know where I am –

**Enid** They'll be telling the truth, won't they? (*Laughs.*) They won't know where you are, any more than Fred will. So he'll just have to get himself a new personal – (*Gestures.*) Won't he? Very soon everyone will have forgotten that you were there, and certainly won't wonder where you are, or whether you're here. No. Least of all that. That's my own view. This is my view anyway. And that's the view that counts from your point of view. And my point of view.

**Terri** The car. They'll wonder where the car is. Freddie, especially. He can't do without it.

**Enid** Oh, how thoughtful of you, my dear, to worry. But I'm sure there's no need. Fred will find himself another car in no time. You know what a man of action he is when it comes to his personal comforts. (*Yaps with laughter.*)

*There is a pause.*

**Terri** (*attempting control*) Why are you doing this?

*Enid shakes her head vaguely.*

There must be a reason! There must be! I know that you're drunk but – but you've arranged it all, getting me down here and all this – for me. Why? Please at least tell me why.

*Enid pats the sofa. Terri hesitates, goes over, sits down beside her.*

**Enid** There. That's better, isn't it? Have a little talk. What I wanted.

**Terri** (*struggling for control*) Yes. Let's have a little talk. Um, you're going to tell me why.

**Enid** Why? Why what?

**Terri** Why I'm here. Like this. (*Suddenly seizes chain, shakes it.*) Like this! (*Then more calmly.*) I mean, I do have a right to know, Enid, don't I? If I don't know, well then, what's the point?

**Enid** I'm chained too, you see, my dear. Chained to him. Wherever I go, whatever I do, I feel the chain of my – need for him – my love for him – my loss – my loss of him. Never a moment without the chain around my heart. His heart. Connected to nothing. As it goes through some hole in the roof of my soul and out of sight. My chain. Like yours. You see.

**Terri** No, I don't see. I mean, this is a real chain and you can take it off. But I can't do anything about this chain of yours you're talking about that's around your heart and not around someone else's heart or whatever, can I? I mean, you can't blame me for your unhappiness, Enid. It isn't my fault.

*There is a pause. Terri looks at Enid. Then, as if suddenly realising:*

Unless you think I – I – Freddie and I – your husband and I are – is that it, Enid? Is that what you think?

*Enid still says nothing.*

If it is, Enid, I promise you – believe me, please believe me – your husband and I have never ever – for one thing, I don't do that sort of thing, and anyway I've only been working for him for six months – no, no, five, just over five months – and I'm not that sort of girl – and Freddie – your husband – is not that sort of boss, he'd never take advantage and I'd never let him – and he's always saying – always – how much he loves you, how very much he loves his wife.

**Enid** Always saying that, is he? Always? Well now, really, really! I can't see Fred dashing about just telling this person and that person – waiters, taxi-drivers, whoever he comes across – 'I love my wife, oh, how I love my wife!' – not his style, not my Fred's. He'd only say it when saying it would make him feel noble, not treacherous. (*Imitating Fred.*) In spite of what's happened – (*Voice throbbing.*) I love my wife, you know. I very much love, I love very much. My wife.

**Terri** (*shaking her head*) No, no, the time I remember him saying it was when there was – when there was some aeroplane crash, he said, 'Oh thank God my wife, my Enid, wasn't on that plane –' and then he said, I'll never forget it because it seemed so – so true and wise – he said how dreadful it was that it took a dreadful accident to make us realise how dreadfully much we love the people we love. Like his wife. His Enid.

**Enid** Plane? Where was I going? No, no, it can't have been me, I never go on planes. Though I expect they're very comfortable if you like them. Do you like them, my dear?

**Terri** No, no, Mrs Parkhurst –

**Enid** Enid.

**Terri** Enid. What I'm trying to tell you – you must understand me, please – if what's troubling you – please listen to me, are you listening to me?

**Enid** Yes, yes, tell me more about your life. Your romantic life. It's very thrilling, isn't it, Ronnie? (*Looking around.*) Where's he gone? Oh, still in there, well, never mind, you – you – and your romances, where were we with your romances?

**Terri** We weren't anywhere – I haven't got any romances. Look, Enid, please try to understand – I'm just a girl – I'm nobody really, just somebody who happens to work for a publisher who happens to be your husband – and I'm not even his PG – PA, I mean – his real PA's got six months off having a baby, so you see, I'm just a temp, that's all I am, strictly temporary, I don't think he's even noticed me – I mean, the only romance in my life is when I go to my classes twice a week –

**Enid** Classes? What classes?

**Terri** Ballroom dancing – my ballroom dancing – the only person I sleep with is my golliwog, Derek. I've slept with him since I was a baby. That's the truth, Enid.

**Enid** Golliwog – didn't think we could have those any more – and there you say you've got one who sleeps with you – actually sleeps with you – and he's called Derek you say – people aren't what they ought to be, that's the trouble, that's always – always the trouble.

*Gets up, stumbles, tries to rally, looks around her.*

I used to want to dance in ballrooms. The waltz – that was one of my dreams –

*Begins to take clumsy, drunken steps, waltzing, as she drinks.*

But we were so clumsy together, his feet, you know, if only he'd let his feet flow – flow like Ronnie's – oh, what a dancer Ronnie is, aren't you, my dear – then Fred and I would have waltzed, oh, how we'd have waltzed! (*Begins to stumble.*) Oh – oh, Ronnie! Ronnie, come and get me, please! Ronnie, I need you!

*Slips down wall, collapses.*
*Door opens. Ronnie comes out.*
*Terri, suddenly aware of him, turns.*

**Ronnie** Hello. I hope you don't mind my using your facilities.

**Terri** What?

**Ronnie** (*gesturing to lavatory*) I hope you don't mind.

**Terri** You mean you've been in there all this time?

**Ronnie** Yes, I'm very sorry, I must have fallen asleep, I tend to do that when I'm sitting – anyway, I'm Enid's friend, Ronald Butterworth. The local vicar. And you must be the young lady from Fred's office – his PG, isn't it, everything all right?

**Terri** Of course it's not all right, I mean, look at me! Look at this, I mean! (*Showing him chain and padlock.*)

**Ronnie** Oh heavens, there's Enid! Is she all right?

*He goes over to Enid.*

**Terri** Yes, yes, she's just passed out. It's the drink.

*Ronnie picks up glass, puts it on table, goes back to Enid, attempts to lift her.*

**Ronnie** Enid – Enid, my dear, it's Ronnie, Ronnie's here –

**Terri** (*taking Ronnie's arm*) Would you mind getting me out of this first, please?

**Ronnie** Ah.

**Terri** The key's up in the house somewhere – somewhere safe, she said. Do you know where?

**Ronnie** Well, no, I don't, not really, it's a very large house, the Big House –

**Terri** Well, think!

**Ronnie** Somewhere safe, well, that could be – anywhere, I suppose, probably in the snuggery, but that's a large room, and it would be a small key – a small key in the Big House in the large snuggery – um, hard to find, I think.

**Terri** Well, go and look, please, or – something to cut through – metal cutters or shears, anything like that.

**Ronnie** No, I don't believe I've got – they look very sturdy, the links – no, I'm sure I haven't got anything that could –

**Terri** There must be something – some way – please! Before she comes around. (*Stares at him.*) You don't want to help me, do you?

**Ronnie** Of course I do. It's just that – well, there's Enid, you see.

**Terri** I won't tell a soul, I promise I won't tell a single soul – ever! Not the police or Fred or anybody in the office. No one. It'll be like it's never happened. Please believe me.

**Ronnie** Oh, I do believe you. I really do. I can see that you're the sort of sensible and womanly, um, girl – who wouldn't want to hurt – especially someone in Enid's sort of state. You'd never want to do that, I know.

**Terri** Well then, help me, please help me to get away!

**Ronnie** (*after a pause*) That's simply not on, I'm afraid. Not without Enid's permission.

**Terri** Enid's permission! Her permission! Look at her! Look at her!

*They look towards Enid who grunts, gurgles, looks blankly towards them, closes her eyes.*
   *Ronnie raises his finger to his lips, lowers his voice.*

**Ronnie** Yes, I know she's – but I hope, I do hope, that soon all will be well. All manner of things shall be well. Including you.

**Terri** Is she doing this because she thinks I'm having an affair with Freddie?

**Ronnie** Have you asked her that?

**Terri** Yes.

**Ronnie** And what did she say?

**Terri** Nothing, nothing that made sense really. Except that there was a chain around her heart that didn't go around someone else's heart –

**Ronnie** Ah. And what did you say to that?

**Terri** I told her I wasn't having an affair with Freddie. With her husband.

**Ronnie** And what did she say?

**Terri** Nothing, nothing, I've told you. But I can't think of any other reason – apart from her being stark, staring mad and so she doesn't need a reason. But does she think I am? Having an affair with Freddie?

**Ronnie** I really don't feel at all comfortable discussing Enid in this way, my dear. Especially in front of her – (*gestures towards Enid*) with her in the room.

**Terri** It's not in front of her, she's not in the room, she's not anywhere. You've *got* to tell me. If you know why she's doing this you've got to tell me. Please.

**Ronnie** Ah, well, you see, theirs has been a long, happy marriage – and she loved him – *loves* him so much, you see – so joyful their weekends up there, in the Big House together, in their snuggery, playing Scrabble, the three of us – she was so, so – well, happy and joyful –

## JUST THE THREE OF US

**Terri** But it's not my fault! It's got nothing to do with me whatever's happened between her and him and you in their snuggery and your Scrabble. You must believe that.

**Ronnie** Well, the issue isn't really whether I believe that – that you and Fred are having a – a thing – but whether Enid believes that you are, and whether believing that you are and doing something about it helps her to get, well . . . (*Thinks.*) Well.

**Terri** But just because she's mad doesn't mean – I mean, you can't just allow her to do this to a completely innocent person. She should be looked after – put in a home, treatment of some sort –

**Ronnie** This is her treatment, you see. Or so she thinks.

**Terri** What is?

**Ronnie** You are. I expect she'll want to be your mistress.

**Terri** Mistress! She wants to be my mistress!

**Ronnie** Oh – oh – in the old-fashioned sense, of course, the educational sense –

**Terri** But I don't want her to be my – anything. In any sense. I refuse.

**Ronnie** Well, look, there's another way of – um – looking at it, that it's – well, that it's perhaps your – (*Takes a deep breath.*) It's your Christian duty to do what you can –

**Terri** My Christian duty to be chained up – is that your idea of my Christian duty, is it really? Really?

**Ronnie** Excuse me, Toni, my dear –

**Terri** Terri. My name is Terri!

**Ronnie** Terri. Well, Terri, if you put it into a – well, global, religious perspective – in some countries the woman taken in – in – (*Gestures*.) In Islam, for instance, you could be stoned to death, is I believe the case. Or flogged. Or both, even. Why, I remember only a few years back – the inhabitants of a remote Dutch village who got wind of what was going on between a young woman and a married chap, she was tied into a horse and cart and dragged around while they all lined up and pelted her with – not stones, it wasn't stones – fruit and vegetables it must have been. What I mean is – is really that with Enid, you won't be stoned or flogged, she's not even going to throw fruit and vegetables at you.

**Terri** Oh, that's nice, that's very nice – no fruit and vegetables even. No flogging, no stones, fruit and vegetables even –

**Ronnie** No, no, she's very kind, she's a very kind, loving, educating woman, Enid, a natural mistress – teacher – teacher! And she needs, she does, she does, Toni, she needs your help. As her student, you see.

**Terri** I'm Terri, Terri, and why should *I* be her student, why should I help, why, why?

**Ronnie** Ah, that cry – that cry that comes down to us through the ages, from Job onwards. Why me? Why *me*? But whereas we can't be specific about Job, it's all very mysterious about Job – God himself is mysterious about 'Why? Why Job?' – there isn't so much a mystery about you, my dear, as a – as a contradiction, you see. A contradiction. Because, on the one hand you say you aren't having a – a thing – with Fred. And on the other hand, other people say you are. Mmm?

**Terri** Other people? What other people?

**Ronnie** Well, Fred. And Enid. And me.

## JUST THE THREE OF US

**Terri** What!

**Ronnie** Well, yes, Fred told both of us. You see. So that's how we both know. So I beg and beseech you, Toni, to accept your plight with Christian –

**Terri** My name is Freddie – Terri, I mean, Terri! What do you mean Freddie told you?

**Enid** (*waking up*) Fred – Fred – do I hear Fred – is there a Fred in the room, my Fred?

**Ronnie** (*getting up, going over to her*) Well, we were just talking – just talking –

*Enid stumbles to her feet precariously.*

Are you all right, Enid?

**Enid** No Fred then? Where is he?

**Ronnie** At a book fair, my dear, in – in – (*Looks at Terri enquiringly.*) Australia, I think it is. Anyway, somewhere well and safe. Come along, come along now, up to the Big House, pop into the snuggery, then have a proper lie-down, a freshen-up.

*He helps her across room.*

**Enid** Yes, yes, lie down in snuggery, freshen up.

*She stumbles, with Ronnie's help, towards door. Suddenly sees Terri, stops.*

Who's that, then?

**Ronnie** That's Fred's PG. Remember, Enid?

**Enid** Oh. Oh, yes. (*To Ronnie.*) What's she doing here?

**Ronnie** She's here to help you.

**Enid** (*to Terri*) Oh. Oh yes, of course. Thank you, my dear, thank you, so kind.

**Ronnie** Come, my dear. You'll see her tomorrow, when you're better. (*Taking Enid off.*)

**Terri** I can't help you, I can't help you – I'm just a temp – that's all –

*As Ronnie and Enid go out. The door shuts. Terri runs after them.*

Just a temp! No shorthand even – (*The chain pulls her up.*) A temp.

*She tries to push chain down over her hips, then up over her waist, can't. Pulls on chain, then looks around wildly. Runs to balcony, is pulled up by chain.*

Help! Help! Help!

*She gives up, goes over to handbag, takes out cigarette from packet, lights it, sits down desolately.*

(*Whimperingly.*) What do I do, I mean? I mean, what do I do now?

*Lights.*

## SCENE TWO

*The following morning. Bed has obviously been slept in. Terri is sitting, sipping coffee and smoking.*

*Enid enters, carrying a basket of flowers, spectacles hanging around her neck. She is flustered and awkward. Throughout the scene, she is a little unsteady, hungover and still slightly drunk from the day before. She stands looking at Terri.*

**Enid** Good morning, good morning – oh, you've found out how the coffee machine works, so complicated these days making coffee, isn't it – I do hope you had a proper breakfast. Yes?

## JUST THE THREE OF US

*Terri doesn't respond.*

Um, well – I brought these, they're from the garden but I can't really claim them as my own, Ronnie does all the gardening, keeps it up so beautifully – but then he loves it –

*She goes to kitchen, fills vase with water, cuts off stems.*

He does the churchyard himself, you know, tends all the old graves, because he can't afford anyone – not that he'd want anyone for that, but for the maintenance, you know, and the roof – he has such trouble with the roof, always trying to raise money – these days in such a small parish and so few people about who believe in God, about nine he once counted it at, such a struggle for him, poor man –

*Stops. During the above she has brought flowers back and put them on the table.*

There – there, well, that should brighten up –

**Terri** (*glares at flowers, pulls herself together*) Mrs Parkhurst –

**Enid** Oh, Enid, dear. We're still Enid and Terri, you know.

**Terri** The vicar said something last night.

**Enid** Ronnie, do call him Ronnie.

**Terri** Ronnie told me something last night. Something that your husband had told you. Apparently Freddie – Fred –

**Enid** No, call him Freddie. That's what you've been calling him after all. Fred to us, Freddie to you.

**Terri** I don't know if you heard him – Ronnie, I mean – telling me what – Freddie – had told you. You were, um, asleep.

**Enid** I know, I know, my dear, I'm so sorry. I've been wondering how to get around to – well, to apologising for my behaviour. I drank far too much, didn't I, and got a little bit out of control and falling asleep like that – it really was disgraceful, disgraceful.

**Terri** Ronnie says that Freddie told you and Ronnie that Freddie and I were having an affair. That Freddie told you that. (*Looks at Enid.*)

*Enid says nothing.*

Did Freddie really tell you that, Enid?

**Enid** Oh, my dear Terri, what is said between Fred and myself is really too private to –

**Terri** But he said it to Ronnie too.

**Enid** Yes, but again, what is said between my husband and my dearest friend is private to themselves.

**Terri** But Ronnie told me.

**Enid** Well, what is said between you and Ronnie is, is – I wouldn't dream of prying into it, my dear.

**Terri** But I can tell *you* what really happened between Freddie and myself, can't I? I don't know what Freddie means by saying we were having an affair – I mean I just don't understand, it isn't true. It was nothing like that. All that happened – and I mean it only happened once, I mean – it was months ago, and we were working late – I mean, we were alone in the office and he didn't have anyone else to talk to about his worries, all his financial worries, and I put my arms around him to comfort him and then suddenly we were on the sofa and – and it happened, that's what happened, that's all that happened, the way it always happens with me, and it ended the way it always ends with me, with him saying after this must never happen again, that's what he said. And you're quite right, quite right, that's when he said, 'I love my wife, you know.' And the next morning he had the sofa taken out of his office.

**Enid** Sofa? I think, my dear, I really do think that what applies to Fred and me and to Ronnie and me also applies to you and Fred – more so, really, because it all seems so very, very private to you and Fred – on the sofa – and I don't want to hear, for my part I certainly don't want to hear –

**Terri** (*pleadingly*) Enid – please –

**Enid** – another word. Not another word. On the subject of you and Fred on the sofa.

**Terri** Well, what can I do? What do I do, I mean?

**Enid** (*after a little pause*) Well, let's talk about the things we can talk about. Your parents, for example.

**Terri** My parents? They're both dead.

**Enid** Oh, I'm so sorry, so sorry. (*Gently.*) How did they die, my dear, may I ask that?

**Terri** (*after a little pause*) In a crash. On the motorway –

**Enid** Oh, dear – cars, you see, cars. And were you very, very young?

**Terri** Five. I was five.

**Enid** And who – who brought you up then?

**Terri** My auntie – my auntie brought me up. Auntie Sheila.

**Enid** And she was kind to you, I do hope she was.

**Terri** She didn't want me.

**Enid** Didn't want you, oh dear, oh dear, all alone with an auntie who didn't want you!

**Terri** (*hesitates, then as if suddenly inspired*) No, no, I wasn't alone, I've got brothers – two brothers. They'll be wondering where I am, they phone every evening – they're bound to come looking –

**Enid** I was an only child too. I enjoyed it, being the centre of attention. But of course I was lucky enough to have parents.

**Terri** I've got brothers. I'm not an only child! And – and – I share a flat with two girls – one of them's a policeman.

**Enid** Policeman? Policeman? Even if she's a man in the police, that can't be the right word for her these days, can it? Now what should one say instead? Police person – no, that doesn't sound right – Ms Plod, the police person – (*Lets out a yap.*) Oh, it's really too difficult, let's just pretend she doesn't exist, shall we?

   *Ronnie enters.*

**Ronnie** Oh, hello, good morning, good morning –

**Enid** Ronnie.

**Ronnie** Um, I just popped down to find out if anyone wants anything. I'm off to the shops.

**Enid** Oh Ronnie, how thoughtful, as a matter of fact I'm out of loo paper up at the Big House – you're all right for that, aren't you, my dear, as I put in six extra rolls. Oh, and some light bulbs – is there anything you can think of, my dear, that you need?

*Terri shakes her head in a kind of disbelief.*

**Ronnie** (*sees cigarette in ashtray*) Oh, you're a smoker. You'll want some cigarettes, won't you? I'll pick up a packet.

**Enid** Oh, better make it a carton, a couple of cartons, to save ourselves your having to pedal back and forth every time Terri runs out.

**Terri** I don't want them. I don't want anything from you. Nothing.

**Ronnie** Really? Not even a packet?

*Terri shakes her head.*

Are you trying to give up? I remember when Enid tried, do you remember, my dear, you made us promise to restrain you physically from going out and buying yourself – (*Realises.*) Um – um – so that's loo paper, cigarettes – no, no cigarettes, light bulbs and – and light bulbs. Well then – well then – I'll look in with all that later.

**Enid** Yes, yes, why don't you join us for lunch? Oh, it isn't for *me* to invite – would you mind, Ronnie dear, if Terri had lunch with us? I mean, Terri dear, if Ronnie – (*Gestures.*)

*Ronnie and Enid stare expectantly at Terri.*

*Terri squawks with laughter.*

**Terri** Oh yes, please come to lunch, please do come to lunch! I mean, why not, why not, I mean?

**Ronnie** Thank you, my dear, that's very kind – and I'll bring along a bottle of Mrs Price's wine. That's a dandelion wine, you know, our Mrs Price makes –

*Terri bursts into tears, picks up empty packet of cigarettes, gropes for a cigarette.*

(*To Enid.*) Perhaps I'd better get some cigarettes after all. (*Makes to go.*)

**Enid** Oh, Ronnie – you haven't forgotten your day's main task, have you?

**Ronnie** What – oh, no, my dear – but I thought this evening – or tomorrow –

**Enid** I think you should do it now, my dear, and be done with it.

**Ronnie** (*hesitates*) Very well, my dear. (*Goes off.*)

**Terri** (*who hasn't taken this in, is crying*) It's so unfair, so unfair, so unfair!

*Enid stares at her at a loss, then goes tentatively towards her.*

**Enid** I know, I know, I expect it does seem like that. There must be lots of girls doing terrible things, really naughty things, and here you are, such a good girl really, I'm sure, on a chain!

**Terri** (*sobbing*) If only you'd tell me how long – how long –

**Enid** Are you uncomfortable then? Here, let me have a look.

*She gently pulls up Terri's shirt, exclaims.*

Oh, it is raw, isn't it? You must have done it during the night, turning and twisting, I expect, in your sleep. Lucky I thought of it. (*Going into bathroom.*) Now, where did I put it – oh yes, here it is. (*Comes out, carrying a carton from which she extracts tube.*) Now you'll be brave, I know, it'll probably sting at first – (*Puts some ointment on her finger.*) I'll be as gentle as I can – (*Moves towards Terri's waist.*)

**Terri** Leave me alone! Don't you dare touch me, don't you dare touch me!

**Enid** (*recoils; after a pause*) I'm sorry, so sorry, I didn't mean to – to – anyway, it's there when you want it.

*Makes to touch Terri on shoulder, doesn't, goes to sit down.*
  *Terri pulls herself together. They look at each other.*

**Terri** I'll go mad too. Then there'll be three mad people, not one of us noticing that one of us is chained. (*Pause.*) So what happens now, Enid? What do we do now, I mean?

**Enid** What a good question, my dear, what a very good question. Well, for one thing, there are the books, all my favourites, which I keep here especially – and lots of lovely Mozart, Vivaldi, Beethoven – there's no Wagner, I'm afraid, not in here – he may be a towering genius, indeed I know he is, but he's quite wrong when it comes to mulling. One can't possibly mull to Wagner. But there are these – (*Taking cassettes out of her basket.*) A couple of waltzes so you can keep up your ballroom dancing, because, you see, my intention – you see what my intention is, don't you, my dear?

  *Terri shakes her head.*

We must find a way of being useful to each other. You will give me your soul. That's how you will be useful to me. I will educate it. That's how I will be useful to you.

**Terri** Educate me?

**Enid** Yes, yes, put the sofa behind you. Behind us both. Our beings will surge way beyond this or that sordid sofa and on into –

*There is a knock on the door.*

**Ronnie** (*putting his head around the door*) My dear.

**Enid** Yes, Ronnie, what is it?

**Ronnie** May I have a word with you?

**Enid** Yes?

**Ronnie** Well, outside. (*To Terri.*) Excuse us, Terri.

*Enid goes half out. She and Ronnie mutter quickly together.*
*Terri goes closer, attempting to listen.*

**Enid** (*turns, comes in*) My dear, do excuse me if I take a liberty. (*Goes to Terri's handbag.*) Oh, here they are, right at the top – (*Taking out car keys.*) So I won't have to invade and forage –

**Terri** Why? What are you doing with them? Give them back, give them back – (*Goes towards Enid.*)

**Enid** (*as she goes out*) No, no, they belong to Fred, my dear, and he can't drive back without them – (*Exits.*)

**Terri** Freddie! Freddie, it's me, Terri, I'm in here, they've chained me up – come in, Freddie! Come in! Come in, come in – don't listen to a word they say! They're lying, they're both loony – Fred, come in, come in!

**Enid** (*enters*) Oh, he can't come in, my dear, he hasn't got time, he's desperate to get back to London and his work. Such a sense of responsibility, hasn't he, Fred, I hope it won't be his downfall one day. Now then – oh yes. Congratulations, bravo, bravo, bravo. That's the message he asked me to pass on to you.

**Terri** He must have heard me, he must know I'm here! You're lying.

**Enid** Lying? My dear! I never lie, and especially not to you. And of course he knows you're here, indeed he does. Hence his message of congratulations, his bravos, you see. 'Hence'. That's one of the things you'll come to understand about me, my dear. I'm a person who actually says 'hence'. You might come to say 'hence' yourself one day when –

**Terri** Congratulations, bravos, hence – what are you talking about, what do you mean, I mean?

**Enid** Oh, it's not what you mean or what I mean, it's what *he* means. And what he means is that he admires you, yes, he truly does, he does indeed, for putting that chain around yourself and padlocking yourself up so in future you abstain from sofas – *hence* his congratulations, hence his bravos, those three bravos he uttered! 'Bravo, bravo, bravo for Toni!' (*Thinks briefly.*) 'Terri', that is. But of course – he's sure you'll understand, my dear – office life, *his* office life has to go on, doesn't it? So he's decided to treat your moral and spiritual resignation as a professional resignation too. He's going to look for a replacement-temp immediately, but you're not to worry, no, not to worry, if he doesn't find one, as his 'permanent' is due to come back quite soon, as soon as she's delivered herself of her –

*Sound of car revving up.*

Ah, there he goes.

*A terrible noise, followed by crashing of gears, car bumping and grinding off.*

**Terri** That's never Freddie. He could never treat the car like that. Not the Porsche. You're just saying it's him to torture me.

**Enid** Torture you? Is that what I've done? Oh, I'm so sorry, my dear, I certainly never meant to cause you pain, not real pain. I was just – just making a bit of a game of it, that's all. Please believe me, my dear. You're quite right, Fred isn't here, of course he isn't, it's just Ronnie, he hasn't driven for years, I don't think he's even got a driving licence and he's got to get it all the way back to London, to somewhere near Fred's office, where Fred might stumble across it – he'll be a complete wreck, poor Ronnie, anyway, I'm sure we won't be seeing him for lunch.

**Terri** And you said you never lie. Especially to me.

**Enid** Yes, yes, well, I won't ever again, I promise. No more silly games, especially if they're going to cause you pain – (*Suddenly ashamed.*) Oh, good heavens, there's something else – what is it? – oh yes, oh yes, of course –

*She takes package out of her basket, hands it to Terri, shyly.*

I found it among some things people have been sending in to Ronnie, for his bazaar – his church roof, you know. *That* bazaar.

*Terri opens package, takes out golliwog, stares down at it.*

There, you see. I mean, I mean, if I may borrow your favourite phrase, my dear, I mean let's forget all about you and Fred up there in London, breaking my heart, the two of you, because now the two of us, Enid and Terri, are down here in Dover, saving our souls. Souls in Dover – Dover soles – (*Yaps.*) sorry, my dear – oh, there's something I ought to tell you, as we mean to be completely honest with each other from now on, with no lies and deceits – you see, I'm Lizzie Heartbourne. Yes,

Lizzie Heartbourne, creator of your beloved Lady Goforth, Queen of Romantic Tosh.

**Terri** I don't care – I don't care what sort of tosh you are, because I already know all that matters about you, you're a drunken loony, that's all you really are, that's all that matters to me! (*Throws golliwog at Enid.*)

**Enid** Oh dear, oh dear, I hoped you'd be pleased that I'd confessed, but of course you're right, my dear, it doesn't matter who I am because I'm still a lush, to give me my proper name. But you see, the important thing is, I've stopped drinking. Just as I promised. That's the important thing. Still drunk, but no longer drinking. (*Pause.*) Now. Let's begin. With – with – it should really be the New Testament but I took it up and forgot to bring it back down so starting from tomorrow we'll read from the New Testament, I've given up on getting Ronnie through it again, he doesn't have the patience if there's a game of Scrabble or tennis going or his blessed roof – a pity really, as he makes the most preposterous mistakes, especially in his sermons, blasphemous ones almost, I sometimes think it's God's will that his roof leaks – but you'll find out, we'll find out together how shrewd and wise and frightening, yes, frightening, the New Testament is, and the language of it, the language – Pick up your golliwog, my dear. (*Her back to Terri.*) Ah, yes. (*Taking book down from shelf.*) Oh, you'll find it so exciting, I'm so looking forward to it, and the great thing is that as they'll be new to you, they'll become new to me, all over again, they see so much more than we do, hear so much more than we do, however ordinary their ordinary non-writing selves might have been, in fact some of them were quite unpleasant, very disagreeable, when they were just being husbands, fathers, wives, appalling some of them, him even, yes, I have to say it – (*rapping book*) even him, but no worse really than

Tolstoy or Hardy or Shakespeare, well, we don't know
about Shakespeare, except we always worry a bit about
his money-lending and then going to law to get it back –
and there are those sonnets, one or two of them – 'they
that have power to hurt and will do none, that do not do
the thing they most do show' – Sonnet 94, full of hatred
and so very personal, it really does make one's flesh and
one's hair stand up and creep, like receiving a nasty
letter, a very nasty letter – to oneself, you know, from a
sort of monster – but they could all be monsters in their
different ways – although not George Eliot, a good
woman as well as a great maker, and the poets, we
mustn't neglect our poets – oh, oh, there's one of them,
Matthew Arnold, who wrote such a beautiful, so moving
– and do you know what about, my dear? This, here –
(*pointing through window*) our own Dover Beach – 'The
sea is calm tonight, the tide is full – ah, love let us be
true to one another, for the world which seems to lie
before us –' oh, oh, but I'm trembling, I must calm
down, not try to rush it all into us at once – (*Takes a
breath, begins to read.*) '*Great Expectations* by Charles
Dickens. Chapter One. "My father's family name being
Pirrip, and my Christian name Philip, my infant tongue
could make of both names nothing longer or more
explicit than Pip. So I called myself Pip, and came to
be called Pip. I give Pirrip as my father's family name,
on the authority of his tombstone and my sister – Mrs
Joe Gargery, who married the blacksmith" –' See, see,
that's what I mean, tombstone, 'the authority of his
tombstone'! Only Dickens, only he could find such a
terrible – such a terrible phrase. An orphan. On the
authority of a tombstone. Oh – (*Flustered.*) But of course
you yourself, you know all about – I'm sorry, my dear,
how insensitive of me, but then that's the thing, isn't it,
about real books, they have a way of hurting us even as
they heal us. (*Sees golliwog.*) What's he doing, still lying

## JUST THE THREE OF US

there, please pick him up, my dear, will you, and let us get on with our reading, please.

*Terri doesn't move.*

(*Imperiously.*) Pick him up, I say!

*They stare at each other. Terri hesitates, picks up golliwog.*

**Terri** Well, Enid – (*Voice trembling slightly.*) Here I am. Indeed, indeed I am. I mean. (*Gestures.*) So, please. I mean. Let's get on with your reading. Mistress.

*Enid adjusts her spectacles, looks down at book, reads, her voice getting stronger.*

**Enid** 'As I never saw my father or my mother, and never saw any likeness of either of them (for their days were long before the days of photographs), my first fancies regarding what they were like, were unreasonably derived from their tombstones –'

*She continues reading, Terri unconsciously cradles golliwog as:*

*Lights.*

# Act Two

### SCENE ONE

*Two months later. It is late evening, the door is open. Golliwog is lying on pillow on bed. There are books and papers scattered about, also flowers. An exercise bike. There is waltz music on the tape recorder. Terri is dancing to music, humming slightly, rapt.*

*Ronnie appears at the door, carrying basket, unseen by Terri. He studies her, then knocks on the side of the door. Terri appears not to have heard. Ronnie knocks again, clearing his throat.*

**Terri** (*turns*) Oh.

**Ronnie** Hello, my dear.

**Terri** Hello, Ronnie.

**Ronnie** May I? (*Stepping in.*) Oh, isn't it charming – I used to enjoy a waltz myself, you know, years ago – though it's probably hard to believe. (*Begins waltzing.*) I was quite good really, though I say so myself.

*He continues to waltz, eyes shut, as if in a trance. Terri watches him, then goes over, turns off music.*

Oh.

*Terri gets on exercise bike, starts to pedal. There is a little pause.*

Well, how are you?

**Terri** Fine, thank you.

**Ronnie** Good. As we haven't seen each other for a bit I thought I'd, well, take the liberty of inviting myself down for supper. I've brought some cold ham. And cheese. And apples. (*Putting them on table as he speaks.*) *And* of course – (*flourishing bottle*) a bottle of our Mrs Price's dandelion wine.

**Terri** Ah. Well, I'm sorry I've already eaten.

**Ronnie** Oh. What did you have?

**Terri** Omelette, asparagus.

**Ronnie** Asparagus? At this time of year?

**Terri** It was tinned.

**Ronnie** Ah. Well – oh, how's the chain, by the way? I expect you scarcely even notice it any more.

**Terri** Of course I notice it. It still clinks every time I move. And gets tighter and tighter –

**Ronnie** Does it? Oh, well, that's perhaps because there's rather more of you to go around – and the thing about those – (*Points to exercise bike.*) I used to use one myself, you know, for a bit – is that they're only good for buttocks and leg muscles, really, they don't seem to do anything for the tummy at all. At least they didn't for mine. (*Laughs, pats his stomach.*)

*Terri gives him a look, gets off bike, goes and lights a cigarette. Ronnie takes out pipe.*

Let's open our Mrs Price's. (*Taking bottle out of basket.*) She started making it, you know, for Mr Price when she managed to get him off the cider and the whisky – he used to turn quite violent – but now she's making him do with this, he's as calm and well-behaved as – anyway, I remember your saying you'd got to like it. Dandelions. The flavour of dandelions.

**Terri** 'Got' meaning 'had'. I *have* to like it because there's never anything else on offer.

**Ronnie** (*laughs*) Does that mean you want a glass or you don't want a glass? (*Looking at her.*) Shall I pour you some or shan't I pour you some?

**Terri** Whichever you like, I honestly don't mind.

**Ronnie** Ah. Well then, I'll –

*Hesitates, pours, hands glass to Terri.*

**Terri** Thank you.

**Ronnie** (*sips*) Perhaps we should try something a little revolutionary – what about adding a dash of sugar – and some lemon, have you got a lemon, I didn't bring one down but I could always nip up to the vicarage –

**Terri** Oh, Ronnie!

**Ronnie** What? Oh, sorry, my dear, am I being a bit irritating, often one never knows when one's irritating, except when people become irritable with one.

**Terri** No, no, Ronnie. You're just being yourself, that's all.

**Ronnie** Really? Are you sure?

**Terri** Quite sure, Ronnie dear.

**Ronnie** Well, that's all right then. At least I suppose it is. And if it isn't there's nothing I can do about it, really, is there?

**Terri** Not a thing. (*Smiles at him.*) Why don't you have your supper?

**Ronnie** Yes – yes, I am rather peckish. (*Going towards table.*) Oh, will Enid be coming down?

**Terri** Yes, I expect so.

**Ronnie** Well, I'll wait until then, she might want to join me – yes, that would be nice, I've seen so little of her, too, recently, I wonder what she's been up to.

**Terri** Oh, Ronnie, you know perfectly well what she's been up to, don't you?

**Ronnie** What do you mean, my dear?

**Terri** And it'll be on your doorstep tonight, probably.

**Ronnie** Mmm?

**Terri** I mean something you're expecting will be on your doorstep tonight, I believe.

**Ronnie** My dear?

**Terri** Well, isn't that the tradition? Whenever Lizzie Heartbourne, Queen of Tosh, gets to the end of a new Goforth, she leaves a copy on your doorstep.

**Ronnie** Ah! So you know all about that – yes, yes, she does. And what a treat – so tonight. Tonight!

**Terri** It's all so silly, all this stuff about her being ashamed. She should be proud. It isn't a burden as she keeps calling it, it's a gift.

**Ronnie** Oh, you're quite right, my dear, you're quite right. I do so agree. A gift from heaven. But it came as such a shock to her – well, to all of us – but of course to her particularly. She was just a teacher then, you see, but goodness, how she loved teaching – sixth-form English in a very good school in Pudsey, no, not Pudsey, it was Putney, Putney. And then one day poor old Fred, well, poor young Fred in those days, he'd just started up on his own, putting out esoteric volumes on, well, anything that wouldn't sell, really, Turkish mysticism, rather bizarre theories about frogspawn and the origins of the universe – well, you know the sort of thing, he's still doing it, after all – and one day in the kitchen – I was there, I was actually there when it happened, well, I was always there – he suddenly gave a moan, a terrible, pleading moan it was, 'Oh God,' he said, 'Oh God, I wish somebody would write a best-seller for me. Any rubbish – any rubbish, I wouldn't be proud!' And Enid – Enid got up as if a button had been pushed in her, it was weird, mysterious – she kissed him on the head and she said, 'You must go away now, darling, immediately. And you mustn't come back until I tell you to.' And Fred just got up and left, as if he understood, yes, that was weird and mysterious too, he did understand. She went to her study and started rattling away on her typewriter, and then one morning, weeks later, she told me to phone Fred and say he could come back now. And he did. And there it was, a whole boxful of romance. And so Lizzie Heartbourne came about. And the whole ritual came about, of Fred having to go away and stay out of touch until she's finished. So you see, what a landmark it's been. In all our lives. Such a landmark. And it was such a thrill, such a relief to hear her up and at it again that night last month, the rattle, rattle, rattle of the old typewriter. And it's so much your doing, my dear, the way you've settled down and accepted – and you've had good times together, you laugh together, the *three* of us have laughed together – chain or no chain!

**Terri** Oh, it's just consequences, Ronnie, my dear, this chain of mine. That's all. Consequences.

**Ronnie** What do you mean, consequences, my – (*Stops himself.*)

**Terri** Well, my dear, as our dear Enid said, it's there in those books – (*gesturing around*) that's what they're all about, my dear.

**Ronnie** Yes, well, I suppose – well, are they all, really? George Eliot and Thomas Hardy and Tolstoy and Dickens and the New Testament – all of them? About consequences?

**Terri** Oh, yes, all of them. There's always this moment when somebody does something, or doesn't do something, like Dorothea in *Middlemarch* choosing to fall in love, yes, *choosing* to fall in love with that pathetic old man just because he's a scholar and deathly to look at so he must be spiritual – and it's no good me thinking, oh, come off it, Dorothea, don't be a silly cow and chuck yourself away on *him* – because at the same time I understand, I really do, because it's what she is and who she is that the terrible things come from, misery, guilt, and in some of them – (*pointing to books*) suicide – and even dead children, in some of them. But it's their characters or their natures, in all of them really, that bring them the consequences, and that's what happened to me too, this – (*plucks at chain*) this is my consequence. Because of my character. Do you understand, my dear?

**Ronnie** Well, yes and no, Terri. That is, in those novels I understand it, and in general – in – in life – I understand it, but – but in your own particular case, my dear, it was just – well, bad luck, wasn't it, that it happened to you?

**Terri** No, Ronnie, it wasn't just bad luck. Because it didn't *happen* to me. I actually did it to myself. Wrapped it around me myself. And clicked the padlock myself. Didn't I? And I can't think of anybody I've ever met in my whole life who'd let a loony and drunken lady get her to chain herself up. Especially when being watched by a furtive sort of clergyman watching from the bathroom, and I bet you were chuckling and grunting and sucking on your pipe like always, knowing perfectly

well that something – something – what word would
Enid use – 'untoward', yes, 'untoward' was going to
happen. Can you think of anybody but me who'd let
something 'untoward' like that happen? And so since
I've started reading those – (*gestures to books*) and
thinking about them and mulling – (*laughs*) yes, *mulling*
them over with Eenie I've asked myself why, no, what,
*what* is it in my character that got me into this chain.
And do you know what I think it is, Ronnie? *Think* it is?

**Ronnie** (*shakes his head*) No, my – no, my –

**Terri** My politeness. I'm always too polite, too willing to
please – was I smiling, Ronnie, tell me, was I smiling
when Eenie told me to chain myself up. Was I smiling?

**Ronnie** Well, um, yes, I believe you might have been
smiling, as I now remember it. Yes.

**Terri** And was it a polite smile I was smiling?

**Ronnie** You were very polite, yes, very, when you, you –
almost as if you were, um, expecting it, actually.

**Terri** Like retribution, you mean.

**Ronnie** Retribution. Ah. (*Ponders.*) For what?

**Terri** Oh, for lots of things, who knows what things,
ever since I was a child I've been expecting retribution. I
used to steal at school, you know, sweets and money and
clothes, especially underwear if it was prettier than mine,
but I was never caught, so the retribution could have
been lying in wait all these years. And then, after all, not
so long ago, I let Freddie take me. I didn't *seduce* him, or
*betray* Eenie or do anything grand and sinful or even
criminal, I just gave him a cuddle, and before I knew it
there he was, with his trousers down and me under him
on the sofa with my skirt up, being polite. And now here

I am now, with my retribution. (*Shimmies*.) What's your retribution going to be?

**Ronnie** Mmmm? Oh, perhaps I've already got my retribution, my dear. In my character.

**Terri** Your character? What is your character, Ronnie, my dear?

**Ronnie** (*laughs*) Well, just as you described me – chortling and grunting and sucking on my pipe. And – and, you see, here's the retribution, it's not just that there's me on the outside chortling and grunting and sucking on my pipe, that's what it feels like to me on the inside. Yes, yes, that's my – my retribution. Being me.

**Terri** Are you 'gay'?

**Ronnie** Mmmm?

**Terri** Are you by any chance 'gay', Ronnie, my dear?

**Ronnie** No. No, I don't think I am, Enid, my dear – Terri. (*Laughs*.) Terri, I mean. That's a part of the problem, perhaps. If I were gay it would give me some shape, some definition. But I've never had any strong lusts, you see. Except for food of course, and cups of tea. And this.

*He shows her bottle, pouring himself and Terri more.*

And this. (*Indicating pipe*.)

**Terri** What about love then? Not lust and that, but love.

**Ronnie** No, no, I don't know about love either. Apart from Enid, of course. And Fred. We were – Enid, Fred and I – in the days when Fred and Enid and I – they were such happy weekends – we played Scrabble, you know, for hours on hours, up in the snuggery at the Big House, they bought it, you know, the Big House, to be near me, in my vicarage. But that's all, that's all I know of love. And what about you, my dear?

**Terri** Oh, I don't know anything about that kind of stuff. I mean, what chance have I had, here with my retribution?

**Ronnie** But still, my dear, oh, my dear, I can't believe, can't quite believe, that you're *merely* what you say you are, a smiling sort of young woman who simply accepts being chained – no, *lets* herself be chained – because, you see, I think there's more to you than you let one see, indeed I do, and that's the reason, the real reason I came down tonight. For a little chat. About the – the Stockholm business, isn't that what it's called, from what I've read and seen on television, where a lot of interdependence develops between the hostage and – and the hostage taker, in other words, are you sure you – well, you really want to be free, my dear? Because, you see, if you really wanted to be, you would be, wouldn't you? You know perfectly well that you only have to ask Enid – you've done so much for her, and you are, in your heart I know you are – a good and gentle young woman, and I know how fond you've become of Enid, but – but I don't want – I won't have her being hurt any more – look, here's the key.

*Holds it out to Terri.*

Take it. Unlock yourself. Go. Before things get really messy –

**Terri** (*ignoring key*) Go? And where would you have me go, Ronnie, my dear? I won't have a room in my flat any more, I haven't got a job –

**Ronnie** A hundred pounds – (*Taking money out of wallet.*) This is a hundred pounds, it'll get you to London, and if people ask where you've been you can say you've had a breakdown, people are very sympathetic to breakdowns these days – but – but – are you sleeping together? (*Little pause.*) You and Enid? Are you?

*There is a pause.*

**Terri** So that's what this is all about then, is it? Poor old Ronnie. My dear.

**Ronnie** Are you? Are you sleeping together? Mmm?

**Terri** What happens between Eenie and me is private to me and Eenie. At least to me. And knowing Eenie, to Eenie too.

**Ronnie** My dear, I beg you – yes, on bended knees – (*Kneeling.*)

*Terri looks at him in amusement, struggles to repress laughter.*

**Terri** Oh, Ronnie, I don't want – really, I don't – (*Out of control with laughter, pulls herself together.*) Sorry, sorry, it's Mrs Price's dandelion muck – but look at you, poor Ronnie – I don't, I really don't want you to be miserable and jealous –

**Ronnie** Jealous! (*Getting up.*) Of you? Oh, you silly, silly girl! You're here because of me. Because of Fred and me. Our love for Enid, Fred's and mine. It was our doing, and it was out of love. Real, grown-up love.

*They stand looking at each other.*

We set out to save her. That's the whole story. In a nutshell.

**Terri** I don't want it in a nutshell. I want the truth, Ronnie. I've got a right to it.

**Ronnie** Yes. Yes, you have. Well – well, let me try and explain then. You see, Fred's a completely faithful man by and large, bless him! He just has these momentary lapses, especially when he's desperate about his finances and thinks he's going down the tubes, which he generally is – but of course you know all that because that's what led to his, with you, on the sofa. Normally Enid would have understood. That's the way it's always gone, you see. Fred lapses, Fred confesses, Enid forgives – it's one of the foundations of their marriage. Absolute honesty from him, followed by honest absolution from her, is how Enid once put it. But this time he confessed *and* asked her to give him a new Goforth, all in the same conversation, I told him afterwards he'd made a terrible mistake, I mean absolution *or* a new Goforth, he couldn't possibly have both, but by then it was too late, she sent him away as she always does, and began her pre-Goforth drinking and breakdown, but this time, instead of homing in on a dog like the last time, that's what your chain was for originally, a dog, but thank God she started writing the day before it turned up and I managed to get it sent back without her even seeing it, a dreadful, snarling creature – or those kittens the time before that Fred and I had to have put – put into a new home – no, this time, she homed in on you. Because that was Fred's other terrible mistake. Instead of having just his normal run-of-the-mill peccadillo, some young writer he'd come across at a literary party, over and done with before she knew she'd even been begun, so to speak, he had to do it with a girl who was going to be there, every day, in his office, always a temptation, always available, that's how Enid saw it, and what was worse, there wouldn't be any more confessions, he couldn't confess about the same girl again and again, could he, so no more honesty – and in no time you'd become an obsession, far worse than kittens or dogs, and her drinking, and she was making herself so ill, so very ill. So – so – when she actually started planning to get you down here and at the end of the dog's – (*indicates chain*) we decided, well, I'm afraid we decided that if you were what she needed to make her well again, and to get on with a new Goforth, then she should have you. You see. But the last thing we thought would – Fred and I, I and Fred – that it would go from – from, well, sofa to chain to, well, bed. And if poor Fred should ever find out he'd be outraged, and wounded, deeply, deeply wounded, yes, wounded by the – the – sheer, the sheer – treachery of it! And knowing Fred he'd blame me. And with some justice. Because after all I'm not a vicar for nothing. Unlike Fred, I do know the difference between right and wrong. And that's where my shame is – that I should have been part in any way, do you know, when Fred saw the state the Porsche was in, the scraped paint and what I'd done to his gears, I actually thought he was going to hit me, and I yearned for him to – to – as my, yes, retribution.

**Terri** So Freddie's known where I am all along, has he?

*Ronnie nods.*

And you helped Enid to trap me, did you?

*Ronnie nods again.*
*There is a pause.*

Well, the truth of the matter, Ronnie, my dear, is that I don't care. Because I'd rather be here on the end of a chain, being educated by Eenie in my soul, yes, soul here in Dover – (*laughs*) than anywhere else in the whole world.

**Ronnie** I can't allow it, I won't, I have a duty, a Christian duty, to free you, whether you want it or not – come here, come here, out of that chain –

*Clutches Terri, attempts to insert key into padlock.*

*Terri pulls away. Ronnie pursues her.
Enid enters, carrying typescript.*

**Enid** Good heavens, what's the matter! You both look – look rather odd.

**Ronnie** Really? Oh well, we're just here, sipping away at Mrs Price's dandelion and – and chatting about Dickens and George Eliot and – and our games of tennis –

**Terri** Tennis? What tennis?

**Ronnie** Well, our tennis. Every morning. Before breakfast we play – Enid and I play –

**Enid** Ronnie dear – (*cutting across him*) it's there on your doorstep.

**Ronnie** Mmm? What?

**Enid** Well, whatever turns up on your doorstep, from time to time, is there again. On your doorstep. The vicarage doorstep. So please go up and have a look at it.

**Ronnie** I will, I will, I can't wait, can't wait. (*Makes to leave, remembers cheese.*) The cheese. (*Indicates cheese, picks it up.*) And apples. Oh, and the dandelion – no, I'll leave that for you in case you feel like a – (*Exits.*)

**Terri** Tennis, Eenie! You've been playing tennis! And with Ronnie! While I've been stuck down here –

**Enid** Oh, it's only for twenty minutes or so, and it's *always* before breakfast, when you're still asleep probably, to warm me up, loosen me up, so I can get away from Enid into Lizzie and do her day's work, and it's done, she's done at last, and it's all because of you, my dear, my salvation you've turned out to be. I mean. (*Laughs.*)

**Terri** Oh, Eenie! And did you write the last bit the way you said you were going to?

**Enid** I don't know. I can't remember how I said I was going to write it. I can't even remember how I've written it, really.

**Terri** Well, read it to me, Eenie. All the way from where you stopped reading last night.

**Enid** Where did I stop last night?

**Terri** She's at the ball, though she doesn't really want to be, but it's a matter of pride – of honour – to show the world her independence, her freedom. Then comes all that humiliation. She runs out of the ballroom in floods of tears, then up the great steps – with everybody watching, all that titled lot, the ladies and the gentlemen, and the servants too, their eyes all fixed on her – but she can't stop, she can't compose herself. She gets out onto the parapet, then slumps against the cold wall, alone, so alone, so forsaken. That's where you stopped.

*Enid, who has been nodding through all this, turns the page, starts reading.*

**Enid** 'She turned her face upwards, and sobbed aloud. And then, then, then – there he was in front of her, filling the emptiness everywhere. He was reaching down, an arm was around her waist, he was pulling her up to him, away from the cold stone into his warm chest. His mouth pressed against hers. His body crushed into hers. The smell of him was the smell of the sea air, the smell of danger and safety, the smell of the man she loved. Her legs trembled, buckled, but there was no release from the ecstasy of her need. "May I have the next dance, please, Lady Goforth?" Later, as they lay naked, entwined, peaceful beyond fulfilment, he dropped a tender hand on the rich curls, the tangled love-soaked bush between her thighs and as he stroked, she –'

*Terri lets out a yap.*

**Enid** My dear?

**Terri** Sorry, Eenie, sorry, I didn't quite get the last – the last –

**Enid** I'll read it again.

**Terri** No, Eenie, don't bother, just go on, keep going straight on.

**Enid** There's no point in my going straight on if you don't know what I'm going straight on from, is there?

**Terri** No, right, Eenie.

**Enid** (*reading*) '– the smell of the man she loved. Her legs trembled, buckled, but there was no release from the ecstasy of her need. "May I have the next dance, please, Lady Goforth?" Later, as they lay naked, entwined, peaceful beyond fulfilment, he dropped a tender hand on the rich curls, the tangled love-soaked bush between her thighs and as he stroked, she –'

*Terri, who has been rigid with the attempt to control laughter, suddenly explodes with it.*
*Enid watches her, half laughing with her but bewildered and hurt.*

**Terri** Oh, Eenie, Eenie, I'm sorry. It's just that – well, there you are looking just like you when you're reading – well, reading Jane Austen – 'Emma Woodhouse, handsome, clever and rich' – 'It is a truth universally acknowledged that a single man in possession of a large fortune must be in search of a wife' – but there were these other words coming out, very different sort of words.

**Enid** Yes, very different words, aren't they? Not what you'd expect from Jane Austen or any other writer that we care for. But they're the kind of words they expect from me – even though I didn't know I'd written them. Anyway, what they sounded like. Until you laughed.

**Terri** But Eenie – Eenie, if you read it as you actually wrote it, without knowing what you'd written, I mean – here, I know how you wrote it. (*Takes typescript from her. Reads.*) 'Later, as they lay naked, entwined, peaceful beyond fulfilment, he dropped a tender hand on the rich curls, the tangled love-soaked bush between her thighs and as he stroked, she flung her head back and sobbed again. But the sobs now were sobs that came from the very pit of the sweet, invaded, precious darkness –'

*Enid lets out a scream, followed by a scream of laughter.*
*Terri, after a second, joins in. They cling together, laughing.*

**Enid** Oh, God! Oh, dear, oh dear, oh dear!

*Terri lies, sprawled on the floor, attempting to get her breath, still laughing.*
*Enid pulls herself together.*

I've never done that before. Perhaps everybody else has, though. Perhaps all over the world people have really been turning my pages and shaking with laughter. Fred probably laughs too – and twice as much, because he sees the royalties coming in. So much to laugh at for Fred. And there's Ronnie now, up there in the vicarage at this very moment – can't you just see him, sucking on his pipe, wagging his head, great, deep chortles of laughter. And afterwards he'll just say what he always says – 'My dear, one of your best, one of your very best' – laughing away inside when he says it. Everybody laughing but me – until now. And if I'd only done it before, when I'd started – laughed at my every sentence as I wrote it – I'd have soon stopped, wouldn't I? I wouldn't have given anyone else anything to laugh at, would I? And so I'd have nothing to be ashamed of either.

*Seizes typescript from Terri, throws it down, bursts into tears.*

**Terri** Oh, Eenie, dear, dear Eenie my dear, I've told you and told you, when I was temping around London, all those dreadful offices where they didn't even see me, hence – hence, Eenie – *hence* – (*Cuddling Enid.*)

*Enid lets out a little laugh, through her tears.*

*Hence*, I always had you in my bag, for the tube or the bus, or under the desk furtively, you kept me going, just as you keep those millions – see, Eenie? Lizzie?

**Enid** You won't keep one of me in your bag any more, will you? Won't need me any more, will you? You've outgrown me.

**Terri** How can I outgrow you, Eenie, when it's you that makes me grow? Now, Eenie, no more tears. (*Goes to tape machine, puts on waltz music.*) Come on, Eenie, time for your lesson.

**Enid** Oh, my dear, Terri, my dear, not yet. Not quite yet.

**Terri** Yes, yet. Quite yet. Get up. Up, I say.

*Enid gets up.*
*Lights dim. They dance in the moonlight.*

Follow me – follow me – I keep telling you, follow me! That's it!

*They dance in harmony.*

Eenie, do you think you're beautiful?

**Enid** (*in a whisper*) No, of course I don't. Because I'm not. Not beautiful.

**Terri** (*laughs*) Well, then – I think you are sometimes. Sometimes I think you're quite beautiful. Your expressions, your eyes – when you're having fun or being suddenly vague. Even when you were at your worst, sozzled and mad. More than quite beautiful actually. What about attractive? Do you find yourself attractive?

**Enid** I hope I am sometimes. When it's – it's important.

**Terri** You're the most attractive person in my world.

**Enid** Oh, Terri, am I really?

**Terri** But then you're the only person in my world, apart from Ronnie, and I think, I really think, indeed I do, that you're more attractive than Ronnie.

*Enid laughs.*

What about me, Eenie, do you find me attractive? (*Pause.*) Eenie? You have to answer. I'm the leader and you have to do what I say.

**Enid** Well yes, yes – in some ways I – in some ways, yes. (*Little pause.*) Very. Very, very, very. Yes. (*Little pause.*) Indeed I do. Attractive.

**Terri** (*swirling joyfully*) Then follow me! Follow me!

*They dance towards the balcony.*

'The sea is calm tonight. The tide is full. The moon lies fair upon the Straits. On the French coast the light gleams and is gone. The cliffs of England stand glimmering and vast –' (*Gives a little laugh.*)

**Enid** 'Ah love, let us be true to one another. For the world which seems to lie before us like a land of dreams, so various, so beautiful, so new, hath really neither love, nor joy, nor light, nor certitude, nor peace, nor help for pain –'

*Puts her head on Terri's shoulder. Takes key out of pocket.*

It's time now, isn't it?

**Terri** Yes, it's time.

*Enid unlocks padlock of Terri's chain.*

**Enid** There. You're free. Free at last.

*Terri puts chain around Enid's waist, padlocking it.*

**Terri** No, I'm not. And nor are you. Ever.

**Enid** Ever? Oh, my dear –

*They kiss.*

*Lights.*

### SCENE TWO

*A week or so later. Morning. The room is empty. The chain goes over the rail of the balcony. Bottle of dandelion wine on table where Ronnie left it.*

*Ronnie enters in his canonicals. He sees the chain, goes on to balcony, pulls up the chain which is attached to the golliwog's ankle. There is a knife through the golliwog's heart. Ronnie exhales compassionately, shakes his head. Goes over to table, picks up bottle of dandelion wine, swigs from it.*

*Terri enters, unseen by Ronnie, watches him.*

**Ronnie** (*sees Terri, starts slightly*) Just back from service. Only four of them to listen to my usual sermon, but four is a quorum, isn't it, and I did manage to get them genuinely worried about the roof, not difficult as there was that brief shower at the time – divine intervention, eh? (*Laughs. Becomes aware of bottle in his hand.*) Oh, good heavens, I'm so sorry, I hope you don't mind – sudden thirst. Quite inexplicable. There it was, you see, inviting me – temptation itself – um –

**Terri** Oh, you're very welcome, it's yours anyway and it's been there for ever, must be deeply disgusting by now.

**Ronnie** Yes – yes, it is. (*Takes another swig.*) Actually she turned up, Mrs Price, just at the end of my sermon, she was in a dreadful state, patch over her eye, one of her arms in a sling –

**Terri** Where's Eenie, I was expecting Eenie.

**Ronnie** Up in the Big House, on the phone – at least she was when I looked in a few moments, um, ago –

**Terri** She *is* coming down, isn't she? We're meant to be going to her favourite pub for lunch –

**Ronnie** Oh yes, the Plough and Bucket. Stars, that is – Plough and –

**Terri** Well, did she say anything? I mean, is she coming down, or am I meant to be going up –

**Ronnie** She made a kind of gesture which meant – I don't know what it meant – as I say, she was on the phone – but I think it meant more down than up, yes, sort of 'see you down there' –

**Terri** (*lighting a cigarette*) Are you taking the opportunity for one of your little chats, Ronnie? Is that why you're here?

**Ronnie** No, no – (*Showing her the golliwog.*) Why did you do this? To poor little – poor little –

**Terri** Oh well, I was remembering that New Testament bit, the not-being-a-child-any-more-and-so-putting-away-childish-things bit – *passage*, Eenie would call it – *passage* –

**Ronnie** I don't believe He – Jesus – meant us to hang our childish things out of the – the – after we've stabbed them through the heart. No, no, he meant us to put them away in drawers, not – not – no, never – (*Unwinding chain.*) Not Jesus.

**Terri** It wasn't Jesus. It was St Paul.

**Ronnie** Mmm?

**Terri** St Paul.

**Ronnie** Oh yes, of course it was, how could I possibly – Corinthians 13,11 – 'When I was a child, I spake as a child, I understood as a child, I thought as a child; but when I became a man I put away childish things. For now we see through a glass darkly –' (*Taking knife out of golliwog, putting it on table.*) There. Safe now. Almost intact again, aren't you?

**Terri** Why don't you keep him, as you're so fond of him, and after all, he's yours, really, sent in for your church bazaar, wasn't he?

**Ronnie** Oh, well, thank you, my dear. (*Picks up golliwog, puts it under his arm.*) If you really have no further use – though these days it'll be hard to find a proper home – we live in such enlightened times that I really wonder if we can see anything clearly any more – except through a glass darkly – yes, you're quite right, one of my chats. Little chats. That's what I've come down for. Sorry.

**Terri** If it's to talk about me and Eenie, I won't. I simply won't, Ronnie.

*Pause.*

## JUST THE THREE OF US

**Ronnie** I expect you think that I'm a weak, morally vacillating, bumbling – you know – sexless, we've already talked about, jealous, we've talked about too, um, indirectly – but the key word is weak, isn't it? That's what you think of me as? Weak?

**Terri** Well, actually, I think you're also quite demanding.

**Ronnie** Yes, yes, of course, I am, aren't I? Demanding. So. So weak *and* demanding. Which means I'm also wicked, doesn't it? (*Nods.*) Wicked. (*Little pause.*) Well, anyway, I've got to do something – something that you'll probably think is rather wicked – look, look, there's this that I have to –

**Enid** (*enters*) You're still here then, are you? Oh, dear! Oh dear, oh dear. (*Vaguely towards Terri.*)

**Terri** Yes, he is and I've been trying to tell him I'm really not in the mood for one of his chats, my – my dears. And where have you been all this time, Eenie, I've been up and down, looking for you – it was much simpler when I was chained up, at least we always knew where one of us was. Why can't we have a phone down here?

**Enid** A phone? In my mulling room! (*To Ronnie.*) You were meant to have finished ages ago.

**Ronnie** Yes, my dear, I'm sorry, I'd forgotten it was Sunday and I had to give the service, and then Mrs Price –

**Terri** Oh, come on, Eenie, let's be off before there's another mix-up.

**Enid** I'm sorry, my dear, I can't, it's all so hectic at the moment, hectic. The phone never stops, everyone begging me to change the title, you're right, Ronnie, as usual – 'Lady Goforth, This is my Dance' – that's the one they want – (*Little pause.*) What I sent Ronnie down to tell you, what he should have told you by now – Ronnie –

**Ronnie** My dear, I really do think it's best if you – you – because I've got to pop up to the vicarage, Mrs Price is expecting me, the wretched Mr Price is back on the cider and is behaving appallingly again, quite appallingly, beating her and smashing up all her bottles of dandelion – (*Making for door.*)

**Enid** Ronnie, what is your reward to be when you've discharged *all* your obligations – all of them? There is a reward, isn't there, for you?

*Ronnie says nothing.*

Well, Ronnie? How much is he giving you?

**Ronnie** Well – only a percentage, a very small percentage of your advance and royalties, was what Fred agreed on – and it's not *my* reward. It's for my church. My church roof. So that people, even if there are only four of them, can stand under it, my roof, protected at last from the elements, for which I thank you, Toni –

**Terri** Terri, I'm Terri.

**Ronnie** – with all my heart and – yes, yes, on bended knees. (*Goes to his knees.*) It's not that I want to raise a great temple to God who may not even exist after all – no, I just want to mend my roof, the roof of a church that goes back – goes back –

**Enid** Oh, get up, Ronnie. (*To Terri.*) I don't know why he does that. They're like little fits, I suppose, and he can't help them.

*As Ronnie gets up:*

Very well, very well. Oh, I wish romantic Lizzie could step in here to tell us about the laughter, the tendernesses, the, yes, loving! Indeed it was loving, wasn't it, my dear, we had, as we cultivated your soul together, here in

Dover. But here is practical old Enid. With a cheque to hand.

*Holds her hand out to Ronnie who has turned away.*

Ronnie, Fred's cheque, please.

*Ronnie hands Enid cheque.*

Oh really, Ronnie, you might at least have put it in an envelope.

*She holds cheque towards Terri.*

Three times your weekly wages for the ten weeks you've been away, minus so much for your board and lodging, as calculated by Fred. A cheque, my dear, for – (*Looks down at sum, hurries on.*) And you'll carry on with your reading, won't you, my dear? Promise me.

**Ronnie** You'll get another job just like that. (*Snaps his fingers.*) I mean, you've shown you needn't be just a temp any more, moving from one little job to another little – (*gestures to Enid*) job, but permanent. Yes, you could get a permanent position. In as much as anything is permanent – um – (*lights pipe*) these days.

**Terri** (*in a whisper, to Enid*) But – but you said you loved me. And you were going to go on teaching me. You said. I mean, I mean – Eenie!

**Enid** (*to Ronnie*) I wish you'd remember, my dear, that it's actually the church's roof, not yours. (*To Terri.*) I think I am – (*nods*) yes, think I am teaching you. This is your final lesson, you see.

**Terri** But I'm your vocation – you said so –

**Enid** I think you misunderstood, my dear. My husband is my vocation, my only true vocation. And Ronnie's roof seems suddenly to be a small vocation on the side. I haven't room for anything more, you see.

**Terri** Oh, Eenie, Eenie, how could you – oh, how could you?

*Little pause.*

**Ronnie** (*to Terri*) You must admit I tried, yes, I did try to persuade you to depart with some dignity, instead of – well, you know, this rather messy, hasn't it been –

*He sucks on his pipe again, grunts, chortles, etc.*
*Terri launches herself at him, slapping him, knocking pipe out of his mouth.*

**Terri** Messy, messy, you're the messy, you're the messy, you're the messy, you – you – with your filthy pipe, your stench stenching up my home, fouling up my home – *my* home! (*Stops.*) This is my home. Until I choose to leave it. Which I now do. Indeed I do.

*She picks up handbag, goes out.*

**Ronnie** Oh, a taxi, do you need a – a –?

*Ronnie puts broken pipe into wastepaper basket, still shaken.*

I expect I deserved that.

**Enid** Well, somebody certainly did, though I'm not sure – not quite sure that it was you.

*Notices cheque is still in her hand, puts it back in her pocket, looks at Ronnie.*

Ronnie dear, do you really have to keep holding on to that doll?

**Ronnie** What? Oh. (*Looking down at golliwog, realising, puts it down on table.*) No, no, it can go into the bazaar, just as she – (*Sits down, pulls another pipe out of his pocket, tamps it down.*) Well, the next bazaar. Oh, dear, it's been such a – such a – far worse than the dog or the kittens that we had to – poor souls – but which one was that? Oh yes, *A Foreigner for Breakfast*.

**Enid** *A Foreigner for Breakfast*! *A Foreigner For Breakfast*! It was *Stranger, Behold the Dawn*, Ronnie.

**Ronnie** Oh yes, yes, sorry, my dear, association of – of – but I haven't had a chance to compliment you on – on – (*Realises he can't remember the title.*) I read it with such delight, my dear, one of your best, your very, very best, I do think.

**Enid** Thank you, Ronnie. (*Seeing typescript, picks it up.*) Oh, and I do hope you noticed my little tribute.

**Ronnie** Tribute? Really? To me?

**Enid** Page one-seven-three, I believe it is, at the top.

*Ronnie takes typescript from Enid.*

**Ronnie** Page one-seven-three at the top. (*Finds page, reads.*) 'And your breasts, proud and pulsing mounds of passion, your arrogant nipples struggling against the soft, transparent silk –'

**Enid** No, no, Ronnie, how could that possibly be a tribute to you!

**Ronnie** Well, it's page one-seven-three, at the top –

**Enid** Try page one-three-seven.

**Ronnie** (*turns pages*) Oh. Ah. Yes. (*Begins to read.*) 'No ordinary vicar, he. A man of compassion and keen, intuitive understanding, a man of the cloth, this shepherd of muscular mind –'

**Enid** (*interrupting*) I wonder when Fred will get here.

**Ronnie** Oh, early evening. (*Brightening.*) Just in time for a game of Scrabble. (*Lighting pipe.*) The three of us again.

**Enid** Scrabble. (*Unconsciously taking a few waltz steps.*) Just the three of us again! Won't that be – delicious!

*Waltzes some more, as:*

*Lights.*

*Curtain.*

# JAPES

Piers
26 May 1947–28 June 1996

**Japes** was first presented at the Mercury Theatre, Colchester, on 23 November 2000. It subsequently transferred to the Theatre Royal, Haymarket, opening on 7 February 2001. The cast, in order of appearance, was as follows:

**Jason** Toby Stephens
**Michael** Jasper Britton
**Anita** Clare Swinburne

*Directed by* Peter Hall
*Set Designer* John Gunter
*Lighting Designer* Neil Austin


Simon Gray wrote other versions of *Japes*, which follow (as he put it) 'the same characters in the same situation in the same house, but tell[ing] a slightly different story through to an almost opposite conclusion . . . or . . . to the same conclusion but by an unexpected (at least by me) route.'

*Japes Too* and *Michael* are published in Simon Gray, *Four Plays* (Faber, 2004). A companion piece to *Japes*, *Japes Too* and *Michael* titled *Missing Dates* was broadcast on BBC Radio 4 in 2008, produced by Jane Morgan, with Jasper Britton and Toby Stephens.

# Characters

**Jason**
**Michael**
**Anita**
**Wendy**

# Act One

### SCENE ONE

*Early nineteen-seventies. Sitting room of family house in Hampstead. The house belongs to Michael and Jason Cartts, brothers. Michael is in his mid-twenties, Jason a year or so younger.*
　*Upstage left, door leading off sitting room to other rooms. Kitchen also off stage left.*
　*Sound of typewriter from upstairs.*
　*Jason is sprawled on sofa in sitting room. He has a bottle of wine beside him, a glass in his hand.*
　*Sound of typing stops. Footsteps on stairs. Michael enters sitting room, walks irritably about, ignored by Jason, goes out again. Footsteps on stairs. A pause. Michael comes back into sitting room, collapses onto chair tensely.*

**Jason** (*after a pause, mumbles*) Hi.

**Michael** Hi. (*Glances at Jason.*) Are you asleep?

**Jason** No. I'm trying to remember.

**Michael** Remember what?

**Jason** 'Sunday Morning'. The last bit. The deer.

**Michael** And can you?

**Jason** Mmm –

　'Deer walk upon our mountains, and the quail
　Whistle about us their spontaneous cries;
　Sweet berries ripen in the wilderness;
　And, in the isolation of the sky,
　At evening, casual flocks of pigeons make

Ambiguous undulations as they sink,
　　Downward to darkness, on intended wings.'

**Michael** 'Extended wings'.

**Jason** Yes.

**Michael** You said 'intended'. 'Intended wings' – 'casual flocks of pigeons make / Ambiguous undulations as they sink, / Downward to darkness, on extended wings.' 'Downward to darkness, on intended wings' was your version.

**Jason** Are you sure?

**Michael** Yes.

**Jason** 'Intended wings'. How depressing.

**Michael** Yes. Makes them into suicides, really, the pigeons.

**Jason** No – no, it doesn't. It could mean the wings were *intended* to carry them upwards, out of the darkness, but they were defective in some way, these wings, probably made in Britain, so the pigeons aren't suicidal, not at all, just badly equipped for flying. Like the rest of us.

**Michael** But still, the way he wrote it the wings are OK. They extend. They extend but the pigeons sink – sink on extended – (*gestures*) is the point. 'Ambiguously undulating' is the point.

　　*Jason pours himself another glass, is aware of Michael watching him.*

**Jason** What's up?

**Michael** Nothing. Nothing's up. Why?

**Jason** Oh, just – just – but you look as if something's up. Are you expecting old Neets, is that it?

**Michael** What?

**Jason** Old Neets, are you expecting her?

**Michael** I wish you'd stop referring to her as old Neets. It makes her sound unhygienic.

**Jason** I got it from you. That's what you call her.

**Michael** No, I don't. Not any more. I've made a point of calling her Anita.

**Jason** So you have. As if it were two words. An Eeta. An Eeta. Like a measurement. Don't you move an eeta or I shoot –

**Michael** I'm on my ninth bloody draft, do you realise that? I've been around the track eight times, over two – what is it? – nearly two and a half years, and I'm not making it better, I'm just making more drafts. I feel completely untalented.

**Jason** Well, you're not. At least three of the six or seven drafts I've read are good enough to be published. Not all three of them, I don't mean, but any one of them. With a bit of redrafting. (*Laughs.*) That one you sent to – that chap, that agent, Weeble –

**Michael** Weedon. His name is Weedon.

**Jason** Weedon. Sorry. Anyway, Weedon wanted to take you on and he should know, shouldn't he? Why don't you trust him?

**Michael** Because at the moment I don't trust anybody, least of all myself. I don't even believe in the title any more.

**Jason** 'Some Fitful Fevers', it's good.

**Michael** What?

**Jason** 'Some Fitful Fevers'. It's OK.

**Michael** That's not the title. That was never a title. It was just a way of identifying it, at the beginning. The very beginning. Instead of 'work in progress'.

**Jason** Well, what's the title now?

**Michael** 'Antelopes in Antibes'.

*There is a pause.*

**Jason** Why?

**Michael** It has a meaning.

**Jason** It must be in the ninth draft. There weren't any antelopes in the ones I read. And nobody went to Antibes.

**Michael** Do you like her?

**Jason** Who? Oh. An Eeta. Yes, I do. Yes, she seems very – very – from what I've seen. Why?

**Michael** Well, I think I need to know what you think of her. How you see her.

**Jason** Oh. (*Takes out joint, begins to roll it.*) Well, as – um, a bit of a waif, I suppose.

**Michael** A waif? Well, yes – of course she is, with her background, those parents, she's bound to be a waif, isn't she, no choice – in fact, what's amazing about her, truly amazing, is not that she's a waif, 'a bit of a waif' as you put it, but that she's a – a strong and individual sort of – sort of waif. Don't you think?

*Jason nods.*

So – so you don't mind her staying here sometimes, spending the night?

**Jason** Not at all. Well, sometimes a bit but never seriously.

**Michael** What times do you mind?

**Jason** Well, when she – oh, the obvious things. You know.

**Michael** No, I don't know. What things?

**Jason** It gets crowded in the kitchen when I'm hungover in the morning.

**Michael** Well then, that makes a lot of times. As you're hungover most mornings. God, I hate the smell of those.

**Jason** Neets – An Eeta doesn't. She smokes them too. Haven't you noticed?

**Michael** Yes, well – I don't like the smell when she does it, either.

**Jason** But you haven't said anything to her, have you?

**Michael** The point is she's not – she hasn't – well, she's still a guest. So of course I haven't said anything. But I might. Soon. That's the point. But what worries me is – is that I've started worrying about her. I mean, when I should be working I start thinking, thinking, well, she ought to be bloody here by now, and where is she, and then a sort of worry grows, just a little one, never specific, not about her being run over or assaulted or – meeting somebody else, for God's sakes, least of all that – it's more – a worry over the mystery of her – of who she is. That's what worries me about her absence, her lateness – not where or what or why – but who. Who is she? Perhaps the point is – the real point is – that I'm in love with her. Never felt like that about any of the others. Have you ever known me feel like that?

**Jason** You used to get very excited about Ingrid.

**Michael** Ingrid! But that was just the sex. She was an addiction. A brief addiction.

**Jason** And a bloody noisy one. You know, there's a funny echo that starts in your bedroom and ends up in mine. Seems to run around in the walls –

**Michael** You can hear us?

**Jason** You and Ingrid, she used to honk, or by the time it went around in the walls it was a honk, like an angry goose.

**Michael** And what do you hear these days?

**Jason** Not much. It's all right.

**Michael** She's very careful, when you're around. Gets embarrassed. But our sex – is – as if – as if we both –

**Jason** Yeah, Mychy, I don't think you should, I really don't think you should – leave it to my imagination, and then leave it to me not to imagine it – I mean, with your 'oops-a-daisy' – one-two and oops-a-daisy –

**Michael** What? What did you say?

**Jason** Well – you know, when you go oops-a-daisy, one-two and oops-a-daisy –

**Michael** Are you – are you suggesting it's obscene or something?

**Jason** No, no, just a bit – a bit public, that's all. Bit difficult to look at when it's going on in front of one. Some – some North Country custom, is it?

**Michael** It's a game. An affectionate expression of – of a kind of *joie de vivre*. I'm sorry if it offends you.

**Jason** No, no, it doesn't offend me –

**Michael** Then why mention it?

**Jason** Sorry – sorry, but as you were asking –

**Michael** I wasn't asking anything. I was explaining. Trying to explain my need to have her here, in here, living with me, officially. That's really what I'm trying to do. Take it into account, from your point of view.

**Jason** You sure you don't want to get married and have done with it?

**Michael** No.

**Jason** Well, that's all right then.

**Michael** What is?

**Jason** That you're sure you don't want to get married.

**Michael** No, what I said is that I'm not sure I don't want to get married. I am, in fact, very far from not sure. But you clearly took me to mean the opposite. Which must mean that you're the one that's not sure I should marry her.

**Jason** It was a misunderstanding – a rather complicated double negative that doesn't come out as a positive – muddled semantics, that's all, Mychy. 'Sure' is one of those words that – that –

**Michael** Christ, I'm trying to have one of the most serious conversations of my life, the most serious –

**Jason** But I'm being serious. I'm doing the most serious listening of my life, Mychy. I'm being – being – Look. (*Stubs out joint, drains off glass, puts it away from him.*) You're in a state. You see.

**Michael** Yes, well. Sorry.

**Jason** I'm only trying to say –

**Michael** Yeah, I know. It's just that – you always have such a casual attitude with your own – (*gestures*) things –

with women. So I assume you're being rather casual with me. About mine.

**Jason** I don't feel at all casual about yours. There's a lot at stake. For both of us.

**Michael** For both of us?

**Jason** Well, all three of us, come to that. But for you and old – her.

**Michael** And for you, you're saying.

**Jason** If you're married then it's all different. Obviously. Completely different from the present set-up.

**Michael** Is it really, when it comes down to it? After all, she's already got a key.

**Jason** She's borrowed a key. No, I mean – you've lent her a key. But she only uses it when you – allow her to, really. She understands the implications – that's why she always rings the bell before she lets herself in.

**Michael** Still, you don't like her having it at all, do you?

*Jason says nothing.*

You don't.

**Jason** Well, actually I suppose I do find it a bit odd, awkward, actually when I come back sometimes and she's let herself in without either of us being here. (*Little pause.*) I mean, as you ask, Mychy.

**Michael** Odd, awkward – to be alone with my girlfriend?

**Jason** Wrong words. Not odd, awkward – it's just, well, finding somebody else in the house, somebody I scarcely know coming and going, when I'm not expecting it. That's all. But now I'm beginning to expect it so I'm getting used to it, I really am. I mean, to hell with the bloody key, it's completely beside the point.

**Michael** But the point it's beside is you. You don't want me to marry her. You think I'm making a mistake. That's the truth, isn't it?

**Jason** Look – aren't we rather forgetting old – Anita in all this? We're rather taking it for granted – I mean, have you discussed it with her?

**Michael** No. I've only just begun to discuss it with myself. Now I'm discussing it with you. Do you think she might refuse me, then? It hadn't occurred to me. Why should she? Do you think she would? (*Looks at watch.*) Now she's really late. Why should she? She loves me.

**Jason** Oh, she's said so, has she?

**Michael** Yes, yes, she has – I think she has, I'm sure she has, anyway she behaves as if she has.

**Jason** And you, what have you said?

**Michael** I haven't had to say anything. She knows. She's very instinctual.

**Jason** Yes.

**Michael** What does that mean?

**Jason** Well, nothing, it means yes. You tell me she's very instinctual and I say yes – Jesus, Mychy!

**Michael** Have you heard something?

**Jason** Like what?

**Michael** About her instincts – instinctuality?

**Jason** No, of course not. (*Laughs.*) Who would I hear it from – except you? Things you've reported. That she's said to you.

**Michael** What sort of things?

**Jason** (*rolling another joint*) That you're not the first and only. There have been others before you.

**Michael** (*sarcastically*) Before me, yes, well, she wouldn't be telling me about the ones she's having at the same time. Or after me. Yet. I trust.

*Jason lets out a strange eruption of laughter.*

What?

**Jason** Jesus, Mychy, I keep telling you I don't know anything about her really except what you tell me. I've scarcely even had a conversation with her.

**Michael** Well, hardly surprising as from your own account you're either hungover or irritated by her turning up. Perhaps if you tried talking to her some time, made a bit of an effort – you know, for my sake.

**Jason** Yes, yes, I will, I will – but what we're talking about at the moment, what we're discussing at the moment is – is not me and her but you and her – and your sexual jealousy, isn't that it?

**Michael** My what? Don't be – don't be so bloody – sexual jealousy!

**Jason** Ah. So it's not that that's made you worried and blocked and suddenly desperate to get married.

**Michael** Desperate? Desperate! I'm not at all desperate! Just considering.

**Jason** Just considering – oh well, that's OK then. That's fine.

**Michael** But what is quite clear, absolutely clear, is that you're against my marrying her, aren't you?

**Jason** No, no, of course I'm not – but – well, what about the house?

**Michael** The house?

**Jason** Yes. Our house. If you set up together, I mean really set up together – permanently – whether married or not – well, I'd have to move out, wouldn't I?

**Michael** Would you?

**Jason** Well, yes, obviously.

**Michael** But this is a – is a – you're virtually making me choose. It's like some Spanish, Spanish – medieval Spanish – it's a kind of blackmail. I mean, where would you go, I'd feel guilty. Treacherous.

**Jason** Why should you, it would be my decision and – and perhaps I need to get away anyway – and there's that job, I've been thinking about it a lot, it's probably still open.

**Michael** Job, what job?

**Jason** The British Council job. In New Guinea.

**Michael** What? Oh, that job! It isn't even in New Guinea. It's in Guyana.

**Jason** Yes, Guyana, the West Indies. One of the islands. And they play cricket. Test matches, now I come to think of it.

**Michael** No, they don't. It's the place it always rains, so they're always cancelled, and it's not even an island, it's a tip of somewhere South American and it's hot, steamy, jungly.

**Jason** Are you sure? Still, it's a place to start, it's a university job, that's what matters, and who knows,

I might end up as a professor, Professor Cartts of the South American jungle.

**Michael** No, you wouldn't, with your – your (*gestures*) health, you'd end up as plain Mr Cartts – Mr Cartts he dead. And you know it. And that's what I mean by blackmail. Because you know I'd never let you – never –

**Jason** And how the fuck – how the fuck – do you think you can stop me? (*Little pause.*) I'm going to go, whether you marry – marry – (*gestures*) or not.

**Michael** Then I'm fucking well not going to marry her, whether you go or not! So you can fuck off anywhere you want to, Japes, just as long as you fuck off! (*Going off.*)

**Jason** I thought people like us weren't supposed to end arguments with language – language –

*Sound of Michael going upstairs.*

(*Suddenly bellowing.*) – of such fucking – fucking –!

*Stops, forces himself to settle down with joint. Takes a swig of wine.*

'Complacencies of the peignoir, and late / Coffee and oranges in a sunny chair –'

*Sound of Michael starting up furious typing, above. Jason looks up, makes a gesture of derision, concentrates.*

'And the green freedom of a cockatoo
Upon a rug mingle to dissipate
The holy hush of ancient sacrifice.
She dreams a little –'

*Sound of front door opening, closing.*

**Anita** (*enters*) Hi.

**Jason** Hi. You didn't ring the bell so it can't be you, can it?

**Anita** Well, it is.

**Jason** Then why didn't you ring the bell – I mean, that's the convention, isn't it, and we have to stick to our conventions at times like these.

*Anita goes over, takes joint from him, sucks in, inhales.*

**Anita** Well, actually, I hoped you'd be here on your own. Because I wanted to see you, you see. (*Looks up at ceiling.*)

**Jason** Yes, that's him all right. And here's me. Here I am, Neets. (*Lifts a finger.*) An-eeta.

**Anita** How stoned are you?

**Jason** Quite. Quite stoned.

**Anita** But you can think.

**Jason** Don't know. Hang on.

*Stumbles to his feet, lurches. Anita catches him.*

Christ! All a bit of a strain really. (*Fumbles in his pocket, takes out a tube, shakes out a pill.*) Pass me – pass me the –

**Anita** What's that?

**Jason** It's a pill.

**Anita** But what's it do?

**Jason** Cleans me up. You'll see. Go on. Pass it to me.

*Anita hands him the glass.*

Well, needs something in it.

**Anita** (*pours some wine into the glass*) Does big brother know you take these?

**Jason** Oh, yes. I tell him they're painkillers. For my leg. That shuts him up. (*Laughs.*)

**Anita** Oh, Japes – I wish you wouldn't get like this. Not just this minute.

**Jason** Well, give me another minute and I won't be like this. (*Stumbles to sofa, sits down.*) Now. Now. How can I help you, An-eeta? (*Gives a little laugh.*)

*Anita looks at him, also laughs.*

**Anita** Oh, Japes. I just want to talk a little, that's all.

**Jason** Good. Because that's what I'm here for these days. To listen. Already done a lot with him. He's in a state. All because of you. You're late, you see. Where have you been?

**Anita** Oh, I just stopped off at that church, the one on the corner by the heath, I wanted to – to, well, think, you see, and it's such a nice church and quiet –

**Jason** Oh, St Mark's, Mummy was very, very fond of it, you know, she was a friend, a friend of St Mark's official, sat on committees, helped to raise money, probably wanted to be buried there, wonder why we didn't – oh yes, there was a lawyer, bloody lawyer kept going on about which of them had died last – anyway, they decided it was Daddy by a nose, so that's right, it was his will that counted and there was something in it about wanting to be buried at sea – why, why at sea, we never understood that, nothing of the old salt about Daddy, not the slightest bit an old sea dog but anyway, there it was, stuck in his will, so in he went, poor Mummy beside him, right in the middle of the Channel, she'd have been much happier in St Mark's – and so would he, probably, but anyway there they are, the two of them, and those are pearls that were their eyes, poor souls, poor souls.

**Anita** What were those you took, those pills?

**Jason** Don't know exactly, called Screamers or Screechers, something like that, good, aren't they?

**Anita** He wasn't really, was he? In a state? Because of me, my being late? I mean mostly he never notices whether I'm there or not.

**Jason** Well, you see, he's only just noticed that he's in love with you.

**Anita** There, I knew it. I told you so.

**Jason** Well, you were right, weren't you? That's why you're in trouble. Being in love with you is blocking his writing. Stops for minutes on end. To pester me about you. Then he's back up there and off again. And it's all – all circular. Like a lavatory roll that never unrolls to the end, just keeps renewing itself. Probably just as well as it's crap, really. Just crap.

**Anita** Crap? Is it really?

**Jason** Delicately thought, finely wrought, maturely paced, ironically poised crap. Well, you've read some of it.

**Anita** Yes, but I wouldn't know, it's all above my head – but – but poor Mychy – (*Looking up.*)

**Jason** (*also looking up*) Terrifying, isn't it? And moving too, in its way. But the thing is, Neets, it doesn't matter. Not really. Because he'll be a success, you'll see. He inherited the success gene from Daddy. And just as Daddy put up houses that everybody bought and nobody wanted to live in, old Mychy will put out novels that – that –

**Anita** And what gene did you inherit, Japes?

**Jason** I think – I think Mummy's driving gene. Yes.

**Anita** That's not funny.

**Jason** Mummy was a very good driver. Ace. Lots of panache. Zipping up and down the motorways, made even old Daddy look pretty glamorous, sitting there beside her as she shimmied and jived through the traffic at speeds of up to and beyond – only made one mistake in her life, apart from me. (*Laughs.*) And if she'd come out of the skid or swerve or whatever it was, he'd have been so proud of her, Daddy would, patted her knee – 'That's it, Debs, darling, well driven, well driven' – so you see. No disgrace in that gene. I think I'll start taking lessons soon. Yup. (*Smiles at her.*) What do you think?

**Anita** I think I hope you never pass the test. What does he mean he's in love with me? Or is he just saying things?

**Jason** No, no, he means – he means – well, the fact is, Neets – (*Little pause.*) He wants to marry you. I think he's going to, you know, pop – pop it at you. The question.

**Anita** Oh, Christ! He can't, can he, I mean, can't you tell him?

**Jason** (*after a pause*) Tell him what?

**Anita** Well – that there's nothing to me really – not the sort of things he needs – the darks, depths and troubled turmoils and –

**Jason** You've got a gift.

**Anita** Gift? What gift – he can't mean my drawing – he doesn't think I'm some sort of artist –

**Jason** No, no, of course he doesn't.

**Anita** What, then?

**Jason** Well, just sort of, you know, being. Being Neets. Old Neets. Very, very desirable old Neets.

**Anita** You mean he loves me for myself alone!

**Jason** Well – (*Little pause.*) And the sex, he says. I stopped the details.

**Anita** (*after a little pause*) Yes, well.

**Jason** The question I ask – very seriously, Neets – is – what do you want from him? Eh? What do you want from my big brother?

**Anita** (*after a pause*) You know what I want. I want the little brother, you see, Japes.

**Jason** But you already have the little brother. Sometimes on the same day as you have the big one.

**Anita** Don't!

**Jason** Sorry. I'm sorry, Neets.

*They both look up at the ceiling.*

Anyway, we're going to stop that. You're just going to be my little – my little sister, possibly even sister-in-law – isn't that the way it's got to work? Because of Mychy and – everything.

**Anita** It won't work for me. I've been thinking about it, Japes, I've never thought about anything so hard – and this is the thing, the difference – when I'm with you and I think about him, even when I try not to – well, even then I'm not ashamed about him. But when I'm with him and I think about you, it's – it's all right – and so that's why it's wrong, you see – oh, I don't know what I mean but you know what I mean, don't you, Japes?

**Jason** (*thinks*) Yes. Mmm. One's natural, one isn't. Is that it?

**Anita** But don't you at least get jealous? Tell me!

**Jason** Yes. But I don't like it. After all, it's only sex. Nothing to get jealous about, really, these days, when there's so much of it around. (*Laughs.*) The only thing I mind, really mind – (*imitating her*) one – two – and oops-a-daisy, one – two and oops-a-daisy, that's disgusting, you're both disgusting when you do that. Pass me my stuff.

*Anita passes his joint stuff, pours herself a glass of wine.*
*Jason starts on joint, passes it to Anita, who passes him glass of wine. They interchange thus during the following.*

**Anita** So what you're saying is, marry him, as far as you're concerned. Right, Japes?

**Jason** No, I'm not. I'm bloody not. What I'm saying is – do what you want – but do it with your – (*gestures extravagantly*) whole self. Existentially, see.

**Anita** I don't want to marry him.

**Jason** Good. Because you shouldn't. Nor should he. He shouldn't marry you. So stop fretting and enjoy your fucking.

**Anita** And what about you?

**Jason** Oh, never mind me, I'm out of it anyway, exactly as we agreed. As a matter of fact I'm going to sort myself out, it's time – (*Nods.*) Might even go away, far away to – to the tropics, set myself up as a university prof. Write my own novel. And it won't be draft after draft after draft, it'll be like Mummy's driving – zoom! I'll zoom over the finishing line. Believe me?

*Anita shakes her head, kisses him.*

**Anita** You're bloody useless, that's what you are, Japes.

**Jason** I've had my uses, though, haven't I?

*He strokes her breast.*

**Anita** (*shudders*) Ooh, don't, don't, Japes.

**Jason** You're such a – such a kitten, you are. That's why we love you really. Because we love kittens. And you're the only one we've got. Purr. Go on. Purr for me.

*Anita makes slight purring noises, rubbing her breast against his hand.*

Oh – oh, shit, Neets.

*Takes her in his arms. They kiss passionately.*

Come on then, come on, we can do it –

**Anita** We can't! Of course we can't!

**Jason** If he stops, we'll stop –

*Anita shakes her head.*

Why not? You haven't lost your nerve –

**Anita** Listen, Japes – now listen. (*Stares at him intensely.*) What if I get pregnant?

**Jason** What! What do you mean, you're on the pill.

**Anita** Still – it happens. It really does. So what if I get pregnant, Japes?

**Jason** Well – well, don't worry, we'll pay for it – one of us. Or both of us, come to that.

**Anita** No, you wouldn't, neither of you. Because I'd never have an abortion, never.

**Jason** Oh, well then, if it's a girl I'll have it. If it's a boy, Mychy gets it.

*Takes her in his arms again.*

**Anita** The thing is, Japes – I'm late.

**Jason** What? Late?

**Anita** Yes, late. Quite a bit late, as a matter of fact. You see.

**Jason** Oh. Well, what the hell –

*They begin to make frantic love. Typing above stops. They continue. Sound of footsteps upstairs. They become suddenly aware.*

**Anita** Oh, Christ!

*Leaps up, dashes out through front door.*
   *Sound of Michael coming downstairs. Jason trying to assume dopey position. Sound of Anita closing front door as:*
   *Michael enters.*

**Michael** Hi.

**Jason** Oh, hi. (*Stirring himself.*) You look – what do you look? Transformed. Fulfilled.

**Michael** Yes, well, suddenly – floodgates – floodgates again – sorry about all that stuff – (*Little laugh.*) Don't know what got into me – but Christ – (*sniffing*) you've been going at it, Japes – actually I had some idea she was here, seemed to hear the bell at some point.

**Jason** No. Absolutely no bell. I'd have heard it.

*There is a ring at the door.*

How's that for timing?

*Michael goes towards door as sound of door, off, opening.*

**Michael** (*off*) Hi, Anita, hi, hi, hi!

**Anita** (*off*) Hi.

*Little pause, then off:*

**Michael** *and* **Anita** One – two – and oops-a-daisy! One – two – and oops-a –

*Jason flinches.*


## SCENE TWO

*Five years later.*
*Anita is lying rumpled on the sofa. Jason is straightening out his clothes. There are pages of a student's essay scattered about.*

**Anita** Are you all right?

**Jason** Yes, yes, thanks, Neets. A bit jet-lagged still, I expect. (*Looks at her.*) Sorry.

**Anita** That's all right. It was great to have you back where you belong.

**Jason** Mmm? (*Picking up pages.*)

**Anita** We always say. You always say.

**Jason** Are there some over there? Some of these?

*Anita picks up pages from sofa, hands them to him.*
Thanks.

**Anita** It isn't then?

**Jason** What?

**Anita** Great to be back – it's been nearly a year. Actually yes, a year.

**Jason** I know. A difficult year. A long and difficult year.

**Anita** Because you've missed being here?

*She has been straightening herself out, feeling about beneath her uncomfortably.*

**Jason** Well, that too, of course. But everything. The faculty politics, island politics –

**Anita** All that stuff you were telling Mychy about last night?

**Jason** Yes, that stuff.

**Anita** (*fishing out page from under her bottom*) There's this.

**Jason** Oh. Thanks. There's still a page missing –

**Anita** Oh. Well, it's not here. (*Looking around sofa.*) It's very precious then? I mean you seem very worried about it.

**Jason** Well, it's a student's essay. One of my best students. That's why I wanted to show it to you. As I'd been talking about it. I thought you – you were showing an interest.

**Anita** Yes, well – I thought you were trying to tell me something.

**Jason** What sort of something?

**Anita** Well, not about Wordsworth. I've never even read Wordsworth, to my knowledge.

**Jason** No, I'm sorry, but then what else, what sort of something else –?

**Anita** About her?

**Jason** Her? Oh, her. Sajit. Yes, well, I suppose I was – because you were asking, you and Mychy keep asking why I went on doing it, teaching English in what Mychy calls the educational arsehole of the world –

**Anita** I've never heard him call it that.

**Jason** Well, that's how he thinks of it, I know he does – and you obviously can't see the point either –

**Anita** Well, for different reasons, probably. Or no, perhaps the same reason – well, we both wish you were back here, don't we, obviously? That's all.

**Jason** Yes, well, I sort of hoped Sajit would explain – this would explain – why I go on doing it, that's all. I mean, look, she's bright, and quick and has a feeling for language, our language –

*Anita has begun to roll a joint.*

– and the only literature she's got is our literature, an accidental literature, here's all this poetry, Wordsworth's – I mean, just think of it – even if you haven't read him you'd know his – his countryside, his world – but Sajit, however hard she tries to imagine it, any of it – glades, bowers, willows, bending willows – they're not in her blood, she probably has to look them up – bowers and – and meadows, even – in a dictionary. But I can help, you see, that's the point for me. I can help her to imagine.

**Anita** Are you in love with her?

**Jason** What! Oh, Neets! She's a student.

**Anita** (*imitating him*) Oh, Japes! So was I, remember?

**Jason** Yes, well – you weren't my student.

**Anita** Wasn't I? Sometimes I feel as if I was. But left half-done. Anyway – anyway, Japes, you're different. Not the way you're usually different when you come back – and it's not just not boozing. It's as if something happened. I mean – are you in love with somebody, well, you're bound to be some day, but I think I've a right to know, honestly, Japes, don't you?

**Jason** You'll be the first to know, Neets. I'm not not drinking and doping because of some – some girl – honestly! (*Laughs.*) It was just that it was getting so bad, that's all.

**Anita** Well, something's happened – something's happened this last year, I know it has.

**Jason** No, nothing, Neets. Nothing's *happened* to do with – to do with – falling in love, anyway. Though actually something did happen to get me off the booze at last. (*Little pause.*) Well, there was this friend, you see – a colleague – taught American literature, as a matter of fact. And we hung about together and drank together and – well, in the evenings, virtually every evening actually, we went down to a rum shop – Angry Annie's – and we got into fights. Well, he did. He's that sort of American. Very political. Thinks anybody who isn't fighting for black independence is a fascist or a coward, that sort of thing – but he's very funny even when he's aggressive, and he liked to stir it up at Annie's, you know, pick out the largest black guy in the room, and go over and sort of cuddle him and – and insult him at the same time – tell him he ought to be out there hanging whitey from the lamp posts, not hanging about with types like him, 'Look at me, the colour of my skin, what's the matter with you, you a faggot, a big black cowardly fascist faggot' – that sort of thing, and mostly they'd just push him away and he'd pass out – me too, sometimes – pass out – but sometimes they'd beat him up. Which is what he really wanted, I suppose. Anyway – anyway, one night he picked out this really tough, really tough – who just beat him and beat him until he was down on his knees, his head hanging, vomiting and blood – and I – I don't know why, I still don't understand it but anyway I – I – joined in. Kicked him with this – (*swings bad leg*) and hit him with – (*Swings stick.*) Harry, I mean. My friend. Not the black – in fact the black had to drag me off him. Off Harry. So – so – Harry went to hospital. I visited him a couple of times. He had no idea – but he was gone really – here – (*Touches his head.*) The Dean sent him home – and I – don't do it any more. Any of it. I stay in my bungalow and I mark my essays and prepare my classes and – get on with my novel. Try to keep myself intact, you see. To be intact and finish my novel. You see?

**Anita** (*after a pause*) Mychy says it's very good. When are you going to let me read it?

**Jason** Oh well, if you really want to –

**Anita** (*angrily*) Of course I want to.

**Jason** Well, he's bringing it back from that agent of his – Weedon – this afternoon. So if Weedon thinks it's OK I'll have the confidence – (*Gestures.*)

**Anita** Huh! (*Little laugh.*) A whole year – you've no idea, Japes, how you've conditioned me somehow, so there's not a day when you're not here, when you're not here –

*She holds her breasts.*

Not a day when I don't go into your room and lie on your bed and – and pray that when you are here, soon, please soon, you'll still want me – Were you ever in love with me? Ever?

**Jason** I've never been in love with anybody else. Never expect to be.

**Anita** (*after a little pause*) Hah! First you give up dope, then you give up booze, now you give up me, then you'll be in love at last. That's the way it'll go. It must.

**Jason** It needn't. It probably won't. But – but the real thing, Neets –

**Anita** Go on. Say it.

**Jason** You know.

**Anita** Still, I want you to say it.

**Jason** Well, we can't. Ever again. I meant us not to.

**Anita** But you couldn't resist me, was that it? Or was it out of kindness? Poor little Neets – old Neets – expecting her – expecting her – Why did you come back at all then, why don't you just keep away, getting yourself more and more intact until you're dead to me. That would be the kindness.

**Jason** But I need to see – to see –

**Anita** Who? Mychy? Or your daughter? Which?

**Jason** (*little pause*) All of you. You're my family. All I have for a family, Neets. And I love you. All of you. And that's why – that's really why –

**Anita** Japes, don't be disgusting. Honest is what you used to be. With your whole heart. Existential.

**Jason** I am being honest. Which is why it sounds – sentimental, I expect. I need you all.

**Anita** Well, I don't see why I should need you any more. I think I should try not to do that. And your daughter doesn't need you, does she, she only knows you in bits of time as it is, so you have no idea of what she goes through in her life, of what Mychy and I go through – You know, Japes, you've betrayed me, you said you couldn't, you were too feeble and frail, you couldn't cope – but look at you, look at you, Jason, standing there perfectly *intact* – wishing if only you hadn't had your usual coming-home fuck – you could have taken the two of us with you, you should have – should have –

**Jason** But how could I have, we don't even know if she's mine.

**Anita** I know. I know whose she is. And so do you.

**Jason** No, I don't. And nor do you. Medically speaking, it's quite impossible for either of us.

**Anita** She's yours, she's yours, she's yours. Do you know how hard it is for me with him? (*Long pause.*) Do you know how hard?

**Jason** But you love him. You said you loved him.

**Anita** I said what you both wanted to hear.

**Jason** Then you shouldn't have.

*Anita runs at him, slapping at him.*
*Jason lurches backwards.*
*Sound of front door opening, closing.*

**Michael** (*off*) Hi. Hi.

*Sound of front door closing.*
*Jason seizes stick, scrambles desperately out of room, as:*
*Anita scrambles to sofa, sits down.*

**Anita** Hi, darling. (*Picks joint out of ashtray.*)

**Michael** (*off, clearly taking off coat, etc.*) It's turned bloody cold, no heating in the taxi – (*Enters, carrying a briefcase.*) Hi, darling. (*Beams at Anita.*) Hi.

**Anita** Hi. Well, you're looking very full of yourself, where have you been?

**Michael** Well, with Weedon.

**Anita** Oh yes, I'd forgotten, well – how was it, how is he, how are his cats, how's his parrot?

**Michael** Cockatoo. (*Raising an admonishing finger.*) We have to remember that it's a cockatoo, not a parrot, and that its name is Dolly, not Polly, and they're all fine and he's fine, at least in some senses of the word, no, no, in no sense of the word is he *fine*, ever, he must have put on half a stone in the last few weeks – (*Picking up ashtray, taking it to wastepaper basket.*)

**Anita** What are you doing?

**Michael** Emptying the ashtray.

**Anita** But I haven't finished it.

**Michael** Oh.

*Looks into ashtray, brings it back, takes out joint, gives it to her.*

Sorry, darling, I wasn't trying to make a point, how could I, when I give interviews about the permissibility of the permissive society – it's just the smell, seems to get into my sinuses these days –

**Anita** Oh, well, I don't really want it anyway. (*Dropping it into ashtray.*)

**Michael** No, no, honestly, darling –

**Anita** Please dump it! (*Checking irritation.*) I've got to pick up Wendy in a minute, so I shouldn't.

**Michael** Oh, then we'll put it over here, you can finish it when you get back.

**Anita** Thank you. Where did he take you, L'Epicure?

**Michael** No, the Garrick. He's been threatening me with it for months, and I've kept stalling him, don't know why, never like the sound of it, I suppose, a club full of actors, lawyers, judges, agents – actually a club full of anyone, really, as I'm completely unclubbable, aren't I? Well, I am, aren't I?

**Anita** Mmm?

**Michael** Unclubbable.

**Anita** Unclubbable?

**Michael** Well yes, you know, I always think of it as Daddy's sort of thing, he was actually on the committee of the Garrick at one time, we used to hate the way he'd say it, with a shy – a shy sort of smirk, Japes does a terrific imitation – so. He sort of swindled me into it. Got me into a taxi, just as he always does when we're going to L'Epicure, and I didn't notice where we'd gone to until we were there. I pointed out that I couldn't go in, as I was improperly dressed – (*Pats his throat.*) so he took one out of his pocket, looped it around my neck and knotted it – all very fluent, as if he'd practised, the bugger. Perhaps it's some rite of passage – when your latest has nestled in among the best-sellers for three months running, which *In Perverted Commas* has, he informed me over his third and my only brandy. He insisted I keep it. As a memento.

*Takes tie out of pocket, hands it to Anita. She attempts to snap to attention, studies it.*

**Anita** God, darling, it's ghastly – where did you get it?

**Michael** From Weedon, darling, I've just told you.

**Anita** Sorry, sorry, Mychy – I was trying to follow, but sometimes you're too quick – you know how dim I am, especially when you've been drinking –

**Michael** I haven't been drinking.

**Anita** I thought you said you'd put away three or four brandies.

**Michael** One brandy. One brandy, I said. Which I nursed. A glass and a half – if that, of claret.

**Anita** Well, that's a lot for you. That's drinking. I didn't say you were drunk. Only that you'd been drinking and I couldn't follow you and – and I've only had that, that bit of a joint and –

**Michael** Neets, Neets, darling, don't get upset. There's nothing to be upset about, I'm not drunk, you're not stoned, we're just talking, or rather I am – so how's your day been, my old Neets, where's Japes, what's he up to?

**Anita** I don't know, haven't seen him, marking his essays and that stuff, I expect.

**Michael** And more sober than his brother, I've never seen him so well, not since he was twelve, who'd have thought of Japes, assiduous, abstemious, dedicated – I must make sure my own head is as clear as his when I pass on all Weedon's comments – and clear with myself, too, you know. The truth is, darling, there's a little bit of me, an ugly little bit of me, that doesn't fancy – what is it, well, sharing *that*, you know, I mean, he's welcome, you know he is, what's mine is his, absolutely his – it is ugly, isn't it, to object to sharing an agent? Oddly, I wouldn't mind if it were you, actually I'd like it, I've thought about it, and actually I think that would be thrilling. So what does that tell us about me? (*Takes her in.*) What is it? Darling!

**Anita** What are you saying? Exactly? I think you've lost me – because you can't really be saying what I –

**Michael** Oh, sorry, sorry, what I'm trying to say is that I don't mind sharing him with you. Or you with him. Whichever way around one wants to see it. Either way around. It would be – be – well, all in the family. But it wouldn't be all in the family with Japes, for some reason. I – I feel I'm making a crucial distinction here. Between obligations marital, and obligations fraternal. I sound like something from one of my own novels. Well, from an early draft – (*Laughs.*) But it's such an unexpected jealousy. And what's its precise nature? Am I jealous of Weedon sharing Japes with me, or of Japes sharing Weedon, yes, it must be that way around, mustn't it? Help me, darling, find my best self for me.

**Anita** (*laughs, slightly out of control*) Weedon – you – Japes and sharing and jealousy and – and – what a problem, what a terrible problem for you, Mychy. Poor Mychy!

**Michael** (*after a pause*) You mean I'm being trivial. Yes. I've admitted as much. But is there something more important, immediately more important – that I should be addressing, perhaps?

**Anita** There's the question – the question of our daughter that you might be addressing, perhaps.

**Michael** Oh. Has there been more trouble then?

**Anita** There has for me. I haven't stopped thinking about her all day.

**Michael** Yes, well, I can't help feeling, darling, that all this talk of her unpopularity from her ground-hogs –

**Anita** Aunts. They're aunts. Ground-aunts.

**Michael** Well, whatever they call themselves, ground-aunts, what does it mean anyway, ground-aunts, they're just nursery school – (*Gestures.*) In other words, a bunch of lumpish unqualified girls who shouldn't really be allowed anywhere near children – (*Realises.*) I mean – I mean, as psychologists and behavioural experts, they should just get on with making sure they're physically safe, don't batter and murder each other, and let *us* worry about the more complex –

**Anita** But it's not very complex, it's quite simple, you've seen it yourself, she doesn't get on with people, her own peer group, or with us – she's always miserable and sullen and ill-tempered, Michael, she is, and tantrums the moment she doesn't get her own way – nobody likes her, nobody likes our Wendy, Mychy, nobody.

**Michael** Now that isn't strictly true, darling, look at – look at – Japes. Absolutely fallen in love with her, when he put her to bed the other night he had her yelping with laughter with his 'Here comes the bogeyman', and he actually got her to sing, all quite gooey really, but there's a real bond there – it's not just that he's brought something out in her, she's brought something out in him, a natural, a natural, that's the word –

**Anita** Yes, well, he only does it a couple of times a year, when he bothers to come back. Let him try doing it every night, then we'd see how gooey – gooey –

**Michael** Well, she's not really Japes's responsibility, in that sense, is she, I only mentioned him because you said that nobody – and anyway she's only four, for God's sake, she's not a hardened war criminal, just a – a perfectly normal, normal difficult child, you know the real problem, the real problem is that we're not allowed

to accept old-fashioned normal difficult children –
nowadays every infant has to conform to some rule of
growth – a touch of colic, a few teething problems, some
mandatory hiccups in the toilet training, well, it didn't
work like that in our daughter's case, did it, every aspect
of her growth so far – from getting her wires crossed at
the nappy stage to gum-boils and thrush and – but then
she didn't just – just pop out of you, did she, in spite of
all those natural birth classes we had to sit through – she
didn't get classes in the womb, there she was, perfectly
innocently upside down or the wrong way around and
suddenly she was being jerked out by forceps and clamps
– put any creature, especially a new one, in a bad
temper, so that's all it comes from really, this famous bad
temper of hers, her beginnings, and all we have to do,
darling, really, is to be patient until she recovers it. Her
temper. Or discovers it. And then her behaviour will be –
well, merely as bad as everybody else's. (*Little pause.*)
And in the meanwhile we can look at some other nursery
schools, where they don't have ground – ground –

**Anita** No, Mychy, no, the truth is – we should keep her
at home. Yes. That's the proper thing, you know it is.

**Michael** At home! But darling, I work here – and you –
now you've really started on your children's story at
last – the Bedbugs, Basil the Bashful –

**Anita** Boris. It's Boris.

**Michael** Boris. I couldn't bear it if you had to give up on
him again.

**Anita** We could get an au pair.

**Michael** An au pair! But we haven't got room for an au
pair! Where would we put her?

**Anita** In Japes's room. Well, it's just sitting there wasted
for most of the year –

**Michael** But darling, it's his. His room. Whether he's in it or not. He still keeps a good part of his life in it.

**Anita** We could shift all that down to the basement. And when he does decide to turn up, he can doss down in here.

**Michael** In here. (*Looks around.*) Japes. Doss down in – (*Laughs.*) Legally half of every room in the house belongs to him, have you forgotten?

**Anita** We could buy him out.

**Michael** No, I couldn't. He'd never sell. And I wouldn't want to buy – buy him – he was born here. I was here when he was born here. It'll always be here for him, wherever he is.

**Anita** Just like you, you mean?

**Michael** What?

**Anita** You'll always be here for him, wherever he is, which is why he hasn't gone anywhere, really, not even to Guyana, not in his – his soul. He's even trying to turn himself into you, not just – just cleaning himself up but becoming a writer and – and trying to muscle in on Weedon, that's why you hate the Weedon business, he's busy sort of – sort of taking over from you, being you –

**Michael** What!

**Anita** Yes. You but without any of the responsibilities of – of a proper grown-up. And you let – no, you encourage him, the heart of him, the soul of him, because he's your little brother and you can't bear to see him get free of you. Your little Japes. Belongs to you. Big Mychy and his little Japes. Well, I want him out, I want that room for my daughter. My daughter's au pair.

**Michael** I thought – I thought you loved him.

**Anita** Love him, love him, what's that got to do with it, it's not my love that won't let him move out, it's yours, and all the guilt, the guilt shit you mix up in it, the way you go on blaming yourself is a kind of conceit, anything that happens to him good or bad, it always goes back to you and what you did to him, so really you end up as a sort of God and he's just your playmate. Thing. Plaything.

**Michael** This isn't you, this isn't Neets, my Neets. It isn't, Neets. It isn't you.

**Anita** You didn't cripple him on purpose, you were just boys, horsing about in a swimming pool, bouncing each other on a diving board, nothing glamorous or dark or hidden in it, just a simple bloody accident, however you tell it after we fuck, your voice droning on and on with the damage you've done to him, oh woe is me, woe is me that I could mangle mine own brother, while all the time your daughter, who's in need, real need of your love and care and attention, is denied – denied – (*Turns away, as if ashamed.*)

**Michael** What? Oh, Neets – my dearest old Neets – (*Goes to her.*) Please, my darling, you can't believe, mustn't believe, ever, that I've made some choice between – between Japes and our Wendy – or you and – and – I love you all. To the very best of my – my – I do. And he is breaking free, you know, Japes – his whole thing over there in Guyana, his struggle to become healthy and strong, his taking his job seriously, his writing – that's all to his making a new life for himself. With the woman he loves.

**Anita** Loves? Woman he loves?

**Michael** I wasn't meant to tell you. He was looking forward to telling you himself. So I mustn't say another word. Except that it's almost certainly the very best thing ever to have happened to him. (*Little pause.*) And it does, doesn't it, darling, put everything you said, make everything you said –

*Jason enters.*
*Michael breaks away.*

**Jason** Ah, you're back then, I thought I heard your voice.

**Michael** Yes, I was just coming to look for you, things to tell you, but I was just filling Neets in on the Garrick Club, remember Daddy in his Garrick Club days, that's where he took me, Weedon.

**Anita** Yes, do your face.

**Jason** My face.

**Michael** That face you used to do that Daddy used to do whenever he was going off to the committee –

**Jason** Oh. Oh, yes, that one – 'Oh, Debs darling, boys, quite forgotten that bloody Garrick pow-wow –'

**Michael** (*laughs, looks towards Anita*) Pow-wow, I'd forgotten pow-wow – only time he ever used the word – anyway, I was just telling Neets, Weedon made me wear a tie he'd brought along especially, wants to put me up for it, he thinks it's a good career move, I suppose, there are editors, possibly even a few literary editors, but just the thought of Daddy, and your smirking his smirk – better off, creatively anyway, on the outside, looking in.

**Jason** Oh, but you're already on the inside, Mychy, at least as most of the reviewers see it.

**Michael** Well then, on the inside looking in. (*Laughs.*) Oh, and look – the fact is, I've been rather indiscreet with Neets, given the game away. About you and your lady in Guyana.

**Anita** (*smiling*) Yes, very naughty of you, Japes, to keep it all so furtive.

**Michael** No, that was my fault, he wasn't keeping it furtive, darling –

**Anita** No, I know, just waiting for the right moment, weren't you, Japes?

**Jason** No, not really, it was more of, you know, not wanting it to seem a bigger – a bigger thing than it actually is, at the moment it's still a friendship, platonic, we're not sleeping together or anything.

**Michael** Really? (*Surprised.*) Oh.

**Jason** Did I say we were sleeping together?

**Anita** And even if they were, wouldn't make it a big thing, would it, Japes?

**Michael** Well, perhaps that's what made it seem a big thing, come to think of it. That you weren't, given your unplatonicky tropical – since you first hit the tropics. Anything that stirred in the jungle – (*Laughs, sees Jason's face.*) Well, as you once yourself –

**Anita** Something else you didn't tell me about. Though why should you, it's man-to-man, brother-to-brother kind of stuff, isn't it, and why should I be interested anyway, I'd just take it for granted, I mean what would be really interesting would be if I knew things you – (*to Michael*) didn't know about. Now that would be really interesting, wouldn't it?

**Michael** You're right, you're absolutely right, Neets, now what sort of thing would you tell her that you wouldn't tell me, and she wouldn't pass on, in wifely fashion? That's a Jamesian, positively Jamesian sort of tease.

**Anita** (*to Jason*) Shall I tell him?

**Jason** Yes, do, because I can't think of anything – Jamesian or otherwise.

**Anita** (*after a slight pause*) Your daughter. (*Little pause.*) I've got to go and fetch our daughter. If I'm late they'll be on the phone again.

**Michael** Oh, lord! (*Looking at watch.*) Do you want me to come with you?

**Anita** No, no, darling, you stay and talk to Japes.

**Michael** Oh yes, there's Weedon, I've got to take you through Weedon.

**Jason** Ah! Sounds ominous.

**Anita** Oh, Mychy – (*Going to him.*) I've been horrible, haven't I, and none of it's your fault, it's just me in one of my moods. Forgive me for being so heartless, I didn't mean it, not any of it, you're too good for me, that's what the trouble is. Your trouble, anyway.

*Puts her arms around him.*

**Michael** (*half embarrassed*) Oh, Neets, it's just – just – normal, I expect –

**Anita** (*intimately*) Come on then, make everything all right with a – one – two – oops-a-daisy, one – two –

*She swings her legs around him.*

**Michael** – oops-a-daisy –

*His hands go awkwardly around her bottom.*

What's this – you've got something – (*Hands go under skirt.*) Here, got it!

*As Anita unwraps herself Michael is holding sheet of essay.*

What is it? (*Glances down at sheet.*) 'Strange fits of passion I have known / And I will dare to tell / But in the lover's ear alone / What once to me befell –'

**Jason** Wordsworth. One of the Lucy – (*Gestures.*)

**Michael** (*reciting, not reading*) 'When she I loved / Looked every day / As fresh as a flower in June / And I to her cottage made my way –'

**Jason** 'Bent'. 'Bent my way'.

**Michael** Yes, of course. 'Bent my way'.

*Hands page to Jason.*

**Jason** (*taking page, reciting, not reading*) 'Beneath the lowering moon –' Sajit's, from the handwriting – well, thank God it turned up before I missed it, I get neurotic about losing pages –

**Anita** Wendy. I'd better get going. (*Going towards door.*)

**Michael** Oh, darling – take a coat. It's turned cold again.

**Anita** Right. (*Goes out without coat.*)

**Michael** (*bellowing*) Neets, a coat!

*Sound of door shutting.*
*There is a pause.*

**Michael** Well, Sajit, eh? Quite a coincidence.

**Jason** Coincidence?

**Michael** Well, as she's your friend, it is Sajit, isn't it, your friend's name?

**Jason** Yes – oh, I see what you mean, coincidence, I must be careful not to let her know where it ended up, she's very sensitive to criticism. Especially mine. As they tend to be partly, well, love letters.

**Michael** Then you certainly mustn't let her know where it ended up.

*There is a pause.*
*Jason, in spite of himself, lets out a little eruption of laughter. As does Michael.*

Yeah. Well, now – Weedon. Shall we go to my study?

**Jason** What, like headmaster, you mean? Actually, here's better for my leg, it hasn't got used to the stairs yet, and as I've only just come down – (*Sits down.*) Every time I come back I notice how vertical everything is over here. Daddy's office blocks. Over there we live life on the horizontal.

*Michael has been opening briefcase, taking out typescript.*

**Michael** So you're not fucking her, in the new version?

**Jason** Sorry?

**Michael** Sajit. From what you told me, I had the impression you never stopped, but then you said to Neets – platonicky.

**Jason** Well, I suppose the truth's somewhere in between. It's a platonic relationship but we – we – do fuck as well. Quite a lot. Just as I – but once we got serious – I got serious – and started thinking – thinking marriage really even – we had a talk and started to go back to square one. Well, to before square one, as a matter of fact, because square one we fucked, actually. So it's, when you think about it, really platonic, we started off with sex, now we've moved beyond it. (*Little pause.*) But with a view to going back to it when we're – we're on a higher plane. So platonic, but with a bit of a twist.

**Michael** What does the doctor say?

**Jason** About what?

**Michael** About everything.

**Jason** The last time I saw him, he gave me a clean bill.

**Michael** A clean bill? Well, thank God for that.

**Jason** If you're worrying about the leg, you mustn't, Mychy, there's no reason that it should ever get any worse than it is.

**Michael** Well, I was saying to Neets, I've never seen you look so fit.

**Jason** Mychy – are you stalling?

**Michael** Yes. I'm afraid I am.

**Jason** He thinks it stinks, does he?

**Michael** No, of course he doesn't. Not stinks, Japes, nothing you do could ever stink. And something you should know about old Weedon, well, we were at the Garrick, so he was a bit boozy, and he's not very articulate at the best of times. Not the world's greatest reader. Or thinker, come to that.

**Jason** Sounds perfect for a literary agent.

**Michael** Well, he suits me, as I don't require him to do either. Still, I always trust his instincts. One has to. All his writers are too successful – not one dud amongst them.

**Jason** And he intends to keep it that way.

**Michael** Oh, he doesn't think you're a dud, come on, Japes – no, he thinks you've got a talent, write beautifully, lots of good jokes about bad sex – 'lovely squalid stuff' were his words, had him falling about – falling about. And he admired – really admired the long set-piece – the American queer getting beaten to death by all those women in the rum shop. Bloody powerful, he called it. 'Bloody powerful stuff.' Reminded him of Tennessee Williams, Truman Capote, that lot.

**Jason** That lot. And what else did he like?

**Michael** Well, everything. Everything except – your tone, really.

**Jason** My tone.

**Michael** Not that he actually disliked it. In fact, he actually rather liked it. In as much as – this is difficult – in as much as – well, in spite of our obvious differences in subject matter – it reminded him, it reminded him too much of me. My tone.

**Jason** Your tone. And you, what do you think?

**Michael** Well, impossible for me to say, really, isn't it? I mean, if it is my tone, then I'd be too familiar with it – I'd be the last to know, so to speak, wouldn't I?

**Jason** I can't imagine any tone less like yours than mine.

**Michael** Exactly. And I can't imagine any tone less like mine than yours. So it obviously cuts both ways. Our over-familiarity. Of course it's not a matter of imitation, the tone, but genetic – neither of us can help having that particular – tone gene. Anyway, that's why he doesn't want – well, the two of us, if you see what I mean.

**Jason** Yes. Yes, I do. I see exactly. So. So. (*Little pause.*) Mychy. I think I'll go tomorrow.

**Michael** Go, go where, to New York, you mean?

**Jason** No, back. To the educational arsehole, I suddenly find myself missing it, and the jungly smells. And Sajit.

**Michael** Oh. If that's what you really want, need, Japes, then – as long as it doesn't have anything to do with Weedon – if I've been clumsy –

**Jason** I just want to go home, Mychy. And I can't imagine I'll be coming back in any regular –

**Michael** No. I suppose it's inevitable. And right. Well then – oddly enough, Neets was just saying that we should start thinking of an au pair, except there wasn't a room. (*Laughs.*)

**Jason** Well, there is now. If you could see to packing up my things and shipping them – the bungalow needs them.

**Michael** And Sajit does too, I expect. If she's to make a home with you.

**Jason** Sajit? Oh, I never let her anywhere near the bungalow. To tell you the truth, Mychy, the actual truth, she's just another of my fucks really.

**Michael** Really?

**Jason** Yes, really. I've been in the habit of saving myself, my best self, for when I came home. You see.

**Michael** Ah. Well then. Perhaps under the circumstances you'd like to sell out. Your half of the house, that is.

**Jason** Oh, I'd never want to do that. Too many important things have happened here. It means far too much to me to let go of it. Ever.

*Turns, goes out of the room.*
  *Michael stands for a moment, makes as if to go after Jason, doesn't.*
  *Lights.*
  *Curtain.*

## SCENE THREE

*Seven years later.*
*Lights up on empty sitting room.*
*Sound of door opening.*
*Michael enters, distraught, stares around sitting room.*

**Michael** (*shouting*) Wendy! Wendy!

*Goes out of room. Hear him shouting.*

Wendy, are you in there? Wendy?

*Re-enters, stands looking around desperately, goes to telephone, picks it up. Realises he hasn't got the number, scrabbles desperately through telephone book, dials.*

Hello? Hello, is that Lady Caroline's School for Girls? Who am I speaking to, please? Mrs Allsop, you're one of the teachers, are you? Oh, I see, well, I'm a parent too – Michael Cartts, Wendy Cartts's father, do you know her by any chance? Oh, well then, do you know my wife, she should be there somewhere, looking for our daughter actually – well then, what about – is Miss Crance, I think it's Miss Crance, the assistant headmistress, the one who's in charge of the party, she was with my wife when I left – well, can you ask, please, it's rather urgent. (*Holds on.*) Bloody child, bloody stupid child – (*On telephone.*) What, gone off where? To one of the classrooms – there aren't any classrooms, it's a party – oh, probably gone to check them, we're looking for my daughter, you see, she's – look, perhaps she's come back to the party while they've gone off to the classrooms – you see, the point is, Mrs – Mrs – would you mind calling out my daughter's name, Wendy Cartts, on the off chance – yes, I know it's very loud, I've just come from there and I can hear it but if you could just – well then, look around for her, can you see a blonde girl – she's eleven but tall for her age, looks thirteen, freckles and – oh, of course, sorry, fancy dress, I'd forgotten, they're all in fancy dress – well, she's there as a wolf – no, no, it's a fox, no, a wolf, I think – she's either there as a fox or a wolf, a girl too tall for her age with freckles as a fox or a wolf – and come to think of it, she may be in one of the corners lying down – is any of the girls there prostrate anywhere, on the floor? Pass me over to whom? Oh, Miss Stokehurst – (*attempting calm*) you're one of the teachers, are you, good – well, Miss Stokehurst, the point is we've lost Wendy – or rather you've lost Wendy – er – anyway, she's vanished from the party, the point is, you see – what? No, let me explain, let me explain – my wife is there somewhere with Mrs – your assistant headmistress – touring the building looking for – you see, the point is she phoned us, Wendy did, about half an hour ago, phoned us at home to say she wasn't feeling well, that she – she, well, as far as we could make out, some girl, some imbecile of a girl had given her pills – (*Little pause.*) Yes, pills, red pills, that she'd somehow got hold of from her mother, presumably from her mother's bathroom or medicine cabinet or – or – anyway, she gave some to Wendy who swallowed them – yes, yes, that's right, that's the whole point, that's what I'm trying to tell you – she swallowed these bloody pills and then when she began to feel faint she phoned us and told us what she'd done and I told her to wait there, there and by the telephone, to try not to sit down or close her eyes, but when we got there she wasn't there so I've come back here in case she'd come here but my wife stayed there in case she was still there and she doesn't appear to be either – or – so she – I suppose she set off from the school on her own – at this hour and dressed like a fox or a wolf and – yes, I know,

very cold, very cold, and if she's coming across the heath
– I mean, my God, across the heath in the dark in the
cold, feeling faint and dressed like a wolf or a – the
police, yes, perhaps we'd better – you'd better – look,
Mrs – Mrs – where are you, where have you gone, where
the hell have you gone? (*Shouting.*) Oh, darling, it's you,
where have you been, where the hell have you been, she's
not here, Wendy isn't here – what? A joke! Not pills,
well, what the hell were they? What, Smarties! Well –
well, where was she then? Hiding in the lavatory, right,
right – well, well, there you are, the two of you – are
you all right? Well, the thing is, darling, to calm down –
anyway, until you get home – no, no, I don't think you
should come now, we don't want to make a meal of it,
she gets into enough – I mean, her reputation – much
better to treat it all as – as, well, as a joke. Which is after
all what it was. So – so, hang on, darling – yes, I know,
I know, hang on another hour and I'll come and pick
you up – yes, in an hour, on the dot, I promise – OK
then, OK – oh, and give her a kiss from me. (*Puts phone
down.*) Stupid child, stupid bloody child – oh!

*Takes off his overcoat, goes over to drinks table,
pours himself a carefully measured drink, goes
upstairs to study.*
　*Sound of typing.*
　*The door opens.*
　*Jason enters. He is dressed in tropical gear, carrying
a bag. He is unshaven, almost bearded. He has his
stick. He puts down bag, clutches himself, shivering,
casts a glance towards the drinks table, goes to it,
picks up a bottle of scotch, takes a terrific gulp. His
hands are shaking. Becomes aware of the music from
Michael's room.*
　*Music stops. Typing stops.*
　*Jason takes another quick gulp, puts bottle down.*

*Moves away from the table, waits.
Michael enters.*

**Michael** (*after a shocked pause*) Japes?

**Jason** Yup.

**Michael** Well then – Christ. (*Little laugh.*) Then you're back.

**Jason** Yup.

**Michael** You know, I thought – I had a sudden sense that you were here, down here. I knew it. Well, let's look at you properly.

*Turns light on, goes to him, stops as if in shock at his condition, then makes to embrace him. Jason averts himself.*

Well – hi.

**Jason** Hi.

**Michael** You're straight off the plane, are you, you must be – you must be – what can I get you? A drink, of course, what would you like?

**Jason** Oh – have you any rum? (*Goes to sit down.*)

**Michael** No, sorry – almost anything else. Scotch, cognac, gin, vodka –

**Jason** Whatever, scotch, I think. Yes. Scotch.

**Michael** Well, what does one say – a surprise, I mean – what a surprise.

**Jason** To me too. I would have phoned, but things were a bit rushed over there, and the lines are always so bad – and at the airport – I didn't understand the coins, how they work in the – the – (*Puts his arms around himself.*) slots. Telephone slots.

**Michael** (*bringing him drink*) You're cold –

**Jason** Yes, I'd forgotten – thank you – (*Taking drink.*) Ice. Like ice.

**Michael** Shall I get you a blanket?

**Jason** No, I'll be fine. More a matter of internal adjustment. (*Takes a controlled gulp.*) That's better. Soon get the heat – nothing on the plane, you see.

**Michael** Nothing?

**Jason** Nothing.

**Michael** You mean you haven't eaten – all the way from Guyana here – you must be famished, let's go to the kitchen.

**Jason** Oh, there was food. Food and water. And the usual rubbish. But nothing like this. No rum. Condition of travel, you see. For me anyway. All alcohol forbidden. (*Laughs.*) They filled me with pills instead. And an injection.

**Michael** Well, is it safe yet?

**Jason** (*who drinks and refills steadily from now on*) Mmm?

**Michael** Should you be having one now? A drink.

**Jason** Oh, yes. Well, must be because I am, aren't I? (*Lifts his glass to Michael, laughs.*) Mychy!

**Michael** What sort of pills? Injection? What for?

**Jason** Mmm.

**Michael** Are you ill then?

**Jason** Ill?

**Michael** If they gave you pills and an injection –

**Jason** Ah. To stop me wanting a drink. Didn't work though. God, I gave them a bad time. (*Laughs.*) Shouted abuse, claimed my rights, made threats – that sort of thing. Very unattractive. But that didn't work either. Had me sort of wedged in my seat so I couldn't get up to do a proper job. Also woozy. No balance. I fell asleep just before we landed. Because of the pills. They got me out of the airport into the taxi, must have because that's where I woke up. In the taxi. Told him to come here. Couldn't think of anywhere else, Mychy.

**Michael** There isn't anywhere else, Japes. (*Little pause.*) So it's that bad, is it?

**Jason** Oh yes, Mychy. That bad. (*Nods.*)

**Michael** And is that the whole trouble?

**Jason** Mmm?

**Michael** Your stomach. It's – (*Gestures.*)

**Jason** Oh, that's nothing. Nothing. Don't worry about that. (*Slapping stomach, which is very bloated.*) Just liquid. That's why it's tight. Drum-tight. Not flabby. Firm. Drum-firm. Hear it?

**Michael** Yes. So you're OK otherwise. Otherwise OK?

**Jason** Otherwise. (*Does a thumbs up.*)

**Michael** That's a relief. That you're not back here for your health. Are you still shivering?

**Jason** Shaking. Not shivering. Mychy?

**Michael** Yes.

**Jason** Mychy – do you mind if I – (*gets up, goes unsteadily to table*) help myself – (*Taking bottle.*)

**Michael** No, no. Of course –

**Jason** I'm used to having control, you see. (*Sitting down.*) Over my own bottle. I get worried if I have to depend on other people. I've come to hate dependence. Need to cope for myself. In the university bar I have my own bottle. They used to put my name on it. Now they don't bother. And at Angry Annie's too.

**Michael** Angry Annie's?

**Jason** Brute of a woman. Vile temper. Got six children. Says two of them are mine. Don't think so, somehow. Somehow don't think so. Wrong colour. Though you never know, do you, whose child is whose, by what evidence. How is she?

**Michael** (*after a little pause*) How is who?

**Jason** Our girl of course.

**Michael** Ah. She's at the school party. End of term. It's a fancy dress. She's gone as a wolf.

**Jason** A wolf!

**Michael** Yes.

**Jason** Neets as a wolf! Grrrr! What a thought! Little Red Riding Wolf, eh, is that it? I can see that. Yes. Quite clearly. Little Red Neets, gone as a wolf.

**Michael** Wendy. It's Wendy that's gone as the wolf.

**Jason** Wendy! Oh yes, of course, our daughter. Quite the terror, isn't she? Quite the terror.

**Michael** Perhaps when you last saw her. I seem to remember she was going through an odd little phase – but she was only three. She's eleven now.

**Jason** Four.

**Michael** She's eleven, Japes.

**Jason**  She wasn't eleven, she wasn't three, she was four when I last saw her, Mychy. That Christmas. When we had that little what's-it over Neets. Almost fisticuffs. (*Laughs, wags his fists.*)

**Michael**  Over Neets? No, we never had a what's-it over Neets, Japes. Though there was a disagreement over Weedon, I seem to recall.

**Jason**  She used to write to me a lot. Sometimes several times a week.

**Michael**  Did she?

**Jason**  You knew that, didn't you?

**Michael**  Well, that she wrote, yes, of course I did.

**Jason**  Some of them were a bit mad, frankly, Mychy.

**Michael**  Were they. Well, that's very much in the past, she's working very hard on her book, her children's book. The illustrations are going to be enchanting.

**Jason**  One-two-oops-a-daisy – one-two-oops-a-daisy, eh, Mychy? (*Laughs lewdly.*)

**Michael**  How's the cold?

**Jason**  Still here. (*Taps chest.*) Can't get to it.

**Michael**  I think – I think you're in a bad way, Japes. Aren't you?

**Jason**  What happened to the dog?

**Michael**  Dog? Oh, wolf, you're thinking of Wendy –

**Jason**  No, Sandy. I'm thinking of Sandy. A labrador. Yours and mine, Mychy.

**Michael**  Oh yes, Sandy. We had him put down – Daddy did – he had distemper.

**Jason** That's it, that's right, running around in circles, foaming, we thought it was funny, didn't we, Mychy, until Mummy started screaming. Wasn't rabid, though, like me.

**Michael** Rabid? Japes, you're not – you haven't been bitten – bitten by a dog in Guyana?

*Jason stares back at him.*

Christ, Japes, well, what have they done, have they given you those shots – is that the injection?

**Jason** What?

**Michael** You said you'd been bitten by a rabid dog.

**Jason** Yes, yes, the Dean – rabid Dean – and the rest of them, the whole pack of them, whole pack of rabid dogs coming at me – grrr! Grrr! (*Roaring, yelping, slobbering.*)

**Michael** Oh – oh, I see. A figure of speech. (*Gives a little laugh.*) Well, what were they coming after you for?

*Jason picks up bottle, cradles it in his lap, closes his eyes.*

(*Looking at him.*) Oh, Christ, Japes. (*To himself.*) Japes, do you know where you are? Japes.

*Goes to him, touches him on the shoulder.*

Japes. I think you need help. Or anyway to lie down, Japes. Old Japes.

**Jason** (*takes his hand, holds it*) Sweet Mychy. You're very sweet. (*Kisses Michael's hand.*) There. I'll be all right. I need to talk to you. Sit down, you're looming again, just the way I always think of you. Go on, Mychy, sit. Please. (*Suddenly roaring.*) Sit, I said!

*Michael sits.*

Thank you.

**Michael** Can you tell me what happened?

**Jason** Mmm?

**Michael** Well, why you're here suddenly. It's the middle of the term, isn't it? (*Little pause.*) Why did they come after you? What did you do, Japes?

**Jason** Christ, Mychy, those reviews you get – I see all of them, always, in the common room, they come late of course, still reading one batch of reviews and there's another novel plopping out, and then while I'm on the reviews of that out plops another novel, and another and another, plop, plop, plop – Christ, I'm proud of you, Mychy, boast about you all over Guyana, made you big in Guyana, what was it you've got, Daddy got too, a CBO, is it?

**Michael** An OBE.

**Jason** And perhaps a knighthood like Daddy, Sir Mychy Cartts – Sir Mychy and Lady Neets Cartts, do you think she'd like that? I would. Wouldn't mind being Lady Neets Cartts myself – (*Laughs. Begins to choke slightly, gets himself together.*) Sorry, Mychy. Sorry. (*Little pause.*) Gets like that, you see. At a certain point. It's the blood. Bad blood. Black. That's why they've sent me to you. Because of the bad, black blood. That's what they say. But it's not the real reason. The real reason is politics. Politics and women. Americans. Three of them. Doing a tour. A tour of Caribbean us. Us.

**Michael** Universities?

**Jason** Us. Us. Us! (*Slapping his chest.*) In the common room. My common room. On their arses. With their grants. Their doctorates. Their publications. Their – their – feminist – feminist – one of them in my chair. Everybody knew it was my chair. My bum shaped it, term in, term out, gave the cushion its – its – depth, its meaning, its value, my bum did. My bum. That's the point, Mychy, it was my bum, my chair.

**Michael** I see. And so you were offensive, was that it?

**Jason** Polite. I was extremely polite, Herman. (*Nods, falls silent.*)

**Michael** Herman?

**Jason** Herman?

**Michael** You called me Herman.

**Jason** Oh. No, he's dead. One of the friendly dead. Australian geologist. I'll probably visit him in Sydney.

**Michael** Please, Japes, you should lie down.

**Jason** Why?

**Michael** Because you're drunk, Japes. Exhausted. And I don't want Anita and Wendy – Wendy in particular – you wouldn't want her to, either.

**Jason** Sitting on their arses in my chair in my common – 'What would you three ladies like to drink?' Don't call us ladies, very offensive, to be called ladies, and I said, what then, what do I call you, and they said anything, anything but ladies, so I said, 'Right then, right, what can I get you three cunts' – (*Begins to laugh.*) Cunts, I called – cunts – 'what would you three cunts' – and then I took it out – (*Stands up, swaying, unzips his flies, gropes for his penis.*) 'Here, cunts, have a look at this, have a look at this!'

**Michael** Yes, Japes, all right –

*He puts his hand preventively on Jason's arm.*

I get the – the –

**Jason** I keep my pension though. And early retirement. Going to sue. And the police. Brutality. Threw me – threw me about and kicked me. And the doctors, those bloody doctors, those bloody fucking doctors. (*Looking at Michael.*)

**Michael** Japes – Japes – come along, Japes, come along. (*Attempting to take Jason's arm.*)

**Jason** (*pulling violently away*) You listen to me, Mychy, you listen to me. This is my house, half this is my house, you can't throw me out of it, Mychy, you can't keep me away from it – I own half and I want it. I've come back for it. I'm taking it and I'm taking my half of everything else, Mychy. My half of our daughter, my half of the wife, the half that belongs to me. Do you understand, Mychy? Understand it?

**Michael** Yes, of course, Japes. You'll have everything that belongs to you. Of course you will.

**Jason** Just half, Mychy, just my half. No more, no less, just my half.

**Michael** Yes – yes, just your half. Now will you come with me and lie down? Just for a while. Just for a little while. When you wake up, there'll be Neets and there'll be Wendy, and I'll be there. And you'll be in your family again.

**Jason** My family again. Oh, Mychy, my family again – oh, Mychy – oh, Mychy –

*He holds his arms out, lurching.*
   *As Michael goes to him, Jason reels away and collapses to the floor. He is making retching sounds, goes still as death, face turned up.*

*Michael goes to him, takes him in his arms, cradles him.*

**Michael** Oh, Japes, my Japes –

*He lets out an animal howl of grief.*

*Lights.*

# Act Two

### SCENE ONE

*Five years later.*
 *There is a student's briefcase on the floor, contents, including purse and keys, scattered about. Also some papers, books. A transistor is lying on the floor, playing popular music, loudly. The television is on.*
 *Anita is sprawled on the sofa, drinking a glass of wine. She has a bottle beside her. Also a drawing pad, a case of pencils, etc.*
 *There is a ring at the doorbell.*
 *Anita registers it, looks towards door. Front door opens, off.*
 *Jason enters. He is carrying a carrier bag. He uses a different, up-to-date, stick, walks more easily.*

**Jason** Hi. (*Then raising his voice.*) Hi!

**Anita** Hi!

**Jason** May I make some silence?

**Anita** What?

**Jason** Turn things off.

**Anita** Oh, yes, yes. I'd almost stopped noticing.

> *Jason turns off television set, goes to turn off transistor.*

**Jason** (*fiddling with transistor*) I don't know how you do these bloody –

**Anita** Oh, just smash it to death is what I long to do – but this is what I usually do.

*Puts bottle down, takes it, opens the back, shakes out batteries.*

Hi, Japes.

**Jason** Hi, Neets.

**Anita** Thanks for coming round.

**Jason** Well, you sounded – you sounded desperate on the phone.

**Anita** Sorry, I was in a state. Actually, I still am. We just had the most terrible row – the most terrible bloody awful row – about this – (*shaking transistor*) being on, and that – (*pointing at television with transistor*) being on, and then she went off and I've been sitting here, with them still on, not even hearing, what do you make of that, Japes, eh?

**Jason** Oh, referred something or other, isn't it called, these days. You know, if you have a pain in your leg, it's actually being referred there from your neck – so if you have a row about noise and then don't do anything about the noise, it's really a referred row – or something. In other words, I can't make anything of it.

**Anita** (*picking up bag, wallet, keys, etc.*) She's left home for good. Without her keys, her money – (*Putting them into bag.*) Oh, and her pot and stuff, so she'll be back, won't she, though will it be for good or for ill, will she be back for good or for ill is the question. What can I get you, tea, coffee, squash –

**Jason** I've brought my own. (*Taking bottle out of bag.*) Saw it in that new health shop in the village, the one with jars of weeds and turds and what have you in the window – and there was this – herbal – costs about three times as much as a bottle of wine – but then

I suppose you're meant to keep the bottle to put weeds and turds in –

**Anita** (*bringing him glass*) I went out to draw, you see. That turned out to be my mistake.

**Jason** Oh. (*Pouring himself a drink.*)

**Anita** (*filling her glass from wine*) Such a beautiful day. And suddenly there was the impulse – it's been years, Japes, honestly, years –

**Jason** Yes, yes, it must be.

**Anita** So. So I was very careful. Thoughtful. Dutiful. Reminded her that her half-term was over tomorrow and she still hadn't gone to the library to do her project on – on – some history, Charles the one of them – and I was very sweet, I really was, knocked on her door, said, 'Darling, isn't it time you were off?', gave her a couple of quid for her tea – hah, hah! – and said we'd see her for dinner, eating a bit late because of Daddy, about eight thirty, that all right, darling, all right, darling?

*Smiles ingratiatingly at Jason. Jason laughs.*

So then I went and sorted out my things, one ear cocked, you know, to make sure she'd actually gone, and then I heard the door open and close and – and off I went, with my pad and my pencils, to St Mark's as a matter of fact, back to my early period, my only period – remember when I used to draw it all the time back then? – and anyway, I didn't, I suddenly couldn't, didn't want my pad or my pencils sitting in the sun trying to do something that it would just make me miserable and resentful not being able to do so came back to the house to find her here, also back in the house, lying on this – (*indicating sofa*) dragging on a joint, with her bloody noise, and it was the – the thought of it, I mean, that she must have loitered about around the corner in the street or something until she'd seen me gone, and then come back and – the television and the tranny and the pot and the whole slatternly, slovenly, rubbishy – and so I went for her, and she went for me – and – (*gestures*) well, no, that's not fair, not fair on me. I tried to do the grown-up crap first, you know, very calm, cold and calm and reasonable, and she grunted, and smirked and sneered – so I got Mychy into it – 'Remember what your father said about kindness, the real meaning of the word' – then I couldn't remember what he said the real meaning of the word was, it was all very complicated, being Mychy – and anyway, anyway, she just sat there, her eyes deliberately glazed and lips – that way she does – (*Pushes her lips out.*) And that's when I – I hit her, Japes. The thing is – (*Begins to cry.*)

**Jason** Oh, Neets.

*Goes to her, puts an arm around her.*

**Anita** Across the face. Like a punch. A punch. Oh Christ, Japes.

**Jason** It's OK, it's OK – it'll be all right, you'll see, you'll see.

**Anita** I wanted to go after her – I wanted to go after her – I really did, but – but –

**Jason** She'll be back. You'll make it all right. You know, she's not – not bad or anything –

**Anita** Well, I'm not bad either.

**Jason** No, of course you're not. You're both good, very good and – and kind actually.

**Anita** Then why are we so bad, so unkind with each other?

**Jason** Well, perhaps because you're both more like each other than either of you recognises, eh, Neets? Sometimes when I'm with one of you it's as if I'm with the other, I forget which is which – the same gestures, even the same sort of jokes, you know.

**Anita** Jokes? She makes jokes with you, does she? How often do you actually see her, Japes?

**Jason** Well, only during her holidays. And even then she's on school trips or somewhere else, isn't she?

**Anita** Yes, but when she is here, like now, how often do you see her?

**Jason** Well, she looks in now and then.

**Anita** At your flat?

**Jason** Of course at my flat, Neets. It's no secret – at least I've never made a secret of it.

**Anita** But perhaps you don't always say, either.

**Jason** Well, if I don't, it's not deliberately. Why? Do you mind?

**Anita** Well, what do you joke about? What sort of things do you talk about together, in your flat?

**Jason** Well, whatever comes up. Whatever's on her mind.

**Anita** Oh. Like her shrink, you mean?

**Jason** Well, no, not like her shrink. For one thing, I don't charge, you see.

**Anita** Do you talk about us?

**Jason** Which us?

**Anita** Any two or three of us. Well, do you?

**Jason** Really, Neets, I've said, she just pops in now and then, and if I'm busy trying to finish an article or don't feel in the mood, I chuck her out, virtually. It's like that, you see.

**Anita** I suppose I sound jealous, do I?

**Jason** No, you just sound as if you regret having to be a mother when you'd like to be a friend.

**Anita** Was that on purpose?

**Jason** Mmm?

**Anita** Did you misunderstand me on purpose? I didn't mean jealous of you with her, I mean the other way around.

**Jason** Then I did misunderstand you, yes. What I love in her is you.

**Anita** Thank you. That's lovely. Thank you. (*Kisses him.*) You're still tops at that sort of thing, Japes. What a gift. But if you love me in her, why don't I love me in her, too? I mean, if I hate myself, does that mean that I hate her?

**Jason** You don't hate her.

**Anita** I do sometimes. Yes.

**Jason** No. You get angry –

**Anita** No, of course I don't hate her. Why did I say that? It's anger – of course it's anger. And it's with myself really, you're right about that too, and it probably all comes down to my being frightened.

**Jason** Frightened?

**Anita** Well, I'm at that age, you know – it does happen – I could go menopausal any minute, I could be menopausal now, which would explain me a bit, my ups and downs and downs and ups.

*She pours herself more wine.*

**Jason** Darling –

**Anita** Mmm?

**Jason** Darling, Neets. (*Shakes his head.*)

**Anita** Am I drunk?

**Jason** Well, you soon will be.

**Anita** And you wouldn't want to see her see me drunk, is that it?

**Jason** I don't want to see you drunk. And you always hate it afterwards.

**Anita** You talk as if I do it all the time.

**Jason** You've done it once or twice recently.

**Anita** But only with you. Well, mainly only with you. Only sometimes with poor Mychy, he hates it so much – especially if she's around, so never when she's around, honestly, Japes.

**Jason** I know, Neets. Where is Mychy?

**Anita** He's doing one of his things, one of his television things. A very, very big one this time.

**Jason** Oh yes, of course. Writers of Our Time.

**Anita** It's going to make him even more famous. Which means he'll come home all humble and depressed. Isn't it funny how it depresses him – you'd have loved it, success and fame – perhaps you should each of you have been the other – but then would I have liked that because then he'd have been here and you'd have been there, being interviewed – would you have liked it that way round, Japes, that's the question, would you, Japes darling? (*Sees Jason's expression.*) Oh, come on, Japes, what's the matter, I'm only talking, you know me, just talking.

**Jason** Just talking. I wonder why we always say that – 'just talking' when talking is about as dangerous as driving, probably ruins as many lives, if not more, really we should set out the same sort of signs – 'sharp curve in next sentence', 'unfortunate joke ahead', 'slippery surface', 'beware soft patches' –

**Anita** And as for talking under the influence – here, here you are, Japes. Uncle Japes. (*Pushes bottle to him.*) Oh, sorry, darling, the smell, I forgot – here, I'll pour it away.

**Jason** No, I'm perfectly capable.

> *Turns to pick up stick.*
> *As he does so, Anita jerks bottle away from Jason who almost falls.*

**Anita** Oh, look, it's almost gone, I might as well – darling, are you all right?

**Jason** Yes, yes, I'm fine.

**Anita** Well then, you mustn't glower. It never suits you. Remember what you once said to me – 'at heart, you were a merry man'?

**Jason** Yes. Yes, I am. You're quite right. (*Little pause.*) So you went up to St Mark's to do a drawing?

**Anita** No, no, I didn't, I told you. I didn't have the nerve, you see.

**Jason** The nerve?

**Anita** I think I'll become a friend instead. They're always pushing stuff through the letter box asking – help keep the grounds up, tend the graves, I suppose, that sort of thing – I mean, if I can't draw it again I can – I can – be its friend instead. Just like your mummy. Yours and Mychy's mummy, Japes.

**Jason** I wish you did more drawings.

**Anita** Why? So I wouldn't be so bored and such a nuisance –

**Jason** You have a talent.

**Anita** That's not what you said back then, when I was being serious and a proper student. You said the only talent I had was as pussy.

**Jason** No, I didn't. (*Little pause.*) I couldn't have said that. Not ever.

**Anita** Yes, you did.

*Rubs herself against him, purring.*

**Jason** Oh! (*Laughs.*) Yes, yes – (*Strokes her head.*) Well, that's all right then, because it's true – except it wasn't, isn't, your only talent. You can draw. You really can. And if you really can't do St Mark's – well, what about your children's book – the woodlice, wasn't it going to be – why don't you get back to that, Neets?

**Anita** Bedbugs actually. Basil and Archie, the Bashful Bedbugs. I burnt them.

**Jason** Burnt them?

**Anita** My Bedbugs.

**Jason** Why?

**Anita** You wouldn't understand. Mychy didn't. Why should you?

**Jason** Well, you might give me the chance at least.

*There is a pause.*

Why did you burn your Bedbugs, Neets?

**Anita** Because when you came back in that dreadful state and nearly died on us – on me – when you were in intensive care and were almost gone for ever for three whole days – I made a deal. You see?

**Jason** A deal? What sort of deal, with whom?

**Anita** How would I know? But I called him God. I made a deal with – with the God one makes deals with. Up at St Mark's, as a matter of fact. I wanted to do it inside, on a pew, but the doors were locked, so I did it in the churchyard. I said it aloud, at eleven thirty-seven on the Wednesday night of April the thirteenth. Straight after seeing you lying there dead, as good as, as good as dead.

**Jason** That if I lived you'd – you'd –

**Anita** Well, it's the only thing I cared – really cared about that I could renounce, wasn't it? I mean I couldn't renounce Mychy or Wendy, could I, all I had to offer was my Bedbugs.

**Jason** That's the most beautiful thing – the most beautiful thing anybody has ever done for me. Thank you. But Neets, my darling Neets, it's over, my illness, and I'm here, and you've got a life to live, a talent – look, Neets, what really brought me back to life was a life support machine, an exceptionally capable liver specialist called Sapperstein, and just possibly – just possibly – my own will to live. (*Little pause.*) Can't you see what a burden you're putting on me by making me somehow responsible – without even giving me a say in the matter. I would never have been party to such a deal –

**Anita** Can we stop this now, please, Japes? It's making me feel sick. It's quite simple, quite simple. If you'd died I'd have been lost. You've always been what's kept me going, Japes, even when you were on the other side of the world, you kept me where I am, and if you'd died – I'd have died too. Been dead too – for them. (*Pause.*) And that's all there is to it, all right? All right, Japes?

**Jason** Of course it's all right. After all, it's not much of a burden, is it, being responsible for your abandoning your talent, insuring your marriage with my brother – not to mention keeping Wendy afloat.

**Anita** Well, we all have our part to play, don't we? I have to be the wife and mother, and whatever you think and whatever you and Mychy think and whatever you and Mychy and the daughter think, at least I try most of the time, and if I have a rotten afternoon sometimes and ask you to come around – well, I still don't ask for much from you, do I? All things considered, do I?

*Jason, after a little pause, shakes his head.*

So you can go if you want. I'm all right now.

**Jason** I don't want to go.

**Anita** Haven't you got any work to do? You're always saying you've got work to do – all those articles on all those poets in all those magazines – I wish I could read them, I would if I could understand them – funny how I can always understand what Mychy writes, but then he's popular, isn't he, and that's why – that's why he's – (*gestures*) and you're – (*Gestures.*)

**Jason** Oh, Neets, oh God, Neets!

**Anita** You think I'm going to do some more drinking.

**Jason** I hope not. For my sake.

**Anita** Do I make you want to drink, then?

**Jason** Not always. But occasionally, when you're like this, I feel an urge to join in.

**Anita** For old times' sake?

**Jason** Well, there are only old times because suddenly there are new times.

**Anita** Really? Really, really, really. New times are afoot, are they, at last, at long last?

**Jason** I mean – I'm staying for your sake. For everybody's sake. And you're not going to drink for my sake. And that's it, Neets.

**Anita** My jailer then, is what you plan to be, is it? And if you're so frightened why don't you –? I think I'll have another drink, and see what happens.

*She heads towards kitchen. Jason hesitates, makes a decision, heads towards door.*

(*Re-emerging.*) Or you can do me a poem. (*Goes to sofa, sits, pats sofa.*) Come on, I promise I'll be good.

*Jason, after a moment, goes to sofa, sits down. Anita moves closer to him.*

Go on then.

**Jason**
'Slowly the poison the whole blood stream fills.
It is not the effort nor the failure tires.
The waste remains, the waste remains and kills.

It is not your system of clear sight that mills
Down small to the consequence a life requires;
Slowly the poison the whole blood stream fills.

They bled an old dog dry –'

**Anita** Stop it, Japes! That's not poetry, it's cruelty! Old dog! Poison! You're making it up to punish me.

**Jason** No, I'm not. And it's a poem all right. I used it as an aide-memoire.

**Anita** Do that one – that one – the crying girl one. Simple and faithless –

**Jason** Let me think. I have to think, Neets.

**Anita** So think.

*Arranges herself, with her head on his lap. Jason looks down at her, strokes her forehead.*

**Jason**
'Stand on the highest pavement of the stair,
Lean on a garden urn –
Weave, weave the sunlight in your hair –'

*Anita reaches up, puts her arms around his neck.*

**Anita** Come on, I know you want to. Well, he doesn't ever, not ever, not even any daisies any more, no one-two-oops-a! So. So why shouldn't we?

*Pulls him fiercely down on her, kisses him.*

There. Got you again at last, haven't I?

*Jason responds.*

Haven't I?

**Jason** Yes, oh, Neets, yes, yes –

*Lights go down dark as over, Jason's and Anita's murmured cries of passion and up slowly on:*
  *Anita asleep on the sofa.*
  *Jason is sitting in the armchair, slumped in despair, staring at her. He gets up, limps around, finds himself drawn to the drinks table. Picks up bottle, takes off*

*top, puts top back on, puts bottle down, goes back to Anita.*

**Jason** (*pulling at her*) Neets. Neets darling. Neets my love –

*Anita makes grunting noises, clings in sleep to his arm.*

**Anita** What are you doing?

**Jason** You should lie down properly. On the bed.

**Anita** (*as he manouevres her across the room*) Why?

**Jason** Because we don't want Wendy coming in on you –

**Anita** Now you hate me all over again, don't you?

**Jason** No. I love you. Don't you see that's the problem?

**Anita** (*as they go out*) Yes, yes, poor Japes, poor Japes –

*There is a pause.*
*Sound of front door opening.*

**Michael** (*off*) Hi! (*Entering.*) Hi. (*He is carrying a briefcase.*) Hi, anyone!

*He puts briefcase down, goes to drinks table, pours himself a small scotch, looks at it, swallows it down, pours himself another one, as if fastidiously. Sees knickers on floor. Goes to knickers, picks them up.*

**Jason** (*enters*) Hi, Mychy.

*Sees knickers no longer on floor, in Michael's hand. Michael, hurriedly raising knickers to his nose, sneezes into them violently.*

**Michael** Sorry. Something up my nose. (*Sneezes again.*)

**Jason** Well – bless you.

**Michael** (*stuffing knickers into pocket*) And where's Neets?

**Jason** She's in bed. On it rather. She fell asleep on the sofa – had a few glasses of wine –

**Michael** In the afternoon. Shouldn't do it, should she? Always knocks her sideways. Shouldn't myself either, especially as I've already had a few.

**Jason** Really? That's not like you.

**Michael** Well, BBC2, you know. After a long interview. And then on to the Garrick. Pointless. All quite pointless.

**Jason** Well, all part of the business of being a writer these days, isn't it? A successful one, anyway. Oh, can I –?

*Takes stick from Michael.*

**Michael** But you're not going, are you?

**Jason** Well, actually – (*Little laugh.*) I don't know.

**Michael** Something on your mind.

**Jason** Seems to be, yes. But I can't quite work out what it is.

**Michael** Well, sit down. Perhaps it'll work itself out.

*Jason hesitates.*

Are you drinking anything? (*Looking around.*) Is this it? (*Picks it up, looks at it.*) You're branching out. (*Sniffs it.*) Mmm. Nice and flowery.

*Pours into Jason's glass, hands it to him. Goes back and pours himself a larger scotch. Jason watches him greedily.*

Well then – (*Sitting down, raises his glass.*)

*There is a pause.*

**Jason** Actually, she zonked out while I was reciting some Eliot to her. 'La Figlia Che Piange'. I couldn't get to the end, as a matter of fact, I seem to have lost it – the bit after 'I should have lost a gesture and a pose. / Sometimes these – these' – I couldn't find them, 'thoughts' doesn't scan, it isn't 'speculations' –

**Michael** (*sips his drink, moves his lips through the later lines, nods*) 'I should have lost a gesture and a pose. / Sometimes these cogitations still surprise / The troubled midnight and the noon's repose.'

**Jason** 'Cogitations', of course. But it's 'amaze', isn't it? 'These cogitations still amaze / The troubled midnight –'

**Michael** Yes, you're right. 'Amaze'. 'These cogitations still amaze / The troubled midnight' – two completely different conditions, really, 'surprise' being a kind of shock to the system, a pulling out of it, while 'amaze' is – is – (*Gestures.*) Oh, where's Wendy?

**Jason** Actually, she's at my place. Or was the last time I saw her. She turned up suddenly, in a bit of a state, she'd had a spat with Neets, you see, and – so forth.

**Michael** Oh. (*Nods.*) What about, did she say?

**Jason** No, well, before she could get into it properly, Neets phoned, so I got her version instead. As far as I could make out it was to do with transistors being on, television being on, school projects not being attended to –

**Michael** Well, she's off again soon, isn't she? Back to school.

**Jason** Tomorrow. She hates it. Her school.

**Michael** Does she? Yes, I expect she does. Although she's never actually said so, about this one. To me, anyway. But then she scarcely gets the chance, does she, poor child, as she's away at school so much. But then I know perfectly well, after all, she's always hated her schools, her boarding schools almost as much as her day schools, when she has to be at home, which she also hates, so what can we do, Japes, given she and Neets seem to have some kind of temperamental problem at the moment, never quite, never really quite – the way one supposes mothers and daughters will, have they? I tried to give her a little lecture the other day when she'd said something particularly surly – about kindness. You know, the real meaning of the word, what *her* kindness implied, but she went vacant-eyed, thrust her lip out that way she has to show that she wasn't taking in a word –

**Jason** She steals, you know. I keep meaning to mention it.

**Michael** Oh, dear. And what does she steal?

**Jason** Oh, money of course. I've taken to hiding my wallet when she's around. So I expect she steals from you and Neets too.

**Michael** Well, it's an inevitable phase, isn't it? After all, you and I used to do a bit of pilfering at her sort of age. For comics and sweets.

**Jason** Yes, well, I suspect the sort of comics and sweets that are available nowadays are rather different.

**Michael** Well, it's just a question of her holding, our all holding on for another year or two, then a university, her own life –

**Jason** Mychy, there's something – Neets told me about that children's book of hers, why she gave it up. I found it rather upsetting.

**Michael** Oh, dear, her Bedbugs, yes. I'd hoped she was getting over it at last. But I suppose humiliation is the one – one – that one never does quite get over. Well, at least she's started talking about it, that must be a good sign.

**Jason** Humiliation?

**Michael** Well, that's how she sees it, failure and humiliation, although Weedon claimed he never actually rejected it outright – the worst he'd been was mildly discouraging, according to him, but the fact is that whatever he said, he completely undermined her confidence. The pity of it was that even if I hadn't been up in the hospital with you, I might have been able to stop her. When I got in, she was crouching in front of the embers, screaming obscenities at poor old Weedon.

**Jason** What, Weedon was there you mean?

**Michael** No, no, obscenities about Weedon I should have said. (*Goes to pour himself another drink.*) Christ, I really shouldn't do this, I've had enough, quite enough, and when Neets wakes up – (*Pours drink.*)

*Jason watches him pour drink, then has to avert his eyes.*

**Jason** It went badly then, did it, the interview?

**Michael** Oh – (*Gestures.*)

**Jason** When are they transmitting it?

**Michael** Next month. Next month there I'll be, in a million homes, think of it, a million and a half, actually, dilating on the theme of my fictions, the recurrent themes, like recurrent colds or sore throats or prison sentences – no, that's concurrent, isn't it, though sometimes, Japes, when I have to go in there, or even worse, come out – (*Gesturing towards study.*) That's exactly what it feels like, a recurrent – loss, loss and betrayal, by the way, my recurrent themes, with an occasional whiff of redemption, he could sniff it, he said, sniff the whiff of redemption. On my prose. Redemption. Hah! (*Little pause.*) And then do you know what he said? At the Garrick.

**Jason** The Garrick? The interview was at the Garrick?

**Michael** No, no, Weedon. I had to meet up with him afterwards. Things he needed to discuss, he said. Although all he really wanted to do was to pay me compliments and gloat. How much money, how many best-seller lists, the American market, the Japanese translations – and then of course the interview, what it'll mean in terms of this and that, on my way to being a household name – and I found myself sitting there grunting at him. Like a grateful pig. And then he said, said suddenly, with a kind of flourish, as if he'd been saving it up for months, for years even, just waiting for the right moment, which was after a major television interview, and the right place, which was the Garrick, he said, 'The remarkable thing about you, Michael, is not just that you're a successful writer, but that you're a successful writer who hasn't got an enemy in the world.' And I looked at his face, and all the other faces around me, those Garrick faces, and I imagined my own Garrick face and I thought, yes, that's it, isn't it, that somehow tells the whole story, I'm a successful writer who hasn't got an enemy in the world – and then I tried to think of one writer I admired, just one, who didn't have at least one enemy, and the only one I could come up with was Jane Austen, at least during her lifetime. But then there was her family, and in families one never knows one's enemies, does one? Or genes, more importantly. The enemy in the genes, eh?

*Jason gets up, begins to move about.*

(*Watching Jason.*) Oh, by the way, did you see that bit about Daddy in one of the newspapers the other day? One of his office blocks is beginning to fall down, the one in East Finchley, they're probably going to have to blow it up.

**Jason** Really, in East Finchley? (*Now standing by the drinks table.*)

**Michael** Actually, it's not bad, the Garrick. You really must let me take you to lunch, at least once. And then if you come, perhaps Neets will come. She's always refused because of their policy about women. But of course she's much more liberal and relaxed about that sort of thing now. So perhaps dinner would be best, that's it, we'll do a dinner à trois –

*Jason lets out an exclamation, moves away from drinks table.*

Are you all right?

**Jason** Yes, yes, fine, just exercising my – my – (*Pats his leg.*)

**Michael** Yes – God, I'm sorry about that.

**Jason** What! You mean this – you don't mean this, Mychy. Christ, it's so much a part of me I never even think of it – least of all how I came by it.

**Michael** Still, I can't help remembering sometimes and thinking that if it hadn't been for me your life might have been completely different. Or if it had been the other way round.

**Jason** The other way round?

**Michael** Yes, if it had been you that had bounced me off the diving board and not me that had bounced you.

**Jason** As I remember it, both of us were doing the bouncing. The difference is that you kept your footing. And whichever way around it had been, I would have still limped and hobbled around your life, if that's what you – (*Gestures.*)

**Michael** Good God, Japes, how could you – how could you think that I meant –

**Jason** No, no, of course, I'm sorry. It's just that I – just that I – look, Mychy, I think it's time for me to go. Away, I mean. I've been thinking of it for quite a while now. Of going away for a bit.

**Michael** (*after a little pause*) How long a bit?

**Jason** Oh, I don't know. But quite a bit, perhaps. I wouldn't mind trying somewhere really cold. Icy even. With stiff winds. Might actually get me back to – to that novel again, eh, a hostile climate. Do we know anything about – about – oh, Nova Scotia, for example?

**Michael** Nova Scotia? Canada, the Eastern seaboard, and there's something – something – oh, yes, isn't that where the *Titanic* went down, off there?

**Jason** Sounds promising.

**Michael** Look, Japes, what I've really been trying to say during all this – been trying to look for a way of saying – awkwardly, I now realise, extremely awkwardly – well, is that it's all right, you see.

**Jason** What is?

**Michael** Well, everything. I mean, if you're thinking of going off – going off for my sake, so to speak, because you and Neets have started – well, started again. Then you mustn't, you know. Go off, I mean. You really mustn't. I don't mind, you see. That's the point. I don't mind. In fact in my view, it's only right. I actually want it. (*Little pause.*) I mean, here we are, we've reached this stage of – of, well, our lives with each other. These could be good years, good years, why shouldn't they be? All we have to do really is accept ourselves for what we are and what we've become to each other. And what's at stake, you know it too, Japes, don't you, really, is her health. If we can just keep everything in harmony. In harmony. Go on loving each other with all – all needs – all needs – fulfilled.

*Goes into a genuine sneezing fit, reaches frantically into his pocket for a handkerchief, remembers, stops.*
*Jason takes packet of Kleenex out of his pocket, hands it to Michael.*
*Michael finishes sneezing, hands the packet back to Jason.*

Thanks.

*Doorbell rings.*

Who the hell is that?

**Jason** Oh, it must be our daughter. She forgot her keys.

*Lights.*

## SCENE TWO

*Ten years later.*
*One corner of sitting room is in a shambles. Books, papers scattered about, chair overturned, etc.*
*Wendy is standing in the room. She puts chair upright, picks up a few books, puts them back, picks up another book, looks at it.*
*Sound of door opening.*
*Wendy puts book back, turns, faces the door.*

*Michael enters, stands frozen.*

**Michael** Neets. (*Staring at her.*)

**Wendy** No, Dad. Not Neets.

**Michael** Wendy? (*Then recognising her.*) Good heavens, yes, it's Wendy. Well – well, Wendy. (*Takes in shambles.*)

**Wendy** Yes, sorry about that.

**Michael** No, no, not at all, that's all right. (*Little pause.*) Um, what happened?

**Wendy** Well, a fit of pique, I suppose it was.

**Michael** (*nodding*) Ah. You had a fit of pique. (*Nodding.*) Well –

**Wendy** Not mine, actually. The bloke I was with.

**Michael** Oh. He wasn't by any chance a youngish man, in an orangish coat and a bit of a beard?

**Wendy** Dark hair? Long dark hair?

**Michael** Yes, yes, definitely darkish. He passed me on the other side of the street just a moment ago, I thought he might have come out of the house. Shouted out to me. My name. Well, I suppose my name. 'Hello there, Sir Michael, all well, Sir Michael?' And then he laughed. And gestured rather – obscenely as a matter of fact.

**Wendy** Yes, that was him all right. His name's Dominic. He's a recovering junkie, and like me he's still a bit fragile in some ways. He suddenly took it into his head that you'd despise him when you saw him, so he did this as a way of getting back at you. It's called 'inferiority rage' one of his shrinks said, it only comes in situations where he feels inferior – but I probably don't have to apologise for him, by now he'll be looking forward to doing it for himself.

**Michael** Oh, tell him there's really no need, no need –

**Wendy** Well, you'll probably be meeting him some time because he's responsible for this. (*Patting her stomach.*)

**Michael** Mmm?

**Wendy** I'm pregnant, Dad.

**Michael** Oh, I noticed you'd filled out, I thought it might be that, I nearly mentioned it but sometimes you know one makes a mistake. And then it can be rather embarrassing.

**Wendy** A friend of mine had a tumour there. And of course everybody assumed she was pregnant. She found it rather – embarrassing.

**Michael** I'm sure she did, I'm sure she did. A tumour. (*Little pause.*)

**Wendy** You look older.

**Michael** Well, yes. But then I am.

**Wendy** No, I mean older than I expected. Elderly. You look almost elderly.

**Michael** Do I? Well, it's been some years since you last saw me after all. Quite a few years it must be.

**Wendy** Seven years.

**Michael** Is that it? Really? Well, there you are. Would you like something? A – a – well, I don't know, what would you like, anything?

**Wendy** No, thanks. But if you want anything –

**Michael** No, no, well, perhaps just a – (*Goes over, pours himself a drink.*) I could do with this.

**Wendy** Yes, I mean coming back and finding your house vandalised and your long-gone daughter standing there pregnant by the vandal must be a bit of a shock. Sorry, Dad, perhaps I should have given you a bit of a warning.

**Michael** No, no, it's wonderful having you just – just – how did you get in?

**Wendy** I hung on to my key, the one thing I didn't let go of. And you hadn't changed the locks. In fact you don't seem to have changed anything very much, have you?

**Michael** Oh, you've been into the other rooms then, have you?

**Wendy** We just peeked here and there. So what's it like to be a grand-daddy, Dad? I expect you'll be pleased to help out the way that grand-daddies do.

**Michael** Well – yes, I will if I can. Of course I will.

**Wendy** Thank you. I could always count on your kindness, couldn't I, Dad?

**Michael** My kindness? Well – I hope so.

**Wendy** I remember one of your little lectures on kindness. Kith, kin, kindness in nature, remember?

**Michael** Yes.

**Wendy** And how it had turned itself into a dead word. No sense of responsibility. No tribal significance.

**Michael** Well, that's frequently the way with words, the important ones, they come away from their stems, drift about like – like petals, into the breeze of this conversation and that – decorative and useless – (*Falters away.*)

**Wendy** Where have you been?

**Michael** Mmm?

**Wendy** Just now, where have you come from?

**Michael** Oh, um, the Garrick. I lunch there most days – these days.

**Wendy** Ah. I thought you might have been up to the church.

**Michael** The church?

**Wendy** Yes, Mum's church, up the road.

**Michael** Oh, St Mark's, yes – no, no, I was at the Garrick.

**Wendy** She's there, though, isn't she?

**Michael** What? Oh, at St Mark's. No, no, I tried of course, but they ran out of room a long time ago – even for 'Friends'. I do walk up there, though, now and then. For the walk and the fresh air and of course –

**Wendy** Well, where is she then?

**Michael** Golders Green. It turned out to be the nearest, the most convenient.

**Wendy** And is that where Japes is too? Beside her?

**Michael** Yes. Well, no. One down as a matter of fact. The plot next to hers had already been taken. By someone called Tuffins. Joseph Tuffins. There was a misunderstanding with the undertakers. I asked for a space in between, meaning to reserve it for myself, but instead of leaving an empty space they left a full one. Full of Tuffins – Joseph Tuffins – died March 13 1984. If you're thinking of visiting I can let you have their numbers. The numbers of their graves. It can be very confusing at Golders Green.

**Wendy** Did you have a joint funeral then?

**Michael** Yes.

**Wendy** Is that usual?

**Michael** Not for me. But then it was a first, wasn't it? I wrote to you about it. I didn't know quite where to get hold of you so I sent it to the clinic – your last address, as known to me, hoping they'd send it on. Did it find you?

**Wendy** No. Well – it may have done but it wouldn't have mattered, I wasn't opening envelopes at that time. Particularly if they had familiar handwriting on them.

**Michael** Still, you seem to know all about it.

**Wendy** Dominic came across something in the newspapers – actually he ended up with quite a pile of clippings. He kept them for me so I'd have news from home when I got out of prison.

**Michael** Were you in for long?

**Wendy** A few months. Five actually.

**Michael** It was something to do with drugs, I assume.

**Wendy** No, fraud actually. I got hold of someone's credit card – although you're right really, it's what they classify as a drugs-related crime when they make up those lists of drugs-related crimes. Anyway, everything I bought fraudulently, I sold for drugs. Did they do it on purpose?

*Little pause.*

Well, some of the newspapers hinted at it. That they committed suicide or even one of them had murdered the other and then –

**Michael** That was nonsense, all nasty newspaper nonsense. It was a simple act of carelessness. They were both careless, you know, in their way – especially when they were – when they were – together. They simply fell asleep, not noticing that the place was filling with fumes from that damn French heating. (*Little pause.*) They were naked on top of the sheets which proves – according to the French – that it wouldn't have been suicide or – or – it's characteristic of suicides to present themselves respectably, *comme il faut* – and there were two empty bottles of Calvados by the bed so they'd also been drinking very heavily – but there was nothing unusual about that, no, no, it was those fumes, those French fumes, that did it.

**Wendy** Japes drinking? But the last time I saw him he'd stopped for ever.

**Michael** Alcoholics do that regularly, don't they? Anyway, he chose to move to Antibes, a legendary place for drunks. Graham Greene, you know.

**Wendy** And Mum, I know she drank a bit but are you saying she became an alcoholic?

**Michael** She was drinking quite a lot, and taking pills.

**Wendy** I don't suppose it was because of me, my disappearing like that.

**Michael** No, no, you mustn't blame yourself, Wendy, you didn't come into it. She had a hard time, you know, with the menopause. And then my attempt to get her back to her Bedbugs, you remember them, those delightful illustrations, it rather backfired, she became obsessed with my agent, my then agent, Weedon, of course you knew him, didn't you, from when you were a child, she embarked on a vendetta against him, threatening phone calls, visits to his office, waylaying him in restaurants, accusing him of ruining her life, it all became very messy, fortunately Weedon was very understanding, although he had to get a restraining order – and then there were the pills, she managed to get herself prescribed all sorts of pills, anti-depressants, pro-depressants, and she went back to smoking a lot of – of – (*Nods vaguely to Wendy.*) All this along with the drinking. I had to leave Weedon, needless to say. I've got a new agent. A young man. Australian. (*Gestures.*)

**Wendy** But you didn't think of getting her into a clinic?

**Michael** Of course I did, but she wouldn't consider it.

**Wendy** I wouldn't consider it either but I seemed to find myself in one anyway.

**Michael** It was different with you. You were still at an age.

**Wendy** Was she living with Japes?

**Michael** Living with him?

**Wendy** Had she left you to live with him?

**Michael** Well, not to my knowledge.

**Wendy** Not to your knowledge!

**Michael** Well, she came to my door. Upstairs. My study door. She knocked. She came in. She said she was going. She was wearing a coat and a – a – she was dressed for going.

**Wendy** For going to Japes?

**Michael** She didn't say where but then she didn't have to. I knew the content of the word, its full content. Every time she came to my door dressed for going and said she was going, I knew she was going to Antibes.

**Wendy** So you expected her back then?

**Michael** Well, of course I expected her back. Just as I always expected her to go, I always expected her to come back.

**Wendy** And you didn't mind?

**Michael** On the contrary. I was pleased she had something to look forward to. Both coming and going.

**Wendy** What about their wills?

**Michael** Their wills?

**Wendy** Yes. Was I left anything?

**Michael** Your mother and I made an elementary will just after we got married, leaving everything to each other. We never got around to anything more complicated.

**Wendy** And Japes?

**Michael** He hadn't left a will. As I'm the next of kin what he had came to me.

**Wendy** So you end up with the lot then? His and hers? What about Mum's personal stuff, did you keep any of it?

**Michael** I gave her clothes to Help the Aged. I didn't know what else to do with them.

**Wendy** Well – (*Little pause.*) What about her other things, her jewellery and that.

**Michael** I sold it.

**Wendy** (*after a pause*) Did you, Dad? Sold it?

**Michael** I sold all Japes's books and personal things too. For the same purpose. There was quite a lot of money. I gave it all to St Mark's. It seems to me that's what she would have wanted. And Japes would have wanted what she would have wanted. (*Pause.*) I had to do everything by instinct. Guesswork, anyway. After all, I had nobody to consult, did I? So all I had to go on were my instinct and my guesses. Perhaps I should have kept it for you, but then where were you, dropped out, vanished, in another country or dead too, for all I knew. And now you turn up, without a word when so much has happened, so much has – changed.

**Wendy** No, it's all right, Dad. I understand how you came to do it, I really do. You wouldn't have wanted me around anyway. Far better for you to keep it between the three of you, as usual – that's what I thought when I got the news that they were dead and how they'd done it – that it was just the three of you, my Dad, my uncle, and my Mum, as usual, I didn't come into it, my proper place was in jail or wherever while all this moving and burying of their bodies and selling of their goods was going on, I'd have been in the way again, and it's not the money or the goods I think I've got a right to at last, it's far more than that, Dad. It's the rest of my life really. Beginning with my past. But then the two are connected, at least that's what my shrink says, so give me back my past, Dad, would you, please?

**Michael** But surely you know your past better than anyone?

**Wendy** One of the things I'm coming to understand is that what one remembers about the past isn't necessarily the past.

**Michael** How interesting. I should have thought that's exactly what it is, the past. One's memories. What else can it be?

**Wendy** But one can keep adding to it, can't one, Dad? Suddenly remembering things one had never remembered before. That suddenly makes sense of the other things one remembered but never understood.

**Michael** How interesting. And of course you're quite right, Wendy. One can't set limits to what one remembers, what would be the use, our memories don't honour any limits we set them, they still come at you around corners you didn't even know were there, let alone that was a glimpse of some *once* waiting to reveal itself – some once that once was, once – in fact, just this morning I was sitting down to write – I do it from habit now, you know, not novels, never a novel again, no, I'm having a go at my memoirs instead, nothing too personal, really a sort of record of my time as I noticed it slipping towards me, around me, away from me – and those lines of Dr Johnson popped into my head, the lines on Dr Robert Levet, a Practiser in Physic – 'Condemn'd to hope's delusive mine, / As on we toil from day to day, / By sudden blasts or slow decline / Our social comforts drop away – I was quite, well, surprised, I hadn't thought of them for years, but then I suddenly remembered, right back *then*, when I was writing one of my early novels, and full of vigour for it, eagerness to get at it – I'd almost rush to my study, you probably remember me, when you were little, rushing to my study, and then I'd see them, you know, the drafts, you know, and just the sight of them – before I actually sat down to begin – the sight of them, on the desk, in the drawers, on the floor, the wastepaper basket stuffed with discards – that was my idea of progress, not a final draft, but a final discard – and a weariness of spirit, not of body or of concentration – no, a weariness of spirit was what it was, and I'd find myself chanting those lines to myself, 'Condemn'd to hope's delusive mine, / As on we toil from day to day' – they'd get into my head like a popular song, I'd even type to the rhythm – (*Simulates typing to the rhythm of the lines.*) And I remembered too how I'd sometimes despised Japes, that he never saw anything through, draft through draft to the final draft, and how I envied him too, that instead he could be out there, out *there* – (*gestures*) with Neets, talking and laughing and –

and with Neets, like a – a – proper – (*Laughs*.) That's the once, no, those are the onces that came at me this morning, as I sat down to my memoirs before I went up to the cemetery. And then when I came back here you were.

**Wendy** Another once from around some corner, that's me, Dad. And I was waiting around the corner, wasn't I? Those years ago while you were in there, drafting on draft after draft, and Mum was out there talking with Japes, and laughing, and fucking and being fucked by him.

**Michael** Yes, I suppose you had to say it, didn't you? It's the – the currency of your lot, isn't it?

**Wendy** My lot? (*Laughs*.)

**Michael** Even though you understood – you perfectly understood that I was trying in my way, the way of my lot, to tell you something. Wasn't that enough?

**Wendy** The proper words for it matter, Dad. To me anyway. To my lot.

**Michael** They certainly seem to, but what do they mean, do they mean anything different, anything more than my words – and it is your lot, not just you, but the lot of you – why I went to the theatre last week, for the first time since – since my one and only play – that long ago – it was called – called *Chokers*, no, no, it wasn't, *Chancers* it was called, *Chancers*, and it was about these people, people, *what* people, they weren't people, not as I understand the term, they were sex drives, over-articulating sex drives, so that when they said, as they did, 'I'm in love with you', not the slightest twitch of 'in love', the state of being in love crossed the stage, no, it turned out that all they meant is 'I want to fuck you' and when they had the impertinence, no, the *hubris* to utter those most terrifying of words, 'I love you', what did they mean by them? They meant 'I've fucked you and now I need to fuck you again, and possibly a few more times after that and I'll be jealous, insane with jealousy if anyone else fucks you', there are four of them, these chokers, chancers, or was it six, anyway, what does it matter how many there were as all they do is fuck each other and all they talk about is how they do it, and who they'd really rather be doing it with or to – and they don't cloak it in their language, they've no use for language as a way of deceiving or purifying once they've made their two declarations, 'I'm in love with you', 'I love you', they're off into their true vocabulary, of cocks and cunts and fuck fuck fucks, no words that even hint at inner lives, no friendships except as opportunities for sexual competition and betrayal, no interests or passions or feelings, as if the man were the cock, the cock the man, the woman the cunt, the cunt the woman, and the only purpose in life to ram cock into cunt, jam cunt over cock, turn and turn about except when they jump the queue and ram and jam when it's not their turn, that's the play, the whole play, and you know – you know the worst thing – the worst thing is that they speak grammatically. They construct sentences. Construct them! And with some elegance. Why? Tell me why? (*Little pause.*) Actually, I know why. So that the verbs and nouns stick out – in your face. In your face. That's the phrase, isn't it? That's the phrase! In your face!

*There is a pause. Michael pours himself another drink.*

Well, good heavens, I didn't mean – I didn't mean – just an evening at the theatre, after all. Probably quite irrelevant. Can't think how I got into it. Still, if you get a chance to see it, this *Chokers – Chancers* – I'd be interested to hear your view. (*Drinks, hand shaking.*)

**Wendy** Thanks, Dad, but after that I feel as if I don't have to see it. Funny though that you'd use the play and all those words, cocks and cunts and jamming and ramming as a way of not talking about Mum and Japes, and what they did. Because that's what they did, Dad, isn't it, and those are the bits of themselves they did it with, aren't they?

**Michael** Your mother and my brother were frequently in love with each other. They loved each other always.

**Wendy** (*after a pause, laughs*) Oh. Well, that's all right then. Put that way.

**Michael** That way conveys it as accurately as I can.

**Wendy** And you knew. Always knew that they loved each other and were frequently – (*gestures*) with each other.

**Michael** I understood it, now and then.

**Wendy** And you didn't mind?

**Michael** Now and then.

**Wendy** Well, what about now, as opposed to now and then? Eh, Dad? What do you feel now? When you go up to visit their graves.

**Michael** A sense of completeness. It's run its course, the story. It's over. (*Little pause.*) I talk to them.

**Wendy** As a couple? Or individually? And what about?

*There is a pause.*

Oh, sorry, Dad. I shouldn't pry. It's really rather sacred, isn't it? But would you mind telling me so that this one – (*pats womb*) can know which one's the grandfather and which one's the great-uncle. There are rights here somewhere, Dad, aren't there? Probably legal ones, too.

**Michael** I don't know. None of us ever knew for sure.

**Wendy** And you don't care, do you? What does that sort of thing matter to you lot from the sodding sixties? With your love, love, love and your freedom and flowers and all belonging to each other so what does it matter where the children came from or who they belong to, as long as they're born in love, love, love and the joys of sex, well, it matters to me, Dad, I don't give a fuck about your lot or my lot, but I give a fuck about this one, and our life together, I want to know whether you're my uncle or my father, Dad.

**Michael** I was your father, Wendy, in every important respect. In every practical respect. My name was on your birth certificate. And on every cheque that was needed for your provision, and for every institution you attended, from your nursery school to your drugs clinic. Japes was only there for you as an uncle, to give you presents and treats.

**Wendy** He was also my best friend. I used to think of him as the only friend I ever had.

**Michael** Then he's unlikely to be your father, isn't he? Why should you want him to be?

**Wendy** I'm not saying I want him to be. I'm saying I intend to find out.

**Michael** I'm sorry, but it seems to me that you'll just have to trust to your instincts. If you want Japes to be your natural father, then have him as such. I'm perfectly happy to remain just your legal one.

**Wendy** (*laughs, shakes her head*) I'm a long way from the nursery school and the clinic now, Dad. I know what's going on around me, things like DNA, for instance. I'm sure you know all about it too, Dad.

*Pause.*

**Michael** Japes was what he was to you, I was what I was. You have your experience of us. What difference will the fact make?

**Wendy** What difference will it make to you? What are you frightened of? If it's just a fact, nothing more.

**Michael** I was the father, to all of you. That was my place. That was what I did. Japes was young and feckless, lost without me. Neets was always the child, I parented her. They played together, as children do. I was the father. That's how it's come to seem to me. That's how it's going to remain, for the rest of my life.

**Wendy** It's too late, Dad. We're here, we're the children now, and we want our dues.

**Michael** Your dues! (*Laughs.*) Well, they won't include any sordid DNA test, believe me, young woman. I'm not having Japes's body grubbed out of the earth so that you can have your dues. What sort of daughter are you?

**Wendy** That's what we're going to find out. But don't worry about grubbing Japes up, we don't have to do the test on him, we just do it on you and me. And if you're not the one, then Japes is. Unless there's someone else entirely that we don't know about.

**Michael** Absolutely not, absolutely not, absolutely not, no.

**Wendy** Then I'll get a court order. And I can, you know. I've been into it all.

**Michael** Really? And on what grounds can a court compel me? I'm not trying to deny that I'm your father. I'm admitting it. Insisting on it.

**Wendy** Insisting on it won't make you it, Dad. But that's where our dues come in, you see. Because if Japes is my father, you're not his next of kin, are you, Dad? I am. And everything you got from him belongs to me. Including half this house.

**Michael** So that's what you want, is it, half the house? When I've already offered to let you have anything you need – you could have just asked for half the value of the house, if you think you need that much, I'd have found it for you.

**Wendy** I don't want half the value, or half the house, I want the whole house, Dad. We'll need the whole of it. This is the only home I've known, and I never got to live in it. Now I want to start life in it again. Our home, I want it to be.

**Michael** And you think I'll just give it over to you – the house that belonged to our parents – our childhood home. The only home *I've* ever known.

**Wendy** One of the things that's coming around the corner out of the past, Dad, one of the onces, is the 'once upon a time' once. The bedtime story once. It's not clear to me yet, we're working through it, my shrink and I, all we've found out is that there was more than just neglect when I was a child, there was trauma and abuse. There was a bogeyman. One of you was my bedtime bogeyman.

**Michael** And will you have me DNA tested for that?

**Wendy** My shrink says the way we're working, we'll get to you in the end.

**Michael** To me.

**Wendy** To one of you.

**Michael** I see. And what did this bogeyman get up to, may I ask?

**Wendy** Well, as he was a bedtime bogeyman, Dad, it's obvious the kind of thing he got up to, isn't it?

**Michael** On the occasions when I put you to bed I read you a Janet and John story. Surely you remember Janet and John? 'This is Janet. This is John. Hello, Janet. Hello, John.' There was one about wellington boots. It was raining but John wouldn't wear his wellington boots. His mother said, 'Wear your wellington boots, John, or your feet will get wet.' His sister Janet said, 'Wear your wellington boots, John, or your feet will get wet.' But John wouldn't wear his wellington boots. 'Silly old wellington boots,' said John. 'I shan't wear them!' Then they all went out into the rain, and soon John said, 'Oh, my feet are wet!' 'I told you so,' said his mother. 'I told you so,' said his sister Janet. So they went home and John put on his wellington boots. Then they went back out into the rain. 'Good old wellington boots,' said John, as he jumped up and down in the puddles. 'Good old wellington boots!'

**Wendy** (*shakes her head*) Pity I didn't remember it though, years ago. It might have stopped me from getting my feet wet, eh, Dad? No, all I can remember is the bogeyman, his voice saying, 'I am your bogeyman' and chasing me around and around, from corner to corner, and when I got past him and hid in bed he'd come up the stairs, clumping up, one foot clumping after another foot clumping, with gaps in between, long gaps, short gaps, saying over and over again, 'I am your bogeyman, the bogeyman has got you', and I'd be quivering with terror and laughter, both, I'd feel him above me, and I'd feel him bend down, he'd wait. And then – wait. And then he'd whisper 'Your bogeyman has got you' and he'd rip the covers right off, and scoop me in his arms. (*Little pause.*) And then when he'd finished with me he'd tuck me in and kiss me on the forehead, and I'd lie there until Mum came in. She'd sit on my bed and sing to me 'Golden slumbers seal your eyes' – (*sings first few lines*) and kiss me on the forehead and go off to bed, and then I'd hear your voices coming up, the two of you, laughing and talking and arguing and after a time I couldn't tell you apart, which was speaking and which was laughing and which was shouting, sometimes you'd both be doing it together as if there was just one of you doing it all by yourself, like a medieval devil. So perhaps that was it, really. You were both my bogeyman, turn and turn about.

**Michael** It's all a lie – a disgusting lie – and you know it.

**Wendy** Well, I don't think that's what my shrink thinks.

*There is a little pause.*

**Michael** There isn't even a shrink, is there? You're just making him up.

**Wendy** I'm not making her up. I just haven't got around to choosing her yet. But it won't be a problem, there'll be hundreds and hundreds of them out there just waiting for the chance. And then we can leave it to the court to sort out, though I expect when it comes to it, if Japes turns out to be my real Dad, I'd like you to be the bogeyman, Dad, as I'll already have got everything he's got, so it's best that you're up for the bogeyman damages. I mean, you're the survivor, aren't you, and after what happened to Mum and Japes there'll be a very, very big story there for you to talk to the newspapers about. And I'll have my own story to sell, with pictures of you ducking about all over their graveyard and oh, that Garrick Club of yours. They'll probably expel you, poor Dad.

*There is a pause.*

**Michael** (*almost to himself*) It's not been like this. Not for other generations. Not in my understanding. We didn't start the world, our lot. We didn't come out of nowhere and just – just start you lot off. We were begot, just like you. We were just three people, struggling with ourselves with each other, in our time. Don't you understand?

*Sound of mobile telephone ringing in Wendy's pocket. Michael jumps.*
  *Wendy takes mobile telephone out of her pocket, puts it to her ear.*

**Wendy** Hi.

*Little pause. Hands mobile to Michael.*

It's Dominic. He wants to apologise.

**Michael** (*puts mobile uncertainly to his ear*) Hello? Oh no, not at all, these things happen, I – no, no, really, there's no need – I see, well, right – that's very kind of you – oh, right –

*Hands mobile back to Wendy.*

**Wendy** (*taking mobile*) Here I am. (*Little pause.*) We'll talk about it later – (*Little pause.*) All right, you can come over on condition.

*Michael moves towards study.*

But no promises, I don't want any more of your promises, from now on you live by the rules or we do without you, Dommy, it's as simple as that –

*Lights beginning to fade.*
  *Michael exits.*

Yes, of course I know you love us (*Patting stomach.*)

And of course we love you – but that's the easy part, anyone can do that, what we've got to do is make it hold together, you see, so that if anything goes wrong, at least we'll know – at least we'll know that we tried, won't we?

*Lights.*

*Curtain.*

# LITTLE NELL

For Simon Callow

Inspired by Claire Tomalin's book
*The Invisible Woman:*
*The Story of Nelly Ternan and Charles Dickens*

# Introduction

Decades ago, when Peter Hall was running the National Theatre, he said he'd like to commission a play from me; had I anything in mind? I said yes, I'd longed for years to write a sort of psychological and theatrical epic about Dickens, but had kept postponing it because even if I managed to write it I couldn't conceive of its ever being produced: it would require an enormous cast and complicated sets, and would be very expensive. He said that the National would be able to provide the cast and sets, and encouraged me to take a crack at it, adding that he might direct it himself.

A few days after this conversation, when I had a long gap between seminars – in those days I was a lecturer in English Literature at Queen Mary College – I sat down at my desk, opened a pad and began to write. That night, at home, I typed up what I'd written, and then went on from there, and on, late into the night. Over the next few weeks, writing in pencil during the day and typing in the evenings, I went hard at it, and made great progress, it seemed to me, almost as if the story had been waiting for me, fully formed – all I had to do was to keep doing what I was doing and I would be there in no time, or at least have a first draft from which I could then proceed at leisure.

I'd got to just before the end of the first act when a cheque arrived from my agent for what was then quite a substantial sum of money. It was the advance from the National Theatre for a play on the life of Charles Dickens, to be delivered in a year's time – the precise date was specified – for production on the Olivier stage. I had never before in my writing life accepted money for work not yet done – all my stage plays had been uncommissioned, and when offered a commission for a television play I always asked for a couple of weeks 'to think about it', then immediately set about writing it, and only after I'd finished it would I accept the commission to begin it. I'd like to think that this behaviour was from principle, a high-minded belief that inspiration would be poisoned by commerce, but really it was from a fear that I couldn't really cut it in a world of advances and deadlines, as real playwrights do.

The fact is that I have always had difficulty in thinking of myself as a playwright. In the space on official forms where you have to put down your occupation I kept on putting down 'Lecturer' long after I'd given up lecturing, and now that that's visibly implausible and I'm afraid that I'd be asked where, and to whom, I put 'Writer' in a loose sort of way, with a little gap between the 'i' and the 't' and a sort of squiggle in it. Wri~ter.

I can't write when I'm afraid to write. If I force myself I become self-conscious, and then I feel bogus, and then I feel ashamed. Not writing, on the other hand, makes me feel that I'm being stolen from, although I don't know by whom, unless it's by time, of course. Or TIME . . .

I decided to give up on the play for a while, get stuck into something else.

Stuck into what? My sense of failure with Dickens lapped into whatever I was writing, as if I were doomed to keep on repeating the experience, though in increasingly minor keys – failed attempts to convert my old stage plays into television films, for instance, or to convert my old television films into stage plays. Furthermore, I blamed Dickens for my inability to write a play about him, coming close to hating him, especially when he was the subject of a seminar. When I read out paragraphs from his novels to illustrate his vitality, his range of tone, his gymnastic jumps from melodrama to tomfoolery and back again, the sheer inimitability of the Inimitable, so forth, so forth, my voice would become feeble and whiny, running against the great-hearted spirit of his prose in spiteful counterpoint – I would have either to falter away into humdrum commentary, deploying the routine Cambridge–Leavis terminology – 'great creative genius', 'completely and fully and richly on the side of life', etc. – or would close the book with theatrical abruptness, and go into reverential dumb-show, raising my hands to the surrender position, working my rather bushy eyebrows, pursing and unpursing my lips like a blowfish. I wonder what effect these displays had on my students all those years ago. Did I succeed in putting them off Dickens for life, as was possibly my unconscious aim?

Realising that both my careers were in rapid decline, I did the only thing I could think to do, which was to return the advance. It was a very significant moment in my life, although I'm sure it was a completely insignificant one in the life of the National Theatre – in fact I doubt if anyone except the accountants noticed, though I remember Peter Hall asking me a month or so later, when I bumped into him at something or other, how the Dickens play was coming on, and having the politeness to appear disappointed when I explained that what with my teaching commitments, plus all the College administration, on top of which my young children, etc., I'd been compelled to give it up for a while.

Now and then, when I thought it wasn't looking, I had a few stabs at tackling it – oddly aggressive imagery now I look at the words, 'stabbing' and 'tackling' to describe an attempt to write a play, but possibly accurate in that I felt sure that I would only manage it by violence and deceit, pretending, when I sat down to the typewriter, that I had hundreds of alternative projects, then suddenly let fly, batter, batter, batter at the typewriter: 'Come out, you bastard! Come out and fight!' sort of stuff.

About thirty-five years later, or about five years ago, to look at it from the other way around, Simon Callow asked me over one of our regular dinners whether I knew *The Invisible Woman*, Claire Tomalin's book about Dickens's long affair with the actress Ellen Ternan. I said yes, I'd read it and admired it when it first came out: it was such an elegant and eloquent account of the sapping logistics of adultery that it had made me realise how deeply he must have cared for her. It had been far more than an affair, it had been a marriage, really, a secret marriage. Yes, Simon said, and potentially very dramatic; he'd been trying to set up a television film based on it but with no luck so far. Would I be interested in doing a script?

I now loved Dickens once more, but the thought of tangling with him as a writer rather than just as a reader made me nervous – I feared that I might turn an old scar into a fresh wound. On the other hand, *that* had been a play, *this* would be a film; a film would be less personal, less impertinent, there would be a director, a script editor, a cameraman and no doubt a number of creatively inputting producers, thus a shared responsibility, dispersed blame etc. So I reread *The Invisible Woman*, parts of it twice, then put it back on the shelf, thinking, well, yes, and on the other hand, no. One night, very late, I took out a pad and a pencil and talked to myself in a hip-hop sort of fashion, conversational notes, really (see below) first about Dickens, and then about Dickens and Ellen Ternan, about them separately and about them together. The next morning I phoned Claire Tomalin, and we arranged to have lunch.

It was quite a long, jolly lunch, at the end of which it was agreed that I'd have a go at writing the film, and if by any chance a believable film producer came along with an offer of money but with a writer of his own she was to let me know, and if I felt I was making no progress, I would stand down, no hard feelings.

I've written lots and lots of films for television, lots and lots of them, and some have even won awards, but when I tried to write a film about Dickens and Ellen Ternan it was as if I'd had no previous experience, almost as if I'd never seen a film, had no idea of how a film flowed from one scene to another, how to see faces in close-up, where the camera should be – yes, that was the nub of it. I could imagine the characters and what they said to each other, but I couldn't imagine the camera. All my scenes took place in rooms with people sitting in a fixed relation to each other, occasionally getting up to walk closer or further away. I spent a year working against the grain – making up snappy new scenes, shortening and eliding old ones, cross-cutting from Ext. Garden, Gad's Hill to Int. Dressing Room, Theatre Royal – until one morning, as the yellow London dawn was breaking, I gave in to my dark and dangerous desire, and sent Claire Tomalin an email saying that actually I wasn't writing a film, I was writing a play. I hoped that was OK by her. She sent me a slightly perplexed email back, saying that it was, she supposed.

It took many months to get a first draft that I dared show anyone. Although I couldn't judge it myself, I had the feeling that it was alive but shapeless, which is better than shapely but dead – the disadvantage being that you can't bury it, *requiescat*, and move on. In fact, a living piece of work is rather like a child in that it imposes obligations, demands attention, allows you to dream, and promises you nothing. I sent it to Simon Callow, who read it and agreed that there was a pulse. I did some more work, and sent it to Claire Tomalin, who thought so too. I did some more work and sent it to Peter Hall, who gave me further hope. Then I did some more work and then I did some more work and then I did some more work until I couldn't think of any more work to do, and then I did some more work.

Bernard Shaw said that writing a play was either easy or impossible. My play wasn't impossible, I'd been at it too long and spent too much of my best blood on it to allow it to be impossible. I reverted to my long-ago tactic of stealing up on it when it wasn't looking, and then batter, batter, batter, 'Come out you bastard, and fight!' etc., but of course I was nearly forty years on, and overweight and short of breath. I decided to give up violence in favour of cheating. I put what I thought to be my best draft on the computer, and then extracted from it drafts galore, sometimes attaching the top half of one draft to the bottom half of another, or a quarter on top of three-quarters, interminable desperate jugglings accomplished by jabbing the copy, cut, paste buttons – synthesised writing, I suppose you could call it. This is the great thing about the computer, for someone of my generation with my sort of temperament, that it gives you the illusion of work – you go to bed at five in the morning with squinty eyes, a befuddled head, and an unnatural but satisfied sense of having cut, copied and pasted yourself to oblivion, from which you will return to copy, paste and cut – what can this be but hard and complicated work? Even if you have the odd moment in which you suspect you've turned yourself into a technological Casaubon.

Eventually I bullied myself back to the typewriter, knowing that at least I would think before I wrote, and with luck, while I was writing. When the typewriter failed I went back to pads and pencil, and when they didn't help I had nothing left to try, really, except perhaps a quill pen on parchment, followed by flint on stone walls, followed by fingernails into flesh finally enraged beyond endurance by the sheer frustration of being me – a bad workman run out of tools to blame.

## LITTLE NELL

In desperation, really, I sent one of the last drafts to the usual trio – Callow, Hall and Tomalin – who replied in their usual encouraging terms, though I had a suspicion that they didn't see in it much difference from the one I'd sent them over a year before. My consolation was that they didn't say that they'd found it any worse, thus sustaining my belief that I hadn't yet beaten or strangled it to death. Nevertheless, I fell into a depressed sloth, and took to wondering why I hadn't taken up a different profession – followed my father, say, into pathology, and then remembered that he, too, was prone to bouts of depression, from spending too much time in the company of corpses, and of women not his wife. But then he was a full Scot, I only half a Scot, so for him the completely dead with lots of life on the side, for me a half-life – those sorts of thoughts, blaming and self-pitying in equal measure, in keeping with my idea of the spirit of the age.

So I was on my knees, my least favourite writing position, when through the ether came an email inviting me to write a play for BBC Radio 4. It was from Jane Morgan, whom I've known and liked for years, and who is a joy to work with, and who knows about cricket, even checking the county scores, as I do sometimes. Furthermore this would be our fifth play together. Oh, how I would love, I said, absolutely love, but alas! I had nothing in me, and on my computer and in a drawer only a large number of nearly finished stage plays about Charles Dickens and his mistress Ellen Ternan. Oh yes, she said, she knew Claire Tomalin's book, could I think of making a radio version? I sent her what I currently thought to be the three best drafts, and we arranged to meet to go through them in detail. We spent long afternoons on the radio play, I spent long nights on the stage play, and lo! in what seemed like no time we had the radio play, and I had three more drafts of the stage play, possibly four – a few hours on the computer could generate another six, ten before dawn, I could see myself back to where I had been, and from there only on and on until kindly Death – but before either prolixity or paralysis could set in I cast the three drafts aside, switched off the computer, and without once looking back, wrote what I knew to be the first and final draft of *Little Nell*.

So to adjust Bernard Shaw's dictum, one could say that writing a play is impossible until it's written. Of course, as Bernard Shaw also said, whether it's any good is a different matter.

## THE NOTES

Of all great writers he's the one who makes the most palpable claim on our emotions, with so many ways of asserting his claim, so many voices and tones, savage, gentle, intimate, melodramatic, boisterous, lyrical, pastoral, comical, historical, hysterical, lachrymose, embarrassing – he never leaves you alone, in every paragraph he's there in front of you, with his hands on your shoulders, or beside you with his arm hooked under yours – and yet you haven't really the slightest idea, not really, of who he is –

One sees the faces, the expressions, the gestures of the characters, but one never, with the exception of Pip and the young David Copperfield, lives inside them, as one does with Tolstoy's, or shares the author's understanding of them, as one does with Jane Austen – for all the vividness and detail, they are actually mysterious. Where could they come from? Possibly an alternative universe, you can sometimes glimpse it, a surreal tavern, say, with inward-sloping walls and a dipping roof, at one askew table Squeers hobnobbing with Bounderby and Bagstock, at another Bucket consulting with Jaggers and Carker. Even in the great narrative passages, the openings of *Bleak House*, *Little Dorrit*, *Hard Times*, the descriptions of the river in *Our Mutual Friend*, you hear an impersonation of a narrator –

I'm looking at the picture of him in my study, not a very good one, it must be said, a watercolour done from a photograph, but it's recognisably him, at the end of his life – tired the face is, lined, much older than his years, rather posed and intense, something a bit fraudulent in the whole effect – a face without a childhood might be a way of putting it, no sense at all of evolution in it, no whiff of the blacking factory. And when you read contemporary accounts of him, of his brightness, his quickness, his merriment, so mercurial, so whimsical, so affectionate, on and on in such terms, you're left with the feeling that he's been encountered in a book, though one not written by himself – he would have made himself more particular, given us the necessary distortions to remember him by. Even people who disliked him somehow failed to see him – they write of his vulgarity, his dandyism and charlatanism, all the externals, and then conclude in a flurry of judgements and abstractions – although come to think of it that's not true of John Forster. His biography makes him seem real even though it's full of lies and omissions, and his Dickens, who has a long and eventually unhappy marriage and, of course, no extramarital sex life, still has a powerful sexuality – but then Forster knew him as only a heterosexual intimate, alert to competitive male impulses, could know him – and Forster had a touch of genius himself.

At one point in his life, towards the ghastly end of it, I suppose, Tolstoy had no time for fiction – fiction was lies, he thought. Nevertheless he allowed *David Copperfield* on his bedroom bookshelf because it was a true book about childhood – and certainly the first half of it is the greatest novel ever written about childhood – and *Great Expectations*, probably the greatest about growing up, and I think, actually, the greatest novel in the English language. Or is *Little Dorrit* the greatest novel in the English language, or might it be *Bleak House* – and so suddenly one is gaping at the enormity of the achievement. How was it possible that a man could sustain a creative life at such a pitch? Balzac I suppose comes closest, I love Balzac and read him now more often than I read Dickens, but really not even *Cousin Bette*, say, put beside *Little Dorrit*, say – so when you're fretting away about who he was, you should keep in mind that ultimately who he was was the man who wrote that and that and that – ungraspable by a man like you, who has written only this and this and this – so perhaps the mystery is just the mystery of his overwhelming genius, your bafflement at being overwhelmed. On the other hand, just like a man like me, he had to live his other life, the life of daily needs in a daily self.

His daily needs in a daily self. How categorise the episodes of sexual lunacy during his twenties and thirties? His grotesque idealising of his dead sister-in-law, for instance, his dancing of the pretty Miss X into the sea at midnight, his creepy mesmeric experiments on young Mrs Y in Italy? Were these just expressions of his superabundant creativity, the mighty life-force spurting down eccentric subsidiary channels? Well, there were also the men-only trips to Paris with Wilkie Collins et al. – lots of fun there, I expect, but nothing for the daily needs, daily self –

Lots of critics claim that he couldn't do women – in my view he could do women, terrifying women at least, better than most – Miss Wade, Mrs Gamp, Mrs Joe, Mrs Skewton, Mrs Merdle, on and on the list – the ghastly joke about them is their sex – their ghastly flashes of sexuality –

just think of Miss Mowcher, the 'id' as a garrulous dwarf. Think too of David's crush on Steerforth, yes, but David's is a heterosexual's crush. In my view.

Sexual lunacy is probably not the right phrase, but I can't think what the right phrase is. Let's just say that his life from early puberty on was a frantic struggle not to 'come out' as a needy, predatory and mostly desperate heterosexual.

How could he not be desperate? All he had for his daily needs and daily self was poor old daily needy Catherine, whose obedient touch he must have come to hate, as he hated her clumsiness, and who gave him all those children to provide for.

He was possibly the most famous man in the world, and certainly the world's most famous family man. To have been caught betraying his wife would have turned him into a sort of Pecksniff of adultery.

So he stuck out his marriage from his early twenties to his mid-forties, all the while tortured by longings that he didn't dare satisfy – at least until at forty-five he seduced Ellen Ternan, an eighteen-year-old actress, who gave him, I hope, sexual freedom at last – though 'I hated his touch,' she is said to have said after his death, when she had become Mrs Robinson, the headmaster's wife.

He should have died in Ellen Ternan's arms, but didn't quite – so she had to smuggle his dying and paralysed body from their little home in Slough to his family home in Gad's Hill, then scuttle off while Georgina, mistress of his household and sister of his dismissed wife, set about organising a respectable death and a respectable version of it – how he'd worked all day in his study in the garden, gone out to post some letters, come back for dinner, begun to stumble, jumbled his speech, fallen sideways – actually I forget the details but they were along those lines, medically appropriate and socially becoming. Ellen was allowed a brief visit, either just before or just after the end, in her role as favourite goddaughter, I can't remember whether she was also allowed to the funeral in Westminster Abbey, I have an idea that she watched from behind a pillar – yes, of course, because that's where she was seen by the vicar, Benham, to whom she later confessed –

And then, well, she had to start life thirteen years behind, so to speak, thirteen unaccountable years to account for, thirteen years of domestic intimacy interrupted by regular and irregular separations, thirteen years of waitings, welcomings, partings. She saw him decline from an exuberant middle-aged man at the height of his powers to the morphine-and-brandy-dependent, gout-and-piles-ridden wreck of the last months while she went from a young woman in her prime to, by the reckonings of those days, a woman well past it. So when one says, 'The affair lasted thirteen years, just think!' one is in fact saying more than one can bear to think, when one tries to think some sort of content into just a few days of the thirteen years.

Let's try to think of them at the halfway stage, six and a half years into their life together, she in their front room, perhaps playing the piano, waiting for his footstep. Did her heart rise or did it sink when she heard it? And his heart, as he approached the door?

The evenings stretching before them possibly tender, domestic and charming as they sang duets. Or interminable and boring, a bit like 'A Game of Chess' in *The Waste Land*, but punctuated with sex. She hated his touch, don't forget. Or so she said.

# LITTLE NELL

He had ten children, wasn't it, by Catherine, if you include the two she lost, and in her subsequent marriage to the headmaster George Robinson she had two, the first when she was nearly forty – so in the course of thirteen years how did it happen that this productive man and this fertile woman failed to produce a child? Of course with hoops and crinoline and all that stuff it would have been hard to tell – And there were her long mysterious spells in France where he visited her occasionally.

Perhaps he dropped the babies off at the nearest orphanage, like Rousseau – much nicer to think that they practised contraception. What sort of contraception could be practised in the 1860s? I must look it up, or ask around.

So after his death, some years as Miss Ternan again, then marriage to George Robinson, and there she was, respectable Mrs Robinson, the headmaster's wife.

Mrs Robinson. Now there's a title.

She could account to her devoted husband George for some – say ten – of the missing years by simply knocking them off her age, the other three by lies about illness, convalescence in Italy, and so forth. Did George sense, in a befuddled male sort of way, that he had a wife not completely his? Something certainly happened that caused him to dwindle from cheerful, robust, responsible into withdrawn, depressed and useless – useless as a breadwinner, possibly useless as a husband and a father – useless at least for the son, Geoffrey –

The son, Geoffrey, had speech difficulties, was it a lisp?

Geoffrey made a career in the army to please his mother, like Coriolanus, fought in the First War, and then retired from the army to run a secondhand bookshop in Slough, where, unknown to him, his mother had lived in sin with one of the world's most famous men. Quite a coincidence, unless he was directed there by some perverse homing instinct. Apart from a mildly unhappy marriage, he led a quiet life in his bookshop in Slough until, thanks to Benham the vicar, he came across gossipy bits in newspapers about Charles Dickens (now fifty years dead) and a young actress called Ellen Ternan (now nine years dead). He must have been first bewildered and then angry – it was preposterous, impossible, salacious, nonsensical, etc. – nothing could have been more innocent than his mother's childhood love of her famous godfather, she'd talked about it often to him, with joy and movingly, she'd read the novels aloud at bedtime. Besides, his mother had never been an actress, she would have mentioned it to him.

Geoffrey obtained an interview with Dickens's son Henry, a distinguished lawyer some thirty years older than himself. All we know about the interview is that after it Geoffrey cleared all the works of Dickens out of his house, divorced his wife, gave up the bookshop, then became his mother's son and went into acting.

He didn't make much of a fist of it, from the little that's known, but there are records of appearances in minor parts in theatres around the Tottenham Court Road area.

**Little Nell** was first broadcast on BBC Radio 4 on 16 December 2006, produced by Pier Productions, with the following cast:

**Sir Henry Dickens** Philip Voss
**Geoffrey Robinson** Crispin Redman
**Ellen Ternan** Monica Dolan
**Charles Dickens** Michael Pennington
**Jane** Maria Miles
**George Wharton Robinson** Nicholas Boulton
**Rev Benham** Nicholas Le Prevost

*Directed by* Jane Morgan
*Technical Presentation* Roy Fraser
*Production Manager* Jane Ellison
*Pianist* Charlotte Brennand


**Little Nell** was first presented for the stage at the Theatre Royal, Bath, in July 2007 with the following cast:

**Sir Henry Dickens** Barry Stanton
**Geoffrey Robinson** Tim Pigott-Smith
**Charles Dickens** Michael Pennington
**Nelly Ternan** Loo Brealey
**Jane** Cressida Trew
**George Wharton Robinson** Edward Bennett
**Rev. Benham** Tony Haygarth

*Director* Peter Hall
*Designer* Simon Higlett
*Lighting* Peter Mumford
*Costume* Christopher Woods
*Sound* Gregory Clarke
*Music* Mick Sands

# Characters

**Henry**
**Geoffrey**
**Dick**
**Nelly**
**Jane**
**George**
**Benham**
**Aldersley**
**Clara**
**Crayford**

*Lights up on the stage of the Free Trade Hall, Manchester. Saturday 22 August 1857.*

*The last moments of the play* The Frozen Deep *by Wilkie Collins.*

*The scene takes place at the back of a cave in the Arctic regions. Wardour, played by Charles Dickens (Dick), is stretched out centre stage. He is dying. Aldersley is lying half propped up, some distance from him. Clara is kneeling by him. Crayford is standing to the side, watching. Lucy, played by Ellen Ternan (Nelly) is standing near Wardour.*

**Crayford** Wardour, look at me! Look at your old friend!

**Wardour** (*vacantly*) My friend? Yes, yes, yes – He looks kindly at me – he looks like a friend. My eyes are dim, friend – my mind is dull – I have lost all memories but the memory of her. Dead thoughts – all dead thoughts but that one! And yet, he looks kindly? Why has his face gone down with the wreck of all the rest? Hark ye, friend? Never let Frank know it! There was a time when the fiend within me hungered for his life.

**Crayford** Hush! Hush!

**Wardour** I took him away alone – away with me over the waste of snow – he on one side, and the tempter on the other, and I between them, marching, till the night fell and the campfire was all aflame. If you can't kill him, leave him, leave him when he sleeps, the tempter whispered me – leave him when he sleeps! I set him his place to sleep in apart; but he crept between the Devil and me, and nestled his head on my breast, and slept here. Leave him! Leave him! the voice whispered. Lay him down in the snow and leave him! Love him, the lad's voice answered, moaning and murmuring, here, in his sleep – Love him, Clara, for helping me! Love him for my sake! I heard the night wind come up in the silence from the great deep. It bore past me the groanings of the icebergs at sea, floating, floating past! – And the wicked voice floated away with it – away, away, away for ever! Love him, Clara, for helping me! No wind could float that away! Love him, Clara – (*His voice dies away and his head sinks.*)

**Aldersley** Help me up! I must go to him! Clara, come with me. (*Approaches Wardour.*) Wardour! Oh, help Wardour! Clara, speak to him!

**Clara** Richard!

*No answer.*

**Aldersley** Richard!

**Wardour** Ah, poor Frank! I didn't forget you, Frank, when I came here to beg. I remembered you, lying down outside in the shadow of the rocks. I saved your share of food and drink. Too weak to get at it now! A little rest, Frank! I shall soon be strong enough to carry you down to the ship!

**Aldersley** Get something to strengthen him, for God's sake! Oh, men! Men! I should never have been here but for him! He has given all his strength to my weakness; and now, see how strong I am, and how weak he is! Clara! I held by his arm all over the ice and snow. His hand dragged me from the drowning men when we were wrecked. He kept watch when I was senseless in the open boat. Speak to him, Clara – speak to him again!

**Clara** Richard, dear Richard, look at your old playmate! Have you forgotten me?

*Music: 'River, River', merging at 'Kiss me before I die!' into 'Those Evening Bells', which lasts until the curtain has fallen.*

**Wardour** Forgotten you?

*He lays his hand on Aldersley's head.*

Should I have been strong enough to save him, if I could have forgotten you? Stay! Someone was here and spoke to me just now. Ah! Crayford! I recollect now. (*Embracing him.*) Dear Crayford! Come nearer! My mind clears, but my eyes grow dim. You will remember me kindly for Frank's sake? Poor Frank! Why does he hide his face? Is he crying? Nearer, Clara – I want to look my last at you! My sister, Clara! (*She falls on him, sobbing.*) Kiss me, sister, kiss me before I die!

*Lucy comes forward, kneels beside Clara, stroking her head.*

*Lights slightly down to create a tableau: Lucy, Clara and the dying Wardour the main grouping.*


*Lights up on the office of Sir Henry Dickens, 1922.*

**Henry** (*scanning a letter*) Hah! We'll see. (*He pushes down button on intercom.*) You can send Mr Robinson in now. (*Puts the letter in front of him.*)

*There is a knock on the door.*

Come in. (*He stands.*)

*Geoffrey enters. He is in his forties, stiff and shy, with a military bearing, He has an occasional stutter, not always specified in the text.*

Sorry to have kept you waiting, Mr Robinson. I asked my secretary to give you a cup of tea – did he do that?

**Geoffrey** Yes. Th—

**Henry** Well, how can I help you, sir?

*Geoffrey has a little trouble speaking.*

In your letter – (*Picking up letter.*) – you mention a legacy.

**Geoffrey** It's a confidential matter.

**Henry** Of course it is. And I am a lawyer. That's why you're here.

**Geoffrey** A family matter.

**Henry** Yes, sir. It's likely to be. Most matters discussed in this office are family matters.

**Geoffrey** (*after a pause, apologetically*) I meant your family. We are connected, you see. In a sense connected.

**Henry** 'In a sense connected.' (*Nods.*) In other words, you are a claimant. I had the feeling the instant I saw the envelope. It had the look of a claimant's envelope. (*Gets up, opens the door.*) Before you go, Mr Robinson, I will give you some professional advice, without charge. Your best course is to end your adventure with this interview. Over the years I've become used to half-brothers, half-sisters, quarter-grandsons – (*Laughs.*) – turning up with doctored documents and fraudulent demands. Several have been lucky not to have ended up in jail. All of them wasted their time and their money – far more of the latter than they could afford. Only my fellow lawyers benefited. Now please – (*Gestures towards door.*)

*Geoffrey doesn't move.*

I can have an officer in two minutes.

**Geoffrey** I'm not here for money. I want information.

**Henry** Information about what?

**Geoffrey** My – my – mm – mother.

**Henry** Your mother? Who was your – Robinson? Wharton Robinson?

**Geoffrey** My father. My mother was Ellen Ternan before she married.

**Henry** Ellen – Nelly. Of course. Nelly Ternan. Why didn't you make your identity clear in your letter?

**Geoffrey** I wasn't sure you would see me. You would take me for – (*Gestures.*) A claimant.

**Henry** And you aren't? Well, now I look at you properly – (*Doing so.*) I can see. My apologies. May we start again?

*He comes around, offers hand. They shake hands.*

Good. Well that's that, then. Let's make ourselves – (*Gestures to chair.*) May I ask you about yourself? You were in the war, I think?

**Geoffrey** Yes.

**Henry** Bad business. Bloody and bad. But I don't need to tell you that.

**Geoffrey** No.

**Henry** Where did you fight?

**Geoffrey** Flanders. Mons. Afterwards I was sent to Persia. Azerbaijan.

**Henry** To keep an eye on the Bolsheviks, eh?

*Geoffrey nods.*

So you must be a bit of a linguist. Russian at least?

**Geoffrey** Learnt it from my aunt.

**Henry** That would be Florence.

**Geoffrey** No, Maria. Aunt Maria. She travelled to Russia and –

**Henry** Oh yes, of course. Maria the traveller and artist. Florence, Fanny, was the novelist. They were remarkable women, your aunts. Adventurous. Ahead of their time. New women –

**Geoffrey** Yes.

**Henry** I was sorry to hear of their deaths. And of your mother's, of course. My father was very fond of your mother, as I expect you know.

**Geoffrey** She was very proud of the connection.

**Henry** And what do you do now, may I ask?

**Geoffrey** I keep a secondhand bookshop. In Slough.

**Henry** Ah. Some tranquillity. After the horrors.

**Geoffrey** Horrors?

**Henry** Of the war.

**Geoffrey** Oh. Oh yes. The war.

*There is a pause.*

**Henry** Well then, well then. You said you wanted information. How can I help?

**Geoffrey** After my mother's death I found a box. It contained a number of things – items – that – that – there was a poster of a play. This –

## LITTLE NELL

*He takes it out of his briefcase and hands it to Henry.*

**Henry** (*taking it*) *The Frozen Deep*! Good Heavens! (*Involuntary smile of recognition.*) I was in it. Well, not in it, but around the edges, an extra. All of us had parts. The children, that is – (*Stops.*) But of course your mother's name caught your eye?

**Geoffrey** It was an amateur production, was it?

**Henry** Yes. Well, no. Half and half, so to speak. You see, in those days when my father got up a production – especially a successful one, like *The Frozen Deep* – he and his friends played the men's parts, but it wasn't thought becoming for women to appear before a paying audience so their parts were played by professional actresses. So your mother and her two sisters – your aunts, Maria and Fanny – and their mother too, your grandmother – the whole family, in fact – all actresses, and all in *The Frozen Deep*. Actually, I'm not sure about Fanny – but your grandmother certainly, she played –

**Geoffrey** She was a professional actress then?

**Henry** Your grandmother?

**Geoffrey** My mother.

**Henry** Yes. She was.

**Geoffrey** She was born in 1850. Or so she said.

**Henry** 1850?

**Geoffrey** *The Frozen Deep* was performed in Manchester on the evening of August 22nd 1857.

**Henry** (*looks down at the poster*) So it was. Good heavens, that's what? Sixty-five years ago. Sixty-five years! Good heavens!

*The cast of* The Frozen Deep *take their bows to ghostly applause and cheering.*

**Geoffrey** So according to her account, my mother would have been seven years old when she played the part of a young woman in *The Frozen Deep*.

**Henry** Ah. I see. Yes. (*Laughs.*) Well, needless to say, she wasn't seven. She was – at least seventeen. Yes, seventeen would be about right. (*Little pause.*) So she told you she was born in '50? Well, you know how women can be about their age, when they're past a certain age. They make subtractions, forgetting that they're likely to create confusion later about earlier periods in their lives.

**Geoffrey** Is that when they met, then? During *The Frozen Deep* in Manchester?

**Henry** Who?

**Geoffrey** My mother and your father?

*Cast exits, Dick holding Nelly's and Maria's hands.*

**Henry** Oh. Yes. I believe so. It seems to me rather odd, Mr Robinson, may I say? That you've come to me to acquire information about your own – own family –

**Geoffrey** My whole world has become very odd, Sir Henry. To discover that my mother had another life – a past quite unlike the one she used to describe to me.

**Henry** Well, there's a likely explanation. In her days, you know, actresses weren't quite – as – as they are now. She married a schoolteacher, did she not? Your father – Wharton Robinson – was a Headmaster?

*Geoffrey nods.*

She probably felt it was wiser, from the point of view of the parents, the governors – and she wouldn't have wanted to burden her child with the responsibility of – (*gestures*) concealment.

**Geoffrey** It wasn't just concealment. She lied outright. She said that Charles Dickens died when she was a child.

**Henry** Once she'd deducted ten years from her age, she had no choice but to make everything fit.

*There is a pause.*

May I ask, in what terms exactly did your mother describe her relationship to my father?

**Geoffrey** She used to tell me that he appointed himself unofficial uncle to the family. And godfather, a sort of godfather, to her. She loved to describe a particular afternoon when he took them all on an outing to Doncaster. The sun was shining, they had such a picnic, with such laughter and jollity – he did conjuring tricks, she sat on his knee as he told stories, they sang songs and at the end of it he made his great pronouncement – that from that day forth he was to be known as Uncle to each and every one of the Ternan ladies, with special godfatherly responsibilities for the youngest of them.

**Henry** The whole family was there, mother and three daughters?

*Lights half up on a park in Doncaster, August 1857. Afternoon.*

*Nelly (seventeen) and Charles Dickens (forty-five) are walking arm in arm. Dick is holding Nelly's arm in a correct, gentlemanly fashion.*

**Geoffrey** She could remember their clothes and the hats they wore. The contents of the enormous picnic hamper he'd brought from London . . . She would always laugh when she remembered it, and cry a little before she'd finished telling me. It was the happiest day of her childhood, because her sisters and mother were so happy too.

*Lights fully up on Dick and Nelly.*

**Dick** I'm so sorry that your dear mother and Maria and Fanny couldn't be with us this afternoon, of all afternoons. Such a beautiful one.

**Nelly** Yes, I hate to think of them in that draughty old theatre. But then they're so pleased to have the parts. (*Little pause.*) We're grateful to you for recommending them.

**Dick** I'm always pleased to be of service. To you. And to your family. I have given you nothing that you don't deserve. You have such hard lives.

**Nelly** Do we?

**Dick** I know – I know something of what it's like for you. The conditions which you have to endure. The little house in Islington.

**Nelly** It's a perfect little house. We love it.

**Dick** Park Cottage, is it not?

**Nelly** Yes. Park Cottage. (*Little pause.*) You've seen it, then?

**Dick** Yes. I followed you home last Wednesday. The three of you. I kept you in my sights. All the way from the stage door of the theatre to Park Cottage, to make sure you got home safely. And then I peeped once, only once and very quickly, through the window.

**Nelly** And what did you see?

**Dick** I saw a devoted mother and her three devoted daughters.

**Nelly** Yes, but what did you see, what were we doing? What were we doing, what were you looking at us doing? Oh, I can't bear it to think of anyone, of you above all, looking at us.

**Dick** You were doing the most ordinary things, that was the charm of you. Fanny was helping Maria off with her coat, and behind them your mother had gone to the kitchen. She was slicing bread.

*There is a pause.*

**Nelly** And I? What was I doing?

**Dick** Yes. What were you doing?

**Nelly** I was coming down the stairs. And I had a feeling – a feeling of being looked at. Through the window.

**Dick** You saw me, then? Yes. Your smile – (*Looks at her, almost touches her on the mouth.*) That I know, I know as if I've known it all my life. But how can that be, how can that be, when we've had so little time together. Tell me, Nelly, my – my little Nell. May I call you that?

**Nelly** But she died, your Little Nell. I shall never forget Ma reading it out to us when we were little. I cried for her, we all cried, Maria and Fanny, and Ma too, even when we knew it almost by heart we still hoped that it would end differently this time, that you'd save her, hoped and prayed that you'd save her, and you never did, not once – oh, it was very hard to forgive you.

**Dick** It was the most terrible thing I ever did. I cried, too, when I knew it had to be done. But you – you have undone it, you see. Here you are. Alive. Alive again. Out of my story and into my life. And so – so very alive.

**Nelly** How do I know you won't kill me again?

**Dick** Will you trust me?

**Nelly** With my life, you mean?

**Dick** (*after a pause*) Yes. Yes, I believe I do mean that. With my life.

**Nelly** What would I have to do?

**Dick** Have to do? Why would you have to do anything, but be? Be. My Nell.

**Nelly** And what would you be to me?

**Dick** What would you have me be?

**Nelly** I don't know. I don't know what is – (*Hesitates.*)

**Dick** What is?

**Nelly** Right.

**Dick** Ah. Yes. Well, would it be right to be your friend? Your friend and protector? A godfather to you? Or an uncle?

**Nelly** My godfather? Oh!

**Dick** You like that, then?

**Nelly** I haven't got a godfather. Or an uncle, even.

**Dick** Then I shall be both. Both your uncle and your godfather.

**Nelly** Uncle would be better. Because I could give you a name, couldn't I? I couldn't call you Godfather Charles, could I, but I could call you –

**Dick** Uncle Charles.

**Nelly** Uncle Charles. Yes. May I?

## LITTLE NELL

**Dick** You may. And may I – may I celebrate the sudden appearance in the world of a fully formed, long established – how long has it been, oh, at least forty-five seconds, now forty-six, seven seconds, which in my soul feels like the longest, deepest, truest lastingest relationship, the relationship avuncular, the relationship protective and the relationship godfatherly, to which you are also entitled. Godly – holy, a holy and most sacred attachment, may I, my dear girl, oh my dear Little Nell, celebrate it with a holy and sacred, avuncular and most godfatherly kiss. (*Kisses her gently on the forehead.*) And how would you like to celebrate it? (*Holding her by the shoulders.*) What will you ask?

**Nelly** Oh – oh, there's nothing – nothing more I could want. Thank you. Thank you –

**Dick** You can say it. Our name for me.

**Nelly** Uncle Charles.

**Dick** It doesn't sound quite right, does it, when it's said. Uncle Charles. Its breeches are very starched, it has a tight waistcoat, because of a tight, round, important stomach, and a waxy moustache and a little spade of a beard that could jab through all the softness and roundness and sweetness of things. No, Uncle Charles isn't the man we took him to be.

**Nelly** There's Uncle Charlie.

**Dick** Uncle Charlie goes to the races, loses his wife's money, gets drunk, fails to come home, falls into gutters – goes to Paris for his pleasures.

**Nelly** Well – (*Laughs.*)

**Dick** What? What?

**Nelly** I quite like the sound of him.

**Dick** So do I.

**Nelly** I should love to go to Paris.

**Dick** And you shall. But not with Uncle Charlie. I can see him, can't you, swaggering his way along the boulevards, one arm tucked under yours – (*Tucks his arm under Nelly's.*) – as jaunty as a dancing master, and behind the two of you trots poor old Uncle Charles, from Gad's Hill, worrying in his pockets whether he's enough cash on him to pay for the two of you, your escapades – and then there'll be dancing, yes. Uncle Charlie will take you to a dancing, and when he arises from the table, offers you his hand, with a perfect little bow, leads you onto the floor. (*Does this.*) Uncle Charles sits with a fixed smile on his face, poor old thing, his foot tapping out of time to the music, because it's at odds with the music in his heart, and you'll look at me with such pity as you sweep by. Indeed, you'll pause, indeed you will, and you'll say, 'Oh, Uncle Charles, why don't you go back to the hotel and rest, Uncle Charlie will look after me –'

*He is sweeping her about, as if to music.*

**Nelly** Oh, I won't, indeed I won't.

**Dick** What will you say?

**Nelly** I'll say – I'll say – 'Now that's enough, Uncle Charlie, quite enough of you and your impertinences! I'm out with my nunky – and it's time he took me home, took me home to – to – to the hotel. He has work to do. He is a great man with great work to do, and we have no time to waste with wastrels like you! (*Taking Dick's arm.*) So you stay here, Uncle Charlie – and settle the bill, if you please!'

*She walks properly along with Dick, but clinging to his arm.*

**Dick** (*stopping*) So it's to be Nunky, then?

**Nelly** Nunky. Well, if I may – if you think it suitable –

**Dick** What are you looking at?

**Nelly** Your face.

**Dick** And what do you see?

**Nelly** Your eyes.

**Dick** Ah, then you see yourself. Because they're full of you. They can see nothing else. Oh, but my beard! You've never seen me without it, have you, Little Nell? Well, I only grew it for the play. I'll shave it first thing tomorrow morning. No. Tonight. As soon as I have my razor in my hand I'll make myself a clean and moral chin again.

**Nelly** No no! I love it – love it as it is!

**Dick** Love it? Do you? Then I promise – a vow, I make a solemn vow that this beard will only perish at your command.

**Nelly** Never!

*She puts a hand out to touch it, but doesn't.*

**Dick** Don't be shy of it! Are you shy of it?

**Nelly** Yes.

**Dick** Why? Why are you?

**Nelly** Because it belongs to you. It is you.

**Dick** Not if you want it. If you want it, it shall belong to you. Take it and see. (*Juts his chin at her.*)

**Nelly** (*puts her hand on the beard, tugs it gently*) It won't let me.

**Dick** Ah well, you can't have him by force, you have to coax him off.

**Nelly** (*strokes the beard, runs her fingers through it*) Oh, it's so soft, so soft, like a baby's beard – oh – oh – so delicate and soft and lovely. (*Pulls it.*) But it's still yours.

**Dick** It is almost yours. You almost have it.

**Nelly** What must I do?

**Dick** There's something you must do.

**Nelly** But what?

**Dick** Only you can know. He's at your mercy.

**Nelly** Perhaps I should bite him. Would he mind if I bit him?

**Dick** Let us find out.

> *Nelly bites Dick's beard. Then nibbles at it, then nibbles around it. Then looks into his face.*

**Nelly** Is he mine now?

**Dick** No. He still seems to be mine. He is clinging to me. He wants – he wants an exchange, little Nell.

**Nelly** What are we to do, then? As I haven't a beard for you to eat, Nunky.

**Dick** Nell, my dearest little creature, with brightest eyes and glowing cheeks and hair a-tumble, tumble, and loveliest, sweetest self within, without, my mouse of a Nelly Nell Nell, there's not a part of you I don't long to eat, to eat. Ah Nell – and full pink lips, did I specify my little Nell mouse's full pink lips, I long to eat and eat –

> *He kisses her gently on the lips, and then more and more devouringly, then stops, walks away a few steps.*
>
> *There is a pause.*

## LITTLE NELL

**Nelly**  What is it, Nunky, what is it?

**Dick**  Nunky – yes, well, now that I'm a nunky – Today we are in Doncaster, no, we are not in Doncaster, we're in our own little paradise that the rest of the world calls Doncaster, but tomorrow we – I – am back in London, in a nunkly world, and in a nunkly world there are nunkly difficulties. And responsibilities. Nunkly responsibilities. Your sisters, for instance. Fanny says she wants to stop acting and become a singer. A trained singer. She is talented, she has a lovely voice, it deserves the best of teachers, which are to be found, I understand, in Italy.

**Nelly**  Fanny – go to Italy? But all by herself, without Mama and me, how will she manage?

**Dick**  Your mama will go with her.

**Nelly**  Oh. But Maria –

**Dick**  Maria will stay with you for a while. Until we find a little house – no, not a little house, like Park Cottage, but a house of a size for happiness. It will be a house with large windows, and outside the air will be clean and healthy, there will be pleasant walks, and a piano – we shall have a piano, and we shall sing duets together by the hearth and we shall be as perfect and compact and neat and harmonious a little family as the world has never before seen or read about.

**Nelly**  (*after a pause*) But how can we be like that – when you already have a family? You are married, Nunky.

**Dick**  Never! Never, never married! Not in my heart, not in my soul – married only in form and in law, a marriage I long ago annulled in my spirit, before it could annul my spirit. My wife is – my wife was – no, I will not speak of her, it would be wrong to speak of her at a moment like this, here, here and now, Mouse, at the beginning of my life. Ours will be the first marriage of my heart and soul, my first and only true marriage. Come, my little Nell. Come.

*He goes to her, holds out his arms. Nelly creeps into them.*

Take my beard and pull – pull the devil out of it! It is yours now, yours, only yours.

*Nelly puts her hand on his beard.*

Pull it hard, pull it hard – it's the devil, don't forget!

*Nelly pulls it firmly, then savagely. Dick lets out a cry, pulls her to him, kisses her passionately.*

My dearest – my dearest – oh, my dearest –

*He pulls her to the ground.*


*Office of Sir Henry.*

**Henry** Uncle and godfather – that is very like my father. He was uncle and godfather to quite a few, over the years – it made it easier for them to accept his help.

**Geoffrey** But why should she pretend that she was a child instead of a young woman?

**Henry** Well, as I've already suggested – from a quite common sort of female vanity. And – as I think I've also said – to escape from her theatrical past. For your father's sake, as a headmaster. (*Pause.*) And of course she was probably anxious to dispel any gossip and rumours – there are always so many after the death of a great man. And if we're not careful they take root, they grow, become accepted. For instance, my own aunt, Georgina, my mother's sister, who looked after the family when my mother left the household, was suspected of being rather more to my father than very dear friend and housekeeper. (*Gestures dismissively.*) My father knew the sort of thing that was going the rounds, he treated it with contempt, needless to say. And there's been other talk, only quite recently, I believe, snippets and fragments of nonsense, nasty nonsense, there always has been, always, but now especially in these times we live in, these salacious and unfeeling times –

**Geoffrey** (*takes a newspaper out of his briefcase, hands it to Henry*) Like this, you mean?

**Henry** Oh that, yes. (*Glancing down.*) Poor old Wright. Thomas Wright. Yes. Precisely the sort of thing I mean.

**Geoffrey** He names my mother. He says he's writing a book –

**Henry** He's been writing it for decades. I doubt he'll ever publish it. And if he does –

**Geoffrey** If he does?

**Henry** His assertions are wild, unsubstantiated. By his own admission, it's thirty-five years since he heard the story, and his only source the gossip of that wretched clergyman, Benham, and he is long dead. Wright's book, if anyone dares publish it, will be received with contempt. Good heavens yes! Contempt!

*There is a long pause.*

**Geoffrey** Sir Henry – (*Hesitates, gets up.*) You've been most helpful, thank you.

**Henry** I'm only too happy to have been of service. Again my apologies for my initial misunderstanding – and as for your mother's little rearranging of history – well, women, you know, they have their secrets. As long as no real harm is done.

*Getting up, he holds out his hand.*

**Geoffrey** (*taking hand*) Sir Henry – um – um – (*He stammers something.*)

**Henry** Mmm?

**Geoffrey** Was she – was my mother in fact – was she your father's mistress?

*They are standing, holding hands.*


*Lights up on Dick and Nelly, some moments after we last saw them in Doncaster. She is on the ground, crouched slightly, as if in shock, her clothes in disarray. Dick is standing some distance from her, looking away from her, as if also in shock.*

**Dick** (*going to Nelly*) Nell. Little Nell.

*Nelly looks at him.*

Don't be unhappy, Little Nell.

**Nelly** (*in a whisper*) I'm not unhappy, Nunky. I've never been so happy – so happy –

**Dick** (*putting coat around her*) You will be more happy. More and more happy. All the happiness that is mine to give, I shall give.

**Nelly** And all the happiness that is mine I shall give. I shall try so hard to be worthy of you. Worthy –

**Dick** Mouse. My mouse. But you are crying!

**Nelly** It's only because I hurt a little. Only a little, a very little.

**Dick** Oh. Oh yes, of course. Poor mouse. Poor little mouse, here, I have a – brought a –

*He reaches in the jacket pocket of his coat, takes out a neatly folded towel, and hands it to Nelly.*

**Nelly** Thank you. (*Dabs her eyes with it.*)

**Dick** It's a towel. I thought you might need a – Poor mouse. Poor little mouse –

*He goes to her, gives her his hand. She takes it. He makes to raise her to her feet, instead kneels, taking her hand.*

We're going to conquer the future, we are, with all the power of our hope. There will be no pain, no more pain.

*He turns her hand over and looks into it.*

I see it in your palm. Did you know I can read palms and tell the future? And in our future there is only happiness. You'll see, my mouse. You'll see.


*Henry's office. Henry and Geoffrey are still holding hands.*

**Henry** (*releasing hand*) His mistress!

*Geoffrey nods his head.*

I was hoping you wouldn't ask me directly. The lawyer in me, I suppose. So yes. Yes, I am afraid she was.

*Geoffrey waits.*

May I offer you some – I have some whisky.

**Geoffrey** Thank you. (*Sits down.*)

*Henry goes to a cupboard, pours two glasses of whisky and brings glass and soda siphon to Geoffrey.*

**Henry** Soda?

**Geoffrey** Thank you.

*Henry squirts.*

Thank you.

*There is a pause.*

Did it start when she was seventeen, then?

**Henry** I believe so, yes.

**Geoffrey** And he was – how old would he have been?

**Henry** Forty-five.

**Geoffrey** And for how long –?

**Henry** Until the day he died.

**Geoffrey** (*nods*) Until the day he died. (*Little pause.*) And that was in – Excuse me, I should know, of course. I expect I do, if I think –

**Henry** Thursday the 9th of June 1870.

**Geoffrey** I see. I see, I see. I see. (*Little pause.*) For thirteen years, then. Thirteen years. (*Looks at him, realising.*) So you must have known my mother, then?

**Henry** Yes.

**Geoffrey** (*after a pause*) What did you feel? About her and your father?

**Henry** She was – everything my father wanted.

**Geoffrey** Was she? Everything? A young woman – almost still a girl – and a man of his age, with the greatest success and fame. Everything he wanted?

**Henry** Oh, I know what you must be thinking. And of course that came into it. Naturally. But there was far more to it. In many respects it was like a marriage. They were even quite sedate. At least, they did the things together that settled and established couples do – for instance, they liked nothing better than to stay at home of an evening and sing duets. For hours and hours. They were in harmony, you see.

*Sitting room in Slough. Summer 1862. Piano over. Dick and Nelly singing a duet.*

**Dick** (*moved*) Oh, Mouse, it's cruel to have us sing that one, it always makes me weep.

**Nelly** No, it's only fair, because you make other people weep all the time, with your writing.

**Dick** (*takes out handkerchief, sits down*) Well then, let the tears be on you, you must mop them up.

*He pats his knee. Nelly sits down on his knee, takes his handkerchief, wipes his eyes.*

**Nelly** There.

*She takes his handkerchief, puts it back in his pocket.*

**Dick** Now I can see again. And what a heavenly sight.

*He kisses her on the neck, on the cheek, on the forehead. Nelly scrambles off his knee as Jane enters, carrying a tray on which is port and a glass.*

Ah! And here's our Jane.

**Jane** Yes, sir. (*Putting tray down.*)

**Dick** And how is your hand?

**Jane** I don't know, sir, quite well I think.

**Dick** Shall I have a look? (*Holding out his hand.*)

*Jane gives him her hand, not eagerly. Dick starts to examine it.*

**Jane** (*looks at Nelly, suddenly takes it away*) Oh, excuse me, sir – I'd rather not.

**Dick** Ah. Why not?

*Jane makes to say something, doesn't. Lowers her head.*

**Nelly** Perhaps because you keep promising her a husband.

**Dick** And a very handsome one. But I've never promised him immediately – only in the distant future.

**Nelly** But perhaps she doesn't want one at all.

**Dick** What, ever?

**Jane** (*shakes her head*) I'm quite happy where I am – I don't want anything else, if that's all right. (*Looks at Nelly.*) And I don't think I – I don't really want to know my fortune until it's on me, if – if –

*She curtsies and runs out of room.*

**Dick** Well. (*Laughs.*) Well, yes, of course she's right. We're better off blind. Sensible girl.

*Nelly pours a glass of port and brings it to him.*

Thank you, Mouse.

*He takes the glass, then takes Nelly's hand, stares into it and raises it to his lips, kissing the palm.*

And thank you, thank you.

**Nelly**  What for?

**Dick**  For being my mouse.

**Nelly**  I sometimes wonder who knows –

**Dick**  Knows what?

**Nelly**  That I am your mouse.

**Dick**  (*shocked*) Well, no one, of course.

**Nelly**  Well then, how do you refer to me, when you're talking to your friends, for instance? Like Wilkie?

**Dick**  I speak of you with – with respect and admiration, and love, of course – how else would I speak of you?

**Nelly**  But how do you refer to me?

**Dick**  It depends on the circumstances.

**Nelly**  You mean you never refer to me?

**Dick**  Everybody who knows me knows that I have a cherished young friend – a sort of niece or goddaughter – who is the daughter of my widowed friend Mrs Fanny Ternan. So of course I call you Miss Ternan or Nelly, depending on – on who it is I am speaking of you to.

**Nelly**  Much easier than with Georgina, then?

**Dick**  Georgina – what do you mean?

**Nelly**  You can't give her a title so nobody really knows who she is.

**Dick**  Everybody knows who she is. She is my sister-in-law.

**Nelly**  But your wife has been sent to live somewhere else. Georgina, who is her sister, dwells in your house at Gad's Hill and cares for your children.

**Dick** (*laughing in spite of himself*) Dwells?

**Nelly** (*nodding*) Dwells. She dwells there. In Gad's Hill.

**Dick** Now come, Nell, come, come – why are we talking about this? You know the situation perfectly well. We've discussed it often enough –

**Nelly** But I still don't understand it, Nunky. You say she wasn't worthy of you and was bad for the children and probably mad, but still, there she is, called Mrs Charles Dickens – so shouldn't poor Georgina have some title to show that she's something more than just Miss Hogarth, your sister-in-law? She's your housekeeper and she looks after your children, and when you're at home, at your home in Gad's Hill, she does all those wifely things for you – though of course none of the things I do for you, but then I don't have a title to go around with either, do I? Except a false one, here in Peckham or when we're travelling together – when I'm wife to Mr Terdle, Teddle, Tiddle, Twaddle, depending on what name you're giving yourself –

**Dick** Come here, come back here, Mouse – (*Patting the arm of chair.*) – so I can answer you properly, you're whirling about so much.

**Nelly** I have been mainly quite still.

**Dick** Well, your words have been whirling about me – Come.

**Nelly** Very well. (*Sitting away from him.*) I'll listen.

**Dick** And what would you like to hear?

**Nelly** Whose fault it is that I have to be a false Mrs, to go with false names like Terdle, Nerdle, Twaddle and Woo – whose fault, Nunky?

**Dick** Whose fault? It is nobody's fault, my little Nell. Or rather, it is the world's fault. Do you wish you'd lived another life, then?

**Nelly** What other life was there for me? Once you'd come into it?

**Dick** You could have remained an actress, I suppose. And I'm sure many men would have fallen in love with you.

**Nelly** And would they have given me their name?

**Dick** The lucky one would have been able to give you his name. And I wouldn't have had my Little Nell.

**Nelly** And then what would you have done? What would have happened to you, if I'd stayed on the stage until someone else had swept me off it, into a respectable and doting marriage? Like Little Dorrit and her Arthur, going down the years to their happiness. What would you have done, if you'd seen me going down the years with Arthur somebody-or-other to a modest life of usefulness and happiness?

**Dick** I would have written myself into an early grave.

**Nelly** Oh. Died of a broken heart, you mean?

**Dick** Yes. I believe I would.

**Nelly** And if you'd never met me?

**Dick** Died of an empty heart.

**Nelly** Your heart could never be empty. It's full of love.

**Dick** But I'd have had no one to give it to. (*Puts his arm around her waist.*) Nell, my dearest, cleverest Little Nell –

**Nelly** (*interrupting*) No, no more, Nunky. I don't want you to say any more, or I shall – I shall – (*Puts her hand* *on his cheek.*) Do you remember when I used to rummage through your beard? Like this. (*Puts her fingers into his beard, pulling it gently.*) It was silky then. Silkier than my hair. (*Little pause.*) You are the world to me, Nunky. And yet it is the world's fault that I can never be a wife to you. So you say. I say it is the beard's fault. (*Pulls his beard.*) Naughty world. Naughty beard. Which is it?

*She leans over, kisses him on the lips. He stands, pulls her to him. They kiss tenderly and sexually.*

*Office of Sir Henry.*

**Henry** I realise that it might be difficult for you – to think that they achieved a, um – a happiness together under such circumstances.

**Geoffrey** Well, it would be a poor son who wished his mother ill in any situation she found herself in.

**Henry** That's very finely said, if I may say.

**Geoffrey** I'm having to get used to a great deal of – of new information. Rather quickly.

**Henry** Of course. Although clearly you had suspicions, more than suspicions, when you came here. In fact, it's why you came here.

**Geoffrey** I had – dread, sir. Dread. But I had some hope too – that it had been a romance – an innocent and unfulfilled romance. In his novels, after all, there is never even a hint – His fallen woman are lost, lost, and his good women are virtuous – There are no adulteries, as far as I remember.

**Henry** No. No adulteries. Although it has often been noticed that the young women in his later novels have a vitality and a charm and sometimes behave somewhat inappropriately. Bella, in *Our Mutual Friend*, for instance. But in the end they turn out to be – as you say – virtuous.

**Geoffrey** She read them to me, you know, all the novels. My own favourite was *Great Expectations*.

**Henry** Mine too, I think. But not his. His was *David Copperfield*, his favourite child. (*Little pause.*) I became Pip for days on end.

**Geoffrey** Yes.

**Henry** He never read them out to me, though. Except when he read them publicly, and I was in the audience.

**Geoffrey** Ah. A case of the cobbler's son.

**Henry** Mmm? Oh, yes, I see. Not being shod. (*Laughs.*)

*There is a pause.*

**Geoffrey** (*abruptly*) You must have hated her. You and the rest of your family. Hated her.

**Henry** Our lives changed because of her. Our mother suffered. He told us she was mad, you know. He told us that she didn't love us, had never loved us, was incapable of love. She was so bewildered, so hurt, so lost and unhappy. And we could see what your mother was, that our mother wasn't. Not simply young, but quick, lively, intelligent. And growing. Growing. Mama never kept pace with him. He always made her feel that. And of course I understand so much better now that he made her worse than she was – more incapable, more clumsy, more stupid, more helpless. Nelly, on the other hand – your mother – (*Little pause.*) We didn't hate her. We liked her. Yes. Even Georgina liked her. They got on.

**Geoffrey** Well, that's, that's – good to know. That she was popular with your family. I'm sorry about your mother, though. I apologise.

**Henry** I don't think – I don't think there's anything you need apologise for.

**Geoffrey** No, no, I know, I don't know why I did – I think I suddenly felt responsible. Ridiculous, of course – as if caught in a web. A web.

**Henry** May I –? (*Getting up, bringing whisky over.*)

**Geoffrey** Oh well, thank you, just a drop. I don't usually – at this time of day – needless to say.

**Henry** Oh, it's not the time of day that matters, it's the circumstance. A circumstance can happen at any time of the day.

*He pours him a decent amount, and then for himself.*

Are you married, by the way? May I ask?

**Geoffrey** No. That is, I am – I was – we are separated at the moment.

**Henry** No children, then?

**Geoffrey** No. My wife was keen but I felt that after such a war – It was difficult to think of bringing children into a world where such wars could happen.

**Henry** But you were a professional soldier? Before the war –

**Geoffrey** It was my mother's ambition for me. From – well, before I was born, I fancy. I – I always wanted to be an actor. Odd, isn't it? Though not so odd now I know that it's in the blood. (*Laughs.*)

**Henry** Acting is quite a dangerous profession in its own way, so I've always understood.

**Geoffrey** Perhaps more so for women.

**Henry** Ah yes. Quite. (*Pause.*) I seem to remember that Nelly – Mrs Wharton Robinson . . . There were two children?

**Geoffrey** I have a sister. She is married. She isn't at all interested in our mother and her previous life. She is perfectly settled, perfectly. For better or worse – So. So.

*Pause.*

**Henry** May I ask further – I hope it's not an impertinence – my mother and your father, I mean my mother and your father – I mean – (*Laughs in embarrassment.*) Oh, what a shambles, I mean your father and your mother, your parents I mean, of course. Was it a happy marriage? Happy enough?

**Geoffrey** She was everything he could have wanted. They sang duets.

*Piano over, playing same tune as Dick and Nelly.*

**Henry** Ah, well that's – that's –


*The song finishes. As they come to the end, Nelly turns her face up to George, who kisses it.*

**Nelly** (*getting up – she is visibly pregnant*) Isn't it time for Assembly?

*George beams intensely at her. Little pause.*

Dearest, you should hurry, I think.

**George** Shan't.

**Nelly** What?

**George** Shan't go to Assembly. Perkins can take it. I shall spend the morning here. With my family. My wife. My son. This one. (*Touches her stomach.*) That's my duty, as I see it. (*Laughs robustly.*)

**Nelly** But – but – what about the boys? You know how they begin to misbehave –

**George** Where is our Geoffrey? Is he still asleep?

**Nelly** No, dear. Jane has taken him for a walk.

**George** Well then – well then – We shall – why don't we –?

*Jane enters, carrying a package.*

**Jane** (*making to give it to Nelly*) This has just come for you, ma'am.

**George** (*almost snatches it from her*) What is it? (*Examines it.*)

*Nelly and Jane exchange worried looks, as Jane goes out.*

Fanny's writing – you open it, and let's see what she's sent you.

**Nelly** I know what it is, it's her new novel – (*Putting it down.*) George, dearest, are you sure that Perkins will be all right? He has a rather feeble voice, and the smaller boys don't really respect him.

**George** The experience will do him good. You know, you girls are remarkable, remarkable. First Fanny's novels and Maria off to all corners of the earth, and published in the newspapers – but then I suppose you could say they're lucky in their husbands. I think of you sometimes, you know, the three of you – three girls, three little girls, so touched with a quality, a specialness.

*He stands over her, beaming down intensely.*

**Nelly** (*carefully*) Oh, I was too sickly and feeble a creature to feel at all special –

**George** (*interrupting*) Ah, but you were the one that the greatest man of his age took to himself as a godchild. He saw the specialness in you, did he not, being so special in himself – he a genius and you his muse?

**Nelly** Oh George, I've never made such a claim – I could never make such a claim. Good heavens! Have I ever made such a claim? I hope I haven't – he was a friend of the family who made himself my godfather because he was sorry for me, and he was such a long time ago – George, I can see that you're upset, what can be upsetting you?

**George** No, no. Happy. That's what I am, Elly.

*He takes Nelly's hands.*

**Nelly** (*puts her hand on his head*) Dearest George. But haven't you Latin after Assembly, with the Third?

**George** (*staring love at her, sinks to his knees*) I am the happiest man.

**Nelly** (*smiling anxiously down at him*) Dearest, dearest, darling George, what are you doing down there?

**George** I am worshipping my wife. My place is at her feet.

**Nelly** And hers is – is – in your arms. George, please do get up, dearest.

**George** I am your obedient George.

*He begins to rise, stands smiling and nodding at her, bursts into tears.*

Please forgive me, forgive me.

**Nelly** Forgive you? Forgive you for what?

**George** I don't know. (*Turns away, tries to compose himself.*) There's something I don't understand, I think there is.

**Nelly** (*takes his hand, leads him to chair, sits him down, sits down beside him*) You haven't been yourself for the last day or two. You have one of your unhappinesses coming on, I can feel it, so we must be careful, dearest, and not let you get – too fraught.

**George** No, no, it's not one of my unhappinesses, dearest Elly – the opposite, it's the opposite. I am overcome by my happiness, you see.

**Nelly** Ah! Well, that can only be good, George.

**George** Yes, wonderful, most wonderful! Except for the feeling that I have done nothing to deserve it. It is such a mystery to me, you see. Do you see?

**Nelly** No, George, I don't. What mystery, where is the mystery?

**George** You, oh my darling, oh my dearest, you are the mystery, Elly. You came into my life from nowhere – nowhere – to give me everything I'd ever hoped for, dreamed of! (*His voice is shaking.*)

**Nelly** This is very like one of your unhappinesses, George – when I have to keep telling you that I didn't come from nowhere. Not from nowhere, George. I didn't come from nowhere, you know very well where I came from, my darling.

**George** Tell me again. I love to hear you tell me, Elly.

**Nelly** (*slowly and urgently, as if to a child*) I came from Italy, from my sister Fanny's, where I had been living since fifteen because of my health, and then when I'd quite recovered, when I was twenty-four, I came to stay with Maria, at Oxford. We met at her house. Where is the mystery in any of that, dearest? (*Attempting to laugh*.) It is the most ordinary way in the world for a young man to meet his future wife.

**George** Twenty-three. You were twenty-three.

**Nelly** Yes. There you are, you see. You remember it all perfectly clearly, I was twenty-three.

*George stares at her intently.*

George, dearest – we are happy. We love each other. We have never loved anyone but each other – at least I haven't. (*Looks at him interrogatively*.)

**George** Oh Elly, my Elly – you know!

**Nelly** Well then?

**George** I wish I – I wish – oh, how I wish –

**Nelly** (*puts her finger to his lips*) You mustn't wish for more than we have, George.

**George** No, no, you're right. I mustn't do that. God might punish me.

**Nelly** God!

**George** Yes, of course God, Elly, who else but God? Why has He rewarded me, rewarded me instead of punishing me, for abandoning Him?

**Nelly** But you haven't abandoned Him. Never. When you decided not to become a vicar –

**George** (*tenderly*) Because you wouldn't marry me, Ellen, if I did.

**Nelly** But I was truthful with you. I could not have been your wife if you had been a vicar.

**George** So you say, so you say, but why? I still don't understand why, why, Elly?

**Nelly** Because I knew in my heart that He never intended me to be a vicar's wife. But I believe, from the moment we came to love each other, that He intended me to be your wife. How can you have abandoned Him? You are a man of faith, George. Parents wouldn't entrust their boys to us unless they believed that you are a man of faith.

**George** But supposing – supposing He has decided that He will no longer allow – that in giving you me – and that is why He makes everything I love, you and Geoff and the school, even this one – (*Touching her stomach.*) – seem wrong to me sometimes, and false? And I become full of dread and suspicions and I don't know what is to become of me – Oh, Elly, Elly, what am I to do?

**Nelly** George! George! What you must do – You mustn't do what you did last time, and neglect your duties. Please listen carefully, George. You have a class now. Is it another Latin class?

**George** Latin, yes.

**Nelly** Then you must go and give it. The boys depend upon you. Their parents depend upon you. You have a great responsibility to them. And to our little Geoffrey. And to this one. And to me. By fulfilling it you earn your happiness from God. You are a good man who deserves everything he has. I love you.

**George** You love me. Yes. I believe it. And I shall go about my duties straight. But first I kiss you, my most, most darling wife, my Ellen, and –

*He clutches her desperately, kissing her. Nelly gazes despairingly over his shoulder, as if seeing Dick . . .*

*... standing at a lectern, reading. He is full of energy – in his pomp, gesticulating violent acts. This in dumbshow. He reaches a climax, stands quivering with excited horror, staring at his audience.*

*Lights up. Church.*

**Dick** And there was the body – mere flesh and blood, no more – but such flesh, and so much blood!!

*Sound of organ very low.*

**Nelly** (*as if struggling*) Dear Father – Dear Father, who art in –

*She stops herself, sits again, upset. The organ sound has stopped. Complete silence.*

*An explosion of organ music, brief, very loud. Nelly winces, shocked.*

*Silence. Sound of footsteps.*

*Benham appears, humming. He walks down the aisle towards the door. He nods respectfully, not recognising her in the dimness. Nelly gets up.*

**Benham** Mrs Robinson!

**Nelly** Mr Benham.

**Benham** Don't say you've been here while I was thundering!

**Nelly** No – well, only a minute or two.

**Benham** A minute or two is all I allow myself. For everyone else it's an eternity.

**Nelly** It suited my mood.

**Benham** Oh. Oh dear! A violent mood, then?

**Nelly** Well, I was thinking of the way things can change when one has – seems to have – a settled and – proper life – but you can never be sure that at any minute –

**Benham** There won't be a clap of thunder and a dreadful storm. Well, peace has returned, for good, I hope – let me leave you to it. Oh, but may I – may I take the liberty of reminding you of a promise you made to me the other month?

**Nelly** Promise?

**Benham** About Charles Dickens. I was showing you my collection – I'd just found a poster, do you recall, announcing a reading he was to give here, in Margate? In the town hall. And you told me about your most extraordinary relationship with him. Well, not extraordinary, I suppose, quite an ordinary one if it hadn't been with him, but he would make any relationship with himself extraordinary, from the point of view of a worshipper like myself – and you were good enough to say, well, to promise, that one day you'll try to describe him to me exactly as you remember him – anything you can remember of his conversation, any detail, even of his dress. I could write it down and show it to you, so that we'd be sure I have it correctly.

**Nelly** I was his mistress.

**Benham** I'm afraid I don't quite understand. You were, you say, I thought I heard you say –

**Nelly** So you see, I need – I need your guidance, Mr Benham. Your help.

**Benham** Of course. Indeed. But I still doubt – You said – Did you say that your were – mm –?

**Nelly** His mistress.

**Benham** (*stares at her*) But – but no. My dear Mrs Robinson – no. You must be using the word in a sense which is not familiar to me.

**Nelly** I'm sure we share the same sense.

**Benham** You were a child – just a child – when you knew him. When he died. You told me –

**Nelly** I am older than I led people to believe. Including George. I am a decade older than George.

**Benham** A decade! I see.

**Nelly** I have told no one else.

**Benham** As far as I'm concerned, Mrs Robinson, you have told no one. He seduced you, naturally.

**Nelly** I don't think so. It was as if I didn't quite know – I was very young – he made me confused. Yes, he confused me –

**Benham** Do you mean, he drugged you?

**Nelly** (*laughs slightly*) No, no. He wasn't – he wasn't – He was very kind to me. He loved me. I was more than just a – (*Gestures.*) He trusted me, my judgement. He read his work to me, every chapter as he wrote it, and then I read it through after he made changes –

**Benham** How honoured you must have felt.

**Nelly** Yes. I always honoured his genius. And served it.

**Benham** But the man, on the other hand –

**Nelly** (*after a pause*) I served him too.

**Benham** And honoured him?

**Nelly** I honoured his wishes.

**Benham** His desires.

**Nelly** It was what I undertook. He was always kind. As I've said. Kind. And he sacrificed so much for me.

**Benham** You sacrificed rather more for him, my dear, I think.

**Nelly** It was impossible not to love him. Everyone who knew him loved him. (*Pause.*) But his touch disgusted me. I hated my life with him.

**Benham** But not him?

**Nelly** Only when he touched me.

**Benham** And now you have a new life.

**Nelly** Do I deserve it? That is what I have come to ask you. Have I a right to it?

**Benham** Deserve? Have a right? But surely, my dear Mrs Robinson – we must accept what God has given us. We know what we deserve and have a right to by what we have.

**Nelly** I have learnt – am learning again – how to endure my shame. I had thought, with his death, my marriage, our child and the child to come, I should have some release. And there was release. But now, with George, it is back, and I must endure it again. He blames me for persuading him away from his vocation, and of course I can't explain to him that I could never be a vicar's wife. My life would have been a lie, a daily lie, our lives ruined if it had been found out, and little Geoffrey's too, his life tainted for ever. And so of course I tell him that God intended him to be a headmaster, though he knows that really he has no gift for it – we are losing boys every term, our position is quite precarious, really very precarious – and the thing is, Mr Benham, whenever I seem to have him calmed down, the name of – of –

seems to pop up in him. Like a snake. I am desperate to help him – what can I do? Would it be better or worse for him if I told him the truth? It would free him – and free me with him. I could stop having to conceal and lie. We would live in honesty and openness – yes, the truth is always best, isn't it, Mr Benham? However painful.

**Benham** But you don't know what he would do with the truth, do you? If it made him angry it might also make him indiscreet – just once. He would only have to be careless or feel vengeful once – confide in just one person just once. Can you be sure he would be able to resist the just once, which would affect the fortunes of the school? The parents would almost certainly have the strongest moral objections – and you say they are already withdrawing.

**Nelly** It might be for the best. It might be for the best to give up the school. We could go away, abroad, start a school for English boys in Rome, start again from what we really are. If we failed then at least he would know why – he wouldn't need an explanation from God.

**Benham** If our only concern was George's welfare. (*Little pause.*) And yours. But we must not be selfish in order to be good. My dear, my dear, you wish to know what I believe? I believe you owe it to his memory not to soil his name. He is one of our greatest men, second only to Shakespeare if not actually equal to him – and in one respect, a most important respect, his superior. In his moral power. It lives on in the world through his works and through what is known of his character. Damage that, and you risk damaging the souls of all those who look to him to accompany them, guide them, on their paths through life. 'By their works shall ye know them' – by their works! No aspect of the life must be allowed to taint the works. No, my dear Mrs Robinson – Ellen –

you must carry the burden of your dreadful secret to the grave. As must I, now that I share it with you. Let me just say – say one thing – that may be in some way consolatory – that if there is that in your connection of which you should justly feel ashamed, there is also that of which you should justly feel proud. God has His purposes.

**Nelly** Thank you, Mr Benham. Good Mr Benham, and my friend.

**Benham** And your friend.

*He takes Nelly's hand.*

How is little Geoffrey?

**Nelly** He is very well, I thank God.

**Benham** Good, and you'll allow us the use of him for the Easter Pageant?

**Nelly** Of course. He adores dressing up.

**Benham** We'll make him into a bunny, perhaps. Or an egg.

**Nelly** He prefers to be ferocious.

**Benham** Ah. Then we'll find a reason for having a lion, shall we?

**Nelly** Yes, a lion. Perfect. Though I like him most of all to be a soldier.

**Benham** Then a soldier he shall be.

*Nelly smiles radiantly at him, makes to go out. Benham watches her, then hurries off to desk, takes out a piece of paper, writes. Nelly is still onstage.*

'My dear Wright, This communciation written in a state of extreme agitation. You remember I told you that I had living in my parish a young woman who, as a child, had actually known Dickens and was in effect a kind of goddaughter to him, and you asked me if I could discover from her anything that would be of consequence in your projected biography. Well, my dear Wright, I have just had with this very woman the most extraordinary conversation, the contents of which I shall now entrust to you, and only you, knowing that you will understand the great responsibility this imposes on you as to how, and in what circumstances, you choose to disclose it to the world. My dear Wright, this woman, whose name is Ellen Robinson, and who is the wife of the headmaster of a boys' school here in Margate, was – so she claims, and I have no reason to doubt her, as she came to me distressed and bewildered and delivered her secret to me in the utmost confidence, and mark this, my dear Wright, her concern was less for herself than her husband, who is driving himself mad with jealousy of he knows not whom – this, my dear Wright, is the ghastly comedy of her situation –'

*During this, lights up on desk, chair . . .*

*Office of Sir Henry.*

**Henry** Yes, it may be odd, but I find myself very pleased. That your parents' marriage was a happy one.

**Geoffrey** Hah!

**Henry** Didn't you say?

**Geoffrey** I said she was everything he wanted. But that's not the same thing as saying that they were happy. Not at all.

**Henry** No. No, it isn't.

**Geoffrey** Where did he keep her?

**Henry** Keep her?

**Geoffrey** Yes.

**Henry** Well, they had a house in Slough. And then in Peckham. Or it may have been the other way around.

**Geoffrey** Slough?

**Henry** And Peckham.

**Geoffrey** Which part of Slough?

**Henry** I don't know, I never – visited – No one in the family ever visited.

**Geoffrey** (*nods*) To think that there I've been, in Slough, all this time – And Peckham, you say. Peckham and Slough. Strange places to keep a – a – my mother.

**Henry** I would imagine that he chose them because they could be reached easily by train. I remember in his last year or so how exhausted he was from the amount of travelling he did – from his readings. Manchester or Birmingham, then back to London, then to Slough or Peckham, then back to London and his office, then home to Gad's Hill, then to Slough, then off to Liverpool or Bristol for a reading. So much of his life seemed to be spent on a train.

**Geoffrey** But then – he liked trains, didn't he? All those pages he wrote about them, whole chapters in *Dombey and Son*. I remember how I admired – My mother used to imitate Bagstock, puff out her chest and put on a deep, blustery voice – and then tell me about how honoured as a little girl, to be his god – his god – daughter and – and you can feel how much – how much he loved going about – in trains.

*He sits staring, rigid, as if in shock.*

**Henry** Yes. Well, not after the dreadful business at Staplehurst Bridge, of course. (*Pause.*) Did your mother ever mention Staplehurst Bridge?

**Geoffrey** (*still staring*) Eh?

**Henry** The Paris Express – coming back from Paris – it crashed at Staplehurst Bridge. My father was in it, and so was your mother. And her mother, actually – your grandmother. All three of them were hurt – could have been killed. He climbed through the broken window of their carriage, was out and about pulling people out of the wreckage, the maimed, the dying. He was heroic, they all said, the newspapers. I don't think he ever quite got over it – the carnage – but it didn't stop him – Well, he had to, you know, he needed the trains to get back and forth for those damned readings – They were enough to kill him in themselves – we all begged him – begged him – but the readings and the trains, the trains and the readings together.

*Geoffrey lets out an odd noise, like a laugh.*

Mmm?

**Geoffrey** Mmm?

**Henry** Did you say something?

**Geoffrey** Oh, I was just thinking of the trains and the readings – and there my mother would be, waiting for him in Slough or Peckham between trains and readings. And then off again and back to Peckham or Slough. And off again – Yes, I can see how exhausting, how very exhausting. Now, I suppose, with the motor car, he'd be behind the wheel, much more restful for him, I should think. Drive straight up to the door. Straight up to her, at the door in Slough or Peckham.

**Henry** (*little pause, bewildered*) Yes, I suppose – um – with a motor car. But I can't quite see why you – where a motor car comes into it.

**Geoffrey** No. No, I don't know why either, the thought just popped into my head. I wonder whether – (*Little pause.*) Has it ever occurred to you to wonder whether – (*Makes to speak, checks himself, changes the subject.*) The readings. My mother used to say that it was one of her greatest sorrows that she'd been too young to go to them, that she'd never heard him read in public –

**Henry** Ah. Well. Of course she heard him.

**Geoffrey** Yes.

**Henry** It would have been hard for her to go to them, you know, especially at the end. It was hard for all of us – to see what it was doing to him – I sometimes hear him now. In my sleep. When I'm almost asleep, somewhere around then. His voice comes into my head – it starts me awake. My wife too. That is, I wake her because of the way I wake – with a cry – I'm sure there are many still alive who sometimes recall the experience in that sort of way, especially if they heard one of his last. He sometimes went beyond, far beyond, at the end –

*Lights up on Dick at lectern, a book open before him. He is gesticulating violently, lurching slightly, a few words and phrases clear, others distorted, as in a nightmare.*

**Dick** The noose was on his neck; tight as a bowstring and swift as the arrow it speeds (*garble*) and hung with his open knife clenched clenched clenched (*garble*) backwards and forwards on the parapet with a dismal (*howling noise*) for the dead striking against a stone, a stone, dashed out his brain!! Dashed. Out. His. Dashed out his. Braiiiins!

*There is a long, eery silence, then cries and applause. Dick stands, swaying, mops his face, drinks water, bows, lurches slightly, bows again, then almost falls off the lectern and limps heavily away, mopping at his face and bowing. He stops, performs one last, unsteady bow, and lurches off.*


*Thursday 9 June 1870. Off, the sound of a dog barking.*

*Lights up on Nelly, aged thirty-one, sitting at a table, reading a manuscript.*

**Jane** (*enters*) Nelly, he's coming. He's just crossing the field.

**Nelly** Who?

*Jane sees Nelly's face, laughs.*

The master, indeed. And doesn't Quilp know it. Do let him out, dear – You know he needs to be the first with a greeting. (*Puts manuscript carefully away.*)

**Jane** (*as she goes out*) He's limping badly. Shall I help him with his bag?

**Nelly** No, put the water on.

**Jane** I've put it on.

**Nelly** Then open the door for Quilp.

*Jane goes out. Sound of Quilp being released, running, yapping excitedly. Nelly goes to window, stares out.*

*Sound of Dick's voice and yapping coming closer, then in the hallway.*

**Dick** (*outside the door*) No, no, you can't come in here, old Quilp, you're too demanding, and I want all the attention.

*Dick enters. He is now fifty-eight. He is carrying a heavy briefcase and a stick, and is limping heavily.*

All the attention.

*He puts down his bag, holds out his arms.*

**Nelly** (*goes into his arms*) You always get all the attention – far more than is good for you.

**Dick** I know – but it's too late now to stop it. People are in the habit. It would be unfair and unkind to try –

*He stops, aware of Nelly's scrutiny.*

Mouse? Your whiskers – (*Touching her mouth.*) – are twitching.

*Nelly takes his finger away from her mouth, then goes to the table, pours him a large brandy, carries it to a small table beside his chair. Dick sits, grimaces with pain.*

**Nelly** Are they worse?

**Dick** I don't believe there's a writer in London that doesn't have them. Tennyson, for example, all he talks about – people visit him expecting music from his lips, instead they get details of his haemorrhoids, and in prose! Well, better than in verse, I suppose. And Wilkie, Wilkie, just the other night he was saying he kept putting off his new novel, couldn't face the thought of sitting at his desk for more than five minutes – (*Adjusts himself.*)

**Nelly** Your cheek is swollen.

**Dick** Yes, damned tooth. I took a spoonful of laudanum. Nearly took some before the reading, when it was raging, but didn't, in case I fell asleep just when I was getting into – (*Checks himself.*) – my stride. (*Drinks deeply, gratefully.*) I saw you there. At least I thought I saw you. It was most curious, though – the sensation I had in my stomach, a slight dizziness, as when I saw you for the first time – She was the twin of you as you were then.

**Nelly** As I was then? Well, perhaps it was the ghost of me as I was then.

**Dick** Now I see you properly, properly, I think she was neither twin nor ghost, not pretty enough, not anything enough. And the man she was sitting with didn't look at all like me – he had a droopy, listless manner and a cough. He coughed during 'The Signalman', and followed it with a wheeze, I caught his eye, gave him a piercing look and a quick snarl, he gave me a friendly little nod and a smile.

**Nelly** And what else did you read?

**Dick** Oh, I started with Mrs Lirriper, the Paul scene from *Dombey and Son*, David's thrashing, Bumble, Pumblechook, the usual repertoire to the usual success – hall full, people standing, leaning through the windows, hanging from the rafters, protruding from the cellars, triumph, triumph, triumph, the whole of Sheffield still reeling from my coming thither and my going thence. Particularly my going thence, lamentations mingled with the applause, triumph, triumph – despair.

**Nelly** And did you do Pickwick?

**Dick** I did.

**Nelly** And did you say Pickwick?

**Dick** I said it very clearly.

**Nelly** What?

**Dick** His name.

**Nelly** Whose name?

**Dick** His. (*Little pause.*) Pickswick.

**Nelly** Pickswick.

**Dick** No. (*Little pause.*) Piskwick.

**Nelly** Piskwick.

**Dick** Is it so?

**Nelly** Can't you hear it?

**Dick** I hear – his name. When you say it and I say it I hear the same name. Very well, it is so. Pick – Pick – (*Stops.*) I'll ask Emsworth what it means, he'll probably tell me it's quite common in gentlemen of a certain age, especially those who insist on showing themselves off to the world –

*Jane enters, carrying a large jug and a bowl.*

**Dick** Ah, Jane.

**Jane** (*putting the bowl down, pours hot water in*) Sir.

**Dick** Have you given up smiling?

**Jane** No, sir.

**Nelly** She worries about you.

**Dick** I know. She's very kind. But when I'm at home there's no need to worry, is there?

**Jane** No, sir.

**Dick** So you can smile. (*Looks at her.*)

*Jane smiles.*

Now I am at home. Thank you, Jane.

*Jane goes out. There is a pause. Nelly refills his glass.*

Yes, Mouse. Home. Home.

**Nelly** You murdered, didn't you?

**Dick** Murdered? (*Laughs.*)

**Nelly** You read the scene from *Oliver Twist*. That you promised me you would never read. Ever. Again.

**Dick** Oh, that murder! No, Mouse, no – how could I, when I made such a promise to you? And to Georgina. And to Dolby. And promised Forster. And promised Wilkie. In fact I can't think of anyone I didn't promise – except the audience, of course. To whom I could scarcely say – (*Puts his arm over his chest.*) – I do solemnly swear and promise that I will not murder this evening. At least in front of you. Nancy is safe. Bill Sikes is safe. And so are you. And so am I.

**Nelly** Look at you. You are exhausted.

**Dick** I was. (*Drinks.*) I feel fresher by the second.

*He takes her hand, raises it to his lips. She puts her hand on his head.*


*Office of Sir Henry.*

**Geoffrey** Were there any children?

**Henry** (*confused*) Children?

**Geoffrey** Do we perhaps have any half-brothers or sisters, you and I?

**Henry** (*pause*) Well, of course there's no way of knowing for sure. There are always these claimants – bogus, as I told you when I thought you might be one of them, but never the slightest shred of evidence –

**Geoffrey** I was an easy birth. She used to joke about it. How many children did he have by your mother?

*Henry stares at him.*

Excuse me. (*Little pause.*) If I may ask.

**Henry** Ten. If you include poor little Dora. She died very young.

**Geoffrey** Thirteen years together. A man who had fathered ten children and a woman who had an easy birth when she was forty. Perhaps he had them killed.

**Henry** (*looks at him, shocked*) My father – my father could never – whatever his faults, he could never –

**Geoffrey** Or put them out as foundlings. Who can say?

**Henry** But surely you knew your mother as I knew my father – how can you imagine –?

**Geoffrey** No sir, no sir, excuse me, but you don't understand. I don't know my mother as you knew your father. You not only knew his past but what he was doing – doing with my – my – She lied to me all my life. If she was capable of that, what else was she capable of? (*Little pause.*) And my father – my wretched father – There was a noise he made, a dreadful howl, like a dog – a dog grieving. Dear Jane, our maid, would put me on her knee and have me stick my fingers in my ears until he'd stopped, stopped his howling, but then there would be his voice, limping on and on and on, and sobs, and Ma speaking so sweetly and gently, never letting him hear her exhaustion and never letting me see her despair.

'The world is a hard place for a man like your father,' she'd say. 'He was born for the Church, his nature was to serve his God, but it wasn't to be.' I never asked why it wasn't to be, thinking that his tendency to howl and weep were enough to prevent him from being anything at all, even a clergyman. But if he guessed – or knew – who had taken his wife when she was a young woman, a girl of seventeen, a child, a child, really – took her and kept her as his mistress and had babies by her which he – which he'd had killed, or farmed out to orphanages – (*Stands up, trembling with anger.*) What manner of man was this man? What manner of man, this Charles Dickens?

*Slough. Living room. Dick and Nelly as before, Dick holding Nelly's hand, Nelly's hand on Dick's head. Dick groans, shifts uncomfortably, bends towards his bad foot.*

**Nelly** I'll do it.

**Dick** No, no, I can –

*He reaches down to his boot, undoes a lace, seems about to topple sideways, rights himself. Nelly bends, undoes his boot laces. Takes off his boot. Dick yelps.*

**Nelly** Oh, I'm sorry, Nunky. Sorry.

**Dick** Not you – the gout! The gout's to blame! (*Laughs.*)

*With great care, Nelly peels off sock, under which are layers of bandage which she begins to unwind.*

**Nelly** (*peeling off the last of the bandages*) Oh, look at this, look at this! (*Holding his naked foot.*) And it used to be such a beautiful foot! Such a springy, bouncy, carry-you-anywhere sort of foot. How could you do this to it?

**Dick** It's not my fault, Nell, you mustn't blame me for the wear and tear –

**Nelly** Whom am I to blame then, myself?

**Dick** No, no, nature, it's nature's wear and tear. Natural, Mouse, natural wear. Natural tear. As a man gets older – and older – and older – (*He seems to drift away.*)

**Nelly** You're not old. You're fifty-eight. That's not old. You're in the middle of a new novel. I thank God for *Edwin Drood*.

**Dick** God? Thank Him for it? Why?

**Nelly** Because you won't let yourself die before you finish it.

**Dick** Don't you mean He won't let me die before I finish it? But I'm putting my all into it. All that I have. And a bit extra. Just for you, my Mouse, because you are my muse and my Mouse – (*Reaches a hand towards her.*) And you're in my heart as I write.

**Nelly** But it's to be a murder story, isn't it?

**Dick** It's a love story, with murder in it. And the murder has love in it – (*Settling back.*) Aaah, Nell, how good you are to me!

*Nelly says nothing. After a pause:*

Yes, I am beginning to feel very well again. (*Little pause.*) Now, shall we sing? I've been back at least twenty minutes and we still haven't sung.

**Nelly** In a minute perhaps. I have a headache.

*She sits down, looks at Dick.*

**Dick** Oh, poor Mouse. Did you ride this morning?

**Nelly** A little trot – then it began to drizzle.

**Dick** Oh, poor Mouse. Poor, poor Mouse. (*Little pause. He seems to drift off.*) No, no, all is settled, all is settled.

**Nelly** What do you mean?

**Dick** What? Oh – oh. I was just remembering an odd thing. On the way back from Sheffield I suddenly had the sensation that the carriage was slipping down to the left, for a second I was convinced that the train had left the tracks – and then when I began to feel safe I started thinking of the dead – the wounded – the cries – and then I made myself think – think that here we are, Mouse, you and I, we came through, we are alive. We still have each other. We still have each other. All is settled in spite of it, was my thought. Is my thought now. (*Smiles at her.*)

**Nelly** And it's a very comforting thought.

*She goes to the piano, tinkles. Stops. Starts again.*

But what I remember now, what I keep thinking of now, is how I was thrown one way and hurt myself, and Mama was thrown another way and broke her arm, and you – you were out and about saving people's lives and your reputation – (*Jangles the keyboard.*) – your reputation!

**Dick** I did all that I could. All that I could think to do – Oh Nell, here we are, here we are, you and I – (*Reaches out a hand.*)

**Nelly** (*after a pause*) You lied to me.

**Dick** Lied? Lied about what?

**Nelly** You read the scene. You murdered. I know you did. I can tell. That's why you're like this. When you left you looked healthy – almost healthy – and you come back, you come back – and you promised. You promised me!

**Dick** I didn't want to. I didn't. But I had no choice. They were expecting it. But I did it very quietly. Calmly and quietly. There was almost no excitement – I kept the fuss and drama to a minimum.

**Nelly** No, you didn't. You were ferocious. You were terrifying. The audience cried out when you beat Nancy upon her upturned face – when you seized the heavy club and struck her down – they moaned aloud – and the look on your face – (*Contorting her face.*) And struck her down! And then you took the dog and dashed his brains out! And what next? Why not yourself? Dashed your own brains out – Yes, it would have been like that – a dashing of yourself to death for the entertainment of your public – their loyal servant – to the end. And beyond – and yet you promised me!

*She goes out of the room.*

**Dick** Nell! Nell!

*He struggles to his feet, stands breathing heavily, in pain.*

**Nelly** (*entering*) What will become of me if you go on like this! You will die and what will become of me? Do you ever think of that?

*A pause.*

**Dick** I'm sorry. I couldn't resist, I wished to see the terror on their faces, and their pity, so it was vanity, I did it from vanity, we both know, but it was for the very last time. How could I do it again?

*He holds out his arms. He is trembling.*

Look at me, Mouse.

**Nelly** I can't bear to look at you, I can't bear it. (*Turning her head away.*) What you do to yourself –! Oh – oh – (*She turns, looks at him.*) Oh, Nunky, lie down, you must lie down.

*She goes to him, takes him by the arm, helps him back onto the sofa. She arranges his body.*

There you are. Now rest.

**Dick** (*takes her hand, carries it to his beard, strokes his beard with it*) What do you make of it now?

**Nelly** (*kisses him quickly on the lips, twines her fingers in his beard, blows into his beard*) Oh, how uncared for it is, like a neglected bush, so tangled, and rough –

**Dick** I never touch it, between going away and coming back. I wouldn't dare, it belongs to you – such as it is, such as it is.

*Drowsily, he catches her hand, kisses it.*

And yet it was you – you who asked me – wasn't it?

**Nelly** What? Asked you what?

**Dick** When we walked that time – our first time – Condaster.

**Nelly** Doncaster, do you mean?

**Dick** If you could feel my beard.

**Nelly** I had to feel your face, to make sure you had one, that you weren't a devil underneath it all.

**Dick** A devil! Hah! I was a poor forked animal –

**Nelly** Perhaps that's the same thing.

**Dick** Not to itself it isn't. To itself it's a poor forked – (*Gestures.*) And look on the poor forked now. Recumbent, groaning on a sofa –

**Nelly** Not even your love can stir it.

**Dick** I didn't say that, Mouse. But of course whether the spectacle of it can stir you –

**Nelly** To what? To my mousy devotions?

*She kisses him on the tip of the nose.*

There. Does that hurt?

**Dick** No. It soothes.

**Nelly** (*runs her hand gently down his body, stops at his crotch, presses slightly*) Soothes?

**Dick** No.

**Nelly** Oh – (*Alarmed.*) Hurts then?

**Dick** (*catches her hand, puts it back*) It enlivens. Brings me back to life.

**Nelly** Oh, any woman's hand can do that. If you shut your eyes you can make it any hand you want it to be.

**Dick** It could only ever be your hand. You always have my soul in your hand, to do as you like with. That is how I know your hand.

*He takes her hand, presses it against his crotch.*

Through my soul.

**Nelly** So it is your soul I press like this – like this – like this –

*She is becoming almost vicious in pressing her hand. Dick lies back, lets out a cry, ghastly in its combination of lust and pain. They look into each other's faces. Nelly forces her hand up to Dick's face.*

My fortune, please.

**Dick** You know I can't – not any more. Not of someone I love so deeply.

**Nelly** Of someone you love so deeply? Someone? Like me, you mean? And why not of someone like me you love so deeply?

**Dick** Because our lives are inseparable. I would be telling my own fortune too, and no man can do that.

**Nelly** Well, we can tell our pasts, can't we? Let us see what's happened to us since you took possession of me. (*Pulls his hand back, compares them.*) Yours is such a wavy line, full of crosses and clutters, here – you see – while mine just goes on in a drear straight line except for the losses, the two sad little losses – could these be they? This little little lump here, and this here – do they show on your hand – well, you have more, here and here and here and here and here – so those could be all your sad little losses, my two just two among them – which would they be? It's hard to tell, they're lost among all the others that belong to you alone, well, to you and someone else that you loved once, must have done, loved her indeed, else how could you have so many losses marked on your palm?

**Dick** Nelly, Nelly, please –

**Nelly** Now where is Staplehurst Bridge? Staplehurst Bridge should be identical on both our palms. How would a train crash show? And dead people, and people who'd lost arms and legs and children – how would their screams show? Can we see Staplehurst Bridge on yours –? Yes, here, this looks like a crash, and this on mine – yes, almost the same, look, your two lines and my two, and at the beginning here, like a stretch of railway track, and on it the Paris Express, from the heart of Paris to the heart of London. You used to say how you loved it, there it goes – (*Runs a finger along his palm.*) Chuff-chuff-chuff-chuff-chuff – chuff – closer to Staplehurst Bridge and closer – (*Getting faster and faster.*) Chuff-chuff-chuff – chuff – Crash! Crash! (*Pause, studying his hand.*) What does this mean here, and here, does it mean – chuff-chuff-chuff, me thrown one way and hurting myself, and Mama thrown another way and breaking her arm, and here you are, here, look at you! Scrambling through the window, pushing away all the broken glass, and then your voice – (*Imitating Dick's voice.*) 'There are two ladies in there! Sharing the compartment, I don't know who they are, but two ladies – two ladies in the carriage who've been hurt – Do see to them while I see to all these others, please look after the two unfortunate ladies I happened to be sharing a carriage with.'

*Dick attempts to struggle to his feet.*

What are you doing! (*Holding him down.*) Be still, lie still!

**Dick** I will not!

*He makes a titanic effort, struggles out of her grasp, stands upright. He is shaking.*

There! Here I am!

**Nelly** Yes, yes. There you are, here you are – now lie down again, Nunky –

**Dick** What for, what for, Nell? Look at me – see me – see what I've come to. You always talk about what you've given – look what I've given. This is all that's left of me, all.

**Nelly** Oh, Nunky, I was only playing. (*Takes his arm.*) Oh, you're trembling – lie down, please lie down, and – and we shall read your next chapter of *Edwin Drood* together, shall we?

**Dick** What, what, who?

**Nelly** Edwin Drood, Nunky.

**Dick** What?

**Nelly** Your novel, Nunky. *Edwin Drood.*

**Dick** (*after a pause, speaking carefully but emotionally*) Dread and dread are dood, stepfoots and I fog my dreet and swearest have pittle litty on her monkey. Nouse. (*Pause. Stares at her bewildered.*) Mell? Nouse?

**Nelly** Oh Nunky – Nunky –

*She pulls him gently to the sofa, settles him, is careful to keep his foot safe.*

There, there, back where you belong. (*Looks at him.*) Oh, look at you, look at you, look at you, Nunky, Nunky, Nunky – oh –

*She kisses him on the forehead, then on the tip of his nose, then on his beard. Kneels, takes his foot, kisses it.*

**Dick** Oh. Oh mlovingmell – Nunce – Nunce –

*He gives a cry, then shudders, goes still.*

**Nelly** (*after a moment lifts her head*) Nunky? Nunky? (*Gets up, looks down at him.*) What is it? Oh. Oh, Nunky – Oh please don't, oh please don't be – (*Taking his hand, clasping it tightly, kneels beside him.*) Jane! Jane!

*Jane enters.*

*Nelly clasps Dick to her.*

*Jane comes and puts her hand on Nelly's shoulder.*

*They stay on stage, as if in a tableau.*

*Office of Sir Henry.*

**Geoffrey** I apologise for my outburst.

**Henry** No need, no need – I quite see how upsetting this must be for you.

**Geoffrey** Until the day he died. Isn't that what you said? That she was with him until the day he died?

**Henry** She was, yes.

**Geoffrey** Did he – did he die in her arms then? As my father did? In her arms?

**Henry** No, no, not quite. But he was with your mother when he had his stroke. He was barely conscious, sometimes not even that, but she managed to get him into a carriage and all the way to Georgina at Gad's Hill, quite alone and by herself she did that. She was determined, for his sake and for the sake of his family, that he should die in his own home. And be universally known to have died there. (*Pause.*) It must have been a frightful business for her, frightful. None of us sufficiently showed our gratitude at the time, perhaps. Whatever your feelings I'd like you to believe that his love for her, and hers for him, was very great.

**Geoffrey** And if I did believe it, would it be a consolation, do you think?

**Henry** No. No, perhaps not. (*Pause.*) And to tell you the truth – the truth for me – is that though I am so much older than you, some things remain as fresh as if we were the same age. Let me tell you that – I once heard Mama – when she thought she was alone in the house – It was a sort – something like a, well, not a howling, no, but a noise, such a noise – Yes. And at that moment I wished them both dead, your mother and my father, for being the cause of such – such a noise from my mother.

## LITTLE NELL

*They sit in silence.*

**Geoffrey** (*gets up*) You've been most kind. And honourable. May I say honourable?

**Henry** (*also getting up*) I hope, in due course, that you'll come to forgive your mother, if not my father. After all, you've already lived so much life, been through a war with great distinction, obviously, and now have your bookshop in Slough –

**Geoffrey** (*shakes his head*) No. Oh no. No.

**Henry** I beg your pardon?

**Geoffrey** I shan't go back to Slough. Never back to Slough. I shall move to London, and – and I believe I will apply for parts.

**Henry** Parts?

**Geoffrey** In the theatre. As I said, I only went into the army because my mother wanted me to. Really, I longed to be an actor. It's in the blood, is it not?

**Henry** Well, yes, I suppose. But it might be a bit late –

**Geoffrey** Oh, I expect I shall have to start very low on the tree, but there are certain character types which would come to me naturally, I believe. Of course I'll take a few lessons first.

**Henry** Well, I'll follow your career with as much interest as if – you were – (*He holds out his hand.*) – some sort of relation. If a distant one.

**Geoffrey** Thank you, sir, thank you.

*They shake hands, hands still clasped as if in a tableau as . . .*

*Lights down on both tableaux.*

*Curtain.*

# THE OLD MASTERS

Alan Bates
(1934–2003)

# Introduction

*The Pig Trade* is about the turbulent relationship between the art expert Bernard Berenson, and the art dealer, Joseph Duveen. It is set in I Tatti, Berenson's famous villa outside Florence, on a summer's night in 1937, with Mussolini at the height of his power, the Barbarians at the Gates. I started to write it as a screenplay about four years ago, fiddling about with it for months, with diminishing interest and belief, until I abandoned it. My problem was that the heart of the story could only be revealed in the course of an epic confrontation between the two morally crippled Titans, which I couldn't write, perhaps because I knew in my bones that however I approached it, and against my every decent inclination, it would come out stagey. The solution, as a friend pointed out, was to write it for the stage, which I did. The first scenes, establishing Berenson and his household, his wife Mary, his mistress Nicky and Duveen's emissary Fowles, came easily enough – in fact I spent a great deal of unnecessary time in their company, in scenes that don't appear in the final play, simply because I enjoyed them so much, and because they delayed the moment when I'd have to get down to my dramatic muttons, with the entrance of Duveen. This comes just after Berenson has had a rather complicated domestic evening, full of love, anger, apprehension and sex, and is now alone in his study, making peace with himself, ready for a final, restful spot of work. He adjusts his lamp, picks up a folder, the door bursts open, the detested Duveen enters, Berenson looks at him aghast, Duveen opens his arms to embrace him – I simply couldn't get myself past Duveen frozen with outstretched arms, Berenson frozen aghast. I did the approach again and again, first changing the closing exchanges between Berenson and Nicky, then changing Berenson's actions in his study, finally providing Duveen with offstage footsteps and coughs, hoping that eventually I'd just find myself writing him into the room and the opening lines of the conversation, their last conversation together, the heart of the play. I stopped, waited for a week or so, started, stopped, waited, started, stopped – one night very late, or one morning very early, with my eyes closed, so to speak, I leapt.

> *Duveen bursts into the room, stretches out his arms. Berenson lets out a laugh of incredulity.*
>
> **Duveen** Happy birthday, BB!

It wasn't Berenson's birthday, actually, but I could sort out why Duveen thought it was, if he did think it was, later, or I could just cut the line or perhaps even decide that it was Berenson's birthday after all – I could do any or all of these things, easy-peasy, now that I'd got them to talk at last – in fact, the problem thereafter was how to get them to stop. *The Pig Trade* has not been produced on the stage in a previous form – in fact, at the time of writing, it has not been produced at all, although it almost certainly might be, some time between now and then, depending on the availability of actors, theatres, producers, directors, honesty and money.

PS. I've recently started looking at *The Pig Trade* again. I suspect that the version published here may turn out to be merely another draft, under the wrong title.

The Pig Trade *was rewritten as* The Old Masters *and premiered at Birmingham Repertory Theatre on 4 June 2004, directed by Harold Pinter. The above is an edited extract from the Introduction to* Four Plays, *2004.*

**The Old Masters** was first presented at Birmingham Repertory Theatre on 4 June 2004, and transferred to the Comedy Theatre, London, on 1 July 2004. The cast was as follows:

**BB**  Edward Fox
**Mary**  Barbara Jefford
**Nicky**  Sally Dexter
**Fowles**  Steven Pacey
**Duveen**  Peter Bowles

*Directed by*  Harold Pinter
*Designed by*  Eileen Diss
*Costumes by*  Dany Everett
*Lighting by*  Mick Hughes
*Sound by*  John Leonard, for Aura Sound

# Characters

**BB**
**Mary**
**Nicky**
**Fowles**
**Duveen**

# Act One

### SCENE ONE

*Garden of Villa I Tatti, 1937. A lovely evening, about seven o'clock. Mary is seated in garden, reading a letter. There is a bottle of wine in an ice bucket. Three glasses. She is sipping a glass of wine. Sound of voices, a man's and a woman's. Mary looks up, picks up the letter, puts the letter under some others, as if concealing it, hurriedly pours herself a glass, settles into what looks like a dozing position.*

*BB enters, with Nicky. BB in late forties, Nicky a little younger.*

*BB is in full flow, to Nicky.*

**BB** – and that soon the duck will imitate him as he imitates him in everything else, but with a dash of Italian originality – black shirts instead of brown shirts, this – (*imitating Fascist salute*) instead of that – (*imitating Nazi salute*) quack quack quack, instead of heil, heil, heil! But which is which? And does it matter? Quack, heil, heil, quack – (*giving alternate salutes*) quack, heil.

**Mary** I do wish you wouldn't do that. The servants might see you, and we don't know their politics.

**BB** Perhaps it's time we found out.

**Mary** Whatever they might think about Signor Mussolini, he is not the duck. He is il Duce, the head of their government. They might not care to have him mocked by a guest of the country. Hasn't it occurred to you that they could get into trouble for not reporting your antics to the police? We have no idea what risks they might be running simply by being members of the household.

*BB turns away, pours himself some wine.*

**BB** Your point is taken. They are good to us and we should respect their feelings. I shall quack *sotto voce* in future.

**Nicky** You've been looking at the bills, Mary?

**BB** The bills? Why?

**Mary** I didn't intend to open them but, once I started, I couldn't stop – like smoking or eating chocolates. (*To Nicky.*) Can we really pay them all?

**Nicky** Well, they shouldn't be very different from last month's, so we'll probably manage.

**Mary** Probably! What do you mean, 'probably'? What does she mean?

**BB** She means, of course, that we shall pay them as always on time and in full. Is there anything for me? (*Noticing letter.*) Who is that from? (*Making to pick it up.*) I recognise the handwriting.

**Mary** (*lurches away from Nicky, snatches it up*) It's from Karin. (*Sits down, stares defiantly up at BB.*) She's coming to stay.

**BB** When?

**Mary** The week after next.

**BB** For how long?

**Mary** She doesn't really say.

**BB** What do you mean – you can't be saying that she's written to you informing you that she intends to impose herself on me for an unknown period – you invited her! Why?

**Mary** Perhaps because she's my daughter, and I'd like to see her. Also she needs a holiday –

**BB** From her husband I suppose. (*Gestures.*) An abominable little man. I believe I can say that without giving offence, as he's not a blood relative, my dear. Actually I'm quite fond of Karin, especially when she's not obliged to play the besieged wife and mother.

**Mary** She'll be playing the besieged grandmother.

**BB** She's bringing those children, all those children –!

**Mary** The children are all in their twenties, as you know perfectly well. She's bringing her only grandchild, little Roger, who is very quiet and likes to read. I believe you're confusing Karin with Rachel. Probably quite deliberately.

**BB** No, not quite deliberately. Your daughters, their children, are confusing in themselves, I do nothing deliberately to confuse them, they – they – well, I shall not be here to entertain them. I shall go away for this unknown period, Nicky will accompany me, of course. Please make arrangements, Nicky. Book us first to Paris, then to London, we shall treat ourselves to a suite in the Ritz of both towns, you shall travel as Mrs Berenson, to save embarrassment, and to keep the expenses down. Go now. Do it at once.

**Mary** (*reaching out her arm for Nicky's support, as she goes back to her chair*) Oh, really, BB, really, really, really – you hate my family because you're jealous of them.

**BB** What, of the attention you give them, is that what you believe?

**Mary** No, it's not what I believe. You're jealous of them for being my children.

**BB** (*to Nicky*) I'm quarrelling with my wife and you're still here. Should you be?

**Mary** Yes, you should be, so don't you dare – and don't you dare, BB, my family is my family – this is my home, I will ask them here. I will ask them here! (*She is clearly upset.*)

*There is a pause, as Mary and BB look at each other.*

**BB** Of course, of course, my dear. And I will make them welcome as always. I was only being irritable. Though I like to think that we too, the ones already in your home, are also your family. (*Goes to her, kisses her on the cheek.*) Now I must go and do some work – Fowles will be arriving at any minute.

**Mary** No, he won't.

**BB** What? What do you mean?

**Mary** He's already here. I forgot about him because you've driven him out of my mind with all your – your –

**BB** Where is he, then?

**Mary** I sent him to have a little rest. Had a very bad journey, some trouble – yes, some trouble with the trains. And there's something else I've forgotten, BB. Your Swedish girl won't be up this evening, to do your massage. Apparently she has to be somewhere at seven, an emergency.

**BB** An emergency. She has to give an emergency massage?

**Mary** Probably someone needs her for something serious.

**Nicky** She looks after the footballers in Florence, she told me.

**Mary** Does she? I didn't know that. Well, there you are, BB, this evening you give way to the footballers of Florence. How many are there in a team of footballers?

**Nicky** Oh, twelve, I think. Twelve or thirteen.

**Mary** Twelve or thirteen! No wonder she won't be up to you this evening, poor thing!

**BB** Quack, quack, quack. When Fowles wakes, tell him I shall be in the library. (*Goes in.*)

**Mary** There. I got my own back. I know. I know. I should be nicer. But then so should he.

**Nicky** I don't think you should be nicer – I think he needs you to be like this, at the moment.

**Mary** Besides, you're nice enough for the both of us. (*Takes her hand.*) I mean that nicely.

**Nicky** Well – I sometimes wish I weren't.

**Mary** But you don't mind about the little Swedish thing, do you?

**Nicky** Of course I do. Did you tell her not to come?

**Mary** No, I'm afraid I didn't. I wouldn't dare.

**Nicky** So she'll be back tomorrow, will she?

**Mary** I expect so. Unless you find a way of stopping her.

**Nicky** I wouldn't dare.

**Mary** You could if you wanted. You have all the weapons, after all. He needs you, my dear.

**Nicky** Much less than he needs you.

**Mary** Oh, let's not get into one of those conversations, it always ends with our deciding that he needs us both, though I can never remember quite what it is that he needs me for. If you're not going to put your foot down, you'll have to accept her as one of the penalties of loving an unfaithful man with an appetite. And you know – much better a Swedish masseuse than something Italian. No emotional nonsense from her –

**Nicky** No, only from him, when she doesn't show up. He's such a child.

**Mary** Perhaps all very exceptional men are. Or so women in our position usually claim.

**Nicky** Yes. (*Laughs.*) I suppose we do. Well, I'd better deal with these bills. (*Picking up bills, moves to go off.*)

**Mary** Yes, it's very bad, isn't it?

**Nicky** No, really, we'll manage.

**Mary** (*to herself*) Bad, bad, very bad –

> *Thinking Nicky's gone, she puts her head back, then her hand to her stomach, clearly in pain. Nicky sees, goes across to her, puts her hand on Mary's forehead.*

Why do you always do that, when I never have a temperature? (*Takes Nicky's hand away, gently holds it.*)

**Nicky** But you have. I felt it. The doctor is coming tomorrow.

**Mary** I don't think I need him.

**Nicky** Yes, you do.

**Mary** Very well then, I don't think I want him. I only have one objective at the moment – to keep going just as I am until Karin and little Roger have visited.

**Nicky** But that's not for another two weeks, you said. And – and why not see the doctor so that you're at your best for them?

**Mary** This is my best! (*Sharply.*) Now leave me alone, there's a good girl!

*As Nicky makes to withdraw her hand, Mary grabs it.*

I'm sorry, my dear, sorry for being an old – old – you see, you see, something's happening to me, it seems to be growing in here – (*gestures to stomach*) like my illness, as part of my illness, it's fear for my children, dread, they're so hopeless with money, they never seem able to manage even with what I send them – so how can they survive if the war comes and we lose everything, and I have nothing – nothing to send?

**Nicky** But you know, Mary, the war hasn't come. Things might get better. Mr Fowles may have brought us the money Joe owes BB –

**Mary** It won't be enough.

**Nicky** Let me.

**Mary** Oh, if only BB would let Joe come here himself and be our friend again. He would find a way of helping, Joe could always pull something out of the hat when we most needed it. Little Fowles, he's very sweet I know, and tries to be helpful, but there's something about him I don't quite – of course he used to be Joe's lift-boy, you know, taking people up and down in the lift from Joe's office, listening to their conversations, then reporting back to Joe – a sort of infant sneak. Well, actually I hope he's still a bit of a sneak, in fact I'm counting on it.

**Nicky** You told him something you want him to report back to Joe?

**Mary** I trust he will. Joe has children, he dotes on his grandchild, he will understand why I am so worried. I only told Fowles what I've just told you – But the message should be quite clear – please, Joe, help me.

**Nicky** But wouldn't it have been better to write direct to Joe?

**Mary** I couldn't take the risk. It would have been evidence of treachery, BB would call it, treachery, so you see nothing may come of it.

*Fowles appears, carrying a picture, wrapped, and a case containing files. He is not yet seen by Mary and Nicky and hears the following.*

Fowles may forget to pass it on, may think it's an old lady's ramblings. I thought of bribing him, he may still just be a lift-boy at heart, with a habit of tips and bribes, perhaps Joe encourages it.

**Nicky** (*seeing Fowles, warningly*) Oh, Mr Fowles.

**Mary** Ah, there you are, Mr Fowles, you're here, good.

**Fowles** Yes, here I am. (*Putting picture down.*) Miss Mariano. (*Goes over, shakes her hand.*)

**Nicky** Mr Fowles.

**Mary** And did you manage a little sleep, Mr Fowles?

**Fowles** Actually, I sat at the window, looking out – couldn't resist – one of my favourite views, you know. And the light!

**Mary** Yes, the light! (*She attempts to struggle to her feet. The extent of her drinking is now clear.*) The light! I think it's time I had a little less of it, myself.

**Fowles** (*going tentatively towards her*) Can I give you a –

**Mary** No, no, I can manage. (*Moves towards the house. Stops, without turning.*) Mr Fowles, you overheard me saying things I wish I hadn't said. Or rather, that I wish you hadn't heard.

**Fowles** Oh, no, no, Mrs Berenson, I was very glad to overhear the little I did, it makes things – well, easier when one understands the situation. People's feelings. They often don't make them clear enough. A great help. And I haven't forgotten our conversation. I'd be glad to give you any help I can by mentioning it to Joe, but simply as a conversation between you and me. I am grateful to you for not offering a tip or bribe. It might have prevented me from performing a friendly service for you, by making it seem something else, and that would have been a pity.

**Mary** (*turns her head, smiles*) That is very gentlemanly, Mr Fowles. I am ashamed of myself. Perhaps one day when you have grandchildren –

**Fowles** I hope I will care for them as you care for yours.

**Mary** Thank you. (*Going off.*) And I think I forgot to ask earlier – the boy is still doing well, is he, at school?

**Fowles** Still doing well, thank you for asking.

*Mary goes off.*

**Nicky** Both still doing well, I hope?

**Fowles** Yes. David's turning into a little classicist.

**Nicky** You could probably do with a glass of wine?

**Fowles** Yes, I could. But I won't. I'm trying not to drink except with meals. If that's all right.

**Nicky** It's perfectly all right.

**Fowles** And how is –?

**Nicky** I'm to tell you he's in the library. You had a bad journey – some trouble on the train, wasn't there?

**Fowles** Oh, yes. Immigration officers, they said they were, but probably the police, really, looking for spies. Took me for a spy – and then they saw his name on one of my papers. Duveen, they said, Joseph Duveen, your employer is a Jew – and Berenson, you are going to visit a Signor Bernard Berenson, also a Jew, possibly? It was all like that, and I kept saying that Mr Duveen was an Anglo-American, I kept stressing American. Joe would have hated that, you know how important being English is to him, especially in America, but now in Italy I've made him into an Anglo-*American* businessman and art lover with a special love of the great Italian artists, and Mr Berenson the world's greatest expert on the great Italian artists – they both worshipped Italy for her history, her beauty, her people, that's what they were, who they were, neither of them in the slightest sense Jewish in the important sense of the word, etc., etc. – but it was all very shameful, especially if I think of the times I congratulated them on all the splendid changes taking place all around us, how wonderfully punctual the train was, going through stations to the minute, how I wished our English trains – it's the atmosphere, the arrogance and brutish stupidity, even my usual hotel in Florence – not – not Italian, really. Not my dear old Italy, eh?

**Nicky** No. I expect you must be anxious to be away, back to London.

**Fowles** Oh, well – it's pleasant enough to be here, in the garden.

**Nicky** No danger in it.

**Fowles** There's always a touch of danger at I Tatti.

**Nicky** Even here? With me?

**Fowles** Ah.

**Nicky** Ah? A diplomatic ah.

**Fowles** Sometimes especially even with you, Miss Mariano. A touch of danger.

**Nicky** If there is, it's you who bring it to me, Mr Fowles.

**Fowles** I was talking about how very – how very charming you always look – that sort of danger.

**Nicky** Thank you. But you are safe. (*Smiles prettily.*) Am I?

**Fowles** Well, there is a little thing – not exactly dangerous, of course not. But it depends on whether I stay on to dinner or not. I'm expected, am I?

**Nicky** Of course. You always stay to dinner.

**Fowles** Well, if I do, you won't have to do anything, because it'll mean I think I've got a chance of persuading BB to do what Joe wants him to do. But if I don't manage it, if things are going badly, I won't stay to dinner. You see? And Joe will take over.

**Nicky** Joe? You mean he's here, he's actually here?

**Fowles** Yes. Well, in Florence. He's come specially to see BB. If I fail, that is. As a last resort.

**Nicky** I don't think BB will want to see him.

**Fowles** Perhaps not, but he thinks that all he needs is someone to open the door for him, you see, so he isn't turned away before he has his chance. Once he's actually in front of BB and gets going – well, you know Joe. He believes completely in his power to charm. Even BB.

**Nicky** And he's right. He gets BB to play with him, and BB hates him for it immediately afterwards. Really, it's a bit like a bad love affair.

*Fowles laughs, rather coarsely, stops himself.*

**Fowles** That's an – a very interesting way of putting it.

**Nicky** He should come after Mary has gone to bed. She adores him, of course, and BB hates seeing them together, it makes him jealous – though I'm never sure which one he's jealous of. Perhaps he isn't, either.

*Fowles laughs again, slightly.*

She's never up much past nine. Tell him to come at ten o'clock sharp, and to ring very lightly, so as not to wake her.

**Fowles** Ten o'clock sharp.

**Nicky** I'll be waiting by the door. (*Smiles.*) But of course I'd much prefer it if you stayed for dinner.

**Fowles** So would Joe, I expect.

**Nicky** May I ask what it is that Joe wants, precisely? That's so important that he'll risk wasting a journey – and BB's insults?

**Fowles** He wants him to change his mind about an attribution.

**Nicky** Oh. The Masaccio that Mellon bought –

**Fowles** No, no. Nothing to do with the Masaccio, but the one Joe really wants him to – to think again about is a Titian. A Giorgione, rather. From Giorgione to Titian. No, I mean the other way around. Sorry. Titian to Gior— (*Gestures.*) You see. The mere thought of talking to BB about it makes me flustered –

**Nicky** It must be *The Adoration of the Shepherds*.

**Fowles** Yes. That's the one. What do you think of my chances?

**Nicky** I think I hope the food is good in your hotel.

**Fowles** And what about Joe's chances?

**Nicky** Ah well, Joe is Joe. It might depend on what he has to offer.

**Fowles** I'll tell him that.

**Nicky** I expect he already knows.

**Fowles** Yes. Well, well – I suppose I'd better be off to the library, and try my luck. Thank you, Miss Mariano, for all your usual – kindness. (*Takes her hand.*) I do enjoy our little –

**Nicky** Trysts.

**Fowles** Yes, well, I don't flatter myself, our little business meetings – Oh. (*Little pause, slightly embarrassed.*) There's something for – from Joe, a little token of his gratitude. (*Fumbling in his pocket.*) To add to your collection. He came across it in Boston apparently. (*Takes out a small box. Is about to hand it to Nicky.*)

   *BB enters.*

**BB** Oh, here you are. (*To Fowles.*) I hope you've had a decent rest. You seem to have had a long one. I've been waiting quite a time.

**Fowles** Sorry, BB. (*Slipping box back into his pocket.*) I was just sorting out with Miss Mariano some things, details – so that I won't need to trouble you with them.

**BB** The detail of a certain Italian count, perhaps?

   *He goes to wine bucket, pours himself a glass of wine, sees Fowles's glass, comes over, fills it with wine, offers some to Nicky, who refuses.*

**Fowles** What?

**BB** Joe recently wrote asking me whether the rumour is true that I've been keeping company with the gentleman.

**Nicky** (*to Fowles*) Gianisanti. Il Conte di Gianisanti.

**Fowles** Oh. Oh yes.

**BB** As I haven't bothered to reply I assume he's put you on to the case.

**Fowles** Yes, well, yes – as a matter of fact he did ask me to ask you whether you'd been advising the Count about the value of some paintings in his collection.

**BB** And if I have?

**Fowles** Well, Joe just wanted me to remind you that he has an exclusive contract with you.

**BB** A contract has to be honoured on both sides, does it not?

**Fowles** In what respect do you think that Joe has failed to honour?

**BB** Well, only on the money front, perhaps? As his *employee* I note that my wages are on an unusual course – as the years pass, they diminish. (*To Nicky.*) Remind me, my dear girl, what my wages were in 1927?

**Nicky** In the region of fifty thousand dollars.

**BB** And now, ten years later?

**Nicky** Twenty thousand dollars.

**BB** From fifty to twenty – and so next year – given that we're still alive next year, and not in captivity to the duck – what can we expect next year, if this rate of decline continues? Ten thousand, five thousand – and he complains because I seek for other sources – no, not seek, I don't seek other sources, other sources seek me.

After all, who else can they turn to? And what can I do under the circumstances, speaking as a man who is likely to have descended from fifty to five?

**Fowles** Well, the thing is, BB, if you'll excuse me, but the fact is that the market is the market, and percentages are percentages, and that's what your contract with Joe deals in – when Joe's income drops your percentage remains the same but your income drops too, in proportion as Joe's drops. It's worth remembering, BB, if I may say so, that while other men were throwing themselves out of windows on Wall Street, Joe not only survived but kept you on as much as twenty thousand dollars a year. Furthermore there's every reason to believe that we may soon start climbing back to where we were, war or no war, and your income would rise in proportion – depending, of course, on contracts being – well – contracts.

**BB** Very well, Edward, I'll accept that. Tell him, my dear, about the nature of my dealings with the Conte di Gianisanti. Miss Mariano accompanied me.

**Nicky** We paid him a visit in Milan, you looked at some of his paintings, he asked for your advice.

**BB** Which – ?

**Nicky** You withheld. You explained that you were exclusively consultant to Joe.

**Fowles** Ah.

**BB** For the while. I decided to wait for your visit. Either that or a cheque. A cheque – I mean you no discourtesy – would have been preferable. (*Little pause.*) As there is still money outstanding, I believe, is there not, my dear?

**Nicky** Eighteen and a half thousand pounds.

**Fowles** Yes. Well, then – I'll ask Joe to settle it as soon as I get back.

**BB** And?

**Fowles** And it'll be settled.

**BB** There. (*To Nicky.*) You've heard that. Marked the time and the date.

*Nicky uses Mary's pen and paper to write it quickly. BB takes both from her, hands them to Fowles.*

**Fowles** I'm sorry you think there's a need for this.

**BB** So am I.

**Fowles** And the Count in Milan?

**BB** The relationship will cease, you have my word on it.

**Fowles** (*handing pen and paper back to Nicky*) Your word?

**BB** Indeed.

**Fowles** Well, that will do for Joe, I'm sure.

**BB** (*pours more wine into Fowles's glass*) I'm relieved to hear it. (*Spotting package.*) And what is that?

**Fowles** It's the copy you asked for. I've done it. The Tacconi. (*Picking up package.*)

**BB** (*clearly at a loss*) You've done it?

**Fowles** Well, I mean, had it done. Picked it up from Madame Helfer on my way through Paris. Here. See what you think. (*Begins to open package.*)

**BB** (*recognising contents*) No, wait, it can wait –

*Nicky looks at the painting, now free of paper.*

**Nicky** Oh. Yes, of course. (*Clearly upset.*) So here it is. She's done it beautifully, as usual, Madame Helfer. If it is the copy. Are you sure it is? She's been so quick –

**Fowles** What? (*Anxiously.*) Well, surely she wouldn't have got them muddled –

**BB** (*almost snatching picture from Nicky, stares at it*) Of course it's the copy. She's almost a genius, Madame Helfer, but look – here – and here – slightest thinness – almost a signature for almost a genius, but a copier cannot be a genius, it's a contradiction – I'm sure Mary needs you, Nicky, shouldn't you go to her, please.

**Nicky** (*to Fowles, collecting paper and letters*) I'll see you at dinner, Mr Fowles, I trust.

**Fowles** Well – (*Gestures ambiguously.*)

*Nicky goes off.*

**BB** I did ask you – I believe I did ask you – to keep this private.

**Fowles** Well, yes, but I didn't think that included – I'm very sorry, it really didn't occur to me –

**BB** When I say private I mean, from the women. Otherwise I don't bother to use the word, as I assume that every detail of our business together is kept private from the world.

**Fowles** I see. Well, it's never come up before. I'll remember it in future, BB, but she seemed to know about it anyway –

**BB** Yes, yes – it's her feelings, her feelings – Mary's too – well, mine, I admit, mine too. I'm not easy about it, and they both sense it, and that makes me even less easy.

**Fowles** But it's for a good cause, isn't it, for some sick men in one of the villages, they'll be getting a bit of money for treatment now, from the sale of the original –

**BB** Yes.

**Fowles** Well, then.

**BB** Not men, boys still. Boys sent by the duck to Abyssinia, poisoned by the duck's own gas. Their priest took us to meet them, we saw for ourselves what it had done to them – and then he took us into his church and showed us what was hanging behind the altar – I could scarcely believe my eyes, but as my eyes never lie, even in the gloom of an unlit church, so – so the priest and I made a deal. And his church will now have this – (*gestures to painting*) hanging behind his altar.

**Fowles** But no one else will know the difference, that's all that matters, isn't it? You should see yourself as providence, God's instrument, that kind of thing. What is there to be ashamed of, BB? The people will think they're looking at the painting they've always looked at, the priest will be able to get treatment for those poor lads –

**BB** – and Joe and I will make a considerable sum of money.

**Fowles** A good deed isn't the less a good deed because everybody benefits. And it won't be that large a sum. At least, all the bids Joe's had so far have been less than he expected.

**BB** Well, that makes me feel much better. Thank you. Tell him if he can't get a decent bid – a decent bid – I'll find someone else who will.

**Fowles** Oh, I'm sure he'll get a decent bid. The lads will get their treatment, don't worry, BB.

*BB looks at him suspiciously.*

And we'll get our profit, don't worry, BB. (*Little pause.*) Oh. There are some photographs – (*reaching into his pocket*) he wants you to look at. (*Hands them to BB.*)

**BB** (*shuffles through them, giving each a fierce scrutiny*) A student's portfolio. School of Pesellino, School of Sebastiano, School of Baldovinetti, school of, school of – we have nothing of value here. What is this, this, what is this?

**Fowles** (*looks at photograph*) Well, that's the Bellini, isn't it, Joe's had it cleaned.

**BB** Cleaned, cleaned, he's had it defiled . . . Defiled!

**Fowles** Well, you know the Americans, they like their masterpieces to look as fresh as paint.

**BB** I haven't seen it, I haven't seen it, make sure I haven't seen it or I shall have to speak about what I've seen. (*Little pause.*) How ghastly this all is, how ghastly!

**Fowles** Sorry, BB?

**BB** Nothing, nothing, I – was addressing myself.

**Fowles** Oh. Can I say, may I just say – I know how you must feel, sometimes, it's difficult to be blessed with a gift that is so valuable to others –

**BB** A gift? Is that what it is? How do you know that?

**Fowles** Well, everybody knows.

**BB** How?

**Fowles** Well, for one thing there are books. Your famous books on the painters of the Renaissance. Your Four Gospels, as everybody calls them.

**BB** Ah, you've read them then, have you?

**Fowles** Well, no, not yet, BB, but I promised myself that one day, when I have a little spare time –

**BB** A little spare time! (*Laughs.*) You'll need a great deal of spare time for my Four Gospels, 'as everybody calls them'. They are in fact my Coffins, my Four Coffins, full of dead prose and murdered – yes, murdered thoughts. (*Stops.*) But if you haven't read them, where does your knowledge of this gift come from? From these conversations we have? Because I speak with such authority? But I may be speaking nonsense with authority. The gift you say I'm blessed with may be the gift of talking nonsense with authority.

**Fowles** Still, it's good enough for Joe.

**BB** And therefore good enough for you.

**Fowles** More than good enough for me, BB, given what I know about Joe, after all – oh, and talking of your authority – he particularly wanted me to discuss an attribution, whether you might care to reconsider –

**BB** Attribution?

**Fowles** Yes.

**BB** Which?

**Fowles** The *Adoration*, BB.

**BB** He wants me to re-attribute it?

**Fowles** Yes, from Giorgione to Titian.

**BB** I have attributed it to Titian.

**Fowles** Yes, I meant of course from Titian to –

**BB** No.

**Fowles** You won't discuss it then?

**BB** No. My attribution is clear and unqualified. There is nothing to discuss. If there was, I'd discuss it. I'm not a man who stands by his mistakes. Which reminds me – and proves my point – the Masaccio Joe has just sold to Mellon?

**Fowles** What? Oh. Yes.

**BB** It isn't a Masaccio.

**Fowles** But didn't you authenticate it?

**BB** Exactly. A mistake. I'm admitting it. You see?

**Fowles** But then – well, if Mellon finds out –

**BB** I shall be publishing my reasons.

**Fowles** Then Joe will probably have to give him his money back.

**BB** I expect so.

**Fowles** And – and you'll have to return your percentage.

**BB** (*after a little pause*) I regarded it as a fee.

**Fowles** Well, percentage or fee – it was for the authentication.

**BB** I will charge him nothing for altering it.

*Fowles makes to say something.*

That was a joke. When I have official confirmation that Mellon has returned the picture and that Joe has returned the money I shall, of course, return my commission. You see, Fowles, I can't afford to stick by my mistakes, whatever the cost. What use would I be with a damaged reputation?

**Fowles** And if Joe finds someone who will support your original authentication?

**BB** I shan't keep quiet. I shall challenge it. And of course my word will be accepted. Because of my reputation. Explain that to Joe. And tell him if I can bear my losses, he can bear his. And I need the money and he doesn't. And tell him further – no, no, don't tell him anything further.

*There is a pause.*

You look unwell – are you all right?

**Fowles** Oh, yes, yes, thank you – I was just wondering whether there was anything else – but I'm sure there isn't – so I can leave you to the peace of I Tatti –

**BB** But you're staying to dinner, surely? You always stay to dinner.

**Fowles** Unfortunately my wife is expecting me home for tomorrow. It's her wedding anniversary, you see.

**BB** Hers?

**Fowles** Ours, I mean. We've never missed one. We've got the boys back from school especially –

**BB** Oh. Well then – (*Holds his hand out.*) Have a good trip back to hearth and home. And happy anniversary to Mrs Fowles. As well as yourself.

**Fowles** (*shaking his hand*) Thank you. And my thanks to Mrs Berenson and to Miss Mariano. Please make my farewells for me.

**BB** Excuse my manner this evening. If I've been a bit – anxious. (*Gestures.*) But these are anxious times, anxious times. They make me ruder than I like to be.

**Fowles** Oh, that's all right, I – I – well, I suppose my trouble is that I'm not Joe.

**BB** On the contrary, your virtue – among many virtues – is that you're not Joe.

**Fowles** (*laughs*) Well, thank you, BB. (*Slight pause.*) And I'll see that the outstanding sum – the eighteen thousand –

**BB** Eighteen and a half, I believe Miss Mariano put it at.

**Fowles** Eighteen and a half, yes. The moment I get back. (*Makes to say something, doesn't, goes.*)

> *BB stands for a moment, takes a few restless paces up and down, sits down, pours himself a glass of wine, takes a sip, grimaces as if finding it warm and sour, flips the contents of the glass onto the grass.*
>
> *Mary enters during this, and stands propped on her stick, watching him.*

**BB** (*suddenly aware of her*) Ah. You're up and about, then.

**Mary** Yes.

**BB** And – what are you doing?

**Mary** I was looking at you. It struck me as odd – that it was a long time since I looked at you without your seeing me.

**BB** Indeed? (*Listening.*) Fowles has gone. He's not staying for dinner. (*Going to her.*)

**Mary** Oh. Pity. I quite enjoy his company at dinner. (*As BB tries to take an arm.*) It's all right, I can manage. You finished your business, then?

**BB** Yes, yes. He was more awkward than usual. More lift-boy.

> *Mary stumbles, almost falls.*

**BB** If you let me take your arm, you wouldn't stumble.

**Mary** (*sweetly*) Perhaps I prefer to stumble.

**BB** (*barks a laugh*) Yes. Perhaps you do. But it's easier to support you than to lift you from the ground.

**Mary** You go in. Tell Nicky to come for me. In five minutes. (*Going to seat, sitting down.*) In five minutes.

> *BB looks towards her, hesitates, goes off. Mary sits. Lights.*

## SCENE TWO

*BB's library. After dinner.*
*BB is sitting at his desk, reading the letter mentioned in Scene One. He is clearly amused.*
*Nicky is sitting at her desk on which there are two ledgers. She is wearing her spectacles, smoking a cigarette, making calculations, as she sorts through the pile of bills from the garden. She glances at her watch, glances at BB, goes back to her accounting.*

**BB** (*not looking up*) Very amusing letter from Kenneth Clark. Particularly about Joe and the National Gallery. Did she have trouble getting to sleep?

**Nicky** Yes.

**BB** More than usual, you mean?

**Nicky** She took a little opium.

**BB** I wish she wouldn't.

**Nicky** She didn't take much. I mixed it myself. But the pain is quite bad tonight. It's been bad all day, I think.

**BB** Yes. We'll get the doctor over tomorrow.

**Nicky** She won't have him. I've already tried.

**BB** Then what are we to do?

**Nicky** She doesn't want us to do anything. Her only plan is to see her family again.

**BB** See the family, take to her bed, die. Is that it? (*Little pause.*) Does she know I love her?

**Nicky** Oh, BB, of course she does. Just as you know she loves you. And don't worry about being disagreeable. She wouldn't have you any other way.

**BB** Yes, yes, And so we live together in rancorous affection. Or affectionate rancour. There may be a distinction. We used to brawl, you know, when we first met –

**Nicky** Brawl?

**BB** As in bar-brawl. Fight. Physically fight.

**Nicky** You and Mary? Why? (*Laughs.*)

**BB** I don't know. It would start from almost nothing. She would find something I said particularly distasteful or wounding – it never seemed particularly distasteful or wounding to me, of course, no different from anything I'd said five minutes before, in fact said most of the time – sometimes just a laugh, or smiling, yes, my merely smiling in a certain way, maliciously I suppose, would do it – she'd be on me, slapping and kicking and scratching at me like a fishwife in a comedy. I would have to catch her wrists, virtually wrestle her to the floor, hold her down. She was very strong. Agile. A brute, in fact.

**Nicky** Mary – a brute! Well, what happened then – after your brawl? Did you make love?

**BB** Sometimes. Or we would just sit together, talking quietly about – well, della Francesca, Giotto, Rembrandt –

whatever I was working on, thinking about at the time. And life, of course. Life. Life. It's a long time since we had a conversation about life. Or Giotto. But then it's a long time since we brawled. Poor Mary.

**Nicky** And poor you, from your expression.

**BB** I sometimes wish – find myself wishing –

**Nicky** What?

**BB** Oh, I don't know – perhaps that she and I had met as unattached man and woman, and then we might never have become attached, or if we had, simply become husband and wife to each other, and left it at that.

*Nicky laughs.*

You find that funny?

**Nicky** Well, the idea that any couple could meet as man and woman, and then simply become husband and wife to each other, and leave it at that! Leave it at that! If only Adam and Eve had left it at that! (*Kisses him.*)

**BB** Do you still love me, then? After so many years?

**Nicky** Oh, stop it, BB. You know I shall always love you.

**BB** But you – you've never shown a hint of jealousy. I don't think I'm altogether flattered by that.

**Nicky** You should be flattered by the fact that I've been completely faithful.

**BB** I couldn't have borne it if you hadn't been.

**Nicky** And yet you expect me to bear your infidelities.

**BB** What do you mean? What infidelities? – You can't mean the Swede? The sex is really just a part of her treatment. With knobs on. (*Lets out a bark of surprised laughter.*)

*Nicky looks at him.*

Yes, yes, very vulgar – well, you bring it out in me. It's one of your most delightful gifts.

*Nicky makes to say something, doesn't. After a pause:*

What is it?

**Nicky** No. Perhaps this is not the evening –

**BB** Yes, it is the evening, it is the evening. You want to say something, so say it. Not to say it would be childish.

**Nicky** Very well. (*Little pause.*) Then you must listen to me, BB.

**BB** I listen.

**Nicky** When I first came here we would spend hours together, you working so intensely, I watching you, learning how to help, I was so in love with you, and I knew you knew what I was feeling, you revelled in it, I could feel you revelling in it –

**BB** And so? They were wonderful hours, wonderful days – you've given me wonderful years, Nicky. I know that. I tell you so. More and more often. It's a form of dotage.

**Nicky** And so. And so. (*Pause.*) Every time you had a female house guest – I'd know whether you'd spent the night with her by Mary's little jokes in the morning. The only times I've ever hated her was when she made those jokes – she would watch my face as I tried to find an expression for her little jokes – you at least had the grace to dodge my look. I am not complaining, I am declaring my love. The nature of it. It has been well and truly tested, from the very beginning.

**BB** Yes. Well then, poor Nicky, too. My poor Nicky.

**Nicky** (*about to go, looks at him in alarm*) I didn't mean! My darling, you look stricken! Don't look stricken – it's nothing – I wasn't complaining – just remembering – teasing –

**BB** No, no, it's not you, it's never you, Nicky, my darling, it's just that I feel as if – as if – I am losing, losing a sense of myself, can it be? That there is nothing there, that really I have done nothing in my life, my life, except acquire, acquire my collections, acquire my reputation, acquire my I Tatti. Just a few hours ago, there I was, with little Fowles, negotiating about money and reputation and the painting we stole from the church and strutting my honour at him over Mellon's Masaccio but I could see that for him there was really nothing to choose between Joe and me, except that Joe is rich, and that I, suddenly, am becoming poor. There is a voice I hear, a piping voice, no, a shrill, jeering voice, that says well, well, it doesn't matter, nothing matters, you and Joe, Joe and you, you have earned nothing, you deserve nothing but each other –

**Nicky** This – this is all because you're having to worry about money, and it's wrong, you should never, ever, have to worry about money, it's an appalling indignity. You have earned and deserved everything you want, and you should have it – how can you speak of yourself and Joe, Joe and yourself? Joe is a businessman, a salesman, an entrepreneur, he is only important in that he is useful to you, and you have every right to use him, every right, because you, my darling BB, are a great man. You've taught people how to look at a painting and see into the soul of artists long dead –

**BB** No, no. Please no!

**Nicky** Well, you have. Yes, you have.

**BB** My darling Nicky, you are a Catholic and half-Russian, you believe that you and I and even Joe have souls, but I, for one, do not. I have only eyes – (*pointing to them*) that can see. A brain – (*tapping it*) that can think. A memory – (*wagging his hand over his face*) that can connect. I have no soul. It is not only the word that has come to disgust me. It is the very thought of the thing itself. It distracts attention from man's achievement, which is that he has evolved from the slime without benefit of soul. He has only his natural faculties, and his determination to cultivate them. No soul. No God. Just this, this, and that. (*Pointing to his eyes, his heart and face.*) And now – now – (*gestures helplessly*) they offer me nothing that can help me. Or so it would seem. So perhaps I could use a soul, after all, eh?

**Nicky** I've seen you a thousand times looking at a painting. Your face – your face has been full of soul, my darling. As a child – in Lithuania – when you used to wander about in the woods – what you described, the way you've described it –

**BB** I described a child in the woods, suddenly seeing the light. I saw the light. With my eyes. Just as now, if I were to look out of the window, I would see darkness. And one day soon we will see the darkness in the light. One morning or afternoon, in the sunshine, there will be the duck quacking at our gates. And then, however bright the sun, we will be living in an eclipse, a man-made eclipse, another human achievement to wonder at. Again without benefit of soul. Quack, quack. (*Lifts a finger, listens attentively.*) Is that a motor? In the drive?

**Nicky** (*suddenly realising, looks surreptitiously at her watch*) I can't hear anything. (*Goes to window.*) I can't see anything. No. No car.

**BB** One is always expecting the police. Those are the times we live in. (*Listens again.*) Are you sure?

**Nicky** Yes. But I'll go and look, if you want – it's time I checked on Mary. (*Hurries out.*)

*BB listens again, makes to go to the window, then forces himself back to his desk, hears something again, goes to the window, peers out at an awkward angle, obviously sees nothing, then goes to the door, opens it, listens. Clearly does hear something. Braces himself angrily, makes to go out, checks himself, closes the door quietly, thinks, goes to his desk, picks up the letter.*

**Duveen** (*offstage*) Miss Mariano, good evening.

*There is a knock on the door. BB pays no attention.*
  *There is another knock, slightly louder. BB pays no attention.*
  *Duveen enters. He is magnificently dressed, or appears to be, from what is visible of his clothes under his astrakhan coat – bottom of trousers, shoes, etc. He is wearing a silk scarf, a flower in his buttonhole, top hat in hand, and a walking stick. He is carrying a shiny, large, oblong case in black leather, with a handle, a form of briefcase.*

**BB** (*goes on studying letter*) Just a minute, if you please.

*Duveen puts down case, stands waiting.*
  *BB turns, looks at him. There is a pause. Duveen holds out his arms.*

**Duveen** Come, BB! BB, come. Let us embrace!

**BB** Don't be ridiculous. And how did you get in? Through a window?

**Duveen** I was about to ring the bell when your enchanting Miss Mariano heard me on the doorstep. She has such a smile – how I envy you, BB, to have such a smile in the house.

**BB** Nevertheless, she knows you're not welcome at I Tatti. She should have turned you away. I shall be very angry with her.

**Duveen** No, you mustn't be. Mary called out and she had to run to her. Fowles tells me that Mary is not well. I'm sorry to hear it.

**BB** She has a problem with her digestion, nothing for you to bother yourself with. But you're incomplete. Something's missing. Oh, of course, your cigar. Where is your cigar?

**Duveen** Ah, the doctors – the doctors forbid! (*Takes one out of his pocket.*) Though I keep one about me – for comfort. The occasional – (*Sniffs it, puts it back in his pocket.*) You are not surprised to see me, then?

**BB** I happened to be thinking about you. You arrived. On the dot.

**Duveen** On the dot?

**BB** On the dot of the thought.

**Duveen** And what was the thought?

**BB** It was occasioned by this. (*Holds up letter.*)

**Duveen** What is it?

**BB** A letter from Kenneth.

**Duveen** Kenneth?

**BB** He keeps me in touch.

**Duveen** Really? What does he say?

**BB** He says here that he thinks you are about to lose your trusteeship.

**Duveen** What? What do you mean?

**BB** Your trusteeship of the National Gallery. Kenneth thinks you're about to lose it.

**Duveen** It is gossip and rumour. Nothing has been settled. It'll become evident, when they look into it properly, that my relationship with the Gallery is completely *comme il faut*, completely proper and *comme il faut*, however certain – (*gestures*) ill-wishers may wish to make it appear otherwise.

**BB** Ah well, in England, you know, the *appearance* of impropriety is the impropriety. You would have understood that if you hadn't spent so much time in America. In America you've got into the habit of thinking of yourself as a sort of king, a position only possible nowadays in a capitalist democracy. And then when you come to England and play the buffoon –

**Duveen** I behave as I believe. That all men are born equal.

**BB** That is what I mean by buffoon. And they love you for it, or so you like to boast – your enthusiasm, your vulgarity, your patter of money and art and – there is the matter of the Sassetta panels.

**Duveen** The Sassetta panels, what about them?

**BB** Kenneth says in your role of trustee you have been negotiating their purchase for the Gallery.

**Duveen** Yes? Well? I am proud of doing so. They will be a splendid acquisition.

**BB** But it has come out they are in fact owned by you and it is therefore from yourself that you are buying them for the Gallery. He writes that this has made your position untenable. He is quite upset, because personally he is very fond of you.

**Duveen** But this is nonsense, nonsense! If I chose to sell the panels on the commercial market, I would make a far greater profit. In fact I will lose money by selling them to the National Gallery. Yes, probably lose money. And certainly time and energy, which I should be hoarding. At my time of life hoarding my time, my money! I have done nothing wrong! In fact I am making sacrifices for the Gallery. It is a sacred trust, to be a trustee –

**BB** Exactly, a sacred trust, a sacred trust, and yet here you are, talking of your time and your money, your profit and your loss, like a mere tradesman. They have been letting you enter and leave by the wrong door, Joe. In future you'll have to go around to the back.

**Duveen** Is that what Kenneth says?

**BB** His language is less delicate.

**Duveen** (*laughs*) Yes, yes, he has a sharp pen. Well – I'll see him as soon as I get back, I shall sort it out. I shall dispose of the panels somewhere else. By the time they get into the Gallery my name will no longer be attached to them.

**BB** I doubt that your name will still be attached to the trusteeship.

**Duveen** They need me.

**BB** They needed you.

**Duveen** I'll tell you what is odd, BB – that of the two of us, the scholar and the tradesman, it is you that should be the cynic.

**BB** It saves one a great deal of disappointment. (*Sees the case. Gesturing.*) What is that?

**Duveen** That? Oh – something I was hoping you'd enjoy casting your eye over later.

**BB** Perhaps now would be best. I shall be going to bed shortly.

**Duveen** Very well, you shall have your way, as you always do – (*Going to case, stops.*) But first let me finish a little business. I have brought a cheque for the sum that you and Fowles established as outstanding. In fact, I went through the figures again with Fowles, you and Fowles were out by a thousand. In your favour, BB, I am sorry to say. Where is it? (*Searching through his pockets.*) It is certainly here – never mind, I'll find it before I go. By which time I hope that we will be partners.

*BB stares at him.*

That is why I am here. I've come by train, boat and car to offer you a partnership, BB.

**BB** A partnership?

**Duveen** A full partnership.

**BB** That would mean, in my understanding, that would mean that I would receive a percentage on any transaction you completed, whether I participated in it or not?

**Duveen** Yes. That is what it means. That is the full meaning of full partnership.

**BB** And what would be the percentage of this full partnership?

**Duveen** Sixteen per cent . . . eighteen per cent . . . twenty, then.

**BB** But I assume that my commissions on any transactions that came your way through my – influence – would remain as they are.

**Duveen** Well, of course.

**BB** And if I ceased to interest myself in any such transactions –

**Duveen** You would have to waive your commission.

**BB** Naturally. I could scarcely claim a commission on transactions I hadn't undertaken.

**Duveen** Any more than you could undertake transactions without claiming a commission.

**BB** By which you mean?

**Duveen** No independent transactions. No deals with other dealers. In other words.

**BB** And if there were no deals at all?

*Duveen shrugs.*

But I would retain my partnership?

**Duveen** Such is your value, BB. And if you decide to involve yourself directly in any deal, your commission would be increased. As befits a full partner.

**BB** By how much?

**Duveen** It would be doubled. It would become fifteen per cent.

**BB** Doubled would be twenty per cent.

**Duveen** Doubled, I mean, from when we first entered into our arrangement.

**BB** I would prefer it to be from when we last nearly terminated it.

**Duveen** You see.

**BB** See what?

**Duveen** How helpless you always make me feel. There should be such a simple opposition, the trader and man of the world against the scholar and recluse – you should have no chance with me at all, and yet I end up yielding everything, everything.

**BB** The value of my name has depended on its not being publicly connected to yours. Our partnership must not be allowed to affect that.

**Duveen** You mean you wish our partnership to be confidential?

**BB** Of course.

**Duveen** So that your authentications will retain their integrity?

**BB** Of course.

**Duveen** But you will continue to authenticate?

**BB** Of course.

**Duveen** Well, that all seems clear and above board.

**BB** And it will be. I have no intention of letting our partnership compromise my authentications. They will be authentic.

**Duveen** As your retractions are authentic. Fowles tells me I will have to reimburse Mellon for his Masaccio. To the tune of half a million, perhaps.

**BB** Your consolation is that it is not a Masaccio. And your honour is preserved.

**Duveen** Our honour now. Our honour, BB.

**BB** Our honour. Which is confidential to us. Our private honour, therefore.

**Duveen** So. You accept then?

**BB** I accept.

*Duveen stands up, opens his arms.*

May we do it my way, Joe?

*Offers his hand. Duveen takes it. They shake. Duveen pulls BB to him, embraces him.*

*Lights.*

*Curtain.*

# Act Two

*The same. A second later, BB is still enfolded in Duveen's embrace. BB detaches himself.*

**Duveen** Well then. That concludes – that seems to conclude with everything settled between us. Settled at last. (*Stares at BB. Moved.*)

**BB** Apart that is, from the cheque. Eighteen and a half thousand pounds – (*Makes a little gesture, with his finger.*)

**Duveen** Nineteen and a half thousand pounds. (*Pats his pocket.*)

*BB looks at him, puzzled. Then, as if remembering, Duveen feels in his pocket, takes out cheque.*

You see what comes when you cuddle your partner? Hah!

**BB** (*laughs*) Well, I suppose this calls for a drink.

*Moves towards drinks.*

**Duveen** Not for me, no drink – no cigar – perhaps a drop of water, though. Eh? No, no, you're right, one must do something, yes, one can at least hold and smell – (*Takes out cigar, sniffs it, rolls it about.*) And a drop of grappa to go with it, just a drop – that local grappa if you still serve it in I Tatti.

**BB** It hasn't been touched since you were last here –

*Brings Duveen glass of grappa.*

**Duveen** (*sniffing it, then sniffing cigar*) Ah! Ah! Those were the days, those were the days. But still, this is the life!

*BB, coming back with drink, sees case.*

**BB** Now what is that?

**Duveen** In a minute, in a minute, now let us just be, just be . . . So good – so good to be here again, talking together again in a way that we used to.

**BB** Yes, well – much of the time we didn't talk, Joe. We often ended up shouting into each other's faces. Once or twice I found myself on the verge of hitting you.

**Duveen** You mustn't blame only yourself, BB. There were flashes of intemperance on my part, too. It's really because we're so fond of each other. For thirty years we've been this and that, on and off, sometimes a good marriage, sometimes a bad one – but how could we not be matched for life! When you think of what you do, and then of what I do.

**BB** And how is Elsie?

**Duveen** All the better for your asking, thank you, BB. She will rejoice at our news. I used to be quite jealous – she admires you so much. But though I could never do what you do – I haven't the eye, the mind, the memory – the genius, yes? But then what is genius but unique? But then what I do – what I do – well, not many men can do as I do, eh, BB, give me that – not unique, but the best. But – to tell you the truth, I sometimes wonder if I can do it any more – the collectors now, the sort of men who want to acquire great works – Frick and Huntington were difficult men, difficult, but at least I could teach them, yes, that was my gift, that made me the best – I could teach men like Frick and Huntington the value of what they were buying – I persuaded them that they – well, that they had – (*Meets BB's eye.*)

**BB** Souls.

**Duveen** Yes. Yes, I know what you think of the word, but Frick and Mellon had something, whatever you call it, that a man like Kress hasn't even a whiff of. Not a whiff of a whatever you call it in Kress. That is my point.

**BB** Kress? Who is Kress?

**Duveen** Kress is the new man. The new American. He is the future. He is Mr Five-and-Dime. Kress.

**BB** Oh. Those stores.

**Duveen** All across America. In every state. And here's something. Let me tell you something. When he was in – he was in . . . (*Looks at cigar, puzzled, fumbles in his pocket, stops, stares at BB, bewildered.*)

**BB** Joe?

**Duveen** What?

**BB** We seem to have lost you.

**Duveen** Lost me? What do you mean? What was I talking about? You've distracted me.

**BB** It was your cigar that distracted you. I believe you were looking for your matches.

**Duveen** (*showing him matches*) They are here. I have them.

**BB** Then perhaps you should use one.

**Duveen** Oh no, BB, no, no, don't tempt me. The doctors forbid. (*Puts matches and cigar back in his pocket. As he does he mumbles something, and the word 'devil' is just audible.*)

**BB** What? What are you saying?

**Duveen** Mmm?

**BB** About the devil. You said something about the devil, I didn't quite hear it.

**Duveen** The devil, eh, the devil, did I, well, I probably said let him take the hindmost, eh, BB? (*Roars out an odd laugh, stops, starting into sudden fluency.*) Yes, there he is sitting in a café in Algiers –

**BB** Who?

**Duveen** Kress, Kress, Samuel Kress – I was just talking about him, when you – (*Gestures irritably.*) And along comes one of those street traders, selling shawls – (*Imitates.*) Shawls, shawls, beautiful shawls – pushing them along in his handcart. So our man Kress, he can't let the opportunity slip by, even in a café in Algiers on his holiday. With a trader who trades he has to trade a little, what else is there for him to do? So he begins, how much are they? Ah, and in dollars how much, ah, and if he buys two shawls now how much in discount, and the discount for three how much, how much, say, if he buys half the stock he sees before him, would he get a couple from the half he leaves behind thrown in free, ah, and how many shawls does this trader have apart from what's on his hand-barrow. Ah, well then, put that stock on top of this stock, how much discount? So on it goes and on, until at the end, he makes his purchase of seven thousand, three hundred and fifty shawls of which two hundred and fifty are completely free, another two thousand, one hundred and fifty shawls discounted down to almost their true worth, the deal of a lifetime, because when he's sold every single one of them, which he will do, he'll have made a clear profit of three hundred and forty eight dollars, which will be a seventy per cent profit. That's it, you see, that's the point, for this man of many millions, he will have pulled off a remarkable coup of a seventy per cent profit. Who cares whether it's in millions or in cents, that's what matters to him, that's the spirit of him, that's the – the whatever of him.

**BB** But surely, Joe, you will educate him. You will make him worthy of his purchases, yes?

**Duveen** I am trying. I am trying. I am trying. But listen to this, BB. Six months ago I let him into my private gallery, into the very heart of it, where I keep one of my most sacred shrines. My Amico di Sandro. (*Nods at BB.*) So you had designated it, BB. I folded my hands, so. (*Folds them.*) And gestured thus. (*Gestures prayerfully with his hands.*) And he looked at this – this truly – of a grace, a charm, a religious tenderness, of a holiness and a lustrousness – as I said to him – whispered to him. Holiness. Lustrousness. (*Whispering intently.*) Luminousness. And he squinted at it for eight, nine, ten seconds, and he said, 'How much?' So. So I doubled the sum that came into my head and added fifty thousand. He said, the room back there, the one we came through, there were six paintings in the room, who were they by? Well, I said, there were two Titians, a Gainsborough, a Tintoretto, a Botticelli and an Uccello. And how much are those, he asked? Well, I said, and I began to give him the price of each. Ah, he said, but if I bought the lot? I named a price, a price, a sum, a sum so huge – ah, he said, now if I bought this sacred and luminous masterpiece here, and three of those other masterpieces in there, what kind of discount would you give me? Ah, and now if I took five and the sacred and luminous masterpiece, ah, and if I took all six and the sacred and luminous, what would you throw in free, and what discount on the other six. And so – and so – I was the street trader in Algiers, BB, I began to bargain, yes, before I knew it, I was bargaining with Mr Five-and-Dime over Amico di Sandro and a fistful of price-reduced masterpieces – No, no, I shouted, no, no, this is not for sale, those are not for sale, not to you, no, they're already sold, they're going to Mellon, all of them, to Mellon. Oh, Mr Mellon, he said, well, why didn't you just say so in the first place? Because I've only just realised, I said, and I haven't told him yet. Well, how do you know he'll buy them, he said? Because, I said, because I'll tell him that if he doesn't they'll go to you. Ah, he said. Ah. He didn't say another word except goodbye and thank you. On the pavement. Well, of course, since then I've had to allow him some droppings from my table, a tidbit here, a tidbit there, just to keep him quiet, but you know the story about the appetite, and what it feeds on. And with Frick dead, Mellon dying, what can I do but trade with Mr Five-and-Dime?

**BB** Mellon is dying?

**Duveen** But not dead. Not yet dead, thank God! We can't have him dead until he's finished his life's work, on which his immortality depends. A few paintings for him still to acquire. One in particular. Yes, one will be enough, if it is the right one. And then he may go. In peace and triumph. With one of the world's greatest collections as his memorial.

**BB** One will be enough?

**Duveen** If it is the right one.

**BB** (*glancing towards the case*) And have you brought it with you, by any chance?

**Duveen** I have.

**BB** That is the pleasure you promised me.

**Duveen** To cap your evening. You will not be disappointed. (*Gets up, goes to the case, looks around, sees a stand, on which there is a picture underneath a light that is off.*) May I? (*Turns on light, looks at picture as he removes it from stand.*) Goya. But you detest Goya.

**BB** That's why I keep him in the dark. I'm thinking of writing a short paper. (*Indicating a corner.*)

> *Duveen places Goya where BB indicated, adjusts the stand for best visibility, goes to his case, takes a bunch of keys out of his pocket, uses a succession of keys to open case, each clicking, opens lid ceremonially, takes picture out. Carries it to the stand, arranges it there, steps away, looks towards BB, who hasn't moved.*

**Duveen** Don't you want to see what it is?

**BB** I know what it is. Your lift-boy let the cat out of the bag.

**Duveen** Well, what?

**BB** It is a copy of *The Adoration of the Shepherds*. By Titian.

**Duveen** No, it is not.

**BB** Well, what then? (*Comes over, looks, looks more closely, in disbelief.*)

**Duveen** You see, BB – not a copy!

**BB** You've been carrying this in your luggage – in cars, boats – through customs –

**Duveen** It was thrilling. Took me back to the old days, BB, when Mary had the false bottoms to her suitcases, and her hat-boxes for the icons.

**BB** And you smuggled it all the way here just to give me pleasure?

**Duveen** And does it give you pleasure?

**BB** Yes. But is it the only reason?

**Duveen** Well, you already know from Fowles, then – I wanted the pleasure of your opinion of it, after you've given it a fresh look.

**BB** Ah! Then I will give it a fresh look.

> *Duveen waits, impatient.*
> *BB goes to painting, studies it with great concentration. He straightens, looks at Duveen.*

**Duveen** Well. What?

**BB** Well what, what?

**Duveen** What did you see? What struck you? Something struck you! I saw it strike you!

**BB** Yes. The exceptional genius of the pupil that is escaping the genius of the master. This is an act of escape, yes. Everywhere the influence of the master, and yet – and yet – it is a creation that is completely the pupil's. A hatching, a moment of sublime hatching. That is what I suddenly felt. As I'd never felt it before. All the times I'd looked at it. However hard I looked. Never had that moment. Thank you, Joe. It was the last thing I expected this evening. Especially when you have already given me so much.

> *Duveen says nothing.*

I am glad it is going to Mellon. It will be a great addition to his collection. And congratulations to you, too, Joe, are of course in order.

**Duveen** (*coldly*) And to yourself, too, as partner. Twenty per cent of the commission will be yours.

**BB** Generous of you, Joe, but I must decline. This is something you achieved before we reached our agreement.

**Duveen** Not that you will be losing much, eh?

**BB** However much or little, it is entirely yours. (*Little pause.*) Well, perhaps I could take my old percentage, if you see fit to use my name. If you think Mellon wants my name attached –

**Duveen** You are laughing at me! (*Shouting.*) Do you think I have come all the way here to be laughed at!

**BB** What about? What am I laughing at you about, Joe, please?

**Duveen** (*pulls himself together*) All right then. Let us discuss it calmly.

**BB** I am calm.

**Duveen** You realise now that you are quite alone.

**BB** Quite alone? Really? In what respect?

**Duveen** *The Adoration of the Shepherds* has been authenticated as a Giorgione by every other expert in the field. But most particularly by Richard Offner. Not even you can deny his authority.

**BB** Indeed not! Nor his integrity. I'm always sorry when he and I disagree. But there we are. I for Titian, he for Giorgione. An interesting debate. History, I suppose, will decide between us.

**Duveen** I can't wait for history. I need it settled now. Once and for all. No loose ends.

**BB** Why?

**Duveen** You know why. Mellon wants a Giorgione, not a Titian. The difference between a Giorgione and a

Titian is a difference of – of – hundreds of thousands. More. A million.

**BB** Why?

**Duveen** Why? What the devil do you mean, why? You know perfectly well why! Because there are lots of Titians and very few, very few – (*Gestures to painting.*)

**BB** But surely what matters is that this is a glory in itself, whether painted by the prolific Titian, or Giorgione – who, I've often thought, would always have hoarded his genius, only releasing it after long intervals of creative contemplation, and that there would be very little of him, even if he hadn't died young.

**Duveen** That's as may be, that's as may be – the fact is he did die young, and – and we owe it to him, to our understanding of his genius, to give him the reputation he deserves.

**BB** But of course.

**Duveen** By assigning to his name his few and precious works.

**BB** But because they're so few and precious we must be particularly careful not to be careless – or greedy – in our assignations. Grant one here – (*gesturing to painting*) merely to increase its market worth, and soon we'll be granting another one, and then another one – why, even in your own terms, Joe, that finally becomes bad business.

**Duveen** There isn't another one, there is only this one, and Mellon wants it as a Giorgione, which it is, it is – it is a Giorgione, not a Titian, and Mellon should be allowed to have it as a Giorgione – he doesn't want it as a Titian. (*Little pause.*) At least accept the possibility that you might be wrong.

**BB** I always accept that possibility. Good God, Joe, these are matters of opinion. Informed opinion. I acknowledge a mistake when there is further information that alters my opinion. Which was the case with the Masaccio. There has been no further information to alter my opinion that *The Adoration of the Shepherds* was painted by Titian. And I have to back my own opinions, Joe, don't I? Or what would be the use of me? What would have been the use of me to you, in the past? The profitable past? I have been, you might say, your golden opinion.

**Duveen** You admit you've made mistakes. What's more, BB, what's more, I've known times when you've gone where the advantage is. (*Little pause.*) The profit. (*Little pause.*) Sometimes when there's been only the slightest, the very slightest, doubt.

**BB** I hope that that is not true.

**Duveen** I could specify them. (*Little pause.*) I will specify them. For instance the Bellini –

**BB** I said it was conceivable that it was not a Bellini.

**Duveen** Then say the same of this. Say it is conceivable – it is conceivable – that it is a Giorgione. I'll settle for that.

**BB** You mean Mellon will settle for that?

**Duveen** He would. I'd see to it.

**BB** Really? And he – you – wouldn't expect me to withdraw my previous attribution to Titian?

**Duveen** (*after a long pause*) No. That won't be necessary.

**BB** Really?

**Duveen** You need do nothing.

**BB** Ah. (*Little pause.*) I see. You will announce that it is a Giorgione, you will announce the source – the eminent source – Offner.

**Duveen** Sources. Sources. Offner and everyone but you. Everyone that matters but you.

**BB** And as long as I hold my tongue –

**Duveen** Hold your tongue, BB? As soon ask a river to hold its flow.

**BB** Well then – we've come a long way. From begging for my authentication of Giorgione to allowing me freedom to repeat my view that it is a Titian. Can that be right, Joe? Do I understand you?

**Duveen** Privately. Privately you can confirm it as a Titian. (*Goes to painting, almost cuddling it.*) Even though you are not a Titian. You are a Giorgione. On every centimetre it is evident, to my eye, Giorgione himself is crying out, this is by me, this is me, here I am, at my greatest, why deny me, how can you deny me my being who I am? (*To BB.*) But you are at liberty to deny me my being who I am. Privately you can pass me off as Titian. You have my permission. You have my blessing.

**BB** Thank you.

**Duveen** Just as long as you publish nothing. That is all I ask.

*BB nods.*

You agree, then?

**BB** (*glances at the painting, then as if drawn to it against his will, goes to it, studies it*) You realise that I've already admitted that without Giorgione this painting could not exist.

**Duveen** Ah – well, if you would say that! Then – then I'd say that you have already earned your partnership, BB!

**BB** Earned it?

**Duveen** Honoured. Honoured would be the better word.

**BB** Would it? (*Turns back to painting.*) These faces – the faces of the two kneeling shepherds – however hard I try, I never remember them properly. I retain an impression of intensity, of devotion, but I never have a sense of them in their individuality, their eyes, their features, their expressions – and now of course I realise why. Because of course he doesn't show us their faces. See, Joe. No faces.

**Duveen** (*peers*) No. No faces. Is that good or bad?

**BB** It is magnificent. You see how everything – (*Stops.*) So this is our understanding. We know, you and I, Joe, that I believe this to be a Titian, but on the other hand, in order to honour and earn, earn and honour our new partnership why not, why not, for God's sake, nod it through as a Giorgione. No need to publish or even speak the lie, just a nod that nods it through, a nod in my sleep, even Homer nodded once or twice, now and then, why shouldn't BB nod, just once, now – what difference? Think of Europe now, think of what awaits us tomorrow, what difference then a little nod in a Tuscan library at midnight, a little nod from BB to Joe?

**Duveen** No difference.

**BB** Except to you and me.

**Duveen** Except to you and me. (*Pause.*) You don't even have to nod. You don't even have to look the other way. You can say what you like to whomever you like, as long as you don't say it in print. What could be better? What could be easier?

**BB** And I will have earned and honoured my partnership.

**Duveen** Yes.

*BB shakes his head.*

What are you doing?

**BB** I am shaking my head.

**Duveen** Why?

**BB** Because it is the opposite of a nod.

**Duveen** But why?

**BB** Because you have been trading, Joe. Since you came here you have been trading the partnership for a nod.

**Duveen** You mean, it's a matter simply of my having put it into words? (*Laughs.*) You can't mean that?

*BB says nothing.*

I never spoke them.

**BB** You spoke them.

**Duveen** I didn't mean them. You misunderstood.

**BB** You meant them. I understood.

**Duveen** And therefore you'll – what will you do?

**BB** I shall publish to the world my view that *The Adoration of the Shepherds* is a masterpiece of Titian's apprenticeship to his great master, Giorgione.

**Duveen** It will go to Kress. To Kress. It will go to Kress. He will buy it and exhibit it – God knows where he will exhibit it – (*Laughs.*) But wherever it will be, it will be an insult. Furthermore, he will probably exhibit it as a Giorgione.

**BB** Then you have the ideal purchaser. One who doesn't give a fig for my views. Still, I can see that it's not a negotiation that you care to be associated with, even by default. Certainly not at this stage of your career, eh, Joe, with your trusteeship of the National Gallery and your reputation already – (*Gestures sympathetically.*)

**Duveen** You think doing this will save yours, is that it? Well then, it's time somebody told you, BB, you no longer have a reputation. Except with Mellon, alas, a dying man clinging to his sad old habits. But among the tellers of reputations, yours is pretty well known these days for the uses to which it has been put over the years. It's losing its value in the marketplace, even. You will have to skulk here in I Tatti with diminishing funds and when you die your collection will be dispersed around the world and I Tatti will become what, an old people's home, a hotel for American or German tourists. Perhaps there will be a suite or a public room named after you, yes, the Bernard Berenson Lounge, where businessmen can do deals and then take cocktails with their weekend girlfriends. And as for your gardens, the chapel – (*Makes gesture.*)

**BB** I like the thought of the weekend girlfriends. That will be preserving something of my spirit. (*Little pause.*)

**Duveen** Or perhaps you hope your reputation will live on through your writings, your Four Gospels. Your own masterpieces. But there are certain doubts there, are there not? About attribution? Rumours have been circulating for some time that the hand that held the pen was not always yours.

**BB** The moment I hear that *The Adoration of the Shepherds* has been ascribed to Giorgione, I shall fire off a contradiction. In fact I shall probably write the contradiction as soon as you leave. Along with a copy for Mellon. Finished business, merely requiring posting.

*Duveen goes to the painting to take it. BB lets out an involuntary cry.*

**Duveen** What?

**BB** Leave it a little longer.

**Duveen** Why?

**BB** So that I can look at it a little longer.

**Duveen** Why?

**BB** Just a few minutes, Joe.

**Duveen** I would prefer to be on my way.

**BB** Joe, Joe, you're being petty. That is not you.

*Duveen hesitates, replaces the picture.*

Thank you. (*Turns away.*)

**Duveen** And what did you see this time?

**BB** Only the picture. No names, no dates, no history. Only the picture. Now I have it here – (*touching head*) as it should be. Worthless. Beyond worth. Mine, for whenever I need it.

**Duveen** I've always longed to look into you as you look into paintings. But your eyes are never still. Can't you keep them still?

**BB** (*coming over to him*) I think I can keep them still when I look into yours.

*They stare into each other's eyes, BB smiling, Duveen frowning with concentration. BB breaks away.*

**Duveen** I haven't finished!

**BB** I saw what you wanted me to see. How long do you have?

**Duveen** (*goes to chair, sits down, as if suddenly collapsed. His speech becomes feebler*) Five years ago they said I would last three months. The five years are now up, I believe.

**BB** I am sorry.

**Duveen** Thank you.

**BB** But I can't buy you a further period of life by changing my opinion about the attribution of a painting, can I?

**Duveen** And if you could, would you?

**BB** For your life?

**Duveen** Any life?

**BB** For the life of someone I loved, almost certainly.

**Duveen** But certainly not for mine?

**BB** (*laughs*) Oh Joe, really, you're being disgusting. You'll probably have yellow eyes for another five years. Ten.

**Duveen** I shall be dead within three months. You have my word on it.

**BB** Very well. I accept it, as always, your word.

**Duveen** Thank you. Is it possible perhaps to say goodbye to Mary? I can't imagine another opportunity, and I've always had the greatest affection . . . It would mean a lot to me, BB.

**BB** I'd rather you didn't. It would mean waking her and – she's easily agitated, these days.

**Duveen** A kiss, perhaps, on her sleeping forehead? I'll be very quiet, very careful.

**BB** (*hesitates*) Her sleep is too precious. I can't risk it. I'm sorry, Joe. I'll say your goodbye for you, in the morning.

**Duveen** And will you tell her what you've thrown away? Fowles tells me that she's concerned about her children. And her grandchildren. She needs money for them. I know she always looks to me when money is needed. Well, I shall have to write to her and explain that it is not my fault that I cannot help her. (*Goes to the painting, takes it to the case, begins to put it in.*)

**BB** Write, by all means. She can sometimes read her letters. Mostly I read them out to her.

**Duveen** It is that serious, then?

**BB** As serious as your own condition, I would think.

*Mary enters. She is in a dressing gown, her hair loose.*

**Mary** I knew someone had come, Nicky said I'd dreamed it – (*Going to him.*) But I didn't dream it was you, dear Joe!

**Duveen** (*as he embraces her*) Yes, here I am – in the flesh!

**Mary** And just what's needed, just to feel you – (*touching his cheeks*) – in I Tatti again. We don't know where we are any more, with those two dreadful men and their hateful politics and Jew-baiting and threats of war – we can't really be in our Italy, our beloved Italy, can we? We're in some nightmare other country – what are we to do, Joe, what's to become of us?

**Duveen** I don't know, my dear, these are terrible times, terrible – but then – but then as my old uncle in Delft used to say, whatever we do the world goes on spinning, each day has its tomorrows, and each tomorrow will have its yesterdays, whether we're on the earth or under it.

**Mary** (*laughs*) Well, thank your Delft uncle, perhaps it sounds more consoling in Dutch.

**Duveen** No, it sounds more depressing in Dutch, but he said it in Yiddish, if he said it at all – I have only my mother's word for it.

**Mary** Oh, yes, yes, I say much the same to my little Roger. But has he offered you anything, a glass of wine –

**BB** My dear, you shouldn't be up, you were feeling a little sickly.

**Mary** You are staying the night, aren't you? BB, tell Nicky to get Joe's old room ready –

**BB** He can't. He's just leaving.

**Mary** Oh Joe!

**BB** A car awaits him, the train, the boat –

**Mary** Well then, what are you doing here like this, just popping in without warning –

**Duveen** I had a little plan that I thought might interest BB. But alas, my dear –

**BB** He wanted my opinion on a painting. That's all.

**Mary** Really? Which?

**BB** One on which I'd already given my opinion, as it turns out, so really the matter is closed, Joe was just taking his leave and you should be in bed. Does Nicky know you're running about like this?

**Mary** (*to Joe*) Which painting?

*Duveen gestures to case. Mary goes over to look down.*

Oh. Oh yes. Of course. It had to be, hadn't it? (*Takes it out, props it on the lid of the box. Gazing at picture.*) Oh! Oh! How I love her face. How did he do it? Oh, I wish we could keep it! – Well – (*Puts it reverently back in the box.*) At least I'll be able to claim that once, for a few minutes, we had Giorgione here in I Tatti.

**Duveen** Hah!

**BB** It is a Titian. In my view. Which is the view that matters. As far as Joe is concerned. (*Goes over to case, brings it to Duveen.*)

**Duveen** Though I should mention – may I mention, BB – to Mary that I came first and foremost to offer you a partnership. A full partnership.

**BB** Perhaps you should also mention that the offer was withdrawn.

**Mary** Why?

**BB** Because I refused to change my opinion.

**Mary** But surely, Joe, you know BB well enough to know that he could never, ever –

**Duveen** Of course I do, my dear. Of course I know my BB, I don't ask him to change his opinion, I merely ask him to refrain from publishing it again. He has published it once, surely that is enough?

**Mary** Ah. But you want him to keep quiet now other people are saying it's a Giorgione –

**Duveen** Not quiet, my dear, he can tell anyone and everyone, *tout le monde*, as long as he doesn't announce it in an unsolicited formal statement signed by himself. That is all I ask. That is all!

**Mary** I don't understand these tumults between you, I don't, when really you're so fond of each other, you have such good times together, jolly times, and yet you always, always have to go through silly little squabbles before you work things out, which you always do. Come, listen to each other, talk to each other, be kind to me. (*To Joe mainly.*)

**Duveen** My dear, who could resist – the offer is renewed, here, in front of you, Mary, my dear. Of a full partnership. In the house of Duveen.

*They look towards BB.*

**BB** Tomorrow morning I send to all the relevant publications, and to Mellon himself, a brief letter stating that in my opinion the Giorgione is not a Titian but a Giorgione – (*realising*) that the Titian is not a Giorgione but a Titian, rather.

**Duveen** (*lowers his head*) And so, Mary my dear – (*taking her hand*) what can I say? I know how hard it's going to be for you and yours, but I think I have to leave this matter now, concluded to everyone's dissatisfaction –

**Mary** (*clutching hand, in a low, urgent voice*) Joe, dear Joe, give him a chance to think, just a few days, please, please!

**BB** (*turning back*) May I remind you, Mary, that in this house, here, in I Tatti, we try to make beggars welcome, but we never beg for ourselves, particularly from beggars, especially from rich beggars, and most especially from rich and dishonourable beggars!

*There is a silence.*

**Duveen** Oh, that reminds me – (*Takes box from his pocket.*) In case I don't see her again – a little something for your charming Miss Mariano – in recognition of her many years of kindness to me, so unexpected in one so young. (*Gestures.*)

**Mary** So young? She's forty-three.

**Duveen** Forty-three is she, indeed? Then so much younger than ourselves, I must admit. It's nothing, really – from an auction in Boston, a widow's estate, my eye was caught by its oddity and charm, the way it seemed to smile up at me – and so I couldn't help thinking of Miss Mariano –

**Mary** May I see it? (*Comes over, holds out her hand.*)

*Duveen places it in her hand.*

(*Studying it in a professional manner.*) But it's French, Louis Quinze, worth a good two, two and a half – and this is for Nicky? Boston, did you say, but it's certainly French –

**Nicky** (*enters*) Oh Mary, here you are! What are you doing, you promised me you wouldn't get up –

**Mary** Joe's got something for you, here – Put it on, Nicky, let's see what it looks like when it's on you – (*Makes to hand it to her.*) No, Joe, you must do it, as it's your – (*Gestures.*) You put it on her.

**Duveen** May I?

**Nicky** (*makes small gesture to resist, attempts a smile*) Of course.

**Duveen** Now where do you think – well, of course I suppose this is the usual – (*Fumbles with it clumsily.*)

**Mary** Like pinning a medal on a soldier. (*Sketches a salute.*)

**Duveen** No, my fingers are thumbs, you'd better do it yourself, my dear. (*Gives brooch to Nicky.*)

*Nicky puts the brooch on deftly.*

**Mary** Now let us look. My dear – your hand – it's covering –

*Nicky lowers her hand.*

**Duveen** (*clamping his cigar in his mouth*) Gorgeous, gorgeous, quite gorgeous, don't you think, BB? Eh, BB? What do you say?

*BB turns away.*

**Mary** (*standing by Duveen*) No, just a minute – don't move, my dear – be still! (*Sharply. Considers Nicky.*) Not quite right.

**Duveen** Really? You think so? What's the matter?

**Mary** Rather common, I think, now I see it on.

**Duveen** Well, of course Miss Mariano has so much natural – natural physical –

**Mary** I may be wrong. What do you think, Nicky, my dear, as you're the one who has to wear it?

**Nicky** Well, I can't see it, can I, but – (*breaking, plucking it off*) it feels, it feels somewhat inappropriate, I'm sorry, thank you. Thank you.

*BB lets out a snort.*

**Mary** (*taking it from Nicky's hand, as she holds it out to Joe*) I'll have it! Well, if Joe wants to give it away, and Nicky doesn't want it –

**BB** Not too common, after all, then.

**Mary** Not for the older woman, my dear – we need a touch of oddity and charm on our bosoms, smiling up at you young men. Unless Joe minds, of course, do you, Joe?

**Duveen** I'm delighted, my dear, that it's found a home on one of the ladies of the household.

**Mary** (*comes to him, embraces him*) I have to hug you tightly, tightly, dear Joe, dear Joe, because this may be the last time, the very last time – (*Steps away.*) Let me look at you. Dear Joe!

**Duveen** (*overcome, lights his cigar, inhales, exhales, emotionally*) Yes, well, who knows – who ever knows – But the thing is, Mary – get well, my dear. And out of this country as quickly as you can, until it's safe again. That's what you must do. All of you. (*Goes to case, picks it up, picks up walking stick.*) Miss Mariano. (*Takes her hand, kisses it.*) I wish I'd had something more – appropriate – to offer.

**Nicky** It was kind of you to think of me.

*Duveen looks at BB. BB lifts his arms for a hug, sardonically.*

**Duveen** May your soul find peace, BB.

**BB** Car. Train. Boat. Now.

**Duveen** (*laughs*) You're right, I must hurry, hurry – (*Flourishes his cigar, goes out in a cloud of smoke. Sound of his laughter.*)

**BB** I spent the whole evening giving him nothing, nothing, at the end he had got nothing from me, nothing, and yet he departs in triumph because the bribe he was giving to one of my women was snatched from his hand by the other! You humiliated me, both of you!

**Mary** Think what he'd have done if the Swede had been here, too. And still remained a gentleman.

**BB** (*turns to Mary*) How could you?

**Mary** (*raises a hand*) Nicky wishes to speak, I believe. My dear?

**Nicky** Anything I did for him I was only doing for you. You know perfectly well you would have wanted me to open the door for him tonight, you know you would, but you'd have been too proud to say so –

**BB** How could you – how could you take things from him! Jewellery! Brooches! What else has he given you?

**Nicky** It's Joe's nature not to trust anyone he isn't bribing, you said so yourself.

**BB** An occasional cheque – even a little salary, as a retainer for your work as a – an intermediary I might understand. But things to wear – to wear in front of me! From him!

**Mary** Why shouldn't she? You never give her anything pretty to put on herself any more. She's been your mistress so long you've stopped noticing how much she loves things like that, and what with spying for him so she could spy for you, and going to bed with you every night and putting up with your Swede in the afternoons while being decent and kind to your old wife in the evenings and being your secretary in the mornings on top of it all, I'd say she earned her brooch, she's slaved for it, and she has a right to it, yes, my dear, you have!

**BB** But she hasn't got it, has she? You've got it.

**Mary** No, I haven't. Joe's got it. I slipped it into his pocket while he was giving me a hug – one of his own tricks. But it belongs to you, Nicky, go and catch him. Say I said you must have it, must! Or pick his pocket, with my blessing, my dear, whatever you like.

**Nicky** I'd rather see you back to bed. You're feverish – and you have to keep strong for Karin and little Roger, remember.

**Mary** She won't be coming. I shall write in the morning, to stop her. It's become too dangerous, you heard Joe, there's to be a war and she'll be glad of the excuse not to come. She's never made to feel welcome, she's made to feel like a beggar. No. Not beggar. I'd forgotten. Beggars are made welcome here, in this house of I Tatti – unless they have something valuable to offer, of course – now, leave me with my husband, please, there's a good girl.

*Nicky goes out. There is a pause.*
*Mary goes to the decanter, pours herself a glass of grappa.*

**BB** That's grappa. It'll harm your stomach, where most of your problems are.

**Mary** (*with a laugh*) Oh no, my dear – no, I don't think that's where most of my problems are. (*Takes a gulp, flinches, puts the glass down.*) It is one thing to refuse money for telling the truth. Or to take money for lying. But to lie for nothing – Why?

**BB** Perhaps because I believe it will do me the world of good.

**Mary** Your reputation, you mean? It's too late. As Joe probably told you, you already have a reputation for dishonesty. You can't change that with another lie. Not even a profitless one. (*Studies him.*) It won't take you back to what you once were.

**BB** To what I never was. But might have been if I hadn't met you.

**Mary** Ah. I corrupted you, did I? Along with Joe, and your Harvard patrons and patronesses, and Nicky too, probably – everyone who ever helped you, admired you, loved you – corrupted you. (*Laughs, nods.*)

**BB** There is a difference between you and the others.

**Mary** Yes. The others used you, or let you use them, which is often the same thing. I loved you earliest, understood you first and still understand you best. I founded you. I have been your anchor.

**BB** No. You founded a lie, and then anchored me to it.

**Mary** Which particular lie among so many – oh, of course, your Gospels, they've been in your wind for a while, I've noticed. Well, my dear, the truth is that you were incapable of writing them yourself, you were waiting for someone to write them for you. If it hadn't been me it would have been someone else, almost certainly a woman – a wife, probably, for all that annotating and indexing, rather like sewing and knitting, that part of it, the higher knitting and sewing. So it would have had to have been a wife, yes, a very clever wife, just like me, performing a higher wifely duty, just as I did, with whom you would one day be having, or have had, or be about to have, just this conversation. From time to time you've been pleased to have your name on them. And proud. But you're perfectly entitled to disown them – why don't you disown them, BB, if you feel shamed by them?

**BB** It would be like trying to disown my own grave. The corpses of the best from here and here –

*Makes gesture to head and heart. Mary mimics him as he does it.*

– are mine, undeniably mine. I can only pray that their spirit has somehow survived the clods of prose you've shovelled – shovelled – shovelled – shovelled – (*Gestures viciously.*)

**Mary** Well, now you've buried the past, tell me what you propose for the future. I need to know what to expect for the rest of my life.

**BB** What the rest of us have to expect, of course. Whatever the future brings.

**Mary** And my family, my family?

**BB** I am your family, family. Oh, you mean your natural family.

**Mary** The family I left for your sake, the family that I gave birth to, cared for, and forsook for – for – (*Gestures at him.*)

**BB** Ah, the family you *abandoned*. Ah, yes, well, they will have to make their way in life unencumbered by obligations to me. And we'll try not to leave any outstanding debts. With luck, all we have to do is to tighten our belts until the war comes and wipes the slate clean. (*Laughs.*) Think of it, my dear. No history, no past, no art, no provenance, no debts, no Jews, no I Tatti – a new age for new men, free men, slate-wipers, clean-sweepers. (*Nodding almost triumphantly.*) They will make the world for your grandchildren to inhabit. So what does it matter, a few lies or a few truths in the attribution of a Giorgione or a Titian, one's as good as the other when there's nobody left to look at them, just the duck and Hitler and the new barbarians, who'll make bonfires of them, along with all the books – Sophocles, Aeschylus, Plato, Titian, Giorgione, Leonardo –

*Mary runs at him, slaps him.*

**Mary** (*slapping*) Don't smile when you say things like that, don't grin your old man's grin when you say things like that, don't. Don't, don't you dare to say things like that –!

*BB at first stands stock still, receiving Mary's slaps, then catches her hands. They stand staring at each other.*

**BB** I didn't mean to grin. I'm not grinning inside. (*Leading her by the hand.*) Come – let's sit down.

**Mary** No. No, I don't want to – I don't want to –

**BB** Yes, you do.

**Mary** I don't.

*Mary allows herself to be led. BB pushes her gently onto the sofa.*

(*Struggling to rise.*) I don't, I don't, I don't –

*BB holds her down. Mary subsides. BB sits beside her. There is a pause.*

You noticed the cigar – how he lit it, flourished it?

**BB** Yes.

**Mary** His usual salute of a triumph. So he must have got something he wanted.

**BB** As I said just a few minutes ago. The sight of me being humiliated by my women.

**Mary** Joe isn't petty. He might have enjoyed that, but he wouldn't have celebrated it with a flourish of his cigar. Well?

**BB** Well. It's true that there is something – yes, something I haven't understood. Of course that's the problem with Joe, you assume there must be a motive within the motive. The fact is, my dear, he didn't get what he came for and I am no longer on his payroll. I'm – I'm –

**Mary** You can say it. You're a free man, at last.

**BB** Well, free of Joe, at least.

**Mary** (*after a little pause*) Perhaps that's what he wanted.

**BB** For me to be free of him? (*Laughs. Stops.*) Oh. You mean he wanted to be free of me. I see. But why?

*Mary says nothing.*

Oh. (*Nods.*) Yes. My reputation. Which is – as you said. And he said. And will no doubt get worse, until it becomes positively unfair, eh?

*Little pause.*

Well, if you're right – at least our final row wasn't about money.

**Mary** Perhaps it was about money as well. Your insisting on sticking by Titian for *The Adoration* – well, my dear, if you can make that mistake, how many others have you made? All your attributions will become questionable. Joe can use them as he wishes – Yes, yes, the great Berenson himself, the great and irrefutable Bernard Berenson, it turns out he can't tell a – a –

**BB** A Titian from a Giorgione.

**Mary** Well, can you?

**BB** I don't know. But it is now my view – my view – for what it is now worth – that *The Adoration of the Shepherds* was probably mostly painted by Giorgione. And that some further work was probably done on it by his pupil, Titian. Or it may have been the other way round. (*There is a little pause.*) I shall write something to that effect at some time in the future. What do you say to that?

**Mary** I say that it is faultless.

**BB** He says – he says he's dying. That he has only three months to live.

**Mary** Oh!

**BB** But he was still bargaining when he said it. He made me look into his eyes – they weren't good. But on the other hand he hugged you like a wrestler –

**Mary** You had better know that I shall never leave I Tatti, BB. I haven't the strength. If this war comes, you will have to go. You're a Jew. You won't be safe here. But I will stay and protect it. I will protect it for as long as I – (*Gestures.*)

**BB** Whatever the future I promise you we will find enough for those you love. Those others you also love.

**Mary** (*nods*) I don't doubt you, thank you, but my dear – you were right about the grappa. It was very foolish of me. I must get to bed. Back to bed.

**BB** I'll take you. (*Rises, holds out his hand to help her up.*)

**Mary** No, no. Nicky does it, I want Nicky.

**BB** (*goes to the door*) Nicky! Nicky! Can you come, please!

> *Mary meanwhile has risen, is standing, one hand on her stomach, in pain. BB goes to her anxiously, hovers, goes back to the door.*

Nicky! Hurry, please! (*Goes back to her.*) Don't you think you'd better let me – I don't know where she is.

**Mary** She'll be here. She's always here.

> *BB is about to go back to the door. Nicky enters, goes to Mary. Mary gives Nicky her arm.*

And did you catch him, and get your brooch?

**Nicky** No, he'd already gone. (*Helping her.*) So I went to my room and cried instead.

**Mary** I don't believe you. Do you believe her?

**BB** (*smiles*) It's possible. Anything's possible with women. They have no shame.

**Mary** What would we need it for? (*To Nicky, as they go off.*) Well, my dear, let's hope for the best for tomorrow, let's hope that at least the Swede is back.

> *BB watches them go off. Sound of their voices, laughter receding. Goes to his desk. Tries to concentrate. Faintly, the sounds of war.*
> *BB hunches himself, as if the sounds are internal, goes to sofa, sits. Closes his eyes, wills concentration.*

**BB** Yes, because one can't see their faces! (*Laughs almost childishly.*) Isn't it ridiculous, that one never remembers that? And yet one should, because that's how it brings the eye – the whole eye – to Mary, Joseph and the baby – just as you'd do it on a stage, a stage grouping, really, as elementary as that – crude almost, until the eye goes beyond, to the boys under the tree, beyond them to the church, then beyond to the mountains, the clouds. Now I've said it I shall remember it whenever needed – (*Little pause.*) – It is needed now.

*Sounds of war louder and louder.*

*Lights.*

*Curtain.*

# THE LATE MIDDLE CLASSES

For Victoria

**The Late Middle Classes** was first presented by the Palace Theatre, Watford, on 19 March 1999. The production then played at Brighton, Plymouth, Bath, Woking and Richmond. The cast was as follows:

**Brownlow** Nicholas Woodeson
**Holly** *in his forties* James Fleet
**Holly** *aged twelve* Sam Bedi
**Celia** Harriet Walter
**Charles** James Fleet
**Ellie** Angela Pleasence

*Director* Harold Pinter
*Designer* Eileen Diss
*Lighting* Mick Hughes
*Sound Designer* Dominic Muldowney

The US premiere was directed by Roger Rees for the Williamstown Theatre Festival in 2000. The cast was as follows:

**Brownlow** Tom Bloom
**Holly** *in his forties* Daniel Gerroll
**Holly** *aged twelve* Benjamin Gerroll
**Celia** Lisa Harrow
**Charles** Daniel Gerroll
**Ellie** Lucille Patton

# Characters

**Brownlow**

**Holly**
in his forties

**Holly**
aged twelve

**Celia**

**Charles**

**Ellie**

# Act One

### SCENE ONE

*Brownlow's study/sitting room. Autumn. Early evening. The present.*
    *A baby grand piano, a sofa, desk, table, an armchair.*
    *Brownlow, in his seventies, is sitting in armchair, dozing, muttering.*
    *Doorbell rings.*

**Brownlow** (*mutters in his sleep, gradually wakes up, listens*) No, I couldn't have heard it – must be a dream –

*Doorbell rings again. Brownlow goes to window, peers out. Knocks on window.*

Is there anybody there? Who's there? Mrs Jameson, is that you? Mr Jameson? Surely you know not to disturb me at this hour, I'm very busy –

*Doorbell rings again.*

Who is it?

*Agitated, he attempts to compose himself, goes out of room.*
    *Voices off, indistinct.*

(*Off.*) Yes? Can I help you?

**Holly** (*off*) I don't know if you remember me. I'm Holliday Smithers.

**Brownlow** Smithers – Holliday Smithers – Yes, yes, of course I remember you.

**Holly** I was just passing and couldn't help wondering if you were still here.

**Brownlow** Yes, yes, still here. Well, please come in.

*Holly enters Brownlow's sitting room, followed by Brownlow. Holly is in his mid-forties. He looks around.*

And, um, where have you come from?

**Holly** Well, from Australia, in fact. Melbourne.

**Brownlow** And you're staying on the island?

**Holly** No, I'm staying in London. But I had to come down to Portsmouth for a few days.

**Brownlow** And so you decided to pay us a visit, after all these years.

**Holly** Well, I had the afternoon off, couldn't resist driving over – odd that, being able to drive over, all the way by road. I still imagined having to take the ferry. I'd have preferred that on such a beautiful day. Especially when everything turned out to be so familiar. (*Looks around again.*) As it is here. Except that it's all older, of course.

**Brownlow** Yes, yes, like myself.

**Holly** Like myself. Do you mind if I sit down?

**Brownlow** Oh – oh, yes, of course, I'm sorry – please. Where would you like? (*Gesturing around room.*)

*Holly walks over to armchair, sits down, watched by Brownlow.*

**Holly** There is a change, though. No, not a change, an absence. Yes, something's missing. Oh yes, a cat. There was always a cat called Kitty-Cat. Kitty-Cat Number Seven. You explained to me that your mother always called her cats Kitty-Cat so it was always the same cat to her. When one died she'd go straight on to the next

Kitty-Cat almost without noticing the pain of loss or the treachery of replacement. But you numbered them in your head. So I knew Kitty-Cat Number Seven.

**Brownlow** They were called Catty-Kit, not Kitty-Cat.

**Holly** Oh yes, sorry. I must have let the chocolate bar get in the way. Well, what number did it get up to, Catty-Kit, before its sequence ended?

**Brownlow** Eleven. Number Eleven I had put down the day after I buried my mother.

**Holly** Ah. The end of the line then.

**Brownlow** It felt like the end of an era.

**Holly** Yes, I suppose it must have done. (*Little pause.*) But have you gone on keeping the same hours?

**Brownlow** Well, I keep the hours, yes. Yes, I do that.

**Holly** Every morning from ten to twelve and every evening from nine, was it, until midnight.

**Brownlow** Nine thirty until midnight. Back then. Now, of course, my time's my own and I start earlier. Whenever I feel like it.

**Holly** You and your beloved talking to each other. (*Glancing towards piano.*)

**Brownlow** Yes.

**Holly** And what do the two of you talk about these days? Anything in particular?

**Brownlow** A concerto. We're working on a concerto. We've been at it for a long time. A long, long time. I hope to complete it before I die.

**Holly** Oh yes, you must. You'd want to hear it, after all. You used to say that you couldn't compose the opening until you knew how the piece would close. So first close, then open, and then on into the middle, which would look after itself.

**Brownlow** Well, of course one has these theories at different times of one's life. One's creative life. Perhaps it's to do with memories. The more memories you have, the more difficult it all becomes.

**Holly** You mean the memories teem about and get in the way?

**Brownlow** Well, no, not teem about. Not quite as lively as that. They bob up.

**Holly** What sort of memories?

**Brownlow** Well, just memories. Of days gone by. (*Little pause.*) You, for instance. You bob up now and then. Quite often, in fact.

**Holly** Do I?

**Brownlow** Do I ever bob up for you?

**Holly** Oh, yes. This afternoon, when I was walking about the island. I went to see the old house, well, the family house, and one thought led to another and that led to another and then finally up you bobbed again.

**Brownlow** Like a jack-in-the-box.

**Holly** No, not really like a jack-in-the-box. The thoughts were quite logically connected, I think. Though there was a bit missing – something I tried to remember and couldn't. The music. The music that seemed to run through it all. It wouldn't come back. It won't come back.

**Brownlow** Really? Can I offer you something? Tea? Coffee? And I do believe there's some sherry somewhere – but very, very old. From my mother's day. Quite a few bottles of it there should be in the larder. Mrs Jameson helps herself to it from time to time but – she's my cleaning woman, you know, she came long after your time – after my mother's too – in fact she's only been here about ten years, I think it must be, and her husband does the gardening. Sometimes I hear them down in the kitchen, laughing and talking, and it occurs to me that they're at the sherry, especially when they're being rather loud. May I ask a question?

*Holly gestures. There is a pause.*

**Holly** (*gently*) A question. You're going to ask a question.

**Brownlow** Are you real?

**Holly** Yes, quite real. Well, at least I think I am. One can never be completely sure on that point, can one?

*Gets up, goes over to Brownlow.*

But here, feel this.

*Holds out his hand. Brownlow tentatively moves his hand, touches Holly's sleeve. As he withdraws his hand, Holly catches it in his.*

There, you see. Not just the garments but flesh and blood.

*They stand, hands clasped for a second. Holly removes his hand.*

**Brownlow** Did you say yes? To the sherry, that is?

**Holly** A glass of your mother's sherry, yes, I'd love to try it at last. Thank you.

**Brownlow** Well, I'll see what I can find. (*Goes out.*)

*Holly goes over to piano, picks along keyboard as if trying to work out a tune. Shakes his head in*

*exasperation, goes back, sits in armchair, takes out cigarette, lights it. Sits back meditatively. As he does so:*
   *Piano music, over, as:*
   *Lights going down as lights coming up on Smithers' sitting room.*

## SCENE TWO

*Spring. Evening. Early nineteen-fifties.*
   *Smithers' sitting room.*
   *Holly, as a child of twelve, playing the piano.*
   *Holly continues to play for a second, stops. He gets up, goes over to sofa, sits down. Takes out exercise book from satchel, extracts a loose sheet of paper, reads it very intensely, then reaches urgently into satchel, fumbles deeply, takes out magazine, begins to go through it, studying pictures, occasionally reading to himself aloud but inaudibly from sheet of paper.*
   *Sound of front door opening and closing.*
   *Holly scrambles to his feet, stuffs magazine and exercise book back into satchel, hurries over to piano, starts playing.*
   *Celia Smithers, Holly's mother, enters, dressed in tennis shorts, top, carrying tennis racket and tennis balls.*

**Celia** She's chucked! That bloody Moira woman has actually chucked! She couldn't phone me before I left so I could have got somebody else, no, she just stepped out as I was cycling past, with her hand raised like a policeman – I nearly pedalled straight into her and I wish I had – she honked out some nonsense about coughs and sore throats, running eyes, her cheeks were like apples, my dear, great shiny apples, by far the healthiest thing I've seen all week – oh, I could kill her! Kill, kill, kill! (*Serves viciously with imaginary ball.*)

**Holly** It's because you keep beating her.

**Celia** Oh, don't be so silly.

**Holly** It's true. Every time you come back from playing against her you crow about beating her six-love, six-love. You do the same with me, so I know how she feels.

**Celia** She wouldn't be so petty. Yes, she would. Everyone on this bloody island is petty. That's why you've got to win a scholarship. To get us off it.

**Holly** That makes complete sense. That's perfectly logical. I understand that.

**Celia** You sound just like your father.

*She bangs her racket gently on his head.*

I. Won't. Have. You. Making. Fun. Of. Your. Father.

**Holly** I wasn't making fun of him. I just don't see why my getting a scholarship would get you off the island.

**Celia** Because if you win a scholarship to St Paul's or Westminster we won't have to pay the fees and we can all move to London where we belong. And if you don't win a scholarship you'll end up going somewhere local where you'll have to be a day boy so we can afford your fees. We've been over and over it.

**Holly** You haven't been over and over it with me.

**Celia** No. I meant your father and I have been over and over it.

**Holly** What's wrong with Portsmouth Grammar School? A lot of boys from around here go there – all my friends – and they say it's jolly good.

**Celia** It may be jolly good for them but it's not jolly good enough for us.

**Holly** Well, I don't think it's fair that everything you want comes down to me getting a scholarship. I probably haven't got a chance. We don't know anybody around here who's –

**Celia** Edwin Tomkins.

**Holly** Oh, *him*.

**Celia** 'Oh, *him*' won a full scholarship to St Paul's, as his wretched parents never stop boasting. And as you despise him so much you could surely do just as well. Now, do get on with your practice, and what about your prep, have you done that yet?

**Holly** Almost. I've just got a bit of French left.

**Celia** Then finish your practice and on with your French. I want it done before Mr Thing-me-bob comes. You're always too tired to do any prep after your piano lessons.

*Holly starts playing piano.*

(*Watches him.*) Oh, you do remind me of someone, you know, whenever you play.

**Holly** Do I? Who?

**Celia** One of the young chaps in the war, one of the fighter pilots. He had the same – same intensity – as if there was nothing else in the world but the music, even though everybody was singing around him.

**Holly** (*plays for a little*) What happened to him?

**Celia** He went for a Burton, poor young devil, like so many of the rest of them.

**Holly** Oh. (*Playing on.*)

**Celia** Tell me something. Something very important.

**Holly** Oh, Mummy, I'm trying to concentrate.

**Celia** You have to answer this. Do you love me?

**Holly** (*sighs*) Of course I love you.

**Celia** Why?

**Holly** Oh, Mummy, you know why. Because you're my mother.

**Celia** I do wish you'd once, just once, come up with a more flattering answer. What is that piece anyway – it's been driving me mad trying to remember – Beethoven, isn't it?

**Holly** Very nearly. It's Brownlow. Mr Brownlow.

**Celia** Golly, really, you mean he writes it too? (*Staring over Holly's shoulder.*)

**Holly** Oh, yes. Thomas Ambrose Brownlow.

**Celia** Ambrose? Thomas Ambrose Brownlow? Is that hyphenated? Thomas Ambrose-Brownlow?

**Holly** No, that's his middle name, I think.

**Celia** Rather precious to use your middle name. Especially when it's Ambrose. But I suppose if your name is Brownlow, Thomas Brownlow, and you want to add a little splash, if you're a composer – what's it called? (*Reading.*) 'Mio' – 'A Bagatelle for Mio'.

**Holly** It's miaow. It's about their cat when it miaows.

**Celia** Doesn't sound at all like a miaow to me. Except it's soft and velvety so I suppose that's a bit like a cat. What does he do with them when he's composed them? Does he have them played by people – concerts, that sort of thing?

**Holly** He says they're doing this on the Third Programme.

**Celia** The Third Programme, golly. Well, perhaps they'll let you play it.

**Holly** Actually, Mummy, I don't want to do the piano any more.

**Celia** What on earth do you mean?

**Holly** I mean I don't like it. And I'm not very good at it.

**Celia** Nonsense! Your Mr Ambrose says you're the best student he's ever had. By far and away the best on the island anyway.

**Holly** Yes, well, he doesn't really mean it, he's just being polite.

**Celia** You need your music, you know you do. You put it down on your scholarship form that you played the piano as one of your main interests.

**Holly** No, I didn't. I put down music. And so if I change to the violin –

**Celia** The violin! How on earth do you think your father's going to afford a violin?

**Holly** Well, we could sell the piano –

**Celia** Sell the piano! It's your legacy from your godmother. You don't just sell off legacies and buy something else you prefer.

**Holly** I know I'd be better at the violin, I know it.

**Celia** But you'd have to start from the beginning and you've gone so far with the piano and – well, you talk it over with him – (*Gesturing to music.*) He'll know what's best.

**Holly** He won't want me to give up the piano. And he doesn't do the violin.

**Celia** Well, there you are. As he's the only music person on the island you'll just have to stick with what he wants.

**Holly** It's not what he wants, it's what I want.

**Celia** It isn't what you want, it's what will get you a scholarship.

**Holly** I'll give up the extra football training if you let me do the violin.

**Celia** Don't be silly, you're captain of the first eleven, they wouldn't dream of letting you. And quite right too.

**Holly** Can't you ask Daddy at least and he can explain to Mr Brownlow and if I only took half my pocket money we could probably find a cheap violin in Portsmouth and somebody there who can teach me.

**Celia** And who's going to ferry you there and back every time you have a lesson? Your father, I suppose, as if he hasn't got enough on his plate – oh, I haven't got time to stand here and argue about something so completely absurd, for one thing I've the evening meal to think about, all I've got are powdered eggs, a bit of lard and almost no butter –

*Holly bangs his hands down on the keyboard in anger and despair.*

Don't you dare do that! How dare you do that!

**Holly** (*after a moment*) Sorry. (*Little pause.*) Sorry, Mummy. It's just that – that I'd love to learn the violin, that's all.

**Celia** Well then, darling, if we get to London you shall, I promise you. And I'll tell your father, I promise. There. I can't say fairer than that, can I?

*Holly nods. He picks up satchel, makes to leave the room.*

**Celia** Where are you going?

**Holly** To my room. To finish my French.

**Celia** You can do it down here at the table where I can keep an eye on you.

**Holly** Why?

**Celia** Because I never know what you get up to in your room these days.

**Holly** What do you mean?

**Celia** You're blushing.

**Holly** I'm not blushing. You were going to go out and play tennis so it wouldn't have mattered to you then where I did my prep.

**Celia** I've had enough arguments for one afternoon. I don't want to talk about any of it. That's your father's job.

**Holly** What do you mean?

**Celia** Nothing. It's just that some things are between fathers and sons.

**Holly** What things?

**Celia** I told you, I don't want to talk about it. It's all perfectly normal, I expect. Not that I'd know.

**Holly** I don't understand.

**Celia** There's nothing for you to understand, I keep telling you. Now you jolly well get on with your prep, young man –

**Holly** You mean when I was praying and you came in? Why are you against my praying?

**Celia** Holliday, not another word. Get on with it before your Mr Thing arrives.

*Holly takes his books over to table, opens books, begins to work.*
*Celia watches him, then goes over to sofa, lights a cigarette. Lies on sofa, smoking, her leg jigging irritably. Suddenly struck by an idea, she gets up, goes to telephone, dials.*

(*On telephone.*) Oh, Bunty dear, it's Celia. It just struck me, lovely afternoon, a bit of a breeze, what do you say to a game of tennis? (*Little pause.*) Well, right now really. I mean, as soon as we've changed. We can be at the court in ten minutes – oh, don't be so silly, dear, you're a very good *natural* player, all you need is practice – and weight has nothing to do with it, many marvellous players are as heavy as you – what? No, no, I don't mean that at all, all I mean is something you said the other day about being worried that you're getting a little – a little – and what better way to get it off? (*Pause.*) Oh, very well, dear, if you really feel I'm inviting you to join a chain gang instead of a mild knock-up – what? Moira? No, no, she's a bit under the weather, she says, and anyway I don't fancy an hour with Moira, all she'll talk about is how marvellous everything is and their wretched holiday in Ireland with all the steaks and butter and fresh cream. Which reminds me, my dear, have you got any eggs from those chickens of yours? I want to give Charles a surprise, he was saying last night how much he yearned for an omelette, but with fresh eggs, not powdered – oh – oh, well never mind, Bunty dear, I was going to offer you some chocolate in exchange but I expect that the last thing you want at the moment is chocolate so it'll have to be dried eggs again, they'll just have to put up with it – what? Wait? Oh, somebody at the door – somebody at the window? Oh, tapping on the window –

well, I really haven't got anything more to – (*Stands, waiting, lights another cigarette, taps her foot irritably.*) Who is it? Moira! Tapping on your window! What does she want? A cup of tea! Moira taps on your window whenever she wants a cup of tea – no, no, thank you, dear, really what I want to be is outside, you see. Give Moira my – my –

*She hangs up.*

Really, these people – these people on this bloody island, I don't know how I put up with them. Always presuming on one's friendship. If they didn't claim to be friends they wouldn't dare to do the kind of thing they do do. Of course it's easy for them, they've both got help, they can play tennis or have their cups of tea with each other whenever they like. While I – what on earth was the point of our winning the war if you end up worse off than before it started? No housekeeper, no maid, while both of them have got both. And Bunty's even got a gardener. Well, she calls him a gardener but really he looks like a convict – pasty-faced and furtive and smoking, and doesn't even know how to say good morning. Doesn't speak at all as far as I know. He may be one of those Eyetie prisoners of war who stayed on. But if you've got an Italian prisoner of war in your garden I suppose you do feel you've won the war and everything's almost back to normal. In spite of Winnie being thrown out.

*She looks at Holly, who is bent over exercise book, writing. Celia sits on sofa, allows her lids to become slack, her eyes vacant.*
*Holly glances towards her, then slides piece of paper out of his pocket, puts it into exercise book, begins to read. Becomes increasingly aware of stillness from sofa.*

**Holly** Mummy? Mummy?

*He stares towards her anxiously as he closes exercise book, puts it into his satchel, goes across to Celia with increasing terror, stares down.*

Mummy – oh, Mummy, what is it? What is it? Oh – (*Wrings his hands, looks around.*) Daddy, Daddy –

*He runs to telephone, dials frantically.*

**Celia** (*looks towards Holly*) What are you doing? Who are you phoning?

*Holly puts down telephone, stares at her with relieved disbelief.*

Who were you phoning?

**Holly** Daddy.

**Celia** Why?

**Holly** Because – because I thought you were dead.

**Celia** Oh, don't be such a fool. I was just lying here thinking about things. Concentrating.

**Holly** (*realising*) No you weren't. You were pretending. You were pretending to be dead.

**Celia** I was doing no such thing. I – I –

**Holly** Yes you were, you were! Why were you? You're always doing things like that – why? (*On the verge of tears.*)

*Celia, suddenly upset, gets up, runs to him.*

**Celia** Oh, darling, I was just being silly, just playing games. I didn't think for a minute you'd believe – and – and – I'm sorry, darling, I'm sorry, there, there. Just a silly game, that's all. Between us.

*The doorbell rings.*

(*Stepping away.*) Oh, there he is, your Mr Thing, I'll let him in, darling, you'd better blow your nose and – (*Going towards door*) What's his name again? Oh, I remember. (*Goes out.*)

*Sound of front door opening.*

(*Off.*) Good evening, Mr Ambrose. He's in there waiting for you, he's been practising all afternoon –

*Holly hurries to the piano. Celia enters, followed by Brownlow.*

There, you see. Warming the keys and finger tips.

**Brownlow** Good evening, Holliday.

**Holly** (*getting up*) Good evening, sir.

**Brownlow** No, don't be up, put yourself back where you're going to be for the next hour.

**Celia** I'm so glad to have caught you for once, Mr Ambrose, I always seem to be out or dashing off just as you arrive, it's usually my tennis hour, you see, but I do hope Holly thinks to offer you a cup of tea, do you, Holly?

**Holly** What, Mummy?

**Celia** Do you think to offer Mr Ambrose a cup of tea, darling?

**Brownlow** Yes, he does, Mrs Smithers, unfailingly. But I always decline. One has to worry too much about the clinking of cup on saucer. It's Brownlow, by the way.

**Celia** (*momentarily confused*) What?

**Brownlow** Not Ambrose. Ambrose is my middle name.

**Celia** (*laughs*) Oh, of course it is, I'm so sorry, I know your name perfectly well, don't I, Holly? It's just that my eye caught Ambrose on the what's-it Holly's playing and it stuck. Well, Mr Brownlow, I'll get out of the way and leave you two to it, shall I?

**Brownlow** Mrs Smithers, may I ask a favour? I'd be grateful if you'd let me take the telephone off the hook. Its ringing can be very disruptive, we've discovered.

**Celia** The telephone? Oh, but there are sometimes calls for my husband. From the hospital, you see. When they want him urgently. He's the pathologist, after all. The only pathologist, you know.

**Brownlow** Indeed, I do know. And I'm sorry, I wouldn't have dreamt of asking if I'd known Dr Smithers was in the house.

**Celia** Well, he isn't, as a matter of fact. So I suppose, now I come to think of it – (*Going reluctantly to the telephone.*) And I'm not expecting anything myself that can't wait.

**Brownlow** They always come, when they come, at the worst possible time. And once one has come, one expects others to follow. The hour becomes about whether the telephone is going to ring and not about the piano. Which is why I refuse to have one in my house.

**Celia** Yes, I do understand. But we must remember to put it back when you've finished. In case my husband needs to call me urgently – well, if he's going to be home late or –

**Brownlow** We will remember, I promise you.

**Celia** Thank you. Well, then. (*Goes out.*)

*There is a pause.*

**Brownlow** (*as if to himself*) Well, here we are again. Just the two of us, surrounded by the foe. And visible this time. (*To Holly.*) But how nice to have had a proper little conversation with your mother. How have you been getting on with my what's-it?

**Holly** Sir?

**Brownlow** Mr Ambrose's what's-it. Have you come to love it yet?

**Holly** I like it a lot.

**Brownlow** You're developing a feeling for it then, are you?

**Holly** It gets easier and easier the more I get to know it.

**Brownlow** Ah. Then you're not developing a feeling for it. It should get more and more complicated the more you get to know it. You'll only know it completely when you come to realise that you're never going to find out its secret. Perhaps because there isn't one. (*Laughs.*) I'm teasing you, mio. That's the way I'd like people to talk about my music. As they don't, I have to do it myself, and so I make it preposterous to myself. Especially when I do it to that. It's merely a finger exercise to make you more agile. Your fingers, anyway. (*Surveys Holly.*) What a strange posture. You look as if you're crouching for a sprint. Waiting for the gun to go off. Turn around, if you please.

*Holly turns around.*

Back straight, if you please.

*Holly straightens his back.*

Arms out, fingers ready.

*Holly stretches out his arms, hooks his fingers.*

No, no, you're not going to savage the keyboard, you're going to caress it, if you please. There. (*Makes caressing movements with his own hands. Little pause.*) If you please, mio.

*Holly begins to make caressing movements with his hands. For a moment they are both making caressing movements.*

Now. Oh, one thing.

**Holly** Sir?

**Brownlow** Who is this 'sir' you keep referring to? I thought we'd got rid of him weeks ago.

**Holly** Sorry, Lowly. (*In a mutter.*)

**Brownlow** You're quite safe. They may be all around us but they're not actually with us. Nobody can hear you except me. Say it again without the apology.

**Holly** Lowly.

**Brownlow** That's better. Once more.

*He puts his hand on Holly's cheek.*

**Holly** Lowly.

**Brownlow** Now explain to me why we decided you should call me Lowly.

**Holly** Because you have low aspirations or why would you be bothering with creatures like me?

**Brownlow** Did I say that?

**Holly** I think so. I think that's what you said.

**Brownlow** Well, now I shan't be able to remember whether I said it or not. I'll just remember what you said I said and hope that it was really I and not actually you that said it.

**Holly** It was, Lowly, I promise.

**Brownlow** (*taking his hand from Holly's cheek*) Now, mio, to Lowly's 'Bagatelle', if you please. Unless you have a greater aspiration.

*Holly turns to keyboard, begins to play 'Bagatelle'. Brownlow stands, listening to music. Lets out a groan. Stands in a posture of despair.*

**Holly** (*turns slowly*) Did I make a mistake?

**Brownlow** No. I did.

*Goes over, takes score off music stand, looks at it.*

**Holly** Don't you like it any more?

**Brownlow** You play it as if I never liked it, mio.

**Holly** I'm sorry. I do like it. Honestly.

**Brownlow** Thank you. (*Stuffs score into his pocket.*) Play something more worthy of your gifts, if you please. (*Riffling through scores on piano, picking one out.*) Here, play this. (*Puts score on music stand.*) At least we'll know where we are.

*Holly begins to play opening bars of the 'Moonlight Sonata'. Brownlow puts his hands in his pockets, walks around the room, nodding his head, staring at Holly. There is a sudden slight discord. Brownlow winces. Holly proceeds to play.*

(*Hissing it out.*) Stop! Stop, stop, stop!

*Holly stops.*

Didn't you hear yourself?

*Holly nods.*

Then why didn't you stop yourself? How do you expect to learn, mio, if you simply ignore your mistakes? Mistakes bury themselves into our natures. They become habits we don't even know we possess. So we must be alert to them, ready to correct them – turn to our teachers for help. That's what I'm here for, aren't I? To help. Answer, if you please. Without mumbling. And no, don't turn.

**Holly** (*pipingly*) Yes, sir.

**Brownlow** (*gently*) Yes who, mio?

**Holly** Lowly, sir. I mean Lowly, I mean.

**Brownlow** And to what, mio?

**Holly** To help, Lowly.

*Pause. Brownlow waits.*

That's what you're here for. (*Pause.*) To help with your mistakes. My mistakes I mean, sir. Lowly.

**Brownlow** (*lets out a little laugh*) Who can say whether the man is playing with the cat or the cat is playing with the man? Eh? (*Goes over to piano.*) Move over, mio.

*He sits beside Holly.*

Now watch my hands.

*Begins to play.*
*He has a velvet touch, his head moves very slightly to the music. He stops, nods at the keyboard and at Holly. Holly starts again.*
*Brownlow at first watches his hands, then, as if against his will, turns, stares at Holly's profile. With an effort, he gets up, walks softly around the room, and as Holly reaches the point of the previous discord, passes it successfully, Brownlow nods to himself. Stares towards Holly, rapt.*
*Celia enters room, makes to speak. Brownlow puts his finger to his lips.*

(*After a moment, gently.*) Holly.

*Holly stops.*

I think your mother wants a word.

**Celia** I'm so sorry to interrupt, such lovely sounds and such a gorgeous piece of music, what a lucky cat! But I've got to make – I've really got to make one telephone call, very important or the whole evening will be a shambles, I'll be very quick, I promise.

*She goes to telephone, lighting a cigarette as she does so. Goes through telephone book.*

M – M – M – M – M – here we are. (*Dials.*) Well, fingers crossed.

*Holds out her fingers crossed, smiles at Brownlow. On telephone.*

Mrs Milton? It's Mrs Smithers here, Dr Smithers' wife – how are you? Oh dear, how unpleasant. I think there's something going around the island, I was going to play tennis with Mrs Authwaite but she had to call it off because she's got exactly the same – runny eyes, sniffles, a slight temperature – my husband always says that they are just little upsets and there's nothing you can do about them really, but you know the famous saying about doctors and their families – um, what I'm phoning about is that when I bumped into you in the village the other day you very sweetly said that sometimes your chickens did you really proud and if ever I were in desperate need it's always worth giving you a ring, so you wouldn't by any chance – oh, you have, how wonderful! Well, I was hoping four – three, I see. Well, I can make do on three, that's very kind of you, the doctor will be pleased, he's been longing for a freshly made omelette. He'll pick them up himself on his way back from the hospital, I'll phone him and tell him straight away – thank you, Mrs Milton. (*Puts down telephone.*) Isn't it revolting how obsequious we have to be these days? Especially with the Mrs Miltons of the world. They don't do you kindnesses, you know, they do you favours – (*Dialling as she speaks. On telephone.*) Oh hello, Dr Smithers, Path Lab, please. (*Pause.*) Laboratory. Pathological Laboratory. (*Irritated.*) This is Mrs Smithers, Dr Smithers' wife – oh, Jean, hello, Jean, Celia Smithers here, can I just have a word? Oh, doing a post-mortem, I see – well, Jean my dear, would you just give him this message – to stop off at Mrs Milton's on the way home and pick up –

*Sound of front door opening and closing.*

Good heavens, who's that?

*Charles Smithers enters.*

My dear, what are you doing here? I'm on the phone to you, I mean leaving you a message about picking up the eggs –

**Charles** I tried to phone to let you know I was on my way but the line was constantly engaged.

**Celia** What? Oh yes – (*Remembering telephone.*) Well, Mr Brown, he likes to have the phone off the hook – (*On telephone.*) It's all right, Jean dear, he's here –

**Charles** No, don't hang up, let me have a word.

**Celia** (*on telephone*) Hang on, Jean dear, he wants a word.

*She hands phone to Charles.*

**Charles** (*on telephone*) Oh hello, Jean. Bad case of the Gremlins again downstairs, Greatorix says he'll have it sorted out by eight and knowing young Greatorix he will. Thank you, Jean. (*Hangs up.*)

**Celia** You're not going to have to go back tonight, darling?

**Charles** I hope not. Sounds clear-cut enough. A drowning. There shouldn't be any urgency.

**Celia** A drowning, oh dear. One of the fishermen, I suppose – oh darling, this is Mr – (*Gestures.*) Holly's piano teacher, you haven't met, have you?

**Charles** (*nods*) How do you do?

**Brownlow** (*coming forward, hand held out*) How do you do, Dr Smithers, how do you do?

*They shake hands.*

**Celia** (*sotto voce to Holly*) Holly, do turn around. There are people in the room.

*Holly turns, gets up.*

**Charles** Well, do stay and – and have a drink. (*Gestures.*)

**Brownlow** How very kind of you, but I really mustn't use up any of your valuable time being sociable.

**Charles** (*surprised*) My time isn't at all valuable. Anyway, now I'm at home.

**Celia** I think, darling, Mr Brown – um – is thinking about Holly's lesson. They're right in the middle, you see. Perhaps we should have our drinks in the kitchen – oh, but first could my husband hear Holly play the thing you wrote for your cat?

**Brownlow** (*smiling politely*) It's not so much a thing as a bagatelle.

**Celia** It sounds very advanced – at least to my ear – but then I've got a tin ear, as you've probably guessed.

**Brownlow** It is quite advanced. But then so is your son. (*Little bow.*)

**Celia** (*to Holly*) There, you see, what did I tell you? Straight from the horse's mouth – and all your talk about violins!

**Brownlow** Violins?

**Celia** Yes, yes, he was full of one of his nonsenses about giving up football and the piano so he could go to Portsmouth to take lessons with goodness knows who.

*Brownlow looks at Holly. There is a silence.*

**Holly** Oh, Mummy, I didn't mean I wanted to give up the piano exactly – I like the piano – but I'd like to know more about the violin.

**Brownlow** I can show you whatever it is you think you'd like to know about the violin.

**Celia** There you are, you see? Everything you want without giving up anything.

**Charles** I'm afraid I'm a little lost in all this.

**Celia** Oh, don't worry about it, darling, we'll just listen to Holly for a minute and then go and have our drinks in the kitchen.

**Brownlow** Well then, Holliday. Perform, please.

*Holly begins to play the 'Moonlight Sonata'.*

Ah, we forgot to change the sheets. (*Puts his hand in his pocket, checks himself.*) Why don't you try it from memory, make a little test out of it?

*Holly begins to play the 'Bagatelle', then starts to encounter difficulties. Celia and Charles listen, smiling politely, unaware.*

Thank you, Holliday. (*Unable to suppress sharpness.*)

*Holly stops.*

(*Recovering,*) Just entering a very treacherous patch – unless you know it by heart – and even then –

**Celia** Still, it was lovely, wasn't it, darling?

**Charles** Very impressive, very impressive. And you wrote it yourself?

**Celia** (*to Charles*) They're going to do it on the Third Programme, Holly was telling me. We must make a point of listening, darling.

**Charles** Yes, do let us know when.

**Celia** Yes, please do. (*Going to drinks table.*) Well, I'll just pour us our drinks, and we'll be off to the kitchen and – oh, darling, we mustn't forget this whole thing about Mrs Milton.

**Charles** Mrs Milton? What does she want?

**Celia** I'm afraid, darling, it's what we want – it's some eggs that I said you were going to pick up on the way back.

**Charles** Oh, I'll drive over in a minute.

**Celia** No, no, that's not fair, you want to put your feet up, especially if you have to go out again. (*Pouring drinks.*) I'll pedal over – or Holly even, won't take him a minute with his young legs. (*To Holly.*) What was it you said the other day? When I told you to go and fetch something and your legs were so much younger than mine – and you said – he said –

> *Coming over, putting drink in Charles's hand, drink in her own hand.*

'Oh, Mummy,' you said, 'wouldn't it be more sensible to use up the old ones first?' (*Laughs.*)

> *Charles grunts a laugh.*

**Brownlow** (*laughs*) Very amusing, very amusing.

**Charles** Are you sure you won't –? (*Holding up drink.*)

**Brownlow** No, no, I think – I really feel that it would be best for me to leave you – (*Gestures.*) You want to be comfortable –

**Celia** No, we can do perfectly well in the kitchen, can't we, darling?

**Charles** What? Oh, yes. (*Struggles to his feet.*)

**Brownlow** No, I'll make up the lesson the next time. But what I think would be a very good idea – so that we're not in your way in the future –

**Celia** Oh, you're not usually, it's just that the doctor's been up since seven –

**Charles** Oh, don't worry about me.

**Brownlow** Still, one wants one's home to be one's home after a hard day's work, whatever hour one gets back. I don't generally allow my pupils to use my piano but Holly has got such an exceptional touch that he won't be a danger to it. Also I think it's time he got the feel of a – if you will permit me to say so – a more delicate instrument. A more responsive one.

**Celia** Well, that's awfully good of you, Mr – isn't it, Holly, darling?

**Holly** Yes. Yes. Thank you very much, sir.

**Charles** Will your prep be all right, Holly?

**Celia** Oh yes, his prep. He always has to do his prep before the lesson, it's an absolute rule.

**Brownlow** He can bring his prep to me. I'll make sure we don't start until he's finished it.

**Celia** Oh. Well, what about his tea?

**Brownlow** My mother can make him his tea. She'll enjoy having a boy to feed, and it'll only be once or twice a week.

**Celia** Twice a week?

**Brownlow** Oh – when we get into something special. An extra hour now and then might make all the difference.

**Celia** (*to Charles*) Is that all right, darling? I mean from the financial point of view?

**Brownlow** Oh, please don't worry about that. Whenever a bit of extra time comes up it'll be entirely my decision, entirely on my account.

**Charles** It's very good of you, but won't this interfere with other arrangements – your other pupils, I mean?

**Brownlow** I haven't got any other pupils, Dr Smithers. I go to a number of boys and girls because their parents feel that their offspring ought to have some piano lessons, even though they're musical clodhoppers – a social matter, really. Holliday, who has a gift – be assured he has a very considerable gift – is my only pupil in any proper meaning of the word. I consider it a privilege to teach him.

**Celia** And I know he feels the same. He feels it's a privilege to be taught by you. (*Looking at Holly.*)

**Holly** Yes. Yes, thank you, sir.

**Charles** Well, then. However, I would prefer to pay for all my son's tuition.

**Brownlow** (*does his odd little bow*) Well, we won't quarrel over it, will we, Doctor?

**Celia** Now that's all settled, do stay and have a quick drink.

**Charles**  Yes, have a drink, do have one.

**Brownlow**  No, I've still got time to get to the fishmonger's, they generally keep a few scraps for my mother. Well, for her cat, I mean.

**Celia**  (*triumphantly*) Oh yes, Miaow.

*Charles looks at her. There is a pause.*

Miaow. Isn't that the name of your cat, the one you wrote the music for? Didn't you say, Holly?

**Holly**  Yes – yes – mi-oh, really, more than miaow, isn't it, sir?

**Brownlow**  Yes, mi-oh. Mi-oh is my cat's name. I mustn't forget to introduce you. (*To Holly.*) I'll be off. (*Makes towards door.*)

**Celia**  Holly dear, show Mr Burnham the door.

*Holly runs ahead of Brownlow, opens door.*

**Brownlow**  Thank you, Holliday.

**Celia**  Oh, Holly darling, why don't you nip on over to Mrs Milton for the eggs, see if you can't wheedle four out of her?

**Holly**  Right, Mummy. (*Hurries out after Brownlow.*)

**Charles**  (*settling back*) Thank God.

**Celia**  Sssh, darling, he'll hear you. (*Closing sitting-room door.*) I suppose it's all right Holly going over there.

**Charles**  A bloody sight better than my coming home and finding him here.

**Celia**  He's a very good teacher, everybody says so, lucky to have him on the island. I must be careful, though, with Moira – he does her two, you know – I'm sure she wouldn't enjoy hearing his view of their musical gifts – what did he call them, 'clodhoppers' wasn't it, 'musical clodhoppers'? (*Laughs*.) Just like Moira on the tennis court – she stood me up, you know.

**Charles** Still, I'm going to pay him for anything extra.

**Celia** But why, darling, if it gives him so much pleasure?

**Charles** I just feel easier, don't want to be beholden, something about the chap, odd – that handshake. (*Grimaces*.)

**Celia** You don't think he's a Jew, do you?

**Charles** Could be. Anyway, something slightly off about him.

**Celia** Well, of course, a lot of them are very artistic and musical. And at least he's not being a Jew on the money front.

**Charles** No, but that's another reason for making sure we're all square. All square and straight.

**Celia** Well, let's see what kind of bill he gives us, he hasn't asked for anything yet.

*Comes and sits beside Charles.*

Have you had a rotten day, my Chaps? (*Stroking his leg*.)

**Charles** It's beginning to go away a bit.

*Celia lights a cigarette, offers it with her mouth to Charles.*

May I? (*Takes cigarette*.)

*Celia lights another for herself.*

**Celia** We'll make it go away completely, Chaps, we will. (*Stroking his forehead*.) You mustn't think about going back tonight to do the drowned man. There's nothing you can do for him that you can't do tomorrow.

**Charles** (*sighs*) Yes, but it isn't a matter of doing for him, it's what there'll be tomorrow as well. Might be wiser to clear him off the decks tonight. As a matter of fact, Ceci, I could have done him this afternoon somehow, could have managed it, but I took advantage of Greatorix not being quite ready – he hadn't finished cleaning the body. So I just left.

**Celia** Well then, you needed to. You would never do that unless you absolutely needed to.

**Charles** Couldn't face it, you see. Now we're back in civilian life, getting used to things as they used to be, although they never will be quite as they used to be, will they? – it's much harder, the death of young men particularly – boys they were, almost, at the beginning, weren't they? – three, four, five a day, no time for postmortems, no need for them, just being an ordinary doctor in an air base – broken bones, burnt flesh – so you think you could deal with the occasional corpse, don't even have to see the pain, hear it – nothing to try to save, just cut it open, sort through the organs, water in the lungs and pneumonia, heart failure, stroke, diphtheria, polio, drowning – anyway, this afternoon quite suddenly I couldn't face it. (*Little pause.*) That's all I mean.

**Celia** Here, come here.

*Takes his cigarette, stubs it out, stubs out hers, puts drinks on table.*

Come on, my Chaps, lay your head.

*Charles puts his head on her breast, she strokes the back of his head.*

You stay here tonight. You stay here in your family, safe and sound, where you belong.

*She rocks him gently.*
 *Charles lifts his head. They stare into each other's eyes, caress each other's cheeks, kiss gently, then passionately. Celia puts her hand between his legs.*

We'll go to bed early and we'll play.

**Charles** Oh, of course. You haven't had your tennis.

**Celia** Jolly good thing too. It's saved me for you. Mmmm – (*Feels him.*)

**Charles** I must try to be worth your saving yourself for.

**Celia** You're always that, Chaps. Oh, my man!

**Charles** Yes, your man. Completely and absolutely yours.

**Celia** That reminds me – *this* reminds me –

*Laughs, putting her hand between his legs again. Charles puts his hand on top of hers.*

Holly.

**Charles** What?

**Celia** Well, he's started.

**Charles** Started what? Oh!

**Celia** Though actually, my dear, I don't think 'started' is quite the word. I sometimes wonder if he ever stops. His sheets every morning – I thought something was up when he began making his bed so tight.

**Charles** You've been carrying out inspections then, have you?

**Celia** I do change the sheets, you know, darling.

Inevitably, as I do all the housework. Anyway, it's not a question of inspections, I couldn't avoid it even if I tried – the other day he shot into the house and rushed upstairs saying he had to get some prep done before tea, and when I put my head around the door to make sure he was really at it – well, there he was, on his knees, can you believe?

**Charles** On his knees? Well, that's rather bold.

**Celia** What do you mean?

**Charles** Well, on his knees in his bedroom and you likely to come in at any minute – that's rather bold in my book.

**Celia** Well, he wasn't actually unbuttoned, and he pretended he was praying, he had his palms pressed in front of his face like this – (*Does it.*) – and his eyes closed, but I could see some wretched-looking magazine under one knee and a piece of paper under the other one.

**Charles** What did you say?

**Celia** Nothing, of course. Well, except that I was sorry I'd interrupted him at his devotions. Then at tea I said, darling, if you're becoming religious there's always church, you know, on Sundays.

**Charles** (*laughs*) And what did he say?

**Celia** That at the moment he wanted to keep it between himself and his God.

**Charles** That's rather a fine way of putting it.

**Celia** But seriously, darling – I know it's silly but I can't help it – I do rather hate the feeling that it's going on, you see. Furtively. Shamefully. And lying about it. It makes it all so nasty.

**Charles** Well, it's better, surely, than having him doing it openly and publicly and boasting about it, darling.

**Celia** Oh, don't be a fool, Charles! (*Laughing in spite of herself.*) But don't you think you ought to have a little talk with him? Let him know that what he's going through is all perfectly natural and normal and – and nothing to be, well, ashamed of. That's what we're meant to do, isn't it, these days in the 1950s – or you, anyway, as a father – be open and honest? And – and natural.

*Charles laughs.*

What?

**Charles** I'm just thinking of my father being open, honest and natural with me, just think of him! 'Charles, after a great deal of thought and consultation with your mother and my colleagues, I have decided that the time has come to discuss with you certain matters connected to the procreation of the species. Not just in general terms but in specific, indeed, personal ones. As you know, your mother and I always believed that both at school and at home it is of the utmost importance that you keep, in the eyes of the world, a clean sheet –' (*Bursts out laughing.*)

**Celia** (*laughing*) But he probably didn't know what you were up to, or if he did, pretended to himself he didn't. Darling, if we had a daughter I wouldn't think twice about doing it myself. Anyway, I've told him.

**Charles** Told him what?

**Celia** That you're going to have a talk with him.

**Charles** Oh, God, you haven't! What on earth got into you?

**Celia** Well, it was really the thought of those magazines, you see. They may be absolutely foul and corrupting for all we know. They may even be against the law. And whatever it is he's been writing, it's been getting in the way of his prep – that's the point, Charles, we don't want him getting muddled and confused and carried away with his scholarship coming up.

*She picks up Holly's satchel, begins to go through it.*

**Charles** (*noticing Celia and satchel*) Really, darling, I'm not sure we have the right –

**Celia** Ah, here you are.

*Triumphantly produces magazine, hands it to Charles.*

'Nature Today'.

**Charles** (*taking magazine, looking at it*) 'A magazine for naturalists' – oh, I see, for nudists. (*Flicking through it.*) Photographs of nudists – rather fleshy – still, young – oh, here's one that's quite pretty –

*Shows picture to Celia, who has found exercise book, taken out loose pages.*

Anyway, nothing that qualifies as corrupting or foul or illegal. A perfectly reasonable way of finding out what a naked woman looks like, surely.

**Celia** But there's this.

**Charles** What is it?

**Celia** I don't know, I haven't looked, I don't want to – here. (*Hands him loose sheet.*)

**Charles** (*takes sheet*) It really does seem wrong, quite wrong – (*Muttering, as he reads sheet of paper.*)

*Celia lights a cigarette.*

(*Shakes his head.*) It's just about some girl he's been peeking at, or imagining he's been peeking at, under water – describing her nipples – and trying to see between her legs. (*Looks up.*) I used to write stuff like this, though actually not as good – well, as literary – and I can remember a time when I didn't know what was between a girl's legs either. Actually, I think I supposed it was rather like what I had between my own legs, only much smaller and daintier, more feminine, in other words.

**Celia** Well, there you are. You can set him right about that, for one thing.

**Charles** (*bursts out*) Would you like to help? Be the demonstrator's model?

**Celia** (*genuinely shocked*) Charles! What on earth's got into you!

*There is a pause.*

**Charles** Sorry, darling, sorry, I – I – it's just the thought of – of –

*Sound of door opening.*

Oh, God!

**Celia** Quick, here, give it to me!

*Charles hands Celia magazine and page. She crams them into satchel, pushes satchel down as they assume unnaturally natural positions as Holly enters, holding brown bag.*

Ah, here you are, darling, we were wondering where you'd been all this time.

**Holly** Mr Brownlow asked me to walk to the village with him. And then I went and got the eggs. Egg, I mean. (*Takes in that satchel is upside down in different place.*)

**Celia** Egg? What do you mean, egg?

**Holly** Well, that's all she had. Just the one left, she said.

**Celia** But didn't you tell her that we need four – at least four – and she promised me three anyway for the doctor's omelette? Didn't you say that, Holly?

**Holly** Well, no, I just said I'd come for the eggs and she handed me this. And I said I thought there'd be more and she said, well, she was very sorry, there weren't, that's all she had left.

*Hands bag to Celia.*

**Celia** Really, this island, these people! And to think how I grovelled to her! You should have gone straight there, Holly, instead of going to the village with Mr – (*Gestures.*) Well, we'll just have to make up with the usual powdered, I'm afraid, darling. (*To Charles.*) I'll get started straight away and you two chaps have a little chat, why don't you?

*Gives a quick meaningful look to Charles, goes out.*

**Charles** Don't tell your mother, but actually I've come to prefer dried eggs.

**Holly** So do I.

*There is a pause.*

Well, I ought to go upstairs with my prep. (*Going to satchel.*)

**Charles** Not finished yet, then?

**Holly** All but a little bit of French.

**Charles** Well, why don't you – why don't you sit down and – for a minute or two? I'm sure that can wait. (*Nods to satchel, realises, lets out a little laugh which he converts into a cough.*) For a minute or two.

*Holly sits down, clasping satchel to his lap.*

So what did you talk about?

**Holly** Daddy?

**Charles** You and Mr – your piano chap. On the way to the village.

**Holly** Oh, just about the piano, really. And music. And the violin. (*Little pause.*) Nothing.

**Charles** You obviously get on with him.

**Holly** Yes, well, he's very good.

**Charles** I often wonder where you get your musical gifts from. Not from my side of the family – at least as far as I know. Oh, there was a great-uncle, your great-great-uncle – Cedric, I think it was – is said to have played the fiddle – but only jigs, and that kind of thing, to please the ladies, I suspect. He was a shameless philanderer, you know. A bit of a gay dog is what that means. A gay old dog, your great-great-uncle Cedric. Well, that's the family mythology anyway. But on your mother's side – well, your mother says she doesn't know of anyone at all on her side to account for you – of course she's almost completely tone deaf, isn't she? Although I'm not actually tone deaf myself – I mean I can carry a tune – but the fact is, apart from great-uncle Cedric, if it was Cedric who fiddled and jigged, we don't know of anyone on either side – (*Gestures.*) But of course that's the thing about a gene, isn't it – just bobs up generations after it was last seen or heard of. So you're what is known as a sport.

**Holly** Oh.

**Charles** It's the word in genetics for what you are. A sudden resurgent gene.

**Holly** Ah.

**Charles** Well, everything seems to be going well then? You mustn't let this business of a scholarship weigh you down, you know, if you do get one – but on the other hand, if you don't, you don't.

**Holly** Mummy says if I don't get one we won't be able to go to London.

**Charles** Does she? I think you must have misunderstood her. Going to London depends on a great deal of other things, not the least of which is whether I can get a job in London. Besides, we may not want to go to London. We may end up somewhere else entirely – here, for instance – or Australia, or South Africa, Canada or New Zealand. Or London.

**Holly** Oh.

**Charles** All I'm saying is that it's not the end of the world if you don't get your scholarship, that's all I'm saying. I'm sure your mother would agree. All right?

**Holly** Thank you, Daddy.

*There is a pause.*

Well then, I'll just – (*Makes to get up.*)

**Charles** There's one other thing. It's nothing very – it's not at all – well, Holly, there are some things in life, you know – well, there comes a time – well, of course there are some things in life, what do I mean there are some things in life? Life is full of some things or other things – some things and other things fill our lives every moment of the day, every second. The point is – well, there comes a time between people – well, father and son – when they need to be – (*thinks*) talked about. Mmm?

**Holly** Yes, Daddy.

**Charles** I wish, you know, that your grandfather had found a way of talking to me. Of talking to me as I'm talking to you now. But then – of course you never met my father, did you?

**Holly** No, Daddy. Well, I suppose I did but he died when I was two, wasn't it, Mummy says?

**Charles** Somewhere about that time it would have been, yes. Anyway, before you were old enough to get a real sense of him. But then I'm not sure I ever got a real sense of him. And he died when I was thirty-three. (*Laughs ruefully*.) I don't mean he was mysterious or there was some dark secret – no, no, not at all. I knew what he did. Like me he was a doctor, though not a pathologist. A straightforward general practitioner is what he was, so of course he knew how to talk to his patients – naturally I don't have to know how to talk to my patients as they're usually dead, although they talk to me in what I discover in this diseased organ or that, samples of tissue – I hear them through my microscope. (*Little pause*.) I've never really discussed my work with you before, have I?

**Holly** No, Daddy.

**Charles** What do you know about it?

**Holly** Well, only that you find out why people died. Isn't that it?

**Charles** (*after a little pause*) Yes. That's it, old chap. Why people died. There's always a scientific explanation, even if I can't always find it. If I had my time again I'd go into psychiatry, all the patients alive and talking for themselves, that's where the medical future lies – financially anyway – and I wouldn't have to put up with all this death – I mean death is – is – (*Frowns, looks into his drink as if lost*.) Do you know what a psychiatrist is?

**Holly** Well, no, not really, Daddy.

**Charles** Well, let's hope you never have to find out, eh? (*Laughs.*)

*Holly laughs. There is a little pause.*

Oh, by the way, that reminds me. Girls, old chap. Do you ever find yourself, um, noticing them? Thinking about them?

**Holly** No, Daddy. Not really. (*Shaking his head.*)

**Charles** Never?

**Holly** Well, sometimes – a little bit, I suppose.

**Charles** Well, I'm glad to hear it. Because otherwise there would be – well, frankly, something odd. (*Takes a sip of scotch, tries not to look as if he's bracing himself.*) Um, masturbation, old boy?

*The telephone rings.*

Oh, blast! (*Picks up telephone.*) Hayling 349? Greatorix – oh hello, you're still there, are you, how are you getting on?

*As Holly gets up, gestures tentatively as he goes out. Charles lifts his hand in vague salute.*

(*On telephone.*) Mmm. Ah. So you think I'd better come over tonight?

*Celia enters.*

(*On telephone.*) Well, I'd like to eat first if the deceased doesn't mind. (*Smiles at Celia.*) It's a damn nuisance, I was looking forward to an evening at home – (*Hangs up.*)

**Celia** Poor darling. (*Pats him on the cheek.*)

**Charles** Well, we had that little talk you wanted. And I'm happy to report it's all just as I said it would be – normal. Perfectly normal at his age.

**Celia** There, I knew it would be. So why you had to make such a fuss about a simple little father–son chat! (*Goes to door.*) Holly? Holly darling, it's supper – hurry, because your father's got to be off. (*To Charles.*) I wish it wasn't mainly powdered eggs but there, I'll put the fresh one in your bit for being such a dear old Chaps.

*Lights.*

### SCENE THREE

*Three months later. Late afternoon. Summer.*
 *Brownlow's study/sitting room.*
 *Holly is sitting at the table, satchel beside him, writing, consulting the dictionary.*
 *Mrs Brownlow (Ellie) enters, carrying a tray of tea, on which is also a bottle of sherry and a glass. Ellie drinks sherry steadily throughout the following scene.*

**Ellie** (*has a Viennese accent*) Come on, Catty-Kit, come on, Catty-Kit, puss, puss, puss, come on – (*Puts tray down on table. Pours herself a glass of sherry. To Holly.*) Are you finished?

**Holly** Yes, I have. I was just checking some words. (*Closing dictionary.*)

**Ellie** Good, good, once more I have the right time, I seem always to know, yes?

*Rumples Holly's hair, goes to door.*

Catty-Kit, Catty-Kit, puss, puss – don't be frightened of him, he's a very kind boy, he will not hurt you. (*Bends down.*) Oh – ooh, Catty-Kit – ooh, come to Mama – oh, silly! Silly frightened thing! (*Stands up, shuts the door.*) It is no good, when you are here she will not come. You must not think it is personal with you, she is not in the habit of guests, you see. We don't have many guests so she thinks you are an intruder, come to take her place even. But still I should leave the door open in case she changes her mind and wishes to be a friend with you at last. Now, here, let us have our tea. (*Lifting lids.*) We have two boiled eggs, we have toast and we have – here, Sachertorte. This is a very special cake we make in Vienna. Before the war it was famous everywhere. Now of course I do not know whether they can still make Sachertorte, it is difficult enough to do it on the island with so little chocolate, but we do not complain because here we have our Sachertorte whether they have it or do not have it any more in Vienna. Eat, please. Eat, Holliday. (*Claps her hands.*) Why must I always tell you to start? Is it that you are shy eating alone with me? (*Pouring him a cup of tea.*) Here, your cuppa, your nice English cuppa. Now you will feel safe and comfortable with your nice English cuppa. You have such good manners, how is the egg?

**Holly** (*swallowing egg*) Very nice, thank you, Ellie.

**Ellie** My boy also has very good manners. But not with me. Never with me. He always makes fun from me – even as a baby he was making fun from me. Do you make fun from your *mutter*?

**Holly** Not really.

**Ellie** Then you have a father and he won't permit you. So lucky *mutter*. My boy was never with a father. Dead before he was born. Did he tell you that?

**Holly** No, Ellie.

**Ellie** He was not a young man, my Emil, but he was very big, very strong. He had a bad heart, you see. A man of good heart with a bad heart. And sometimes he was angry, very angry. I think he would have been angry with my boy quite often. He was not an artist, he was a banker. And a soldier. Brave. What is it like today outside? Catty-Kit, Catty-Kit – I thought I felt her, did you see her? Was she there?

**Holly** No, I didn't see her.

**Ellie** (*going to window*) It is beautiful outside, I can see that, but is it cold, is there a wind?

**Holly** Not very cold, Ellie, no. Don't you like going out then?

**Ellie** No, I do not go out.

**Holly** Never? I mean, don't you ever go out?

**Ellie** No. I stay here, inside, where I have trust, you see. Safety. When I arrive in this house I think, now I will never have to go outside again. It was very bad for me, you see, in Portsmouth, in the war. Because of my accent. Everybody thinks I am a Nazi from the Gestapo. Such silly they think. When I go to shops – it is very terrible for my boy, they think he is a little Nazi Gestapo when I speak. Or black market when I have coupons. Or a Jew even. You, Holliday, do you think we are Jews?

**Holly** No. I mean, I don't know, I've never thought about it, Ellie.

**Ellie** Of course you have. And your father and your *mutter*. I know you English, they are always looking very close. So?

**Holly** I don't think you're Jews, Ellie. Nor do my parents. Well, they've never said, honestly, and I expect they would have said something if they thought you were.

**Ellie** Well, it is true they have only seen my boy. They look at him and they say straight away, no, he is not a Jew. But if they hear my voice – me – my voice, you understand? Then they would be confused. But now you can tell them yourself everything about me. Yes, Holliday? You are the only one he brings back to see me, ever. Oh, Teddy sometimes – when we were in London – but he was not his pupil, he is grown-up. Like him, poor soul. Grown-ups. Hah! Do you know what I mean?

*Holly shakes his head.*

That is good. I am glad of that. There must be no trouble. I cannot move again to another house. I will not move. This is my home. This is my last home. Do you understand?

**Holly** Not really.

**Ellie** That is good. There is nothing for you to understand. What we say is private, yes?

*Holly nods.*

You cross your fingers?

*Holly nods.*

Well then, cross your fingers.

*Holly crosses his fingers.*

You are a little gentleman. Now you shall have some Sachertorte. There. (*Cutting slice, putting it on a plate.*) Eat, please.

*Holly makes to pick it up.*

No, no, there is a fork. You must always eat Sachertorte with a fork, otherwise it is not Sachertorte, it is only chocolate cake. Now.

*Putting fork into Holly's hand. Stands, watching Holly as he eats.*

There. What do you think of Sachertorte?

**Holly** Oh, it's – very nice, Ellie.

**Ellie** Very nice! All you English, you say that about everything – everything is always very nice – I am very nice, you are very nice, we are very nice, the house is very nice, God himself is very nice – or it's a very nice bomb, nice gas, nice, nice, nice – England is very, very, very nice – what a pity it isn't also very, very, very kind, huh? Because kind is nicer. Much nicer.

*There is a pause.*

**Holly** It's delicious. Really delicious.

**Ellie** (*claps her hands*) Thank you. Thank you, thank you, thank you. For that you will have some more.

**Holly** Oh no, no thank you, Ellie – no, really.

**Ellie** Why not?

**Holly** Well, if I eat anything more I'll be too full to play the piano properly.

**Ellie** And my boy will not like that, huh? If you sit there with a big stomach, playing the piano – (*Does piano movements with her fingers.*) Your stomach – woof – all big – woof! He is a very good teacher.

**Holly** Yes.

**Ellie** He is very serious.

**Holly** Yes.

**Ellie** He is a genius. You don't think so?

**Holly** Oh yes, yes – I mean, I expect he is. I'm sure he is, Ellie.

**Ellie** One day you will see. I hope only that I live so long, it is my hope. No, it is not my hope. After I am gone, then he can be a genius to all the world. Now he can be my genius and your genius, we keep him to us. Our little secret, eh, Holliday?

*Goes to him, rumples his hair, kisses him.*

Ah, yes, my little English gentleman, we shall have our genius to ourselves, mmm?

*Laughs, caresses him on the cheeks.*

Is he nice to you, like me?

*Stares intently down at Holly.*

Sssh –

*Picks up bottle of sherry and glass, takes a quick gulp from glass, then puts them behind flowers on table, goes to door, opens it.*

Catty-Kit, Catty-Kit, puss, puss, puss – Oh, there you are, back then, we didn't hear you come in.

*Brownlow enters, carrying his coat over his arm.*

**Brownlow** That wasn't me you were calling then, Mutti?

**Ellie** What's your name, Catty-Kit, suddenly? (*Taking his coat, putting it on back of chair.*)

**Brownlow** Ah, Number Seven, you mean. He or she was hurrying out of the kitchen when I came in, carrying something or other between his or her jaws. A mouse, do you think? A mouse, Mutti? A mouse, Mutti, for Number Seven?

**Ellie** You're teasing me, you're teasing me again, Thomas. (*Slapping at him playfully.*) It wasn't a mouse and it is a girl, you know very well. And her name is Catty-Kit.

Why are you back so early? Look, he is still drinking his cuppa.

**Brownlow** The Merrivale twins had colds so I refused to teach them. I went for a walk by the sea and if I'm early – (*glances at his watch*) it's only by five minutes. (*To Holly.*) You haven't practised for me yet, then?

*Holly shakes his head.*

Ah.

**Holly** I was just going to.

**Brownlow** Were you? (*Fixes him with a look.*)

*Holly lowers his eyes, looks away.*

**Ellie** Oh, you mustn't be unkind with him, it is my fault, I was talking and talking and talking.

**Brownlow** Now, Mutti, you can stop talking and talking and talking and let us get on with our work.

**Ellie** You be kind to him, he is a good boy.

**Brownlow** Yes, I know. A little gentleman, isn't he?

*He turns Ellie around.*

Go, Mutti, and do the washing-up.

**Ellie** (*as she goes out*) Ah, there you are, waiting for me, come –

*Brownlow closes the door.*

**Brownlow** Where did she put it this time?

**Holly** Behind the flowers.

*Brownlow goes to flowers, takes bottle of sherry, raises it, studies it.*

**Brownlow** (*still holding bottle of sherry*) I trust you keep all our little family secrets to yourself, mio.

**Holly** Of course I do, Lowly.

**Brownlow** Because never forget, they're your family secrets too now, aren't they? What was she talking and talking and talking about this time?

**Holly** The same as last time, really, and the time before. What she always talks about. Though I never quite understand it, really.

*Brownlow sits in armchair, puts bottle of sherry on floor beside him.*

**Brownlow** And what do you tell them when you go home, about what transpires here – our transpirations here? Mmm?

**Holly** Nothing.

**Brownlow** They don't ask questions then?

**Holly** Well, only the first time. About what I had for tea, mainly, and what Ellie was like – what your mother was like. I said they were both very nice. That's all. They haven't asked anything since.

**Brownlow** Secrets, secrets. So much of our life is spent not saying who we are, what we really do, what we really think. (*Little pause.*) What we really feel. We live in secret almost all the time. When I was walking along the shore, I listened to the waves and the wind, the cries of the seagulls, and I thought – I thought – here, mio, here mio, come on.

*Pats his lap. Holly goes over, sits on Brownlow's lap, stiffly.*

And I thought – what did I think? That if I were Bach or Brahms or Mozart or Beethoven, I would hear so many different sounds – the deep movement of the sea, the soft wind – how it can become a scream – and the seagulls, within their ugly shrieks I would hear other songs, sad songs, of restless souls, whatever, whatever, whatever – I thought I am not Brahms or Beethoven, I can only imagine what they might imagine, and do I even want to hear it, what their imaginings want to hear? Not Ludwig van Beethoven but Thomas Ambrose Brownlow – well, Thomas Ambrose Brownlow, what do you really want to hear? Do you want to know, mio, what I really wanted to hear?

**Holly** Yes, Lowly.

**Brownlow** Yes, mio – yes, Lowly. (*Little pause.*) That's what I truly wanted to hear. Your voice saying 'Yes, Lowly.' So. So. Perhaps you will have to be my muse. Perhaps you are already my muse. But then – but then we have a contradiction, haven't we? A paradox. Why – why, if you are my muse, do you make me feel impotent? Do you know what impotent means?

**Holly** It means not being able to.

**Brownlow** And of course you know what a paradox is.

**Holly** I think so.

**Brownlow** What is it, mio? What is a paradox?

**Holly** It's one of the ways you say things when you want to show off.

**Brownlow** (*laughs shakily*) You are very clever. Am I the only person who knows how clever you are, mio?

**Holly** I don't know. They think I am at school, I think.

**Brownlow** And do they ever punish you for it?

**Holly** No. Why should they?

**Brownlow** Ah, so another duty falls on me. I will punish you for your cleverness.

**Holly** (*after a pause*) Why?

**Brownlow** (*coldly*) Yours not to reason why, little Englishman.

*Pushing Holly off his knee.*

Go and stand there – there, by the piano. Now, you know what to do.

**Holly** But it's not – it's not –

**Brownlow** And you know what not to do.

*Stares at Holly. Holly stands to attention, raises his arms, facing Brownlow.*

**Brownlow** It is through the punishment that we shall find the sin. Another paradox. A paradox that will be received this time in silent respect, not to say humility. A becoming humility. (*After a pause.*) What am I to do, mio, if the muse I need so much is a bad muse? A muse who takes away my power. (*Staring fixedly at Holly through this.*) You see, this is not showing off, this is giving up my secret. That's what my bad muse makes me do, give up my secret.

*Door opens. Ellie enters.*

**Ellie** Excuse me, please, I'm so sorry, but how can I wash the dishes if I do not have dishes to wash? (*Crosses room. Looks at Holly.*) What are you doing, is this a new exercise? Is he teaching you a new trick? (*Groping behind flowers on table.*) What is he doing? (*Sees sherry bottle beside Brownlow.*) He mustn't stand like that too long, the blood will leave his hands, then how can he play the piano? (*Picks up tray.*) Put it on the tray, please.

**Brownlow** (*in German*) Go away, Mutti, no more for you until tonight.

**Ellie** (*in German, hissingly*) And what about you? I know what you're up to, you will cause us trouble again, you will be in disgrace, we'll have to leave – give me the bottle, give me the bottle!

*Brownlow puts bottle of sherry on tray.*

(*In English.*) Thank you. (*In German.*) But for God's sake be careful, control yourself, you must. (*Goes out, leaving door open.*)

*Brownlow gets up, goes to door, closes it. Looks at Holly, goes over to him, takes handkerchief out of his pocket.*

**Brownlow** That was very good. Well done, mio. You didn't move your eyes, even though they were running.

*He wipes Holly's cheeks. Holly makes to lower his arms.*

A minute more, that's all. Let's have a minute more. You can manage that, I know you can. (*Going to piano, playing.*) And then you'll have earned your chance with my – beloved. As you stand there think how privileged you are and tell yourself – (*still playing*) that you must talk to him as I talk to him. Then perhaps he will talk to you as he talks to me. Eh, mio? (*Turns, looks at Holly. Suddenly begins to wheeze.*) Quickly – quickly –

*Holly runs to jacket, fumbles in pockets for inhaler. As he does so, doorbell over, not noticed by Brownlow and Holly.*

*Holly comes over, squirts inhaler into Brownlow's mouth in a practised manner as:*

**Ellie** (*loud, over*) They're not playing the piano so it will be all right, I'm sure it will be all right – (*Warningly.*) Thomas! Thomas! (*Opening door.*) There's someone to see you, it's the *mutter*.

# THE LATE MIDDLE CLASSES

*Brownlow breathes in, still wheezing, beginning to recover. Celia enters.*

**Celia** What on earth is going on?

**Holly** Mr Brownlow, he's having an attack, Mummy.

**Celia** What of?

**Ellie** Oh, it's his asthma. I always tell him he must not get excited.

**Celia** Oh. Are you all right?

**Brownlow** (*squirting inhaler, breathing in, recovering*) Yes – thank you. Thanks to your son's quick thinking. I left this – (*indicating inhaler*) over there. I should always have it on me. (*Getting up.*) There. Mrs Smithers.

**Celia** Well, I just came – I couldn't resist coming, I wanted him to have the news straight away. He's won a full scholarship to Westminster. Congratulations, Holly. (*Shaking Holly's hand.*)

**Holly** Thank you, Mummy.

**Brownlow** Indeed, indeed congratulations, my boy. (*Shaking Holly's hand.*)

**Holly** Thank you, Lowly – Mr – Mr Br—

**Ellie** (*rampaging across*) Oh, how wonderful, what a wonderful, clever boy!

*Clutches Holly to her.*

But please – please, you will have some tea with us, you will have a cuppa and some cake – but no Sachertorte, I'm sorry, no Sachertorte left, we have finished it together, haven't we, Holly? But there is cake – sherry, would you like a glass of sherry?

**Celia** No, no, I won't, thank you very much – um, I've got my tennis, you see. I just wanted to give the news. (*To Holly.*) See you later, darling.

*Ellie accompanies Celia out.*

**Ellie** (*off*) Such a boy, such a boy you've got. And such a little gentleman, such a little English gentleman. How lucky you are.

**Brownlow** Well then. That means you'll be leaving us for London, doesn't it?

**Holly** Yes. Well, I mean it's in London, Westminster, so I suppose –

**Brownlow** A scholarship. To Westminster. In London. How proud you must feel. Are you feeling proud, mio?

**Holly** Well, I haven't had a chance to think about it yet. What it means.

**Brownlow** What it means is that you're on your way. The little English gentleman is on his way. Away from all this. (*Sweeps arm contemptuously around room.*) And back to his proper little England.

*Sits down at piano, begins to play and sing 'Rule Britannia' savagely.*
  *Holly watches him as Ellie opens door in state of excitement, joins in, makes encouraging signs to Holly. Holly joins in, sings more and more full-bodiedly. They sing through to end.*

**Ellie** Oh, that was so good! So good for the spirit! Such a grand song!

**Brownlow** Thank you, Mutti.

**Ellie** And such a lovely lady, Holliday, *dein Mutti*.

**Brownlow** She is indeed. Thank you, Mutti. (*Nods at her pointedly.*)

**Ellie** Well, I leave you, I leave you. And your clever, clever boy. (*Going out.*)

*Brownlow laughs. Holly laughs.*
*There is a pause.*

**Holly** They're talking of coming back some time. In the summer. They say once they're away they'll probably miss it, really. And the beach.

*Brownlow looks at him.*

I'm sure they will, Lowly. Honestly. And anyway it's not for three months and so we'll have lots of time.

**Brownlow** Time for what, mio?

**Holly** (*after a little pause*) Well, to teach me.

**Brownlow** I should like, if I may, to teach you now. This minute.

*Gets up, moves away from piano. Holly goes to piano, sits facing Brownlow, stretches out his arms, does his finger exercises. Brownlow gives a slight nod. Holly turns around, begins to play a hitherto unheard piece of music. Chopin Etude?*

*Lights. Curtain.*

# Act Two

### SCENE ONE

*A few weeks later. Early evening.*
 *Smithers' sitting room.*
 *Holly is at the piano. Celia is lying on the sofa, smoking.*
 *Holly completes passage, gets up quickly, stuffs score into his satchel, goes towards door.*

**Holly** Bye, Mummy.

*Celia doesn't answer.*

Mummy? (*Goes over to Celia.*) What is it this time, going dead again or gone blind again? Mummy, please, I'll be late, what is it?

**Celia** (*as if coming out of a trance*) Sorry, darling. I've been away somewhere, I think. A bit of a headache.

**Holly** Oh. Well, you must take some aspirin.

**Celia** (*patting sofa*) Just give me one of your rubs. Just for a minute.

**Holly** But, Mummy, I –

**Celia** Just for a minute, darling, please.

**Holly** He gets very fed up when I'm late.

*He goes behind Celia, beginning to massage her neck.*

**Celia** Well, you can tell him you've been looking after me for once. Or I'll write him a note, if you like.

**Holly** Oh, Mummy. (*Laughs.*) A note.

**Celia** Mmm – mmm – deeper, deeper – oh, you've got such a feel for it. You seem to know my neck like your piano, I suppose. Holly, do you love me?

**Holly** Oh, Mummy, of course I do. Because you're my –

**Celia** No, no, not that, not the usual. I'm being very, very serious. I just want you to say it and nothing more.

**Holly** Well, I've said it.

**Celia** Well, say it again. Think about it first and then say it. Holly, do you love me?

**Holly** (*after a little pause*) Yes.

**Celia** You don't know how lucky you are being a boy. Look at me – I may not be stupid but I'm almost completely uneducated, really. You're far more educated than I am already. And when you grow up you'll have your freedom, you'll be able to make all kinds of choices. Be what you want. But what am I good for? I can't do anything except what I do. And sometimes that just seems to be nothing. Nothing at all.

**Holly** But you used to teach girls gym, tennis – and lacrosse.

**Celia** I can scarcely go back to that now, can I? Do you know, I wouldn't even know how to go about getting a job any more.

**Holly** But you drove ambulances at the air base. You're always saying how much you loved it.

**Celia** Oh, they don't want women driving ambulances now the war's over. They don't need us to be anything except what we've always been now they don't need us for carrying wounded men about.

**Holly** Mummy, are you crying?

**Celia** (*sniffing*) No, not really. Just a little.

**Holly** But why? Just because you're not educated?

**Celia** (*laughs*) Yes, I expect that's it. And because I feel a little sad too, I expect.

**Holly** But why are you sad?

**Celia** Oh, things, darling, things. Things I wouldn't dream of burdening you with. You wouldn't understand and I don't want you to.

**Holly** What things?

**Celia** Grown-up things, darling. Which are just childish things, really, that happen after a certain age.

*Sound of front door opening and closing.*

Oh, there's your father. Early. So he'll be going out again this evening, won't he?

*Holly has gone to pick up his satchel.*
*Charles enters.*

**Charles** Oh, hello, darling. (*Sees Holly.*) Off already?

**Holly** Daddy?

**Charles** Well, it seems that every time I come in you're going out. Rather like a French farce. At least we've both got our trousers on, eh? (*Laughs.*)

**Holly** (*laughs*) I've got my piano.

**Charles** Well, yes, I assume that. It's been virtually every evening, hasn't it?

**Holly** He's teaching me some preludes – Chopin – and they're rather difficult.

**Charles** And you want to master them, do you?

**Holly** Yes, Daddy.

**Charles** Well, now your scholarship's in the bag I suppose your time's your own for a bit. After all, you've earned it. Earned your Chopin. So. Off you go then.

**Holly** Thanks, Daddy.

**Charles** (*slightly surprised*) Not at all, Holly.

*As Holly goes to door.*

Oh, Holly, there is one thing. You might ask your Mr – Mr – um – no, it's all right, it doesn't matter.

*Holly goes out.*

I was going to ask him to find out when I can expect a bill at last. I know he said he wouldn't charge me for the extra hours but I don't feel right about it. It's all a bit awkward, if you ask me. Still, mustn't complain, I expect his London tinkler will want it in cash and on the dot – but there's something about him, Mr – Mr – why can we never remember his name?

**Celia** You're going out again, I take it.

**Charles** A little girl just come in, four years old. We're all hoping to God it isn't polio that did for her, though from what Greatorix says – (*Looks at Celia.*) Are you all right?

**Celia** A slight headache, that's all.

**Charles** Have you taken an aspirin?

**Celia** Yes, I took two.

**Charles** When?

**Celia** About an hour ago.

**Charles** And you've still got it?

**Celia** Yes, I've just said.

**Charles** Poor Ceci, poor Ceci.

*Kisses her forehead, goes behind her.*

Here, let's see what I can do.

*Begins to massage her neck.*

You feeling it?

**Celia** Yes. It's making it worse.

*Walks around room, her hand to her head.*

**Charles** Oh. Sorry. (*Little pause.*) Shall I get us a drink?

*Celia nods.*
*Charles goes and pours drinks, glancing anxiously at Celia, who lights a cigarette. Charles goes over, hands her a glass.*

There we are. (*Smiling.*) May I?

*Makes to take cigarette from between Celia's lips. Celia moves cigarette away.*

Darling – (*Stops.*) Oh, isn't it your period about now, old girl?

**Celia** Don't you know?

**Charles** Well, not the precise date, how could I?

**Celia** So you're guessing. Because I've got a headache and I'm feeling low and miserable, it must be old girl's period.

**Charles** Well, if it's not, then what is it?

**Celia** I suppose people can feel low and miserable because they're actually low and miserable, even if they are women, wives and mothers and aren't allowed to be low and miserable, except when they've got their periods.

**Charles** Is it the island again? The gang getting you down? (*Little pause.*) Has Moira said something?

**Celia** What sort of something?

**Charles** Well, the sort of something she's always saying that upsets you.

**Celia** No, Moira hasn't said anything she's always saying that upsets me.

**Charles** Well, anybody else in the gang? I know how much you hate them but, darling, we're away from here soon – a new life. There'll be a new life.

**Celia** Yes. A new life. A new life. (*Walking about, smoking. Laughs.*) But there's no getting away from the old life, is there? Ever?

**Charles** No, I suppose not. But the old life merges into the new life and things change directions and – I don't quite know what you mean, Ceci.

**Celia** I'm trying to talk about the old, old life, not this that will be the old life when we get to London, but the old life that was before we came to the island. Do you remember?

**Charles** Yes, of course I remember. Well, there was quite a lot of it, wasn't there, quite a lot of life before we came here. There was the war, for example. (*Little laugh.*) I mean, which part of the old life?

**Celia** Well, there were certain special moments, I suppose, even in the war, special moments for us – there must have been, mustn't there?

**Charles** Yes. Yes, quite a few of them. Which ones are you thinking of? I mean, darling, what are you talking about, really?

**Celia** Well, Whitstable. I think I must be talking about Whitstable.

**Charles** Whitstable?

**Celia** Yes. Do you remember us in Whitstable?

**Charles** Yes, of course I remember.

**Celia** We went there for the oysters.

**Charles** Well, darling – yes, the oysters – but we went there to become lovers. Surely that's what you remember about Whitstable.

**Celia** Yes, yes. All that embarrassment over getting the room for the night.

**Charles** Rooms actually. We had to take a room each because of that ghastly little landlady – she knew perfectly well what we were up to – so all my shuffling up and down the stairs in the dark . . . (*Laughing reminiscently.*)

**Celia** Yes, that's how it began. You shuffling about in the dark, me waiting for you in that horrid room with the curtains that didn't close and the window you couldn't open.

**Charles** (*laughs*) Yes, well, I suppose quite a lot of couples got off like that. It was all we could get of romance.

**Celia** Yes, quite a lot of us. Quite a lot of others must have got off like that. Got off on the wrong foot. Deceiving people right from the beginning. Whatever we pretended to each other, we knew it was furtive and it was wrong.

**Charles** Furtive – wrong? It was just how we had to go about things before – before we were properly married. As far as society was concerned, our parents and – for form's sake. Discreet, we were being, that's all.

**Celia** But still, we were different, you and I. We wanted to be different from the others. And that's why we kept saying that whatever happened in our lives together we would always be straight with each other, at least. That was to be our rule. Unbreakable. That we would be straight with each other. We made that rule the very next morning. In Whitstable.

**Charles** Well – yes. And we always have been.

*Celia shakes her head.*

What? What do you mean?

**Celia** Oh, Chaps, not me. I haven't been straight. I haven't been straight with you, Chaps.

*Charles stares at her.*

I had an affair, you see, Chaps.

**Charles** An affair? In Whitstable? We were only there for three days!

**Celia** Oh, don't be so stupid, Charles! Of course not in Whitstable. Afterwards. After we'd just got married. At the base.

**Charles** (*after a pause*) Who? Who, may I ask?

**Celia** It was Johnny.

**Charles** Johnny? You don't mean Johnny Miller!

**Celia** No, not Johnny Miller.

**Charles** Which Johnny then? There were several Johnnies, I seem to remember.

**Celia** Johnny Seafield.

**Charles** Seafield. (*Thinks.*) Johnny Seafield! The one who used to tinkle the piano and lead the sing-songs in the mess?

**Celia** That's right. Piano Johnny we used to call him.

**Charles** That's not what some of us called him, some of us called him *Pansy* Johnny – and worse.

**Celia** Oh yes, I know you did. That was part of the – well, the joke, really. You thought he was like that because he was boyish and delicate and had a gentle manner.

**Charles** He was effeminate and – and he had a kind of lisp. He made our skins crawl.

**Celia** (*laughs*) You were such stupid chaps. Blind, the lot of you. We women knew what he was really like. And he was brave. Brave and doomed.

**Charles** They were all brave, and a lot of them doomed. He wasn't the only one to buy it, you know.

**Celia** I know. Oh, how I know. He and Julian Lownes and Dickie Storbuck. All in the same afternoon.

**Charles** But it was him you had a fling with, was it? Or did you have a fling with all of them? All three?

*Celia gives him a look.*

**Celia** It wasn't a fling. It was a sadness. The saddest time in my life. I used to watch the skies for him and when I saw him coming back I'd think, well, that's one more time, one more time at least, God has given us.

**Charles** One more time God had given you – *God* had given you – for you and he to – to – Where did you do it?

**Celia** Rose House.

**Charles** Rose House. But that was the vicarage! You did it in the vicarage!

**Celia** The vicar was Johnny's uncle. He was the only person who knew. And he understood. Understood everything. Sometimes he stood with me watching the skies. Both of us looking for Johnny's plane.

**Charles** Well, we watched the skies too, wondering who was coming back – how many we could patch up – how many we could send up again, knowing that the more often we sent them back, the more likely it was – and that went for your Johnny too. For all the Johnnies we had to put back in the skies. Pansies or not.

**Celia** It wasn't your fault.

**Charles** What do you mean it wasn't my fault? Of course it wasn't my fault that you and your Johnny –

**Celia** No, no, I meant it wasn't your fault that you weren't up in the skies with them. You did the only job you could do. Just as I did in the ambulances.

**Charles** Are you saying I should be ashamed? That while you were having your – your – with him up in the skies – I should be ashamed for being down there on the ground?

**Celia** No, I'm saying you shouldn't be. That's it, you see, that's what I'm trying to explain. You and I – well, we had a chance and a future. For us, we could hope it would be over one day, there'd be peace and our lives to live. But Johnny – and the others too, of course – didn't have that hope –

**Charles** Look – (*Getting up.*) I know – I know what sort of thing went on. I'd supposed you were exempt from all that panic and living-in-the-moment stuff. But if you weren't – well, God knows how many stories there are to tell that shouldn't be told – what on earth is the bloody point –?

**Celia** Of being straight, you mean? When we promised we would be. That was our rule.

**Charles** Well, it's a bit late, isn't it? A dozen years or so late.

**Celia** I couldn't have told you then, not while it was going on – and I couldn't have told you afterwards – after he'd gone. It would have been unfair on Johnny – to my memory of him – if he'd been the cause for unhappiness between us.

**Charles** Well then, why now? Why now, when he's been at the bottom of the sea for seven or eight years and it no longer matters? You don't have to be straight when it no longer matters, there's no point to it. No – no moral value even. I mean – I mean, for God's sake, woman, I come home from a day's work, this morning's post-mortems behind me, and tomorrow's – no, tonight's probably – a child of four – a little girl of four and it could be polio, here on this island – if so, God help all of us who have children – looking forward – just looking forward to being alone with you, having our usual drink, our usual – our usual – and this. I get this. Why?

**Celia** But you see, Chaps, you see, you talked about a new life in London and I'm afraid, you see. So afraid.

**Charles** Of London? But you've been begging to go to London! Everything I've done has been to get you to London! We're only going there because of you.

**Celia** But what I'm afraid of, Chaps – my dear old Chaps – is that it won't be a new life. Because we'll be taking our old life with us, you see.

**Charles** Taking what you've told me with us, you mean? So why did you tell me? Because if I didn't know there'd be nothing to take with us, would there?

*Celia looks at him.*

What?

**Celia** There's Holly to take with us.

**Charles** Holly? What do you mean?

*There is a pause.*

That's not true.

**Celia** He'll have to know. One day. One day soon. We've got to be straight with him. Or at least I've got to be. He can't grow up in a lie and find out somehow, people always do, and that would be the worst. Going on lying to him, going on pretending – (*Shakes her head.*) We've got to be straight.

*Charles has gone over, poured himself another drink.*

**Charles** Everything's upside down. Just some minutes ago it was right side up and now it's upside down. Everything. (*Sinks into sofa.*) I never thought the day would come when I'd – when I'd hate you. Have you any idea what you've done? Do you realise what it'll be like from now on for me to be me? How I'll look at you and him? How I'll think of you and him? Every time I look at you and him together I'll see you at Rose House and I'll see him at Rose House and I'll see that pansy at Rose House, the three of you at Rose House – how can I hope to go on?

**Celia** Oh, you foolish man, how can Holly be anything else but yours? I wanted to enjoy this, I really wanted to, I wanted to let you stew away, I was looking forward to it. I think I deserved that. And so did you. But the awful truth is I love you and I can't get away from that so I can't bear to see you hurt.

**Charles** You mean – you mean this is a joke? Is it a joke? Is that what it is? One of your stupid games, like pretending you've gone blind or that you're in a coma or are having a stroke, one of your dramatising, one of

your attention-seeking silly games? Can it really be?
Something like this – something as dangerous as this?
God damn you, Ceci, God damn you!

**Celia** I have a right! Because I wanted you to feel what I've been feeling. It was my revenge.

**Charles** Revenge? Revenge for what?

**Celia** Moira, damn you! Moira, Moira, Moira!

**Charles** Moira? What has Moira got to do with any of this?

**Celia** You might as well be straight, Charles. She told me herself, you see.

**Charles** (*after a long pause*) She told you.

**Celia** And how many others have there been?

**Charles** Never anyone. Only her. I swear, darling.

**Celia** Why should I believe you?

**Charles** Because you know me.

**Celia** No, I don't know you. We don't know each other, that's what we're discovering.

**Charles** You do know me, Ceci. Everything about me that matters. The whole me. You're the only person in the world who knows the whole of me.

**Celia** I know the whole of you has been unfaithful – lied to me – betrayed me – and with my best friend.

**Charles** Oh, now, darling, your best friend? You can't stand her.

**Celia** She's still my best friend on this bloody island anyway. My only friend. Well. Are you going to tell me what happened and how it wasn't your fault really?

**Charles** Of course it was my fault. I accept that completely. Though it wasn't entirely my fault. I mean – I mean – Look, darling, what happened was that she phoned me. At the hospital. She needed my professional advice.

**Celia** Your professional advice? Why? Was she dead?

**Charles** It was about Richard. She wanted to talk to me about something that was wrong with Richard. And she asked me not to mention it to anyone. Not even you.

**Celia** Ahah.

**Charles** So I looked in on the way back –

**Celia** And when was this?

**Charles** I don't know – about two months ago it must have been, I suppose.

**Celia** Two months. Go on.

**Charles** I looked in on the way back and she gave me a cup of tea.

*There is a long pause.*

**Celia** (*helpfully*) She gave you a cup of tea.

**Charles** Well – then she told me about Richard.

**Celia** What did she tell you?

**Charles** Well, actually, darling, it's still – well, confidential. A matter of professional etiquette.

**Celia** Oh, I see. And it doesn't matter that she goes about blabbing about you and her because she hasn't any professional etiquette to worry about, has she?

**Charles** He's impotent.

**Celia** Oh, dear. Poor Moira. So you were called in as a replacement?

*Charles, in spite of himself, lets out a little bark of laughter.*

**Charles** (*after a pause*) He absolutely refuses to discuss it with her so she wondered whether I could find some way to – to help him.

**Celia** And how had you planned to do it? Go up to him and say, 'Oh, Richard, old boy, I was rogering Moira the other afternoon and she happened to mention that you're having a little problem, so perhaps you'd like to pop home and watch me when I'm at it.'

**Charles** You say you want to find out what happened but you won't let me tell you, tell you properly.

**Celia** Oh, I'm so sorry. Do go on. Please.

**Charles** Well, it seems things are pretty bad between them. In every possible way, really. Richard's not making out too well in his new job – well, like the rest of us, he was out of things for nearly five years and now there are much younger chaps coming into insurance straight from National Service and the universities – so he feels lost. Afraid of getting the sack, drinking far too much and – and – well, taking it out on Moira and sometimes quite violently. You see. Then she has to put on this front for the rest of the world – you know how she is, always cheerful and laughing – and suddenly there she was, breaking down in front of me. And I put my arms around her and she seemed to assume – and I didn't know how to refuse. Yes, that's what it comes down to. I was frightened of hurting her. You see, Ceci? I know it sounds feeble but that's what really happened.

**Celia** Where did you do it, by the way?

**Charles** Why?

**Celia** In their bedroom, was it?

**Charles** (*indignantly*) Of course not.

**Celia** Where then, darling? On the floor – on the sofa, perhaps?

**Charles** In the spare room. Spare bedroom.

**Celia** Oh, I don't think so, darling. I've seen that spare room, it hasn't even got a bed, it's got a cot, it wouldn't support Moira on her own, let alone the two of you. I should think you had to do it in their bedroom.

**Charles** It was in the spare room –

**Celia** And did you enjoy it, darling? Because that's the main thing, isn't it?

**Charles** Celia, really!

**Celia** Oh, don't be such a prude, Charles. You can tell your wife, surely?

**Charles** I don't know – I don't know – I did it because it seemed the right thing to do – that's what I'm trying to explain – even though I knew it was the wrong thing, at that moment – at that particular moment it seemed – (*gestures*) the right thing. I don't think I was trying to enjoy it, I was just trying to – to do it.

**Celia** And the other times?

*Charles shrugs.*

How many other times have there been?

**Charles** Five, I think. Yes, five.

**Celia** And how did you manage them, your little visits? Oh, of course! When you have to go out in the evenings.

To the hospital. To visit your corpses. For their post-mortems that you hate doing, poor lamb.

*There is a pause.*

**Charles** Needless to say, there won't be any more – any more –

**Celia** So you'll be keeping the little polio girl for the morning after all, will you? Really, Charles, how sickening. (*There is a pause.*) But of course, in London, where there will be lots and lots of fat little Moiras laughing and cheerful with impotent husbands, it'll be so much easier for you. You won't even have to lie to me.

**Charles** Damn Moira – why did she have to tell you, why? I simply don't understand.

**Celia** She didn't have to tell me. She just couldn't help herself. After tennis the other day she suddenly started on Richard. She said she's fairly sure he has a floozy in London and that's why he'd lost interest in her and why he was drinking. And I said – I said – hah! (*Laughs.*) I said, '*Fairly* sure? But you must know. I mean, I'd *always* know if Charles had been with another woman – *fairly* sure wouldn't come into it. I'd just *know*. Just by looking at him.' And she said, 'Oh, how close you and Charles must be if you'd know about him just like that. That's what I call a real marriage, darling.' And I caught her look – a little gleam in her eye, a sort of grin in her eye. That's how she told me. The grin in her eye. I didn't know anything about it from you, however often I'd looked at you. Even now I wouldn't know anything about it just from looking at you. (*Pause.*) I could have had an affair with Johnny. He wanted me to. And I was so – so proud of myself for not. Because I was attracted to him. Very attracted. But then I could never do anything like that to you, could I? I couldn't stand the pain of the pain

I'd be giving you – knowing you as I do. But now – what difference would it have made? None at all. Except to me, of course. (*Smiles at him.*)

**Charles** (*attempts to smile back*) Everything's going to be all right. I'll make sure.

*Puts a hand out towards her. Celia looks at him in sudden horrified bewilderment.*

**Celia** But I don't believe you. It's true – I've never known you. Never really known you. So how can I live with you any more – in London or anywhere? (*Little pause.*) I'm not going to be like all those others. You've been like those other men but I'm not going to be like their women – standing by my man when I don't know what man I'm standing by. No, Charles, I've got to leave. I've got to take Holly and leave. Even though I've got nowhere to go because you've left me with nothing – there's nothing for me, nothing I can do in life, nowhere to go. But I'd rather nothing than be with you, just another man I don't know and can't trust.

*Gets up, goes towards door, collapses, sobbing.*

Oh, Mama, Mama, help me, help me – oh – oh!

*Charles, appalled and distressed, goes to her.*

**Charles** Oh, my Ceci, my poor darling Ceci! What have I done? Oh, please, Ceci, please –

*He attempts to put his arms round her.*

**Celia** (*pushing him away*) No, leave me alone! Leave me alone!

**Charles** Ceci, Ceci –

*He forces his arms around her, holds her tightly. Celia rocks and keens in his arms. Keening fades*

*away. They cling together as if saving themselves. They become aware of a noise off, separate quickly, desperately trying to compose themselves as:*
  *Door opens. Holly enters, followed by Brownlow.*

**Celia** Oh, hello, darling, what are you doing back so soon? (*Seeing Brownlow.*) Everything all right?

**Brownlow** Oh, yes, indeed. It's just that I've had a rather exciting telegram from a friend of mine in London – a conductor. Teddy Schefflen. Apparently they're going to be playing a small piece of mine at his concert on Saturday.

**Celia** Oh, how exciting, eh, darling?

**Charles** Yes, yes, congratulations.

  *There is a pause.*

**Celia** Would you like a drink?

**Brownlow** Thank you, if I may. But we mustn't stay long, we haven't begun our lesson yet.

**Charles** We're drinking gin and tonic. Will that do?

**Brownlow** Thank you.

**Celia** Do sit down.

**Brownlow** (*sitting down*) I wondered if you'd let Holly come with me. Stay over on Saturday night, coming back on Sunday evening. I think it could be very educative – there are a number of other concerts over the weekend – and I'd make sure, of course, that he would be well looked after.

**Celia** Well, that sounds – that sounds – what do you think, darling?

**Charles** Well – here, Holly, give this to Mr –

*Hands Holly drink. Holly takes drink over to Brownlow.*

**Brownlow** We studied music together, Teddy and I. And his wife. All three of us. She's a flautist. Now they have a delightful baby, very chubby. Their house is in Fulham – very convenient for the concerts. He's conducting two of them, the one with my piece and another on Sunday morning. He really is becoming something of a maestro, Teddy.

**Celia** It would be awfully good for him, darling. And I mean, as we're going to London, he'll already know something about music halls.

**Brownlow** We'll be visiting several. Concert halls. Though I'm not so sure about music halls. (*Gives a little laugh.*) Anyway, he'll learn a lot. We'll all conspire to make sure of it.

**Celia** (*to Holly*) And you'd like that, darling, would you?

**Holly** Oh, yes – yes. Very much.

**Charles** (*making an effort*) But you must let me know about the tickets, the train and any expenses. I insist on that. Insist on it.

**Celia** My husband is very pernickety about things like that, aren't you, darling?

**Charles** I just don't want Mr – um – anybody to be out of pocket.

**Brownlow** Oh, I shan't be, I'll make sure of it.

**Charles** Yes, please do.

*There is a pause.*

**Celia** How's the cat – Miaow – how's Miaow?

*Lights.*

## SCENE TWO

*The following Sunday. Nine p.m.*
  *Brownlow's study/sitting room.*
  *Ellie is at the piano, accompanying herself as she sings a Viennese folk song. She plays well, sings well. She is drunk. She concludes song triumphantly and theatrically, drinks from glass on piano.*
  *Sound of doorbell.*

**Ellie** (*in German*) What? Who is this now at this hour? Has he forgotten his keys? (*Goes to window, taps on it.*) Thomas? Thomas? Is that you there, Thomas?

  *Sound of voice off.*

(*In English.*) Who is it? (*Obviously can't hear. In German.*) Oh God, it's the police, it's the police, they've come to take me, come to take us! (*Cowers.*) Thomas, Thomas, why aren't you here?

  *Doorbell rings again imperiously.*
  *Ellie goes out. Voices off.*

**Charles** (*off*) Is my son here?

**Ellie** (*off*) Your son, *bitte*?

**Charles** (*off*) Yes, my son. Holly. Is he here, please?

**Ellie** (*off*) Oh, Holly, yes, yes, of course, of course! He's with Thomas.

  *Ellie holds door open. Charles enters.*

(*Attempting to conceal drunkenness.*) So you're the father, the father of Holly. I'm so sorry, I couldn't see you, I thought it was the police, you see.

**Charles** The police? (*Anxiously.*) Why did you think I was the police?

**Ellie** *Bitte?*

**Charles** Why are you expecting the police?

**Ellie** Oh, no, no, it's just that sometimes when it's late – so. You are the father of our boy.

**Charles** I'm Holly's father, yes. I thought you said he was here.

**Ellie** *Bitte?*

**Charles** My son and your son, isn't it, you said at the door they were here. Didn't you?

**Ellie** Ah yes, well, they were here before – for a long time – and then I went upstairs to rest and I came downstairs and you were at the window, no, you were at the door and – the kitchen, perhaps they are in the kitchen having a cuppa. (*Goes to the door, screams out.*) Thomas – Thomas – Holliday – Holliday, here is your father, are you there, are you there? (*Comes back in.*) No, there is no light, they are not in the kitchen, no. Well, they must have gone out for a walk, yes?

**Charles** A walk? At this hour?

**Ellie** Can I offer you a drink? It is only sherry but it is new, a fresh bottle.

**Charles** No, thank you. When did they get back?

**Ellie** Back? *Bitte?*

**Charles** When did they get back from London?

**Ellie** Oh, I don't know, let me think – back, back – this afternoon early, I made them some lunch, I remember, yes, soup and corn beef –

**Charles** But they were meant to be coming back on the last ferry, which was two hours ago – we've been getting worried, very worried – and you say they've been here all day virtually? Why didn't he phone us at least?

**Ellie** Yes, I know, so silly, I keep telling him he must have a telephone for his asthma but no, he will not –

**Charles** But why are they back so early?

**Ellie** I think my boy there was in some quarrel with his friend in London – Teddy – sometimes they have terrible arguments – shouting, anger, tears, you know with friends. Yes, probably there was a fight, I don't know.

**Charles** I see. A fight with his friend – Teddy. (*Little pause, thinks.*) But there's a wife, isn't there, and a baby?

**Ellie** Teddy, a wife, baby? (*Laughs.*) No, no. Not for Teddy a wife and a baby.

**Charles** But your son said – I remember distinctly – a wife, a baby – his friends, a husband, a wife and a baby.

**Ellie** Ah, that is Teddy's sister, Debbie. She has a baby, yes. But not husband. He ran away – poof! And no wife for Teddy.

**Charles** And what have they been doing here all day?

**Ellie** Doing? Who?

**Charles** My son and your son, what have they been doing since they got back? (*Just controlling anger.*)

**Ellie** Nothing. Playing like always. Always they play. Like children they are. Except when Holliday is at the piano and my boy is teaching him. Then goodness, my goodness, very serious, very strong. Yes, the music, that is always serious. But he is a genius. One day he will be a great artist, famous everywhere – oh, if I should live to see it, that's all I hope for! And your boy too, your Holliday – my son, he hates to teach all the children here – (*in German*) lumpen fingers – (*in English*) he calls them, how you say? Yes, their fingers are lumps. They have no music in their heads, their bodies, only English stupidity and nice – all so nice. But his Holly, him he loves and worships, he has a beautiful gift, a beautiful soul – not English and nice but a free soul like his, dancing, dancing – so they dance together. (*Wagging her head, crooning.*) Like this, like this, they are, to make you cry.

**Charles** Really. And you don't know where they are now?

**Ellie** Oh, no. Perhaps on the beach. By the sea. They like to hear the sea, to inspire them.

**Charles** Do they. And what sort of games do they play when they're not at the piano?

**Ellie** Just ordinary games. They pretend – you know – pretend they are at anger between them, and cruelty – and then if he cries they are friends again. Like children, you see. Playing, crying, holding each other – (*Stops. Looks at Charles, suddenly worried.*) You are angry. Oh, please do not be angry, do not be English – be nice, not like English nice, there must be no trouble, no more trouble – it is not his fault if he loves to teach, people do not understand – we cannot move away, oh, we cannot move away again – please, Mr Holly's father, please be kind. (*Begins to cry, sags into a chair. In German.*) Oh, what have I said, what have I done?

*Charles stares at her in disgust.*
*Door opens. Brownlow enters.*

**Charles** What have you done with my son?

**Brownlow** I've just taken him home. To your home. Your wife told me you'd come over here so I hurried back.

**Charles** He's been here all afternoon, I gather.

**Brownlow** Yes, well, we came back early – the lunch-time concert was cancelled – and as I knew you weren't expecting him back until the last ferry –

**Charles** The last ferry is at six o'clock on Sundays.

**Brownlow** Oh, is it? I assumed it was the same time as in the week. I'm very sorry – but even so we're only an hour or so later than –

**Charles** That's not the point.

**Brownlow** What is the point?

**Charles** The point is – the point is that I've been talking to your mother. I think I have a fairly good idea – no, I won't call it a good idea – but an idea of the sort of thing that's been going on between you and my son.

**Brownlow** Indeed? What has been going on between your son and myself, may I ask? What is this idea you have of what has been going on?

**Charles** Let's just say that you are to have nothing further to do with him. Do you understand me?

**Brownlow** No – no, I don't understand. I've done nothing wrong. We did nothing wrong together. I would never do anything to harm your son. Never. So please, please don't stop his lessons – he will never find another teacher who understands him as I do, who knows his talents –

**Charles** If I catch you anywhere near him, I'll go to the police.

**Ellie** (*in German*) The police, the police – there, I warned you!

**Brownlow** I don't care – go to the police, I'm not frightened, I'm not ashamed, I have nothing to be ashamed of.

**Charles** Yes, you probably believe that, that's just it, isn't it, with a type like you? You don't know what decency is, you have no idea, no sense, no understanding even of what it is to be straight. You filthy, little – Jew.

**Ellie** No, no, we are not Jews! Not Jews!

*Charles turns, goes out.*

(*In German.*) See? See what you've done? He'll go to the police and we'll be finished.

**Brownlow** What did you say to him? What did you tell him about me – about Holly and me?

**Ellie** (*in German*) Nothing – nothing – I said how good you were to each other, how happy, how you taught him and sometimes that you were strict, that you loved each other like children –

**Brownlow** Loved each other – loved each other like children –

*Sinks into a chair, puts his face into his hands, his shoulders begin to shake. Ellie goes over to him, kneels beside him, strokes his head.*

**Ellie** (*in German*) There, there, Thomas, my poor, poor Thomas.

*Puts her arms around him, begins to rock him.*
*He rocks with her.*
   *Lights.*

### SCENE THREE

*The same.*
   *Smithers' sitting room.*
   *Holly's overnight bag by sofa. Holly is sitting at piano stool, facing away from piano, drinking cup of tea.*

*Celia is lying on sofa, smoking.*

**Celia** I must say, darling, it does sound all terribly Bohemian and hothousey. And what was it about, this ferocious row?

**Holly** Oh, a bit of music – well, that's what started it anyway, I couldn't follow the rest of it, it was all about people I don't know, but it was the Berg that did it in the first place.

**Celia** The Berg? What Berg?

**Holly** The composer, Alban Berg. They were trying to remember the first bars of some piano piece, I don't know which one, but they had a bet on it, you see – well, what happened was that Teddy began to play it and Lowly –

**Celia** Who?

**Holly** Mr Brownlow, that's what everybody calls him in London, Lowly. Anyway, he, Mr Brownlow, said that Teddy had got it wrong and it started like this and he showed him, and then they had their bet and then Teddy couldn't find the music and Mr Brownlow said he was hiding it because he knew he'd lost the bet and – and so, you know, that's when it went all over the place.

**Celia** But, poor darling, how embarrassing for you. What on earth did you do?

**Holly** Oh, I just went back to our room.

**Celia** Our room? Whose room?

**Holly** Well, the bedroom.

**Celia** Oh. So you and Mr Brownlow shared a bedroom, did you?

**Holly** Oh no, not really, I was on a sofa thing in the hall but I left my stuff in the room he was sleeping in so I went there and got the score for the lunchtime concert they'd given me.

**Celia** Then Teddy threw you both out, did he?

**Holly** No, no, he didn't throw us out, Mummy. It was all quite friendly after that, except it turned out the concert had been cancelled or something so he, Mr Brownlow, said let's go back and enjoy the weather and we said goodbye. It was all friendly and as if nothing had happened really.

**Celia** Well, I suppose musicians and people like that tend to have tantrums and melodramas. It's probably all quite fun in a way. And what was the little wife and baby doing during all this?

**Holly** Oh, she didn't pay much attention, as if she were quite used to it.

**Celia** Even so, you should have been more thoughtful, darling. He probably doesn't think about parental worries and fears when children are late – trains do crash, ferries do sink – so you should have popped in to let us know you were safe at least.

**Holly** Well, he didn't think you'd expect us back, he explained to you, Mummy, he just got the time wrong for Sundays, that's all.

**Celia** Well, the next time – (*yawns*) you'll know what to do. Your father really was getting into quite a state.

**Holly** Well, I'm sorry. Do you mind if I just play something? It was in the concert last night and we've been practising playing it from memory this afternoon but I'm afraid it'll slip away if I don't do it once more before I go –

*He notices that Celia isn't paying attention, turns to piano, begins to play thoughtfully.*
  *Celia goes on smoking, Holly goes on playing.*
  *Celia, suddenly becoming aware of Holly, looks at him. She stubs out cigarette, looks at Holly again.*

**Celia** (*sternly*) Holly, come here.

*Holly goes on playing, as if unaware.*

(*More loudly and sternly.*) Holly. I said come here. This minute.

*Holly sighs, gets up, goes over.*

**Holly** What, Mummy? I was just –

**Celia** Sit down.

**Holly** (*going to sit down*) I was just getting to the bit I wanted to –

**Celia** Not there. Here. (*Pats side of sofa.*)

*Holly sits on sofa.*

Now, look at me. Straight in the eye, my boy. I want the truth.

*There is a long pause.*

**Holly** Well about what, Mummy?

**Celia** You know what about. (*Pause.*) Do you love me?

**Holly** Oh, honestly, Mummy.

**Celia** I want an answer.

**Holly** Of course I do. You know I do.

**Celia** Why? Tell me why.

**Holly** Well, because you're my mother.

**Celia** That's not good enough.

**Holly** Why not?

**Celia** Because I'm not your mother. You're adopted. There. What do you say to that?

*Holly stands, trembling and swaying, as if in shock.*

(*Suddenly alarmed.*) Darling – darling!

**Holly** (*holds up his hand*) Mummy, I think that's the most terrific news I've ever heard. I always knew it – well, I always hoped it anyway. Thank you, Mummy.

*Celia grabs him, begins to tickle him. Holly squirms, giggling helplessly, pulls himself away.*

Now I've got to get back –

**Celia** Twiddle my toes. Twiddle my toes first, go on. They feel stiff and crampy. Just for two minutes.

**Holly** Ohh. Two minutes. Exactly two minutes. (*Looks at his watch, sits down.*)

*Sound of front door opening, closing.*

**Celia** Ah, there's your father.

*Charles enters, taking in Holly massaging Celia's toes.*

Oh, there you are, darling, and here he is, as I expect you already know.

**Holly** (*gets up*) Hello, Daddy.

**Celia** Darling, what is it?

**Charles** Holly, sit down, please.

*Holly sits down.*

**Celia** What is it, Charles?

**Charles** I've just been speaking to that creature.

**Celia** What creature?

**Charles** That creature and his mother. I know what sort of thing's been going on. What I don't know is exactly how far it went. (*Little pause.*) Holly?

**Celia** Charles, shouldn't we –

**Charles** Holly.

**Holly** I – I don't know what you mean, Daddy.

**Charles** I think you do. When you 'played' together, for instance.

**Holly** We just played Beethoven – Chopin –

**Charles** No, not when you played together on the piano. When you 'played' together like children. What did you do then, when you 'played' together like children?

**Holly** He – he – sometimes he pretended to get cross – that's all – when I went wrong on the piano. And – and it was just a game. He didn't mean anything. I didn't mind. It's just – just his way of teaching me, to make it more – to make me concentrate more.

**Charles** And your dancing together, was that to make you concentrate more?

**Holly** Dancing?

**Charles** Dancing.

**Holly** Well, we didn't – I mean – there's a bit of Handel he used to play and he taught me a few steps –

**Charles** Show me.

**Celia** Charles.

**Charles** Show me, please, Holly.

*Holly, after a pause, takes a few steps, a pirouette, then a few more steps, bows.*

So he played and you did that for him. (*Little pause.*) When you were in London with his friend – Teddy – what then?

**Celia** There was Teddy's wife and the baby.

**Charles** In London with his friend, Teddy, and Teddy's sister and her baby by someone who's left her, what then?

*There is a pause.*

What did you do, you and Mr – (*Gestures.*) Your dancing master. What did you do together in London?

**Holly** Nothing. We went to a concert in the evening and a walk and then there was a quarrel over music and then the concert was cancelled and then we came back and we didn't know you were waiting for us and – and that's all.

**Charles** And what were the sleeping arrangements?

**Holly** Well, I slept in the room with the baby.

**Celia** Yes, he was just telling me about it, Charles.

**Charles** You and the baby?

**Holly** Yes. And then the baby woke up and the mother came in and I slept in the hall on the sofa.

*There is a pause.*

**Charles** I told your friend that he's not to see you again. You will stay away from him, Holly. Is that understood?

*Holly nods.*

Good. If I had my way I'd drive him off the island. There's nothing I'd like better. But as we're leaving ourselves, it would probably just cause a lot of fuss and we don't want the fuss following us to London like a plague, and there'd be bound to be talk about you, what you let happen to you –

**Celia** Darling!

**Charles** You know this island, for God's sakes, better than anyone. Whatever the truth, there'd be gossip.

**Celia** (*turns to Holly*) All Daddy's saying is that people are so silly and nasty and quick to make silly and nasty things up – that you should – should, well, keep mum.

**Charles** (*as if ignoring her*) The point is, you're starting your scholarship with a clean sheet as far as everybody else knows, you'll just have to make sure you keep it that way. Now we won't discuss this any more ever again. All right, Holly?

*Holly doesn't reply.*

Now off you go.

**Holly** Where, Daddy?

**Charles** To bed, of course.

**Celia** Yes, darling, you should, you've had a – a long day – a nice hot bath and then tomorrow everything will be back to normal.

**Holly** But he didn't do anything wrong. He was always very nice – kind – kind to me. Honestly.

**Charles** I told you, we're not going to talk about this any more. And I told you to go to bed.

*Holly sits for a moment, as if to speak, then gets up, goes to door, turns defiantly to the piano, sits down,*

*begins to play a brief melange out of which 'Rule Britannia' emerges.*
   *Charles, after a moment, gets up, goes to Holly.*

Go to bed, I say. Go to bed!

*Holly continues playing. Charles makes as if to strike him.*

**Celia** Charles!

*Charles just controls himself, looks from Holly to Celia, goes to door, turns.*

**Charles** Pansy Johnny's boy. That's who you are. Pansy Johnny's boy. (*Goes out.*)

*Holly continues playing, stops.*

**Holly** What did he mean, Pansy Johnny's boy?

**Celia** (*gets up, goes to him*) Nothing really, darling. Just a grown-up sort of thing. One day you'll find out all about it, I expect. But there's no rush.

*Puts a hand on his head, looks towards door, goes out. Holly sits for a moment, then turns to piano, continues playing 'Rule Britannia'.*
   *Lights going down as lights coming up on Brownlow's study, Holly still playing.*


## SCENE FOUR

*The present. A few minutes after Act One, Scene One.*
   *Brownlow's study/sitting room.*
   *Holly is sitting in armchair, smoking, bowl as ashtray cupped in his hand.*
   *Brownlow enters, carrying tray on which decanter and two glasses.*

**Brownlow** And when are you planning to go back? To Australia, I mean, Melbourne?

**Holly** Oh, when I've cleared up a few things, settled a few things.

*Brownlow has put tray on table. Picks up decanter, holds it up, inspects it.*

**Brownlow** I can't see any sediment, rather a lovely colour, what would one call it? Tawny? No, no, of course not, that's for port, isn't it? Topaz, what about topaz? Oh yes, there are one or two black spots floating around, I must try and keep them out of your glass.

*Pours sherry into a glass, brings it over to Holly, puts it beside him. Gives a little cough.*

**Holly** Oh, I'm smoking, I'm sorry, I forgot.

**Brownlow** (*stepping away*) No, no, that's all right. As long as I keep my distance. (*Pouring himself a glass of sherry.*) So much dust in the room anyway, in the corners, I'm always telling Mrs Jameson to get into the corners but I don't think she ever does. There. (*Sitting down at table.*) I'm quite safe over here.

**Holly** (*indicating bowl*) Is it all right to use this as an ashtray?

**Brownlow** Oh, yes, yes, indeed.

**Holly** It's pretty. (*Looking at bowl properly.*)

**Brownlow** Yes, very useful, for little odds and ends. My mother used to have it by her bed. For her teeth, actually.

*Holly puts bowl down beside him.*

And your parents, how are they, are they still with us?

**Holly** Not my mother. She died fifteen, no, sixteen years ago. Cancer.

**Brownlow** Oh, I'm so sorry. She always seemed so – so vivid to me.

**Holly** Yes, she seemed vivid to quite a few people. Perhaps still does. I hope so, anyway.

**Brownlow** But your father, he's well, is he?

**Holly** Oh, yes. He's retired, of course. Lives on the Isle of Wight with his second wife and their two children.

**Brownlow** The Isle of Wight? That's – that's convenient. Now that you're here, you can just pop across –

**Holly** Yes, but I doubt if I'll have the time.

**Brownlow** But you found time for me.

**Holly** Yes. Yes, I did.

*Pause.*

**Brownlow** So. Life – life, um – and you? What has become of you, may I ask?

**Holly** I'm a doctor.

**Brownlow** Ah. And are you also a pathologist like your father?

**Holly** No, I'm a psychiatrist.

**Brownlow** A psychiatrist? Ah. So you abandoned your music then, after all?

**Holly** No. No, I think it abandoned me. My daughter has a gift, something of a gift. She's only ten but her mother keeps her at it. She's a professional cellist – my wife, that is.

**Brownlow** Oh. So it's the cello for your daughter, not the piano.

**Holly** The violin, actually. But her brother likes to play the piano when he's in the mood and can't find anything better to do.

**Brownlow** Well, it sounds a happy life. And a complete life. A happy and complete life that you've made for yourself in Australia.

**Holly** Yes, I suppose it does sound that. Though one never knows, does one, almost from minute to minute, what lies ahead – what memories lie ahead, even. Or don't lie ahead, as it turns out. Like the music. The music that won't come back.

**Brownlow** I'm sorry?

**Holly** I think I mentioned it before you got the sherry. Which is actually remarkably drinkable, by the way. It was a bagatelle.

**Brownlow** A bagatelle, was it?

**Holly** Yes. You wrote it especially for me. 'A Bagatelle for Mio' you called it. It was played on Radio 3. The Third Programme, I mean. Ring any bells?

**Brownlow** No, it doesn't, I'm afraid. But it was a very long time ago, wasn't it? Some thirty years.

**Holly** But might you still have the score somewhere?

**Brownlow** No, I've thrown everything out from those days.

**Holly** Oh. But could it still be in you, lurking – waiting to come out again? Perhaps if you tried on the keys for a few minutes, see if anything bobs up? I'll recognise it from just a few notes, I know I will. (*Little pause.*) Would you mind? Um, giving it a go? On the keys?

*Brownlow gets up, goes across to piano, sits on stool, puts his hands out as if to play. Turns.*

**Brownlow** I'd rather not. I'd really rather not. There hasn't been music for years – no concertos, no bagatelles, not even dreams of concertos, not even memories of bagatelles – nothing, for years and years. So why have you come here? You come looking me up like this, from so long ago, out of the blue, out of the darkness, remembering this, trying to make me remember that – what do you want? What do you want? To punish? To forgive? (*Laughs.*) It's too late – far too late –

*Begins to wheeze, gropes for inhaler in his pocket, drops it to the floor. Holly, after a moment, comes over, picks up inhaler, puts an arm around Brownlow, supports him, puts inhaler in his hand, helps him to apply it. Steps away. Brownlow begins to recover.*

**Holly** Are you all right?

*Brownlow nods.*

I'm so sorry. I just wanted to remember the bagatelle. You see, I remember everything else as clearly as I want to, I really do. But the bagatelle, not remembering it has been driving me mad. I shouldn't have been so pressing, I'm sorry. Though oddly enough – for what it's worth – I think – (*Hums.*) Isn't that it?

*Brownlow shakes his head.*

No, it isn't, is it? Oh well, it'll just have to nag away at me until I forget to try to remember it. (*Hums again, shakes his head.*) No. (*Laughs.*)

*Brownlow laughs.*

(*Looks at his watch.*) Good heavens, I'd better be on my way. Leave you in peace. Here –

*Holds out his hand. Brownlow takes it.*

There, you see. Still real, I hope.

**Brownlow** (*clutching Holly's hand*) No, stay. Stay and talk a while. We have so much to say to each other, we've hardly said anything – anything that matters.

**Holly** (*removing his hand, gently but firmly*) I can't, I'm afraid. I'm meeting somebody in Portsmouth. She's my what they call 'bit on the side', you see, so of course she doesn't like to be kept waiting. And nor do I. (*Smiles.*) But if I'm ever in the old haunts again – Goodbye, Lowly. (*Goes out.*)

**Brownlow** (*stroking his hand*) Still real. Still real.

*Brownlow goes to the piano, starts to play the 'Bagatelle'. As he does so, lights up on Smithers' drawing room, young Holly at the piano. Brownlow and Holly play the 'Bagatelle' as lights go down.*

*Curtain.*